APICS CSCP

EXAM
SUCCESS

A GUIDE TO ACHIEVING
CERTIFICATION
ON YOUR FIRST ATTEMPT

HOWARD FORMAN
DAVID FORMAN

T0350704

ISBN-13: 978-1-60427-129-4

Printed and bound in the U.S.A. Printed on acid-free paper.

10 9 8 7 6 5 4 3 2 1

Library of Congress Cataloging-in-Publication Data

Names: Forman, Howard, author. | Forman, David (Certified supply chain
  professional), author.
Title: APICS CSCP exam success : a guide to achieving certification on your
  first attempt / by Howard Forman and David Forman.
Description: Plantation, FL : J. Ross Publishing, [2018] | Includes index.
Identifiers: LCCN 2017055897 | ISBN 9781604271294 (pbk. : alk. paper)
Subjects: LCSH: Business logistics—Examinations—Study guides. | Materials
  management—Examinations—Study guides.
Classification: LCC HD38.5 .F67 2018 | DDC 658.50076—dc23 LC record
available at https://lccn.loc.gov/2017055897

Direct all inquiries to J. Ross Publishing, Inc., 300 S. Pine Island Rd., Suite 305, Plantation, FL 33324.

Phone: (954) 727-9333
Fax: (561) 892-0700
Web: www.jrosspub.com

CONTENTS

PREFACE

We want to thank you for purchasing our *APICS CSCP Exam Success: A Guide to Achieving Certification Success on Your First Attempt*. Our study guide provides information on concepts, terms, relationships, and calculations needed to help you prepare to pass the CSCP certification exam. If you follow the information in this guide, it will help improve your probability of earning your CSCP certification.

The objective of this study guide is to present the various supply-chain-related concepts in a simple and user-friendly fashion. In order to do this we provided numerous examples to help the reader better understand how to apply learned concepts. It's our intent to increase your knowledge to better prepare you to take and pass the CSCP exam on your first attempt. Our study guide is designed for both the novice and the experienced supply chain professional who are searching for a user-friendly study guide and for any individual who did not earn their CSCP certification on their first try.

The beginning section provides useful information to help prepare you for the exam. Remember that your first step is to develop and follow a CSCP study plan. Once you develop your plan, you can begin to read the material in this study guide. We have segmented the concepts into sections to help you perform calculations and to learn key concepts, terms, and relationships.

We made a number of assumptions that you: have purchased and read (or will) at least the 2016, 2017, or the 2018 version of the APICS CSCP Learning System; reviewed the APICS CSCP Exam Content Manual course outline; and studied the key terminology list to identify key concepts, terms, relationships, and calculations. We also assume that you have access to and are using the online APICS CSCP Learning System as a study tool. If not, this reduces your probability of passing the exam. Our study guide is not meant to be a replacement for the APICS courseware. However, if you don't have the latest revision of the courseware, you might find it beneficial since we've incorporated the latest revisions in our study guide.

Inside this study guide, we have arranged the material into a number of chapters. Each chapter is broken down into different sections where we have identified key concepts, terms, relationships, and calculations. We have also provided a comprehensive list of key terms found in that chapter along with a number of exercises and practices to enhance your learning.

Chapter 1 provides an overview and an understanding of supply chain management—its objectives, how to make it more efficient and responsive, and the different integration types. It also provides an understanding of the value chain, value stream, and value stream mapping.

Chapter 2 discusses the importance of the Supply Chain Reference Model (SCOR)—its background, the various types of supply chain structures, SCOR Level 1 and 2 metrics, plus the various manufacturing environments and their attributes.

Chapter 3 deals with logistic fundamentals, supply chain integration, logistics service providers, substituting information for inventory, reverse logistics, and the waste hierarchy.

Chapter 4 covers the functions of logistics, warehousing activities and their functions, ownership versus leasing, the impact of adding or removing warehouses, temporary material storage, intermodal types, line haul shipping costs, value and packaging density, transportation stakeholder goals, carrier types and selection, transportation modes, shipping, pickup and delivery conflicts, and mechanized systems and equipment type attributes.

Chapter 5 addresses import/export logistics, its participants, global order flow air participants, import/export financial consideration terms, Incoterms, multicountry strategy, intellectual property, software, and technology licensing.

Chapter 6 deals with sustainability, regulatory, and security procedures; risk standards; the committee of sponsoring Organizations of the Treadway Commission (COSO) enterprise risk management framework components; the International Organization for Standardization (ISO); and sustainability and regulatory compliance.

Chapter 7 covers marketing and their processes, the four P's attributes, business plan, supply chain network modeling, operations research, identification of segments, marketing management, voice of the customer, communication and its processes, and measuring customer service.

Chapter 8 discusses demand management, demand, forecast processes, and its required information; basic time-series forecasting methods; historical sales data; simple and multiple regression; seasonal index; forecast error measurements (including the mean absolute deviation calculation); and the demand manager's role.

Chapter 9 deals with customer relationship management strategy, the differences between a transactional marketing strategy and customer relationship management, its implementation process and strategy by customer type, technology tools, the four levels of customer relationship management implementation, successful customer relationship management implementation key activities, customer lifetime value, customer relationship management implementation challenges, cultural issues impacting customer relationship management, and supplier relationship management.

Chapter 10 covers product design, its impact, product life cycle stages, and the various product design approaches.

Chapter 11 focuses on manufacturing and planning control, master planning, the planning hierarchy, sales and operations planning and its process flow, process steps, process ownership, aggregate strategies including level and chase, the sales and operations planning communications process, and manufacturing environments delivery lead times.

Chapter 12 extends the discussion to strategic and business strategy, organizational strategy, business strategy types, the five competitive cost strategies, functional versus innovative products, the balanced scorecard, organizational design, and the different supply chain management evolution stages.

Chapter 13 focuses on master scheduling, master schedule disaggregation, the differences between sales and operations planning and master scheduling, time fences and zones, commitment decision points, the projected available balance calculation, master scheduling time-phased records, the available-to-promise calculation, and rough cut capacity planning.

Chapter 14 demonstrates material requirements planning and distribution requirements planning, including the calculation process, and planning changes. It also discusses bills of material, single and multi-level bills of material, and distribution push and pull systems.

Chapter 15 deals with production activity control and capacity management, capacity management attributes and its hierarchy, the capacity requirements planning process, validation methods, resource planning process, capacity strategic objectives, input/output control, load profile, work center capacity versus load, capacity corrective action, and the various capacity calculations.

Chapter 16 focuses on continuous process improvement, lean, just-in-time philosophy, the Toyota Production System, Six Sigma, DMAIC, DMADV, the takt time calculation, Theory of Constraints, total quality management, total productive maintenance, various improvement tools, and the cost of quality.

Chapter 17 covers supplier relationship management and purchasing, their functions and benefits, the make-versus-buy cost analysis, total cost of ownership, offshoring, buyer-supplier relationship types, tactical and strategic sourcing, understanding the differences between single, sole, and multisourcing suppliers, supplier selection strategy, hard and soft negotiations, creating alliances with suppliers, alliance development steps, the supplier certification process, portals, trade exchanges, horizontal marketplace, auctions, and measuring suppliers.

Chapter 18 discusses synchronizing demand and supply, their principles, implementation challenges, supply chain integration, and inventory synchronization between trading partners.

Chapter 19 covers inventory management and types; independent and dependent demand; inventory ordering systems including order point, economic order quantity, safety stock, and safety lead time; inventory locations and echelons; Pareto analysis; inventory policy; periodic inventory versus cycle counting; aggregation inventory management; inventory types and functional types; inventory-related costs; and storage locations.

Chapter 20 deals with financial and managerial accounting concepts such as financial statements and financial analysis; financial report components; standard and overhead costs; *first-in, first-out* and *last-in, last-out* calculations; tax impact; financial metrics; and benefit-cost and net present value analysis and calculations.

Chapter 21 addresses the concept of economics, microeconomics, macroeconomics, the economic business cycle, aggregate demand-aggregate supply, understanding of the aggregate demand-aggregate supply model curve shift, economic attributes, and marginal analysis and cost calculations.

Chapter 22 addresses risk management in the supply chain, managing the supply chain risk process, the risk register, the risk response plan, risk probability and impact assessment, risk level categories, risk cost estimate table, expected monetary value, net impact expected monetary value, decision tree, sensitivity analysis and simulation, the four basic risk response types, supply chain risks, and business continuity and plan implementation.

Chapter 23 focuses on technology, its architecture, the evolution from material requirements planning to enterprise resources planning, software selection considerations, other software applications, and middleware.

Chapter 24 addresses data acquisition, storage, communication tools, the capture of timely and accurate data, static and dynamic data, data collection, data integrity and accuracy, big data, data mining, scanners and bar codes, automatic identification system, automatic identification and data capture, and radio frequency identification tags.

Chapter 25 focuses on understanding electronic business and commerce and its various types, traditional versus electronic business, the different business-to-business and business-to-consumer e-commerce layers.

Chapter 26 covers project management, the various process group activities, variance analysis, and its calculations.

The final chapters include sections on test readiness, a practice exam, a discussion on the CSCP Exam sign-up, the exam process, how to segment the exam, and potential mistakes to avoid when taking the exam. It discusses what to do at the conclusion if you pass or don't pass the exam.

We have also included a master listing of over 1,000 terms which you will find very beneficial to learn. Knowledge of all of these terms will aid the test taker to identify the correct answer. We have also included a listing of over 100 calculations found in the CSCP Learning System with samples of actual calculations to further aid your learning.

If you find any errors in this study guide, if you think something is missing, or if you desire an additional example or exercise, please let us know. We will promptly respond to you and make a correction, if needed. We will reference your name and contribution in an acknowledgment section if you find an error. E-mails should be addressed to pimassociates@yahoo.com.

INTRODUCTION

If you are reading this sentence right now, you are in one of two groups of supply chain professionals. If you are in the first group, then you have already made that important decision to improve your career by earning an APICS Certified Supply Chain Professional (CSCP) certification. You may have already purchased the CSCP Learning System, sat through an instructor-led course, taken an online course or performed self-study, and are now looking for a study guide to help you prepare for the exam.

If you are in the second group, you are just beginning the process of understanding how a CSCP certification can improve your career, help you earn more money, jump-start a stagnant job, or switch careers. You may have spoken with a CSCP certified individual or coworker, read information on the value of earning your CSCP certification, and/or attended an APICS chapter professional development meeting. However, before making the final decision to earn your certification, you want to ensure yourself that it will benefit your future.

As the need for global supply chain professionals continues to expand in the marketplace, the desire for individuals who have earned their CSCP certification becomes a key employer requirement and differentiator. To validate this need, we suggest you look at employment search engines, want ads, or recruiter sheets to notice the numerous companies that are looking for CSCP certified individuals. We also suggest you perform a search for supply chain or operational employment positions in your area, and see if this presents an opportunity for you. If the answer is yes, make it your goal to obtain your CSCP certification and see how far it can take you!

Before we start to examine what's in this study guide, it's important to note that this book isn't a replacement for reading the CSCP Learning System, using the APICS CSCP online practice questions, reading supplementary materials, studying, or attending an instructor-led or online CSCP course. Its main purpose is to highlight and emphasize the contents of the CSCP Learning System with our own thoughts, descriptions, suggestions, examples, and comments. It's designed to help you identify and resolve your CSCP body of knowledge gaps, and to better learn and understand the various concepts, calculations, and relationships. Reading this study guide will aid you in getting the maximum benefit out of the CSCP courseware.

In order to get the full benefit from this study guide, it's imperative that you have completely read the current version of the CSCP Learning System. Our study guide reflects the latest revision, which was rewritten in January 2016 and most-recently updated in January 2018. It includes the added and enhanced topics of risk management, economics, communications, and project management that weren't included in earlier versions. If you have studied from an earlier CSCP version, these chapters will help you to learn these key concepts. However, we do highly recommend that you obtain the latest version of the CSCP Learning System to increase your probability of passing the exam.

Not only does this book help to explain key concepts and provide additional examples, it also includes:

- Free 45-day online access to over 700 practice questions, enabling readers to perform practice tests by CSCP group and/or simulate actual full exams, with feedback on incorrect answers (see the inside front cover for the link to the test bank and your unique serial number)
- Test-taking tips
- How to read and analyze exam questions
- Over 40 exercises to help you learn and reinforce concepts
- Downloadable content such as CSCP acronym lists (see WAV page xxvii for more details)
- Over 100 calculations shown with working examples to help you better understand the logic behind the math
- Over 400 practice questions to help identify APICS CSCP body of knowledge gaps
- A comprehensive list of key terminology used throughout the CSCP Learning System

Our review of key terminology found in the CSCP Learning System identified approximately 1,100 terms. This far exceeds what APICS has highlighted in the exam content manual, and we believe that having knowledge of these additional terms will help you to be better prepared to answer exam questions. We have always stressed to our students that learning vocabulary is a key step in their exam preparation.

Feeling motivated? Let's get started on earning your CSCP certification!

PREPARATION

We recommend that your first step toward becoming certified is to download the APICS CSCP Examination Procedures Bulletin for either North America or outside of North America. This bulletin will provide information on the CSCP eligibility form, how to schedule the exam, the Authorization to Test (ATT) process, the cost of the exam, and other terms and conditions as established by APICS.

CSCP Eligibility Form

After downloading and reading your bulletin, submit your online CSCP eligibility form. Don't delay in performing this activity—it will determine if you are eligible to take the exam. Remember, you can't register for the CSCP exam unless APICS has approved your eligibility application.

APICS Membership

The third preparation step we recommend is to join APICS as a Plus member. Selecting the APICS Plus membership option will allow you to obtain discounts on ordering the CSCP Learning System, taking the exam, and on any other reference materials you may elect to purchase from APICS. The decision to join will have an immediate return on investment. While we believe that APICS membership has great value, this is your decision. You don't need to be an APICS member to take the CSCP exam.

CSCP Learning System

By purchasing the latest version of the CSCP Learning System, you will be provided with courseware that includes the CSCP Exam Content Manual (ECM) as well as one year of access to the CSCP online practice questions. The CSCP Learning System can also be ordered through the APICS Tappan Zee Chapter, if you live in the United States. Go to www.apicstz.org to place your order. If you order it this way, you will be provided with an extra 100-question practice test at no extra cost in addition to the practice questions in our book. Remember that APICS Plus members can obtain a discount on this material, so consider joining before you order.

Once you receive your CSCP Learning System, start by reading and reviewing the ECM to help you to better understand what will be on the exam. The ECM is found in the front of Module 1, Book 1. It will help you focus your studying to key areas.

APICS Dictionary App

If you have a smartphone, we suggest you download the free APICS Dictionary App to help you learn the CSCP key terminology. If you don't have a smartphone but are an APICS member, you can request a free copy of the APICS Dictionary. Nonmembers can purchase a copy from APICS—and it's worth the investment. Highlight the key terms found in the APICS CSCP Learning System ECM in your copy of the APICS Dictionary, and make sure to learn those terms. We also suggest you learn all of the terms found in our extended list. This step will help you to be better able to answer test questions by eliminating those terms that you know are wrong.

Authorization to Test (ATT)

Sign into the APICS website and go to My APICS where you can either purchase an exam credit or use an existing one to schedule your exam.

APICS requires a test taker to request and receive an ATT e-mail before scheduling their exam. This process validates a person's CSCP eligibility status and the existence of an APICS identification number. You need to validate that the name that appears next to your APICS identification number matches the stated member name on your primary and secondary identification documents. If you have discrepancies in your APICS documentation, or lack an APICS identification number, contact APICS customer service and request assistance. You won't be permitted to take the CSCP exam unless your documents match your APICS record.

The APICS computerized system will ask if you want to take the test in North America or outside of North America. Select your option and follow the APICS instructions to register for the exam. The CSCP exam is offered worldwide, only in a computer-based testing (CBT) format, and is scheduled through Pearson VUE.

Once you have logged into the APICS website, you can proceed to register. Select a test site using a chapter-supplied exam credit or pay for the exam with a credit or debit card. This site also permits you to reschedule or cancel your exam.

CSCP Study Plan

The use of a study and time management plan will provide a road map to help you prepare for the CSCP exam. We suggest you perform the following steps to determine your study start and end dates:

- Determine your desired CSCP exam date.
- Back schedule from your desired exam date to determine the number of available reading/study days.
- Leave at least ten days for your final review before your expected test date.
- Divide the number of CSCP Learning System pages by the number of days before the exam to determine the number of pages you must read each day/week.
- Plan to spend at least one hour per day reading the courseware and answering the questions found throughout the session. You will also need additional time to read our study guide.
- You should spend at least one to two hours (maybe more) per week answering the CSCP practice questions found in the online CSCP Learning System and our study guide and online test bank.
- You should spend at least one to two hours per week on body of knowledge gap analysis to help you better understand why you answered a practice test question incorrectly.
- You should spend at least one hour per week reviewing CSCP flash card/dictionary terms and doing some supplemental reading. The flash cards can be downloaded from the APICS CSCP online website or you can use the APICS Dictionary App.

We suggest you spend at least 10–15 hours per week on reading, taking practice tests, and resolving your CSCP body of knowledge gaps. Keeping up with the reading can be challenging, so establish milestones and track your progress. If you find you can't achieve your planned milestones, move out your exam test date. Don't take the exam if you haven't completely read the APICS CSCP Learning System, our study guide, and taken the online CSCP practice tests.

ACKNOWLEDGMENTS

We would like to take a moment to thank a number of people who assisted us in making this study guide possible.

First, we would like to thank our spouses, Harriet and Michelle, for their ongoing encouragement, support, faith, and love. Also, a special thanks to Joshua and Andrew for bringing love and joy into our lives.

Second, we want to thank Renee Myles for her editing skills, keeping us on track, constantly pushing us to finish this study guide, and for making us better writers. A special thanks to Anthony Myles, Ph.D., for his advice and all the time he spent checking our mathematical calculations and key concepts. This study guide would never have been finished without their hard work, encouragement, love, and ongoing efforts to cheer us on.

Third, we would like to thank the APICS Tappan Zee and Mid-Hudson Chapters for permitting us to teach APICS CSCP, CLTD, CIRM, and CPIM certification courses for them for the past 20 years. We also want to thank the hundreds of students who have attended our certification courses and tutorials. Their questions and feedback made us better instructors, which led us to write this study guide.

Fourth, a special thanks to Drew Gierman, Stephen Buda, and the team at J. Ross Publishing for their editorial guidance, technical knowledge, understanding, and patience—and for giving us the opportunity to write this study guide and prepare it for publication.

Finally, we also would like to thank all of the individuals who reviewed various sections of this study guide. We appreciated your encouragement and feedback.

ABOUT THE AUTHORS

HOWARD FORMAN

Howard Forman is president of PIM Associates Inc., a leading provider of operations and supply chain consulting, education, and training. He has over 35 years of experience in operations and supply chain management as a practitioner, consultant, and educator. His industry experience includes aerospace and defense, automotive, chemical, consumer, electrical/mechanical, financial, food, medical, pharmaceutical, remanufacturing, and service companies. Howard worked as a management consultant for Coopers & Lybrand, KPMG, Grant Thornton, and J.H. Cohn. He specializes in aiding companies who desire to reduce their inventory levels; make operations, warehouse, and process improvements; enhance cycle counting processes; optimize enterprise resources planning implementation systems; and improve demand management processes.

Howard has been a member of APICS since 1977. He has held numerous chapter board positions at the APICS Tappan Zee and the APICS Northern New Jersey Chapter, including Chapter President. He served the APICS Society as a member of its board of directors and Region 2 VP and as a member of its Chapter Development and its Voice of the Customer Committees. Howard was a section author for the APICS Operations Management Body of Knowledge Framework and a contributor to the CPIM Basics of Supply Chain Management and Master Planning of Resources courseware. He also participated in APICS CPIM and CIRM test question development sessions.

Howard has been recognized as a leading provider of APICS CSCP, CLTD, and CPIM certification courses, the APICS Lean Enterprise Workshop, APICS Principles courses, and the Basics of Supply Chain Management course. He has taught approximately 60 APICS CSCP and CLTD courses and over 175 CPIM certification courses for numerous APICS Chapters and the APICS Society. He has also developed and delivered tailored educational and training classes at over 85 companies in numerous industries.

Howard presented the first CSCP instructor webinar for the APICS Society and taught the first public CSCP certification and Lean Enterprise Workshop Series course in the country. He has presented the APICS Master Planning of Resources and the Detailed Scheduling and Planning CPIM certification tutorials at APICS International Conferences. He has also developed and freely shared numerous study aids and exercises to students worldwide.

Howard frequently speaks at APICS chapter dinner meetings, workshops, and seminars. He has also been a frequent speaker at the 6-Packed Conference, Seminar1, and Congress for Progress. He has presented at the DC Expo, BAAN, and American Software User Conferences as well as multiple APICS Volunteer Leadership Workshops held at APICS International Conferences and numerous APICS region and district meetings. He was honored at the 2012 APICS International Conference as the APICS Volunteer of the Year. He has also been honored by the APICS Tappan Zee Chapter, the APICS Mid-Hudson Chapter, and the APICS Northern New Jersey Chapter as their instructor of the year numerous times. The APICS Northern New Jersey Chapter has also recognized Howard twice with its Lifetime Member of the Year award.

Howard is a graduate of Fairleigh Dickinson University with a BS and MBA in Business Management and has had the privilege of teaching an operations management course there. He previously earned his APICS CSCP, CLTD, CIRM, and CFPIM certifications. Howard has also had articles published in Manufacturing Systems and Plant Maintenance magazines.

DAVID FORMAN

David Forman is a graduate of Johnson and Wales University with a BS in Business Management. He is currently the Senior Manager of Business Projects at a leading manufacturer of residential and commercial electronics. David is also a senior associate with PIM Associates Inc., a leading provider of operations and supply chain consulting, education, and training. He has over 15 years of experience in operations and supply chain management as a practitioner, educator, and consultant. His industry experience includes SAP project management and internal consulting in SAP customer relationship management and R/3, as well as being a subject matter expert in material management, production planning, material requirements planning, sales and distribution variant configuration, supply chain management, demand management and forecasting, and operations and business process improvement. David also specializes in global supply chain management, global enterprise resources planning implementation, warehouse management systems, customer relations management, supplier relations management, service and repair, and logistics management. His experience includes industries such as electrical/mechanical products, consumer products, food products, finance, remanufacturing, and service.

David earned his APICS CSCP and CLTD certifications and has taught courses for the APICS Tappan Zee and Mid-Hudson Chapters since 2014. He has also developed and delivered tailored educational and training classes at numerous companies. These courses have included such topics as inventory management, material requirements planning, sales and operations planning, master scheduling, cycle counting, and supply chain analytics.

David has held numerous chapter board positions at the APICS Northern New Jersey Chapter, including chapter president. He was honored by the APICS Northern New Jersey Chapter as their member of the year in 2012. He currently serves on the board of directors of the APICS Tappan Zee Chapter and teaches the APICS CSCP and CLTD certification courses.

PIM ASSOCIATES INC.

PIM Associates Inc. has been a nationally known provider of consulting and education services since 2000. They specialize in providing APICS CSCP, CLTD, and CPIM certification courses, as well as generic and tailored education and training. In addition, they also provide consulting services to help reduce inventory levels, improve inventory accuracy, help implement or improve cycle counting, take physical inventory, and improve MRP systems.

PIM Associates Inc. is dedicated to providing exceptional consulting and education services to emerging, mid market, or Fortune 100 companies. Their experience is based on many years of improving operational performance, reducing costs, improving customer service, and increasing company profit. They are able to quickly review operations and make recommendations to improve operational and financial performances. They have developed and delivered supply chain management, lean, S&OP, MRP, inventory improvement, and process improvement workshops along with APICS CSCP, CLTD, and CPIM classes to thousands of managers and employees.

This book has free material available for download from the
Web Added Value™ resource center at *www.jrosspub.com*

At J. Ross Publishing we are committed to providing today's professional with practical, hands-on tools that enhance the learning experience and give readers an opportunity to apply what they have learned. That is why we offer free ancillary materials available for download on this book and all participating Web Added Value™ publications. These online resources may include interactive versions of material that appears in the book or supplemental templates, worksheets, models, plans, case studies, proposals, spreadsheets and assessment tools, among other things. Whenever you see the WAV™ symbol in any of our publications, it means bonus materials accompany the book and are available from the Web Added Value Download Resource Center at www.jrosspub.com.

Downloads for *APICS CSCP Exam Success* include answers to the 25 exercises found throughout the book and the 75 question practice exam presented in Chapter 27, and a table that will help test the reader's understanding and recall of key terms and concepts.

J. ROSS PUBLISHING TESTING CENTER ACCESS

If you have purchased a new physical copy of this book, please check out the inside front cover for the link and serial number you will need to gain 45 days of free access to the CSCP online test bank. Happy studying!

1

SUPPLY CHAIN MANAGEMENT

This chapter focuses on the importance of supply chain management (SCM) to an organization. It examines how supply chains add value, the differences between an efficient and responsive supply chain, and vertical and horizontal integration. It also explores value chains, value streams, and value stream mapping.

SUPPLY CHAIN OVERVIEW

A *supply chain* is a network of participating entities, linked together, that is used to manage resources and materials, transform materials into a product, move and store products, and pass information from suppliers to their customers. Each organization seems to have its own unique definition of *SCM*. They range from improving supply chain related activities, to helping create customer value, planning and managing the movement of materials, and coordinating and integrating supply and demand management to plan, source, make, and deliver a product across all channels. One thing that all of the definitions have in common is that SCM helps to create net value, has value-creating activities, balances competing internal and external organizational interests, and manages the group dynamics of states, countries, and cultures to improve the overall process flow. This results in lower costs, improved delivery performances, visibility, and velocity—leading to enhanced customer value.

SUPPLY CHAIN OBJECTIVES

Companies strive to achieve five primary supply chain objectives in order to create value and gain financial benefits. The five objectives are adding value for customers and stakeholders, improving customer service, effectively using system-wide resources, efficiently using system-wide resources, and leveraging partner strengths.

Customer service supports customers before, during, and after the sales process and adds value to the customer experience. It can involve face-to-face, computer, phone, mail, or self-service interactions. The goal of customer service is to support, measure, and improve customer satisfaction.

Value is defined by the customer—and it's more than the monetary worth of an asset, item sold, or service rendered. The customers compare their perception against perceived cost benefits. This value comparison process can be quite subjective as customers perceive value differently based on cost, brand name, usage, and image in the marketplace. The process of adding value for customers and stakeholders is all about making supply chain investments that create customer service value while managing self-defeating internal and external tradeoffs and conflicts. Value ensures that the risk of extreme cost cutting is avoided because it can negatively impact customer service. Finally, adding value guarantees supply chain financial gains among all stakeholders so that everyone benefits.

A *stakeholder* is anyone who has an interest or concern regarding an organization's objectives, goals, actions, or policies. Examples of stakeholders include customers, employees, investors, suppliers, the government, and the community at large. Each group has a different definition of value, and companies need to consider how increasing the value for one stakeholder may impact the others. This requires carefully balancing the needs of one party against others so that everyone can benefit. A *primary stakeholder* is usually an internal stakeholder (employee, supplier, customer, or creditor) who is engaged in an economic business activity within the business itself. *External stakeholders* are those outside of the business who are affected by the business (investors, lenders, communities, and government).

The process of excellence in customer service addresses customer wants and needs. Common customer service metrics include on-time customer product delivery, reliability, availability, customer satisfaction, and operational performance. Companies target underperforming measurements and then implement supply chain improvement programs to correct areas in which they are weak.

The process of the effective use of system-wide resources refers to how well companies handle their own resources. Resources can be labor, equipment, material, or even money. The process measures resources against planned capacity. The process of efficient use of system-wide resources compares actual output to expected standard output in order to track performance. This metric is inward-focused, as it measures the efficiency of supply chain velocity, visibility, costs, and resources. It tracks a company's process in producing and distributing the right product, at the right time, to the right place, and at the right cost to meet customer service requirements. *Velocity* refers to speed. It's the rate at which products move through a supply chain, order process, manufacturing process, or get delivered to a customer. *Visibility* is the ability to see from one end of the supply chain to the other. Enhanced visibility improves velocity throughout the supply chain. Companies have learned that focusing on operational efficiency alone may lead to poor quality, which results in no additional gains. They have also learned that in order to be successful, they not only have to be efficient, they must also be effective.

Leveraging partner strengths is a supply chain objective that allows a company to focus on their core competencies or core capabilities. It leads to improved sales, design improvements, productivity gains, cost reductions, access to new markets and customers, new product ideas, and enhanced competitiveness. *Core competencies* or *core capabilities* are activities that are performed by companies and have been defined as being critical to their success. They consist of a number of different areas that help gain competitive advantages, enhanced strategic growth, and added value to products. Core competencies/core capabilities involve improving market access for their products, economies of scale, resource advantages (utilization or access), improved communications, improved organizational skills, technology advantages (software, data usage, or processes), financial strength, and geographic expertise or capacity advantages (global reach). Core competencies/core capabilities can be further broken down into decision making (planning and enabling) and execution activities (sourcing, making, delivering, and returning). Economies of scale are the competitive advantages that a company may have over its competition. Examples include high manufacturing volume, bulk purchases, or operating a warehouse seven days a week for three shifts per day.

EFFICIENT SUPPLY CHAIN

The *efficient supply chain* is driven by forecasts for make-to-stock (MTS) products that have stable customer demand and low forecast error. These products have a long product life cycle (PLC), limited market changes, and infrequent product introduction. The efficient supply chain permits a company to focus on high volume with low variety. This helps drive down operational costs and improve customer service. Examples that require an efficient supply chain are commodity products such as tomato soup, salt, or underwear.

Efficient supply chains focus on minimizing their cost structures. Companies using this method maintain a high equipment utilization and efficiency rate. They maintain minimal inventory levels that are sufficient to achieve desired customer service levels and select suppliers based on their ability to quickly deliver low-cost, reliable, and quality products. Products are forecasted based on historical demand.

RESPONSIVE SUPPLY CHAIN

The *responsive supply chain* is driven by customer orders and has low demand predictability. Products in this supply chain have a short PLC with frequent market changes and new product introduction. They are higher-margin make-to-order (MTO) or assemble-to-order (ATO) products *pulled* against customer orders. These products are desired by their customers but have low volume, high variety, and higher operational costs. *Supply chain resilience* is the ability to quickly adjust and restore supply chain operations back to their original state after a disruption.

A responsive supply chain manufacturing strategy focuses on delivery speed, agility, and higher profits. The company maintains flexibility with their operating facility and equipment and they keep excess capacity available to meet ever-changing customer demands. They also maintain higher raw material and component inventory levels, keep buffer (safety stock) inventory levels, and select their suppliers based on the ability to quickly deliver inventory. In the responsive supply chain strategy, products are forecasted based on qualitative techniques, and the forecast error can be quite high. The transportation strategy focuses on speedy delivery to meet customer requested lead times.

The key attributes and differences between the two forms of supply chains are displayed in Exhibit 1.1.

Exhibit 1.1   Efficient and responsive supply chain comparison

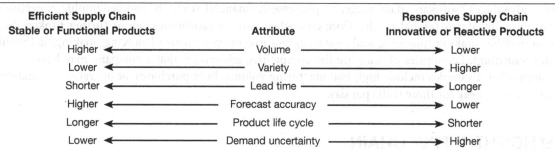

Efficient Supply Chain Stable or Functional Products	Attribute	Responsive Supply Chain Innovative or Reactive Products
Higher ←	Volume	→ Lower
Lower ←	Variety	→ Higher
Shorter ←	Lead time	→ Longer
Higher ←	Forecast accuracy	→ Lower
Longer ←	Product life cycle	→ Shorter
Lower ←	Demand uncertainty	→ Higher

SUPPLY CHAIN VERTICAL INTEGRATION

Vertical integration is when a company owns and controls all aspects of its upstream and downstream supply chain. It provides a stronger foundation for future growth by permitting the company to bring new products to market more quickly. A good example of vertical integration is the Ford Model T. Ford controlled its entire supply chain starting with the upstream iron mines, ships to move the iron ore, iron smelters, stamping presses, machine shops, and the downstream assembly areas. Although vertical integration gives a company strong internal control, it lacks the flexibility to incorporate product variability.

SUPPLY CHAIN HORIZONTAL OR LATERAL INTEGRATION

Horizontal or *lateral integration* creates a leaner, more agile business model in which a company focuses on its core competencies and outsources non-core activities. A good example of this is Apple, which performs its own sales and marketing, product design, and the operation of its retail stores. However, they outsource their manufacturing processes to third parties. A *business model* is a conceptual picture of an organization's strategy that is developed to project a future view of the business. It gets included in the business plan and includes attributes such as speed, quality, financial goals and objectives, market share, sustainability, resource management, and employee welfare. A business model focuses on satisfying customers.

SUPPLY CHAIN KEIRETSU INTEGRATION

Keiretsu is an intermediate form of integration that is used by Japanese companies. It's a business group in which member companies own small portions of each other's companies, have interlocking business relationships, buy and sell products and services to each other, and is centered on a core bank that provides funding.

Exercise 1.1 will test your knowledge and understanding of the three supply chain integration types—vertical, horizontal, and Keiretsu. Read each question and write in the answer that best applies. The answers to this exercise are available from the Web Added Value™ Download Resource Center at www.jrosspub.com.

Exercise 1.1 Supply chain integration types—vertical, horizontal, or Keiretsu

Attribute	Answer
1. Which type applies with a supply chain that has an agile business focus?	
2. Which type controls the entire supply chain?	
3. Which type focuses on a core competency?	
4. Which type focuses on economies of scale?	
5. Which type focuses on improving visibility?	
6. Which type is best for improving the income and cash flow statement?	
7. Which type is centered around a core bank?	
8. Which type is focused on backward integration?	
9. Which type is focused on long-term planning?	
10. Which type is focused on outsourcing?	
11. Which type is focused on interlocking business relationships?	

SUPPLY CHAIN VALUE CHAIN

A *value chain* identifies *value-added activities* within a company. These are high-level, primary, and support functional activities that a company considers its core competencies. Companies believe these activities are their strengths and add value in the eyes of the customer. A non-value activity is to be eliminated or outsourced. Examples of supply chain activities that can be outsourced include manufacturing, warehousing, transportation, and purchasing.

SUPPLY CHAIN VALUE STREAM

A *value stream* looks at processes or activities that are required to satisfy a customer need. It starts with an internal customer, such as a distribution center, and moves across functional departments including order entry, purchasing, and operations. It then ends at the external customer. A value stream examines each activity to determine its worth. The goal is to eliminate non-value process activities—resulting in reduced costs and improved velocity and visibility. An example of a supply chain value stream activity that can be eliminated is paying the supplier's invoice by check when it can be replaced by an electronic funds transfer.

SUPPLY CHAIN VALUE STREAM MAPPING

Value stream mapping (VSM) is a lean technique used to document a product or service value stream by using a one-page visual process picture. VSM starts with the customer and ends at the supplier. It encompasses various order processing, operational, inventory, and technology functions and activities. VSM begins with a one-page visual conceptual picture of the current *as-is* process and ends with a future *to-be* state that is used to identify supply chain process improvement opportunities.

Exercise 1.2 will test your knowledge and understanding of where to apply value chain, value stream, or value stream mapping. Read each question and write in all answers that apply. The answers to the exercise are available from the Web Added Value™ Download Resource Center at www.jrosspub.com.

Exercise 1.2   Understanding value chain, value stream, and value stream mapping

Question	Answer
1. Which are used to display a strategic business process model?	
2. Which are used to identify wasteful activities?	
3. Which best creates a future activity view?	
4. Which best displays delivery activity processes for a product and service organization?	
5. Which best displays process metrics?	
6. Which best shows a functional collaboration view?	
7. Which displays all information with a one page view?	
8. Which is a lean tool?	
9. Which is focused on showing a core competency view?	
10. Which shows an end-to-end supply chain view?	

KEY TERMINOLOGY

Understanding key terms and the concepts they represent is key to passing the Certified Supply Chain Professional (CSCP) exam. In this chapter, the following important terms are identified in Table 1.1.

Table 1.1   SCM key terminology

Business model
Core capability
Core competency
Customer service
Efficient supply chain
External stakeholder
Horizontal integration
Keiretsu*
Lateral integration
Primary stakeholder
Responsive supply chain
Stakeholder
Supply chain
Supply chain management (SCM)*
Supply chain resilience*
Value
Value chain*
Value stream*
Value stream mapping (VSM)*
Value-added activities
Velocity
Vertical integration
Visibility

* Key term found in the CSCP Exam Content Manual (ECM)

CSCP EXAM PRACTICE QUESTIONS ON SCM

The questions shown in Table 1.2a cover the concepts presented in this chapter on SCM. They are examples of what to expect on the actual exam.

Table 1.2a   CSCP exam practice questions on SCM

No.	Questions
1	Henry Ford's flow production process lacked a critical concept found in today's more customer responsive supply chain environment. What was it missing? a) Velocity b) Flexibility c) Quality standards d) Flexible workforce
2	A product which has little need for real-time information and uses a simple connectivity technology is best described by which supply chain strategy type? a) Stable b) Unstable c) Reactive d) Efficient reactive
3	The practice of bringing the supply chain inside one organization refers to: a) Chase integration b) Lateral integration c) Vertical integration d) Horizontal integration
4	A form of integration in which suppliers and customers aren't completely independent, but instead own limited stakes in one another, is best called: a) Cartel b) Kanban c) Keiretsu d) Poka yoka
5	Which of the following may hamper a lateral supply chain? a) Focus b) Control c) Expertise d) Economics of scale
6	Supply chain management is about creating: a) Net value b) Cost reduction c) Leaner supply chain d) Process improvements

Continued

7	What is the real challenge in developing a value stream? a) Seeing it from the customer's perspective b) Seeing it from the supplier's perspective c) Eliminating non-value-added activities d) Seeing it from the producer's perspective
8	What will most likely increase in a traditional manufacturing business if driven by economies-of-scale thinking? a) Agility b) Velocity c) Flexibility d) Inventory
9	Which of the following isn't the best indication of a company using a responsive strategy? a) Faster delivery speed b) Quicker order fulfillment c) Higher customer satisfaction d) Higher work center efficiency and utilization
10	Zara, a global manufacturer and retailer of clothing, has a supply chain strategy that is best based on: a) Cost efficiency b) Speed to market c) Configure to order d) Outsourcing manufacturing
11	The MIP Company decided to pursue cost efficiencies and increase velocity due to changes in market conditions, but not at the exclusion of: a) Speed b) Flexibility c) Process flow d) Product volume
12	A company that has a relatively stable demand and a high level of forecast accuracy will focus primarily on: a) Agility b) Efficiency c) Reliability d) Responsiveness
13	Which of the following isn't an attribute of a response-focused supply chain? a) Fixed capacity b) High forecast errors c) Multiple warehouses d) Short product life cycle (PLC)

ANSWERS TO CSCP EXAM PRACTICE QUESTIONS ON SCM

The answers to the practice questions on SCM are shown in Table 1.2b. Any question you answer incorrectly indicates a gap in your body of knowledge and encourages the need for additional study time.

Table 1.2b   Answers to CSCP exam practice questions on SCM

No.	Answers
1	Answer: B Flexibility was missing in the Ford flow production process. The company built only black model Ts which increased volume, but limited product mix flexibility.
2	Answer: A A stable product has a stable demand pattern and doesn't require real-time information.
3	Answer: C This question requires knowledge of the APICS Dictionary definition of vertical integration. Vertical integration means that the company does everything themselves. Horizontal and lateral are the same term, and chase integration is a made-up term.
4	Answer: C This question requires knowledge of the APICS Dictionary definition of Keiretsu. Keiretsu is a Japanese network of integrated companies with interlocking business relationships and cross-ownerships.
5	Answer: B A lateral supply chain doesn't have direct control over functional activities because they are being performed by other parties.
6	Answer: A Supply chain management is about creating net value, not cost reduction. Creating net value includes answers B, C, and D within it.
7	Answer: A This question requires knowledge of the APICS Dictionary definition of value stream. It's hard to view a value stream from the customer perspective because it may be in conflict with internal objectives.
8	Answer: D Traditionally, economies-of-scale thinking drives a company to produce large production quantities which result in increased inventory levels.
9	Answer: D Higher work-center efficiency and utilization means that a company is making longer and larger production runs. Customer service is impacted as the company focuses on a forecast or low-cost strategy, rather than a responsive strategy.
10	Answer: B Zara considers speed to market (velocity) as their strategic order winner, as described in the CSCP courseware.
11	Answer: B The company must still be flexible even if it impacts cost so that it can increase product delivery when and where it's required.
12	Answer: B A company that has relatively stable demand and a high level of forecast accuracy will focus on efficiency. This permits it to lower costs as pricing becomes the key market driver.
13	Answer: A Fixed capacity restricts the amount of products a company can produce and limits the flexibility to respond to customer needs. This then limits the response-focused supply chain as the company needs flexibility to respond quickly to customers. For this reason, fixed capacity cannot be an attribute for a response-focused supply chain.

2

SUPPLY CHAIN
REFERENCE MODEL

This chapter focuses on the importance of the APICS Supply Chain Operations Reference (SCOR®) model to an organization. It examines the various business activities, supply chain stages, and manufacturing environments. It also explores the SCOR Level 1 and 2 metrics.

SCOR BACKGROUND

The *Supply Chain Council* (SCC) was organized in 1996 by Pittiglio, Rabin, Todd, and McGrath and Advanced Manufacturing Research (AMR), along with representatives from a cross mix of 69 different manufacturers, retail stores, and distributors. The SCC merged with APICS in 2014, and is now called the APICS SCC.

The APICS SCC is tasked with continuing to establish a common cross-functional standard for defining supply chain processes, identifying performance improvement opportunities, and developing measurements to track the performance of different supply chain entities. The standard is designed to help companies improve their overall supply chain by benchmarking internal performances against best-in-class performances. *Benchmarking* compares a company's performance against other company or industry performances.

The SCC created SCOR which is now called the APICS SCOR model. SCOR makes it easier for companies to benchmark their individual performance against other companies. This allows companies from different industries to use the same performance criteria as a standard set of metrics to monitor and track supply chain performances based on industry best practices.

BASIC SUPPLY CHAIN MODEL

The APICS SCOR basic supply chain model consists of three high-level entities called the *supplier*, *producer*, and *customer*, and is displayed in Exhibit 2.1.

The SCOR model further breaks down into six distinct supply chain processes—plan, source, make, deliver, return, and enable. These six processes are common building blocks that are used to describe

Exhibit 2.1   Basic supply chain model

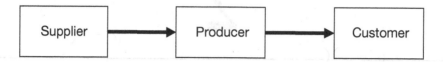

simple to complex supply chains. This allows different industries to be linked together with a standard set of processes. The APICS SCOR basic supply chain model displays only two levels in either direction.

The six supply chain management processes use a standard language that all companies can easily understand. *Plan* aggregates demand and supply to develop a course of action to improve the planning, how to source, and how to deliver supply chain activities. *Source* (*sourcing*) involves the procurement of goods and services. *Make* is used to transform raw materials and components into a product, meeting planned or actual customer demand. *Deliver* includes the order management, transportation management, and distribution management processes. *Return* is the process associated with returning products back from a customer. *Enable* provides guidance on how to support the other five supply chain building blocks using the *plan-do-check-act* model.

Exercise 2.1 will test your knowledge and understanding of the six SCOR processes (plan, source, make, deliver, return, and enable). Read each question and write in the best answer. The answers to the exercise are available from the Web Added Value™ Download Resource Center at www.jrosspub.com.

Exercise 2.1   Understanding of SCOR processes

Question	Answer
1. Which process is focused on reducing scrap?	
2. Which process is focused on selecting suppliers?	
3. Which process is focused on end-of-life activity?	
4. Which process is focused on specifying packaging?	
5. Which process is focused on scheduling shipments?	
6. Which process is focused on using recovered materials?	
7. Which process is focused on determining material needs?	
8. Which process is focused on using eco-friendly packaging?	
9. Which process is focused on minimizing hazardous materials?	
10. Which process is focused on determining how to best dispose of hazardous materials?	
11. Which process is focused on supporting best recycling practices?	

SUPPLY CHAIN STRUCTURES

The retail, manufacturing, service, and return environment supply chain models are displayed differently when compared to the basic supply chain model. The retail supply chain adds a new entity called *retail* that is placed after the producer but before the customer. Retail is the initial customer of the producer who receives product delivery and can perform a service before selling products to their customers, as shown in Exhibit 2.2.

Exhibit 2.2   Retail supply chain

A *manufacturing environment* looks similar to the basic supply chain model but the supplier is called a *Tier 1* supplier. The Tier 1 supplier procures goods or services from a supplier's supplier. The supplier's supplier is called either an end supplier or a *Tier 2* supplier. In a Tier 2 model, two new storage entities are also added. They are called the *central warehouse* and the *distributor warehouse* and both support the customer, as shown in Exhibit 2.3.

Exhibit 2.3   Manufacturing supply chain

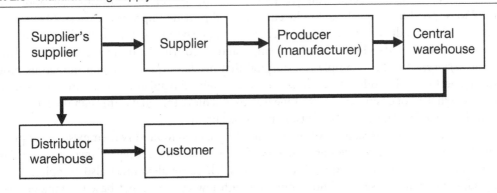

Examples of *service* providers are an instructor selling APICS education courses, a utility, or a person cutting grass. They perform the producer function and deliver a service directly to a customer without performing any manufacturing or warehouse activities, as shown in Exhibit 2.4.

Exhibit 2.4   Service supply chain

In the basic, retail, manufacturing, and service supply chains, the flow of information travels both ways, products or services move from the producer to the customer, and the flow of cash moves from the customer to the supplier.

The return supply chain is slightly different from the others. The flow of information still travels both ways, but products move back from the customer to the producer, and the flow of cash moves from the supplier to the customer, as shown in Exhibit 2.5.

Exhibit 2.5   Return supply chain

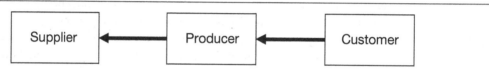

An emerging trend for companies is the establishment of nontraditional supply chains that often require specialized activities to meet the unique attributes of their operations. In those situations, supply chains need to respond more quickly, at reduced costs, and provide improved services. One example of this is humanitarian and disaster relief services. They need to respond quickly, plan deliveries to locations with poor infrastructures, develop local relationships, and build trust in order to provide needed relief supplies and services. Another example is a hospital that needs to quickly obtain numerous products, track delivery, perform full product traceability, comply with local regulatory requirements, reduce costs, and provide a high level of customer service. One way they achieve this goal is through the requirement of a *unique device identifier* (UDI) for tracking and billing accuracy.

Traditional retailers, such as Staples, Walmart, and Macy's, need to modify their existing supply chains to have multichannel distribution centers. They need to maintain high levels of inventory and product variety, provide quick delivery, and do this at low costs. These retailers must also complete this while providing superior customer service and competing with low-cost, internet-based companies, such as Amazon and Alibaba.

SCOR LEVEL 1 AND LEVEL 2 METRICS

Level 1 SCOR metrics display *key performance indicators* (KPIs). KPIs are quantifiable measurements that are linked to a corporate strategic goal or objective that is used to track ongoing performance. Level 1 SCOR measures and tracks KPI performance attributes, which include *reliability, responsiveness, agility, costs*, and *asset management*. The first three attributes are customer-focused and the last two are internally-focused. Companies use these metrics to benchmark themselves against competitors and to establish *level-of-service* improvement targets. Level of service is a metric that tracks whether or not a company is achieving customer delivery goals in terms of requested quantity, on-time delivery, and other customer specified requirements.

Level 1 metrics can be further broken down into Level 2 metrics and classified by manufacturing environments including make-to-stock (MTS), make-to-order (MTO), assemble-to-order (ATO), engineer-to-order (ETO), and retail. Level 2 metrics also provide a greater level of detail in performing supply chain diagnostic and root cause analysis based on the manufacturing environment.

Reliability is a customer-facing metric that is used to track supply chain performance to determine if the customer order is delivered as requested by the customer. Measurements include fill rate and perfect order fulfillment. *Fill rate*, also known as *order fill rate* or *customer service ratio*, measures the speed at which a company can fully satisfy customer orders. Other variations of the order fill rate are unit fill rate, line item fill rate, and monetary value fill rate. Table 2.1 provides an example of the order fill rate.

Unit fill rate is determined by taking the percentage of units that can be fulfilled and comparing it against the ordered unit quantity. In Table 2.1, 14 units have been ordered, but only six units are available to be shipped. The unit fill rate is 42.9% (6/14). *Line item fill rate* is determined by taking the percentage of order line items that can be fulfilled and comparing them against the ordered amount. In Table 2.1, four line items have been ordered, but only two line items are available to be completely shipped. The order line item fill rate is 50.0% (2/4). *Monetary value fill rate* is determined by taking the percentage of the monetary value of the requested line items and comparing them against the costed amount. In Table 2.1, the value of the ordered line items is $54, but only $20 worth is available for shipment. The monetary value fill rate is 37.0% ($20/$54). *Perfect order fulfillment* measures the percentage of customer orders that were delivered 100% complete. In other words, the shipment has the right quantity and is shipped at a specified time, to the right location, to the right customer, and with the right documentation. For example, if 98 orders out of 100 meet this condition, the perfect order fulfillment rate would be 98%.

Responsiveness measures the supply chain velocity (speed) in delivering products to a customer. It's based on order fulfillment lead time, which counts the number of days from customer order receipt until delivery at the customer's location.

Agility is the ability of the supply chain to quickly respond to changes in the marketplace in order to assist a company in gaining or keeping their competitive advantage. There are four metrics used to track supply chain agility. They are upside supply chain flexibility, upside supply chain adaptability, downside supply chain adaptability, and overall value at risk (VaR). Per SCOR, *upside supply chain flexibility* is the number of days required to achieve an unplanned, sustainable 20% increase in delivered quantities. *Upside*

Table 2.1 Order fill rate example

Item	Cost	Stock	Order	Quantity
7777	$3.00	7	1234	4
7787	$3.00	2	1234	1
8555	$2.00	0	1289	2
8577	$5.00	1	1296	7

supply chain adaptability is the quantity of increased production that an organization can achieve and sustain for 30 days. *Downside supply chain adaptability* is the reduction in order quantities that are sustainable for 30 days prior to delivery with no inventory or cost penalties. Overall *VaR* is used to measure and quantify potential financial loss in value within the supply chain. VaR is calculated by taking the sum of the supply chain functions (plan, source, make, deliver, and return).

Order fulfillment cycle time measures the time required from customer order placement to the customer receipt of the ordered product. This is also referred to as *customer order cycle time*.

Supply chain costs include those costs associated with operating a supply chain to deliver products and services to customers. *Total cost to serve* includes the sum of supply chain direct and indirect costs to plan, source, land, produce, manage orders, deliver, and return products. Its analysis is used to inform management of where costs are incurred and how they get consumed throughout the supply chain.

Supply chain asset management refers to how well an organization effectively manages its resources (assets). This includes fixed and working capital. It uses cash-to-cash cycle time, return on supply chain fixed assets, and return on working capital to measure how effectively assets are being used.

Table 2.2 provides an example of how two Level 1 metrics can be broken down into Level 2 metrics according to the SCOR documentation.

The SCOR model identifies processes that influence the performance of Level 1 metrics and associated Level 2 metrics. Level 2 metrics serve as a diagnostics tool for Level 1 metrics. They identify Level 1 metrics that aren't performing to expectations, and then analyze them to identify issue root causes.

Companies use Level 1 and Level 2 metrics to measure and monitor their own supply chain. A company aggregates its supply chain performances and benchmarks them against their competition to target improvement opportunities. A company can't be the best in all areas, so each company must select key metrics that will help it become more successful.

The Level 1 *total cost to serve* metric can be broken down into two Level 2 metrics. They are supply chain management cost (SCMC) and cost of goods sold, as shown in Table 2.3.

Exercise 2.2 will test your knowledge and understanding of the Level 1 SCOR metrics. Read each question and write in the best answer. The answers to the exercise are available from the Web Added Value™ Download Resource Center at www.jrosspub.com.

Table 2.2   Level 1 metric disaggregation into Level 2

Attribute	Level 1	Level 2
Responsiveness	Order fill rate	Forecast accuracy
		Inventory days of supply
Reliability	Order fulfillment cycle time	Order fulfillment lead time
		MTS items from order entry to order shipment
		MTO items from order entry to complete manufacturing to order shipment

Table 2.3   SCOR Level 2 supply chain financial metrics

Level 2 Metrics	Definitions	Calculations
Supply chain management cost (SCMC)	Sum of the costs associated with the SCOR Level 2 processes to plan, source, deliver, and return Cost of raw materials and make costs are generally accounted for in COGS	SCMC = cost to plan + source + deliver + return + mitigate supply chain risk
Cost of goods sold (COGS)	Cost associated with buying raw materials and producing finished goods. Costs include direct costs (labor and materials) and indirect costs (overhead)	COGS = direct material costs + direct labor costs + indirect costs related to making product

Exercise 2.2   Level 1 SCOR metrics

Question	Answer
1. Which Level 1 metric best represents downside supply chain adaptability?	
2. Which Level 1 metric best represents order fulfillment cycle time?	
3. Which Level 1 metric best represents overall value at risk?	
4. Which Level 1 metric best represents perfect order fulfillment?	
5. Which Level 1 metric best represents return on supply chain fixed assets?	
6. Which Level 1 metric best represents return on working capital?	
7. Which Level 1 metric best represents the cash-to-cash cycle time?	
8. Which Level 1 metric best represents total cost to serve?	
9. Which Level 1 metric best represents upside supply chain flexibility?	
10. Which Level 1 metric best represents upside supply chain adaptability?	

MANUFACTURING ENVIRONMENTS

An MTS item is a functional product that requires immediate product delivery to a customer. It employs *repetitive manufacturing* or continuous production manufacturing techniques. MTS items are high-volume, low-variety forecasted products with short manufacturing cycle times. Cost reduction is a major focus. The factory will have high utilization that keeps the overhead and cost of goods low, but the line will have limited flexibility. In this environment, the master schedule represents the anticipated build schedule that is required to maintain inventory at desired levels. Examples of MTS items are tomato soup and basic computers.

An MTO item is a functional or innovative product that is produced to a specific customer order. Volume is low and variety is high, with lead time being a major concern. In this environment, the master scheduler plans actual customer orders. MTO items are usually produced in intermittent batches. Demand is irregular with product variety being the driver. Examples of MTO items are unique machine parts or furniture with different colored fabric.

ATO, *finish-to-order* (FTO), and *package-to-order* (PTO) are all similar terms that are used to describe functional or innovative products that are being produced to specific customer orders. Quite often sub-assemblies, modular units, or bulk products are the first parts produced to stock, based on a modular bill of material. This permits manufacturing to quickly assemble and package a product based on customer defined specifications. For example, a customer wants to purchase a laptop computer with extra memory, a large hard drive, and a number of preloaded software applications. The base laptop modular unit, along with extra memory, and a large hard drive, is pulled from inventory. It is then quickly assembled, loaded with software, and tested. This is an example of a *final assembly schedule* (FAS). Other examples are automobiles, silverware with different-sized place settings, or different-sized packaged food products.

Configure-to-order (CTO) items are functional or innovative products that are assembled to meet unique customer needs upon the receipt of a customer order. Customer orders are processed using a configurator that handles one product at a time. Products are assembled from prebuilt components and subassemblies. Volume and variety are high and lead times are shorter. In this environment, the master scheduler plans according to actual customer orders. Examples are window shades or computers where the customer specifies different sizes, colors, or components.

ETO items are unique and innovative products that are designed, the materials are requisitioned, and then the item is produced after the receipt of a customer order. Volume is very low and variety is high with lead time being a major concern. In this environment, the work center builds according to actual customer orders. ETO items are produced one order at a time. Examples are unique, specially designed factory packaging equipment, a cargo ship, or an airplane.

The various manufacturing environments have unique attributes pertaining to volume, variety, delivery speed, cost structure, planning, and carrying costs, as shown in Table 2.4.

Table 2.4 Manufacturing environment attributes

Type	Volume/Variety	Delivery Speed	Cost Structure	Planning/Carrying Costs
MTS	High volume, low variety	Fastest	Lowest	Low/high
ATO	Low volume, high variety	Faster	Lower	Lower/moderate
CTO	Low volume, high variety	Fast	Low	High/low
MTO	Low volume, high variety	Slow	High	High/moderate
ETO	Low volume, high variety	Slower	Highest	High/low

Strategic and marketing decisions determine the type or types of manufacturing environments that a company selects. They will often select different strategies for different product lines (functional versus innovative) and define a different master scheduling approach for each product line.

KEY TERMINOLOGY

Understanding key terms and the concepts they represent is crucial to passing the Certified Supply Chain Professional (CSCP) exam. In this chapter, the following important terms are identified in Table 2.5.

Table 2.5   SCOR model key terminology

Agility
Assemble-to-order (ATO)*
Asset management
Benchmarking
Central warehouse
Configure-to-order (CTO)
Customer
Customer order cycle time
Customer service ratio*
Deliver
Distributor warehouse
Enable
Engineer-to-order (ETO)
Fill rate*
Final assembly schedule (FAS)
Finish-to-order (FTO)
Intermittent
Key performance indicators (KPIs)*
Level of service*
Make
Make-to-order (MTO)*
Make-to-stock (MTS)*
Manufacturing environment
Order fill rate
Order fulfillment cycle time
Package-to-order (PTO)
Perfect order fulfillment
Plan
Producer
Reliability
Repetitive manufacturing
Responsiveness
Retail
Return
Service provider
Source
Supplier
Supply chain asset management (SCAM)
Supply chain cost
Supply Chain Council (SCC)
Supply Chain Operations Reference Model (SCOR®)*
Total cost to serve
Unique device identifier (UDI)

*Key term found in the CSCP ECM

CSCP EXAM PRACTICE QUESTIONS ON THE SCOR MODEL

The questions shown in Table 2.6a cover the concepts that were presented in this chapter on the SCOR Model. They are examples of what to expect on the actual exam.

Table 2.6a   SCOR model practice questions

No.	Questions
1	Addressing and managing waste disposal is found under which SCOR model process? a) Plan b) Make c) Source d) Delivery
2	What SCOR cost entity lies between cost to source and cost to return in a total cost to service calculation? a) Cost to plan b) Cost to make c) Cost to retail d) Cost to deliver
3	Calculate the piece fill rate based on the data provided below: Item Cost Stock Order Qty 7777 \$3.00 5 1234 4 7787 \$3.00 2 1234 2 8555 \$2.00 0 1289 2 8557 \$5.00 3 1296 4 a) 36% b) 75% c) 64% d) 71%
4	A repetitive manufacturing process most likely is used to produce: a) Low-volume, low-variety products b) High-volume, low-variety products c) High-volume, high-variety products d) Low-volume, high-variety products
5	A repetitive manufacturer has all of the following advantages over a job shop except for: a) Shorter cycle times b) Lower overhead rates c) Lower cost of goods sold (COGS) d) Greater product flexibility
6	In the supply chain community, who resides at the end of the supply chain? a) Retailer b) End user c) Wholesaler d) Distributor
7	Source and return processes are only performed by which supply chain member? a) Supplier b) Customer c) Supplier's supplier d) Customer's customer

Continued

8	What does a company need most if it experiences high supply chain demand variability in the marketplace? a) Agility b) Flexibility c) Efficiency d) Reliability
9	Which of the following is most important to satisfy the customers' requested delivery dates and quantities? a) Efficiency b) Reliability c) Responsiveness d) Level of service
10	Which of the following is most important to satisfy the customer's requested delivery dates and quantities of unique products? a) Repetitive process b) Continuous process c) Intermittent process d) MTS environment
11	A metric defined by management that has been linked to a specific strategic goal or objective is most likely using: a) An attribute b) A measurement c) The Balanced Scorecard d) A KPI
12	A key performance indicator nonfinancial metric must be linked to a/an: a) Tactical goal b) Strategic goal c) Operational goal d) Supply chain goal
13	Management established a KPI linked to a strategic customer service replenishment goal. Management noticed that the goal hasn't been achieved. What action will they most likely take? a) Reduce the goal b) Assess the root cause c) Contact the customer d) Collect replenishment data
14	Order fulfillment dwell time is best described as: a) Total supply chain cycle time b) Time an order spends waiting to be shipped to a customer c) Time an order spends waiting in queue d) Time an order spends waiting to move to the next processing step
15	Which of the following SCOR metrics measures reliability? a) Perfect order fulfillment b) Order fulfillment cycle time c) Upside supply chain flexibility d) Upside supply chain adaptability
16	All of the following SCOR metrics measure supply chain agility except for: a) Overall value at risk b) Order fulfillment cycle time c) Upside supply chain adaptability d) Downside supply chain adaptability

Continued

17	Which of the following isn't a broad approach to benchmarking? a) Surveys b) Process benchmarking c) Competitive benchmarking d) Best-in-class benchmarking
18	Which of the following isn't an availability performance measurement? a) Fill rate b) Consistency c) Stockout frequency d) Orders shipped complete
19	Which is the formula for perfect order fulfillment? a) Total perfect line items/total number of orders received b) Total perfect orders/total number of orders c) Total number of orders/total perfect orders d) Total number of orders/total order line items
20	What term best refers to the least amount of time required to achieve the unplanned, sustainable increase when considering source, make, and deliver components? a) Upside supply chain flexibility b) Upside supply chain adaptability c) Downside supply chain flexibility d) Downside supply chain adaptability
21	The MIP Company needs to quickly respond to a reduction in customer orders. What SCOR supply chain attribute needs to be measured? a) Agility b) Velocity c) Flexibility d) Adaptability

ANSWERS TO CSCP EXAM PRACTICE QUESTIONS ON THE SCOR MODEL

The answers to the practice questions on the SCOR model are shown in Table 2.6b. Any question you answer incorrectly indicates a gap in your body of knowledge and encourages the need for additional study time.

Table 2.6b Answers to CSCP exam practice questions on the SCOR model

No.	Answers
1	Answer: B Managing waste disposal is found under the SCOR *make* process. Review the SCOR Reference Guide (outside reference).
2	Answer: D Knowledge of the total cost to service Level 1 metric and the SCMC Level 2 metric formulas are required to answer this question. The formula for SCMC is the sum of the cost to plan + source + deliver + return. The correct answer is cost to deliver because it lies between cost to source and cost to return. The cost to make is excluded from this calculation when calculating total cost to serve. It is however included in the COGS.

Continued

3	Answer: B
	The piece fill rate first adds up the number of ordered items (12). Next, it compares the number of items ordered against what can be delivered from stock. For example, item 8557 requires four pieces, but only three pieces are in stock. This review is repeated for each ordered item. A total of nine pieces are available to be shipped. The piece fill rate is calculated by taking the number of delivered pieces (available), divided by the total number of pieces ordered, to calculate a piece fill rate of 75% (9/12).
4	Answer: B
	A repetitive manufacturer requires high volume and low variety in orders. The company will make only a few high-volume products which limits their product variety.
5	Answer: D
	A repetitive manufacturer requires high volume and low variety in order to keep the line active. They make only a few high-volume products, which have short cycle times. The factory has high utilization, which keeps overhead low and COGS low. However, since they only make a few products requiring long production runs, flexibility is limited.
6	Answer: B
	The end user resides at the customer end of the supply chain. The retailer, wholesaler, and distributor are all intermediate customers who sell to someone else. This means that none of them can be at the extreme end of the customer side of the supply chain.
7	Answer: D
	The customer's customer only performs sourcing and returns. They don't make or deliver anything as they are the end customer.
8	Answer: A
	Companies experiencing high supply chain demand variability in the marketplace require agility to quickly react to change. Flexibility and reliability are part of agility. Efficiency is the ability to produce a product faster than the defined process routing standard.
9	Answer: D
	This question requires knowledge of the APICS Dictionary definition of *level of service*. Answers A, B, and C refer to level of service.
10	Answer: C
	The key words in this question are *unique products*. A *unique product* is best described by the term intermittent process. The use of an intermittent process permits the company to make unique products one at a time for customers. MTS, continuous process, and the repetitive process are all used to build inventory to a forecast.
11	Answer: D
	This question requires knowledge of the APICS Dictionary definition of KPI. A balanced scorecard isn't a metric, but rather a process.
12	Answer: B
	This question requires knowledge of the APICS Dictionary definition of KPI. A KPI refers to a strategic goal or objective and not to a tactical or operational goal, which are both more detailed. A supply chain goal isn't strategic, but rather more tactical or operational depending on what it's trying to measure.
13	Answer: B
	The company needs to assess the root cause to find out why the goal hasn't been achieved. A, C, and D are incorrect because reducing the goal doesn't solve the problem, contacting the customer may be required after assessing the root cause, and collecting replenishment data isn't needed as they have already collected data.
14	Answer: D
	Dwell time is the amount of time an order spends waiting to move from one stage of processing to another.

Continued

15	Answer: A Perfect order fulfillment measures reliability, which is the process of delivering what is required, in the quantity required, and when it's required. Order fulfillment cycle time measures responsiveness and upside supply chain flexibility and upside supply chain adaptability measure agility.
16	Answer: B Agility is the process of responding to changes in the marketplace. Order fulfillment cycle time measures supply chain responsiveness. The fourth agility measurement is upside supply chain flexibility.
17	Answer: A The three broad approaches to benchmarking are competitive, best-in-class, and process. Surveys are a benchmarking tool.
18	Answer: B Consistency isn't a direct measurement of product availability. Answers A, C, and D do measure availability.
19	Answer: B The perfect order fulfillment formula is total perfect orders divided by total number of orders.
20	Answer: A This question requires knowledge of the APICS Dictionary definition of *upside supply chain flexibility*.
21	Answer: A Agility is the ability for the full supply chain to respond quickly to market changes. Velocity is the speed at which changes are made, flexibility is the ability for the factory to change (which provides agility within the factory), and adaptability is the overall ability to change.

3

LOGISTICS FUNDAMENTALS

This chapter focuses on the varying roles of logistics in the supply chain. It examines the meaning of logistics, the need for supply chain and logistics integration, the role of logistics service providers, and reverse logistics.

LOGISTICS

Logistics is the part of supply chain management (SCM) that plans, executes, and controls the movement and storage of goods throughout the supply chain. It refers to the movement of products from an upstream point of origin to a final point of use and involves the integration of these functions to permit seamless distribution and warehousing. Logistics functions include transportation, warehousing, inventory management, packaging, material procurement, light assembly, product labeling, clearing customs, distribution to customers, and reverse logistics. All of these different steps are needed to support customers throughout the supply chain.

The logistics *value proposition* involves balancing costs against services. It focuses on implementing internal and external activities that are considered important by the customer or by performing services better than a competitor. The *total cost concept* compares meeting customer service expectations against total cost savings. It looks at the areas of delivery speed, inventory, management, and service costs. These costs are benchmarked against other companies to determine who provides the best service at the lowest cost.

SUPPLY CHAIN INTEGRATION

Supply chain integration requires a number of critical steps to be undertaken before constructing an effective global logistics network. These steps are:

1. Start by identifying all forward and reverse supply chains by country. Perform a location analysis to determine what location would make the logistic function more efficient and effective. The goal is to place a facility in the right country.

2. Develop an effective export-import strategy by examining freight volume, customer locations, and *stock-keeping units* (SKUs). The goal is to determine where to best store inventory based on distance to customers and delivery lead time.

3. Select the optimal number of warehouse locations based on their distance from global markets and customers within a distribution network. The goal is to identify where to place the required number of warehouses and which country best meets strategic objectives.

4. Select transportation modes and carriers that will efficiently connect all supply chain participants. The goal is to reduce costs and improve delivery times.

5. Select the right number of partners to effectively manage the forward and reverse logistics supply chains. They must have the knowledge of local markets and custom regulations. The goal is to better manage the movement process and improve delivery times.

6. Develop a state-of-the-art information system to track and control material movement regardless of the global location. The goal is to improve demand transaction speed and data accuracy.

LOGISTICS SERVICE PROVIDERS

Outsourcing is the process of transferring internal manufacturing activities and capabilities to an external service provider. An example of this is a company that moves an in-house manufacturing process to a third-party provider whose factory is across the street.

Some companies consider logistics to be a core competency, while others don't. The ones that don't decide to outsource this function to a third party. A *third-party logistics* (3PL) provider performs these services—such as warehousing, transportation, or product repair for these companies. A *fourth-party logistics* (4PL) provider acts as a general contractor of multiple 3PLs to design, build, integrate, and operate outsourced supply chain processes. Companies outsource functions that they don't consider a core competency.

A company that plans to allow a third party to perform its logistics functions needs to be aware of outsourcing caveats. These caveats include understanding how internal cost structures compare against proposed 3PL provider costs in order to validate expected savings and benefits. The company must determine if the 3PL provider has the expected special skills and strengths to enhance its customer service level, in which the company may be lacking. It must also determine whether the 4PL plans to hire the most qualified partner or if it will select a favored *subcontractor* who may not be the best or cheapest service provider. Finally, the company must decide if the benefits of outsourcing are worth the loss of operational and budget control.

Outsourcing permits a company to focus on its core competencies. The benefits of outsourcing functions to a 3PL or 4PL provider are: improved business focus, access to the latest technology, reduced costs and enhanced cash flow, and improved efficiency, velocity, flexibility, and operations. In outsourcing, one disadvantage is loss of control.

Contract success requires both sides to benefit financially and operationally from the relationship. A company needs to predefine success goals, identify who commits to perform what functions in the relationship, show how rewards and risks will be shared, specify regular communication meetings, predefine performance metrics, and properly manage the relationship to include confidentiality, arbitration, and escape clauses.

Exercise 3.1 will test your knowledge of 3PL or 4PL activities. Place an *X* in the column if you think it applies. The answers to the exercise are available from the Web Added Value™ Download Resource Center at www.jrosspub.com.

Exercise 3.1   3PL or 4PL functions

Activity	3PL	4PL
1. Who performs a specific supply chain related function?		
2. Who manages and directs multiple external service providers?		
3. Who will make the investment in the latest technology and services?		
4. Who may select a partner who may not be the best or cheapest service provider?		
5. Who has the responsibility to assemble, manage, and integrate resources, along with the capability and technology to design, build, and run a comprehensive supply chain solution?		

SUBSTITUTING INFORMATION FOR INVENTORY

Substituting information for inventory is an important part of the logistics process. It permits inventory levels to be reduced along with supply chain *friction* through improved velocity and visibility. Friction is caused by any process or activity that slows down the supply chain. Visibility can be improved through communications and using tracking inventory tools such as *global positioning systems* (GPS), radio frequency identification devices (RFID), and bar codes. Additional improvements can be obtained by keeping inventory in transit, the use of *postponement centers* (which delay final assembly until receipt of customer orders), and mixing multiple SKUs together in one shipment. A company can also reduce having to wait in the customs line by preclearing customs using the *Customs-Trade Partnership Against Terrorism* (C-TPAT) in the United States (U.S.) or the Authorized Economic Operator (AEO) in the European Union (EU) and other countries.

REVERSE LOGISTICS

A supply chain flows both ways. The process of products flowing back to a supplier from customers is called *reverse logistics*. Although the flow of information still goes both ways, returned products require a financial credit to go from the supplier to the customer, and returned materials flow from the customer to the supplier. A *reverse supply chain*, also known as product returns, moves products back from the end, downstream customer to the entity that is responsible to perform the analysis, repair, or product disposal throughout the product life cycle (PLC).

A *waste hierarchy* or *reverse logistics hierarchy* identifies five waste management activities and ranks their sequence based on what is most environmentally sound. The five hierarchy levels are *reduce*, *reuse*, *recycle*, *recover*, and final *disposal* of materials in a *responsible landfill*. A responsible landfill generates low emissions during incineration due to special equipment. A landfill is the least desirable option and companies should first look to reuse or recover materials.

A company can benefit from reverse logistics. For example, consider how a reduction of waste disposal can result in cost savings for a company. It can lead to the creation of new jobs to process returns, disassemble and salvage parts, and sell recycled and waste byproducts to other companies. Aluminum soda and beer cans that were once thrown away as garbage are now collected and reprocessed into new cans. *Total waste management* (TWM) deals with garbage, sewage, and other waste products in a cost-effective manner while addressing environmental regulations and compliance issues, avoiding organizational risks and liabilities, and doing this in an ethical manner while protecting the company's reputation.

Waste exchange is where one company's waste or byproduct is used as a raw material by another company. This reduces waste disposal costs through reuse. Complying with government regulations can improve a corporate image and enhance customer loyalty by preventing pollutants from entering landfills. Reverse logistics can also lead to new revenue sources by selling or reusing raw materials, components, *byproducts*, and refurbished materials, and by the sale of *service contracts*.

Exercise 3.2 will test your knowledge of the reverse logistics waste hierarchy. Write in the hierarchy level name that best applies to the stated activity. The answers to the exercise are available from the Web Added Value™ Download Resource Center at www.jrosspub.com.

Exercise 3.2   Waste hierarchy

Activity	Level
1. Ship products in a returnable plastic tote	
2. Redesign the wall thickness of a water bottle	
3. Send returned products to a responsible landfill	
4. Convert plastic bottles into a salable raw material	
5. Perform a conversion process to capture energy from burning waste	

KEY TERMINOLOGY

Understanding key terms and the concepts they represent is crucial to passing the Certified Supply Chain Professional (CSCP) exam. In this chapter, the important terms are identified in Table 3.1.

Table 3.1   Logistics fundamentals key terminology

Byproducts
Disposal
End-of-life management*
Fourth-party logistics (4PL)*
Friction
Global positioning systems (GPS)
Logistics
Maturity
Outsourcing*
Postponement centers
Recover
Recycle
Reduce
Responsible landfill
Reuse
Reverse logistics*
Reverse logistics hierarchy
Reverse supply chain*
Service contracts
Stock-keeping unit (SKU)*
Subcontractor
Third-party logistics (3PL)*
Total cost concept
Total waste management
Value proposition
Waste exchange
Waste hierarchy

*Key term found in the CSCP ECM

CSCP EXAM PRACTICE QUESTIONS ON LOGISTICS FUNDAMENTALS

The questions presented in Table 3.2a cover the concepts that were presented in this chapter on logistics fundamentals. They are examples of what to expect on the actual exam.

Table 3.2a   Logistics fundamentals practice questions

No.	Questions
1	The logistics value proposition attempts to balance logistics costs against: a) Delivery speed b) Inventory levels c) Customer service d) Manufacturing costs
2	How can a company best replace physical inventory? a) Keep inventory in transit b) Precisely track inventory c) Implement a fixed location system d) Substitute information for inventory
3	The process of having suppliers provide goods and services that were previously provided internally is best called: a) Insourcing b) Offshoring c) Outsourcing d) Foreign sourcing
4	What is most likely impacted when transportation delivery times decrease? a) Cash-to-cash days go up b) Transportation costs go down c) Customer service costs go down d) Inventory handling costs go down
5	A company desiring to eliminate friction in the marketplace will need to: a) Change a process b) Acquire the competition c) Restructure their organization d) Become an environmentally responsible business

ANSWERS TO CSCP EXAM PRACTICE QUESTIONS ON LOGISTICS FUNDAMENTALS

The answers to these practice questions on logistics fundamentals are shown in Table 3.2b. An incorrect answer indicates a gap in your body of knowledge and it indicates the need for additional study time.

Table 3.2b   Answers to CSCP exam practice questions on logistics fundamentals

No.	Answers
1	Answer: C The logistics value proposition matches customer service against logistics costs. Delivery speed is a requirement defined by the customer, and it may have value.
2	Answer: D A company can best replace physical inventory by substituting information for inventory. Answers A, B, and C relate to keeping or moving existing inventory.
3	Answer: C Outsourcing is the process of having an outside supplier perform a function that was previously provided internally.
4	Answer: C Improved transportation will reduce overall customer service costs. Faster delivery will reduce needed inventory levels, so cash-to-cash goes down.
5	Answer: A Friction is eliminated by changing a process to improve its velocity (speed). Answers B, C, and D are all forms of change.

4

LOGISTICS FUNCTIONS

This chapter focuses on the logistics functions that are required to move, store, pack, and ship products. It examines ownership versus leased warehouses, warehousing functions and activities, the impact of adding additional warehouses, intermodal types, line haul, value and packaging density, transportation goals, types of carriers, and mechanized systems.

LOGISTICS

Logistics is the moving and storing of products and is part of supply chain management (SCM). It involves planning, as well as executing the plan, to move the right product, in the right quantity, at the right time, in the right packaging, for the right cost, and with the right degree of quality. SCM includes the logistics process but takes it to a higher level of sophistication. This chapter will review the various logistics movement activities to and from the customer, storage, inventory, and mechanized systems and tools.

WAREHOUSE OBJECTIVES

Warehousing is an integral component of logistics and has numerous objectives that need to be managed. These include minimizing inventory to reduce receiving, storage, and shipping costs and processing times; minimizing variances in logistics services; supporting the entire product life cycle (PLC); and performing reverse logistics. Warehousing achieves these objectives by maintaining a high quality level, engaging in continuous process improvements (CPI), responding rapidly to changes in the marketplace, quickly meeting customer order delivery requirements, and consolidating product movement by grouping shipments.

OWNED VERSUS LEASED WAREHOUSES

Companies have to strategically decide if it's better to retain *private* ownership of a warehouse, use a *public* warehouse, or enter into a *contract* for a warehouse through a third party. They may even want to use a combination of all of them. Each type of ownership has financial and operational benefits and disadvantages, which requires a company to consider the tradeoffs of each decision based on the factors shown in Table 4.1.

Table 4.1   Warehouse ownership attributes

Attribute	Private	Public	Contract
Overhead costs	Higher	Lower	Lower
Capital conflicts	Yes	No	No
Resource flexibility	Limited	Higher	Higher
Startup location costs	Higher	Cheaper	Moderate
Uses latest technology	No	Yes	Yes
Asset and profit impact	Negative	Positive	Positive
Provides tailored services	Limited	Yes	Yes
24/7 resource utilization	No	Yes	Yes
Economies-of-scale savings	No	Yes	Yes
Located closer to customers	Yes	Depends	Depends
Expansion time-frame capability	Longest	Shortest	Short

WAREHOUSE FUNCTIONS

Warehouse functions begin with a material *receipt* and paperwork transaction processing. Materials move through the *inspection* process and then get *put away*. Customer or work orders require raw materials, components, or finished goods to be *picked*. The picked materials are sent to the production area or the *packing* area where they are either assembled and/or packed. The final warehouse activities are shipping and then invoicing customer orders.

WAREHOUSE ACTIVITIES

Many different processes occur in a warehouse, and each one of them is crucial, depending on the customer's requirements.

Mixing is the process of receiving full vehicle shipments of different products from multiple plants. Shipments are broken down and reassembled into a requested customer product mix along with other internally stored warehouse items. This permits customers to obtain full truckload (TL) shipping rates, reduces the need to process multiple smaller shipments, and makes better use of warehouse space.

Anticipation, also called *stockpiling*, is the process of receiving seasonal products from multiple suppliers. Material is unloaded and stored in distribution centers until it's required. It's later loaded onto outbound trucks and shipped to seasonal customers. Anticipation permits manufacturers to be more efficient by allowing them to level load production and eliminate their need for additional manufacturing capacity during the peak season. Customers benefit by obtaining full TL transportation rates and it reduces seasonal product stockouts. Examples of anticipation are holiday lights, seasonal candy, or bottled water needed for the summer months.

Assortment is the storing of products in a warehouse close to its customers. It's similar to stockpiling, but has a wider range of goods such as clothing of different colors and sizes. Assortment permits customers to obtain shorter delivery lead times, reduces the need to process multiple small shipments, and allows the customers to obtain exactly their required product mix.

Spot stocking focuses on preordering and storage of strategic inventory in advance of actual need in key markets. It's used to avoid maintaining high inventory levels throughout the year. An example of spot stocking is storing rock salt in advance of the winter months.

Break-bulk is the process of a customer receiving a TL of similar items from one supplier location and delivering them to a customer's break-bulk warehouse. The load is disassembled and then reassembled to meet various customers' requirements. Break-bulk permits customers to receive one *fuller* shipment. This results in lower shipping rates, reduced receiving dock congestion, and it reduces the need to process multiple shipments.

Cross-docking is the process of receiving products from multiple companies or plants. Material is unloaded and moved directly to the shipping area. It's then loaded immediately onto outbound trucks without being moved into a warehouse for storage and later picking. Cross-docking improves velocity, reduces the amount of stored inventory, and reduces customer receiving dock congestion.

Consolidation is the process of a customer receiving shipments of different products from multiple suppliers to their warehouse. Products are consolidated and then reshipped to other customers. The biggest difference between cross-docking and consolidation is that in consolidation, materials can be stored in the warehouse. Consolidation permits customers to receive one *fuller* shipment, which results in lower shipping rates, reduced receiving dock congestion, and a reduction in the need to process multiple shipments.

Postponement is the process of receiving materials from multiple suppliers and storing them at a postponement center until they're needed to support a customer order. The received materials can be modular units or they can be partially assembled. Material is pulled and configured as a final product based on actual customer orders. Postponement permits finished products to be quickly assembled into a final product and shipped directly to a customer. This improves delivery performance and lowers costs and finished goods' inventory levels. Postponement is used for products such as computers, toys, and personalized checks.

Exercise 4.1 will test your knowledge of warehouse capabilities. Write in the answer that best describes the warehouse capability type. The answers to the exercise are available from the Web Added Value™ Download Resource Center at www.jrosspub.com.

Exercise 4.1 Warehouse capabilities

Scenarios	Answers
1. This activity ships different clothing sizes to a retail store.	
2. This activity ships materials from a manufacturing location to a warehouse and then breaks them apart before shipping them to a customer.	
3. This activity stores products until they're required by seasonal customers.	
4. This activity receives full shipments of different products from multiple manufacturing plants. It breaks them apart and labor reassembles a shipment with the stored warehouse products to meet a customer order.	
5. This activity ships materials from multiple manufacturing plants to a warehouse and then ships them directly to a customer.	
6. This activity stores products in a warehouse from multiple suppliers until required by a manufacturing plant.	
7. This activity receives materials and immediately ships them to a customer without going into a warehouse.	
8. This activity finalizes a product at a warehouse to customer specifications before shipping it.	
9. This activity receives and stores materials from multiple suppliers. It later ships a full truckload of requested materials to one factory.	

IMPACT OF ADDING WAREHOUSES

Strategically, company management needs to decide on the proper number of warehouses to either own, enter into third-party contracts with, or lease. This decision is based on numerous factors including desired customer service, transportation costs, inventory levels, speed of delivery, and/or financial and overhead cost considerations. The more warehouses a company has, the higher the inventory levels and fixed costs. Company benefits include quicker delivery, reduced transportation costs, and improved customer service. For example, a company expands from one to two warehouses. This permits them to ship a full TL to the second location, rather than shipping a *less-than-truckload* (LTL). The company receives a lower shipping rate based on a TL, rather than paying more for the LTL. The addition of a second warehouse results in the reduction of overall system costs. This is due to a decline in transportation costs. Unfortunately, after three warehouses, the transportation savings no longer offsets the higher warehousing and inventory costs.

Exercise 4.2 will test your knowledge and understanding of the impact of adding or removing warehouses. Read each question and write in the best answer. The answers to the exercise are available from the Web Added Value™ Download Resource Center at www.jrosspub.com.

Exercise 4.2   Impact of adding/removing warehouses

Question	Answer
1. What is the impact on total inventory by adding warehouses? (up or down)	
2. What is the impact on transportation costs when going from one to three warehouses? (up or down)	
3. What is the impact on customer delivery speed when going from one to three warehouses? (up or down)	
4. What one word best describes why a company may want to add or remove a warehouse?	
5. What two words best describe what has the greatest impact on transportation costs when going from one to three warehouses?	
6. What happens to overhead costs if a company goes from one to three warehouses? (up or down)	
7. Which manufacturing environment has more finished goods stored in a warehouse?	

TEMPORARY MATERIAL STORAGE

Customers often require temporary material storage due to internal or external warehouse space constraints. A customer can park trailers or containers in their parking area for short-term material storage. Large retail stores often use this method to temporarily store seasonal merchandise. Customers can also request that suppliers invoice them, but leave their products on the supplier's dock for a few extra days. In this situation, the supplier is happy to get paid upfront, and the customer doesn't have to worry about space constraints. Another option is having the shipping company take an extra-long delivery route before dropping off the merchandise. This buys the customer a few extra days to make room in their warehouse. Last, the customer can have the product shipped, but change the final destination en route.

INTERMODAL TYPES

Intermodal transportation is the process of using multiple freight modes such as planes, ships, carriers/trucks, and trains/rails with minimal handling or container reloading when changing from one mode to another. This process improves overall productivity and efficiency while reducing delivery time and costs.

Piggyback (train/rail), *fishyback* (ship), and *birdyback* (plane) involve the placement of a container on a railcar, in a boat, or on a plane. The shipment moves part of the way in one mode, and then switches to another. A container placed on a railroad flatcar is called a *container on flatcar*. If a truck trailer with a container is placed on a railroad flat car, it's called a *trailer on rail flatcar*. A *ship* with containers is called a *containership*. Containers can also be placed on *barges* to move over water. If railcars are placed on a barge, it's called a *trainship*.

A *land bridge* is used to move cargo from one seaport to another. It travels over water after first crossing a land mass. For example, a shipment leaves China by ship heading to the west coast of the United States, and then moves across the U.S. by rail or truck to the east coast. It will then be placed back onto a ship and sail to Europe. The U.S. has acted as a land bridge.

Delivery patterns or *shipping patterns* reflect how consumers purchase and receive merchandise from retail suppliers. The delivery location impacts supplier warehouse placement, mode of shipment selection, cost structure, and delivery speed. There are five types of delivery patterns, as shown in Table 4.2.

Table 4.2   Delivery patterns attributes

Attribute	Manufacturer storage with direct delivery	Manufacturer storage with drop ship	Manufacturer to distribution center to a retailer	Independent distributor with omni-channel network	Independent aggregator with e-business network
Delivery lead time	Long	Long	Short	Short	Very fast
Intermediary involvement	None. Product shipped direct to customer	Yes. Distributor or retail store takes customer order, places an order with the manufacturer who makes and then drop ships directly to customer	Yes. Regional distributors stock inventory Products sold and delivered to local customers	Yes. Independent distributor buys from multiple suppliers and sells directly to customers	Yes. Independent distributor buys from multiple suppliers and sells directly to customers
Sales channels	Customer has numerous ways to order—direct, catalog, and website	Distributor, retail store, or direct sales takes order and places it with manufacturer	Retail stores order from the distributor's warehouse	Independent distributor sells directly to customers or to other distributors	Independent distributor sells directly to customers or to other distributors
Manufacturer customer relationship	Manufacturer has direct contact with customers	Indirect customer contact (3rd party has direct customer contact)	None. Retail store has direct customer contact	None. Omni-channel has direct sales and customer contact	None. Independent distributor has direct sales and customer contact
Typical manufacturing environment	Make-to-order	Make-to-order or assemble-to-order	Make-to-stock	All types	All types
Product variety	High	High	Low	Selective	Selective
Finished product inventory maintained	None	None	High levels kept at manufacturers, distributors, and retail stores	High levels kept at manufacturers, distributors, and retail stores	High levels keep at manufacturers, distributors, and retail stores
Inventory carrying costs by manufacturer or order taker	Low. No finished inventory maintained	Low. No finished inventory maintained	High. Echelons carry inventory	High. Echelons carry inventory	High. Echelons carry inventory

Continued

Control	Manufacturer has direct control over inventory	Manufacturer has direct control over inventory	Each party in supply chain has direct control over just their inventory	Each party in supply chain has direct control over just their inventory	Each party in supply chain has direct control over just their inventory
Logistics costs	High	High	Low	High	High
Example	Dell/Apple	American Standard	H&M/Zara	Sephora/ Starbucks	Amazon/Alibaba

Retail delivery and direct-to-consumer are two methods used to deliver purchased materials. The *retail delivery* method moves small-to-large packages to distribution centers (DCs), where they are shipped by either TL or LTL to a retailer. The packages are then picked up by the consumer. *Direct-to-consumer* moves small packages to a DC where they're shipped directly to consumers via delivery service companies such as UPS or FedEx.

LINE HAUL SHIPPING COSTS

A shipping company has *fixed costs* and *variable line haul costs*. These costs become the basis to calculate their shipment cost. Things such as infrastructure are fixed costs, as well as equipment, depreciation, warehousing, security, vehicles, and insurance. Variable line haul costs are labor and operating charges per miles traveled including costs related to overhead, oil, gas, tolls, and room and board. Additional charges can also be applied based on the number of stops, loading and unloading, special handling, and fuel surcharges.

The further a shipment travels, the higher the transportation mileage charge will be, regardless of the shipment weight. The mileage charge is almost always linear based on the distance, but cost per pound decreases as additional weight is placed on the truck. For example, assume that a *line haul cost* is $4,000 to go 3,000 miles for a direct shipment from New York to California. If a company initially decides to ship cargo weighing 25,000 pounds directly to California, they will need to pay the TL rate of $4,000, or $0.16 per pound. However, if the company chooses to increase the weight to 40,000 pounds, the cost remains $4,000, but the rate then drops to $0.10 per pound. The cost per pound declines because the fixed and variable shipping costs of a full load can spread over more pounds. This results in a rate decrease per pound.

VALUE AND PACKAGING DENSITY

Density is the weight per cubic foot of a product being shipped. *Value density* refers to the product value and weight of an item being shipped. Expensive items can be lightweight, such as diamonds, and have a high value density. They can also be very heavy, like motorcycles, and have a high value density. Inexpensive items, such as a shipment of iron ore, can be very heavy and have very low value density. They can also be very light, like sponges, and have very low value density per traveled mile.

Packaging density refers to the space an item occupies on a vehicle in relation to its weight. A product like iron ore has high packaging density and can easily exceed the weight limit of a vehicle before it's completely filled. The less an item weighs, the lower the packaging density.

A product's *shipping density* is determined by weight and dimensions. Dimensions refer to the product's length, width, height, and shape. The higher a product's density is, the lower its cwt. In the U.S., cwt refers to hundredweight which is 100 pounds; whereas in the United Kingdom, cwt is 112 pounds.

For packing density, a shipper needs to consider the size and volume of the item being shipped. While a sponge is low in density, has a low mass per unit volume, and can be easily handled, an iron pot is dense and heavy and can be much more difficult.

There are a few additional terms associated with density. *Nesting* is the process of placing one product inside another. An example is placing one garbage pail inside another. This permits more products to be placed inside a truck, increasing its density. *Stowability* refers to product placement and positioning on the chosen motor (carrier) method for shipment. Odd shapes, weights, lengths, hazardous materials, fragility, or packaging can impact the transportation process. *Assembled* or *disassembled products* can also impact it. Assembled products take up more floor space in a container or truck. For example, companies ship bicycles in a disassembled state to reduce required space.

TRANSPORTATION STAKEHOLDER GOALS

Suppliers need to select a carrier to transport products to or from a customer. The three active logistics participants in this process are the shipper, *recipient*, and *carrier*. It also encompasses the government and the public who have a vested interest in the shipment of products. The selection decision to pick a carrier is based on numerous factors, as identified in Table 4.3.

Table 4.3 Carrier selection

Goal	Shipper	Recipient	Carriers	Government	Public
Pickup time	Convenient	————	Convenient	————	————
Delivery time	————	Scheduled	Convenient	————	————
Cost focus	Low	Low	Profitability	Regulations	Fair pricing
Liability	Limited	None	Limited	Regulations	————
Infrastructure ownership	Public and good	Public and good	Public and good	National defense route	Convenient and cost-effective

Exercise 4.3 will test your knowledge and understanding of the various transportation stakeholders. Read each question and write in all answers that apply. The answers to the exercise are available from the Web Added Value™ Download Resource Center at www.jrosspub.com.

Exercise 4.3   Understanding various transportation stakeholders

Question	Answer
1. Which transportation stakeholder has no shipment liability?	
2. Which transportation stakeholders want a convenient pickup time?	
3. Which transportation stakeholder wants a convenient delivery time?	
4. Which transportation stakeholder is the most concerned about profitability?	
5. Which transportation stakeholder wants a scheduled pickup/delivery time?	
6. Which transportation stakeholders are the most concerned about establishing safety regulations?	
7. Which transportation stakeholder is the most concerned about fair pricing and no discrimination?	
8. Which transportation stakeholders want convenient, cost effective, and environmentally sound infrastructure	

TRANSPORTATION MODES

A shipping company has a number of transportation modes available to them for shipping their products. They have to select the mode and carrier which best meets their needs for speed, cost, scheduling, flexibility, and security. Table 4.4 demonstrates the unique attributes of each type.

Table 4.4   Transportation mode attributes

Attribute	Rail	Carrier/Road/Truck	Water	Pipeline	Air
Ride	Rough	Moderate	Smooth to choppy	Smooth	Very smooth
Delivery speed	Slow movement plus time needed for consolidating and transferring	Very fast movement with door-to-door pickup and drop-off	Slow movement plus time needed for consolidating and transferring	Very slow movement plus time needed for storing and transferring	Very fast movement plus time for consolidating and delivering
Cost rate per cwt	Low	Somewhat low	Very low	Very low	Very high plus delivery costs
Flexibility	Limited access with fixed routes and drop-off points	Easy access with unlimited routes and drop-off points	Limited access being restricted to ports and dock areas	Inflexible, restricted access to pumping and storing stations	Restricted to landing strips, heliports, and water
Scheduling	Requires advanced notice and planning	Easy movement requiring no advanced planning	Requires advanced notice and planning	Requires advanced notice and planning and moves in only one direction	Requires some advanced notice and planning

Continued

Fixed costs	High costs for equipment and rail bed	Low to high costs for vehicles	Low to high costs for container ships and barges	High costs for pipeline, pumping stations, and maintenance	High capital equipment and maintenance costs
Load types	Heavy and bulky materials	Everything and anything from light to heavy weights, small to large packages and quantities, and Hazmat	Everything and anything from containers to packages	Oil, gas, water, and some slurry liquids without any packaging	Small to medium packages of expensive materials

Exercise 4.4 will test your knowledge and understanding of the various transportation modes. Read each question and write in all answers that apply. The answers to the exercise are available from the Web Added Value™ Download Resource Center at www.jrosspub.com.

Exercise 4.4   Understanding of the various transportation modes

Question	Answer
1. Which mode is the fastest?	
2. Which mode is the most reliable?	
3. Which mode is the most expensive?	
4. Which mode has the least flexibility?	
5. Which mode can carry the most weight?	
6. Which modes have the lowest fixed costs?	
7. Which mode has no intermodal capability?	
8. Which modes have the lowest rates per cwt?	
9. Which modes have the highest variable costs?	
10. Which modes have to maintain their own infrastructure?	
11. Which mode has the greatest risk of damaging cargo?	
12. Which mode has the lowest risk of being impacted by weather?	
13. Which mode doesn't require advanced planning and scheduling?	

TYPES OF CARRIERS

As previously stated, suppliers need to select a carrier to transport products to or from a customer. The four carrier types used by companies are *common* (public) *carrier*, *private carrier*, *contract carrier*, or *exempt carrier*. A supplier determines which carrier type to use based on numerous factors, as identified in Table 4.5.

Table 4.5 Carrier type attributes

Attributes	Common	Private	Contract	Exempt
Published rates	Yes	No	Negotiate	No
Discrimination allowed	No	Yes	Yes	Yes
Operate in public interest	Yes	No	No	No
Authority granted by government	Yes	No	Yes	No
Government regulations on rates	Yes	No	No	Yes
Able and willing to provide service	Yes	No	No	No
Core competency	Yes	No	Yes	Yes
Examples	YRC	Walmart	UPS	Farm

SHIPPING, PICKUP, AND DELIVERY CONFLICTS

There are a few additional terms associated with transportation. *Dwell time* refers to the time a vehicle remains idle waiting to pick up or deliver a shipment. *Demurrage* is an extra charge for holding a freight car or truck beyond the specified time allowed in a contract. *Backhauling* is when a vehicle obtains a load for the return trip after making a delivery. *Deadheading* is when a vehicle returns empty after making a delivery. *Shipment reconciliation* validates that a shipped carton quantity matches the delivered carton quantity.

The selection of a *shipper* is needed to transport products from a supplier to customers—who, by nature, all have conflicting objectives and constraints. These conflicts can range from lot size and its impact on inventory storage, product variety and its impact on inventory retention levels, inventory shipment size and velocity and its impact on transportation costs, and delivery lead time and its impact on transportation costs and customer service levels. The shipper decision is based on many different attributes, as identified in Table 4.6.

Table 4.6 Delivery type attributes

Attribute	Supplier	Shipper	Customer
Product mix	Limited	Indifferent	Assortment
Customer service	High	High	High
Variety or volume	Volume	Indifferent	Variety
Delivery speed cost	Cheapest	Indifferent	When needed
Weight (truckload or less-than-truckload	Truckload	Indifferent	Less-than-truckload
Timing (pickup/delivery)	On call	Convenient	Scheduled

MECHANIZED SYSTEMS

Companies have the option of selecting and using a number of different types of material handling equipment based on internal requirements. The use of this equipment can lead to improved velocity, productivity, efficiency improved space utilization, and reduced labor costs. The disadvantages of using different types are capital costs, integration efforts, equipment inflexibility, breakdowns, and maintenance requirements. The selection decision is based on the attributes found in Table 4.7.

Table 4.7 Equipment type attributes

Equipment Type	Operator Required	Capital Cost	Setup	Required Space
Automated guided vehicle systems	No	High	Programmed to follow markers, tape, or wires in the floor	Minimal
Automated storage and retrieval systems	Yes for initial material loading and unloading No for material retrieval	High	Programmable Requires fixed floor space Can be integrated to an ERP system	Fixed floor space Maximizes floor space by going upward
Bridge cranes and wagon cranes	Yes	Moderate to high	Operator training (U.S. Occupational Safety and Health Administration [OSHA]) Bridge cranes require a fixed overhead ceiling location Wagon cranes can be easily moved Manual or automated setup	Bridge cranes require no floor space as they are mounted on the ceiling Wagon cranes require minimal floor space
Conveyors	Manual = yes Automated = no	Low to high	Manual = fixed or movable Automated = fixed or programmable	Manual = fixed or movable on floor Automated = fixed or mounted on ceiling
Forklifts	Yes	Moderate	OSHA (U.S.) required driver's certification	Minimal—can go up or down, left or right
Live racks	Yes for initial material loading	Mid to high	Located on shop floor or warehouse	Gravity moves the first-in item downward on the rack Example: a soda or milk display in a supermarket

Continued

Pick-to-light systems	Yes	Low to moderate	Fixed to a storage location Requires integration to the enterprise resources planning and warehouse management system Programmable	Minimal Mounted to a storage location rack
Robotics	No	High	Programmable	Fixed location
Sorting systems	Manual = yes Automated = no	High	Programmable, fixed location often attached to a conveyor, and can adjust speed	Located on shop floor or warehouse
Tow line	Manual = yes Automated = no	High	Fixed floor location	Fixed on floor permitting the product pulling
Tow tractors with trailers	Yes	Moderate	OSHA (U.S.) required driver's certification	Minimal—can go straight, left, or right

Exercise 4.5 will test your knowledge and understanding of the various mechanized systems. Read each question and write in all answers that apply. The answers to the exercise are available from the Web Added Value™ Download Resource Center at www.jrosspub.com.

Exercise 4.5 Understanding various mechanized systems

Question	Answer
1. Which mechanized systems reduce the need for labor to pick materials?	
2. Which mechanized system is the most expensive?	
3. Which mechanized system can lift and move materials in all directions?	
4. Which mechanized system is programmed to automate material movement?	
5. Which mechanized system is programmed to build a unit load?	
6. Which mechanized system is programmed to enhance order picking?	
7. Which mechanized system is programmed to move along a predefined path?	
8. Which mechanized system maximizes floor storage space?	
9. Which mechanized system requires an operator to move materials?	
10. Which mechanized system makes efficient use of floor space?	

KEY TERMINOLOGY

Understanding key terms and the concepts they represent is crucial to passing the Certified Supply Chain Professional (CSCP) exam. In this chapter, the following important terms are identified in Table 4.8.

Table 4.8 Logistics functions key terminology

Anticipation
Assembled products
Assortment
Automated guided vehicle systems (AGVS)
Automated storage and retrieval systems (ASRS)
Backhauling
Barge
Birdyback
Break-bulk
Bridge crane
Carrier
Common carrier
Consolidation
Container on flatcar
Containership
Contract carrier
Contract warehouse
Conveyors
Cross-docking*
Deadheading
Delivery patterns
Demurrage
Direct-to-consumer
Disassembled products
Dwell time
Exempt carrier
Fishyback
Fixed costs
Forklift trucks
Inspection
Intermodal
Land bridge

Continued

Less-than-truckload (LTL)
Line haul costs*
Live racks
Mixing
Nesting
Packing
Packing density
Picked
Pick-to-light systems
Piggyback
Postponement
Private
Private carrier
Private warehouse
Public carrier
Public warehouse
Put-away
Receipt
Recipient
Retail delivery
Robotics
Ship
Shipment reconciliation
Shipper
Shipping density
Shipping patterns
Sorting systems
Spot stocking
Stockpiling
Stowability
Tow line
Tow tractors with trailers
Trailer on rail flatcar
Trainship
Truckload (TL)
Value density
Variable costs
Variable line-haul costs
Wagon cranes

*Key term found in the CSCP ECM

CSCP EXAM PRACTICE QUESTIONS ON LOGISTICS FUNCTIONS

The questions presented in Table 4.9a cover the concepts presented in this chapter on logistics functions. They are examples of what to expect on the actual exam.

Table 4.9a Logistics functions practice questions

No.	Questions
1	Which mechanized system doesn't require an operator to operate? a) Live rack b) Tow tractor with trailers c) Automated guided vehicle system d) Automated storage and retrieval system
2	Which of the following wouldn't be a benefit found in a transportation management system? a) Reduced dwell time b) Reduced demurrage c) Reduced deadheading d) Reduced backhauling
3	The process of moving inventory immediately from receiving to the shipping dock without being stored in a warehouse is called? a) Consolidation b) Cross-docking c) Quick response d) Break bulk operation
4	Which automated equipment type will free up the most factory floor storage space? a) Towline b) Conveyer c) Bridge crane d) Automated storage and retrieval system
5	Which of the following isn't an advantage of a pick-to-light system? a) Elimination of pick lists b) Computer generated pick sequencing c) Flexibility to move pick-to-light devices d) Reduction in operator physical movements
6	Variable shipping costs are least impacted by: a) Stowability b) Load weight c) Distance shipped d) Number of containers
7	Which transportation stakeholder is the least flexible about scheduling? a) Carrier b) Shipper c) Recipient d) Customer
8	A truck delivers a load of steel to a company in the northern portion of Maine. It returns empty after delivering its load. The return trip is best called: a) Backhauling b) Deadheading c) Distributed load d) Reverse logistics

Continued

9	The intermodal concept provides all of the following benefits except for: a) Efficiency b) Flexibility c) Reliability d) Reduced costs
10	Which of the following is the best description of break-bulk? a) Reselling b) Repackaging c) Reassortment d) Remanufacturing
11	Materials received from multiple companies that move immediately to a customer after being received at a distribution center is an example of: a) Mixing b) Consolidation c) Cross-docking d) Break-bulking
12	Allocating inventory to a warehouse in advance of heavy demand in selected strategic markets is best called: a) Staging b) Stockpiling c) Spot stocking d) Postponement
13	Breaking down shipments from more than one manufacturer in a warehouse and reassembling them into customer desired order quantities is best called: a) Mixing b) Break-bulk c) Stockpiling d) Assortment
14	Which type of U.S. legal motor carrier has the greatest amount of economic regulations, governing rates, and scope of services? a) Private b) Exempt c) Contract d) Common
15	Which carrier type may be required to lose money on a delivery? a) Exempt b) Private c) Common d) Contract
16	What is the greatest advantage of being a private carrier? a) Lower total cost of ownership b) Putting advertisements on their trucks c) Free from all government regulations and restrictions d) Total control of what, how, and when goods move
17	Which of the following isn't generally a contract warehouse benefit over a private warehouse? a) Markup b) Flexibility c) Tailored services d) Geographic market
18	Which supply chain entity would most likely want small lot sizes delivered daily? a) Retailer b) Supplier c) Distributor d) End customer

ANSWERS TO CSCP EXAM PRACTICE QUESTIONS ON LOGISTICS FUNCTIONS

The answers to the practice questions on logistics functions are shown in Table 4.9b. Any question you answer incorrectly indicates a gap in your body of knowledge and encourages the need for additional study time.

Table 4.9b   Answers to CSCP exam practice questions on logistics functions

No.	Answers
1	Answer: C The automated guided vehicle system doesn't require an operator to function while the other devices do. A live rack is similar to a gravity feed roller conveyor which requires an operator to load materials from behind the unit. A tow tractor with trailers requires a driver. The automated storage and retrieval system requires an operator to remove materials from bins.
2	Answer: D A company would want to increase backhauling to prevent deadheading (having the truck return empty). Answers A, B, and C are all benefits found in a transportation management system.
3	Answer: B This question requires knowledge of the APICS Dictionary definition of cross-docking. Cross-docking is delivered products being moved across a dock without going to a warehouse.
4	Answer: C A bridge crane is suspended from the ceiling and doesn't require any floor space. The other types of equipment require factory floor space.
5	Answer: C Flexibility is lacking in pick-to-light devices as they have to be physically mounted to a location.
6	Answer: A Stowability is how material is placed in the truck and is least impacted by variable costs. Load weight increases costs since more weight is being shipped. Variable shipping costs include tolls, labor, and fuel, which fluctuate with the distance driven. The number of containers can incur additional handling and storage costs, especially if the items are being shipped in a less than full truckload.
7	Answer: A The carrier is the stakeholder that is least flexible about scheduling. They prefer to pick up or deliver shipments whenever it's most convenient for them. They don't want to base it on the needs of the supplier or customer. The recipient and customer are one and the same, which eliminates these two answers. It's often difficult for the shipper (supplier) to know when the shipment is going to be ready, so they need flexibility.
8	Answer: B Deadheading means the truck returns to the truck depot empty.
9	Answer: C A company using the intermodal concept cannot be 100% certain that the materials will be delivered on time and in good condition. Answers A, B, and D are all benefits of the intermodal concept.
10	Answer: B Break-bulk is the process of receiving a shipment that is split apart (repackaged) into individual orders and then shipped to a customer. The process says nothing about a reassortment function being performed.

Continued

11	Answer: C This question describes the cross-docking process. Break-bulk has only one plant, and mixing has more than one. Consolidation has multiple suppliers.
12	Answer: C This question defines spot stocking. The key words are the phrase *selected strategic markets*, which are *spot* locations. Stockpiling is similar, but it builds up inventory levels in anticipation of seasonality demand.
13	Answer: A This question is defining mixing, which is the process of receiving different products from multiple plants. These delivered products are stored in an assortment warehouse. Products are then pulled and shipped to a customer based on the ordered mix product quantities.
14	Answer: D A common carrier is granted the authority to enter transportation markets by the federal government. They have more government regulations to follow than the other answers. Private and exempt don't normally have any regulations concerning rates. Contract has some regulations, but rates are negotiated between two parties and most rates are outside of the government's scope.
15	Answer: C A common carrier is required to take all legitimate business within the scope of their licenses, even if it comes at a loss. For example, a carrier may have to drive a long distance and then come back empty. Exempt, private, and contract carriers have the ability to reject or charge higher rates for these types of deliveries.
16	Answer: D A private carrier (a company moving its own products) has the advantage of being in total control of what, when, and how they elect to move products.
17	Answer: A A contract warehouse charges a markup for services, which can be higher than if performed by a company on their own.
18	Answer: A Retailers would like to receive as little inventory as possible and receive quick replacements daily. End customers (consumers) want small lot sizes, but only when needed.

This book has free material available for download from the
Web Added Value™ resource center at *www.jrosspub.com*

5

IMPORT/EXPORT LOGISTICS

This chapter focuses on the import/export financial process and explores a multicountry strategy. It examines the water and air import/export process including the various participants, forms, and documents needed to prepare a finished product for shipment.

IMPORT/EXPORT LOGISTICS PROVIDER PARTICIPANTS

A company selling a product to a customer in another country is performing an *export* function. The customer who purchases the product is the *importer*. Products can be transported via a number of different modes. *Motor carriers* (trucks), *trains*, *ships*, *planes*, *pipelines*, or a combination of two or more of these modes, is called intermodal. The shipper can use any one of these to move products from one location to another.

In the water shipping process, four key participants are involved in moving a product from the supplier's dock to the shipping dock. A *freight forwarder* (also known as a *foreign freight forwarder* or *forwarder*) picks up freight directly from a supplier or suppliers. The freight forwarder consolidates shipments from multiple suppliers and/or consolidators and arranges inland transportation to a port or non-vessel operating common carrier (NVOCC) location. The freight forwarder's only responsibility is to physically transport commercial cargo. They don't buy or resell vehicle or container space on other carriers.

A *consolidator* combines small shipments from multiple suppliers into a larger shipment that fills a vehicle or container. This action permits the consolidator to obtain a full container discount from the shipping company, which then allows them to offer the customer a reduced shipping rate. The supplier can choose to work with an *NVOCC* or a freight forwarder.

An NVOCC pre-purchases bulk container space on a carrier (ship) at a deep discount. They resell this container space to companies looking for a lower shipping rate than the carrier offers directly. The NVOCC provides labor to load, consolidate, and later unload the products from containers. They fill containers that are going to foreign destinations with products from one or more companies. The NVOCC owns their own shipping containers and they try to obtain cargo to backfill the containers for the return trip. The ship is the fourth participant in the water shipping process as it moves cargo to and from one port to another.

IMPORT/EXPORT PARTICIPANTS

The *export trading company* (ETC) buys and sells goods for export. It often seeks out importers to purchase imported merchandises and make export arrangements as well as comply with various custom regulations. The ETC is also called a *general trading company* or a *sogo shosha* in Japan. The *export management company* (EMC) is a foreign trade specialist which acts as a consultant to exporters. They have special knowledge of local custom requirements and government regulations and have connections in local areas to help ease goods through customs.

The *custom house broker* assists importers in preparing and processing documentation so that it's accurate and complete when freight moves through customs. The broker submits electronic documentation to the United States Automated Broker Interface System (AES*Direct*) and the Canadian Pre-Arrival Review System (PARS) and pays any required custom duties to local authorities under power of attorney granted by the importer. However, liability for any unpaid duties remains the responsibility of the importer.

The *export packaging company* provides specialized packaging services to assist shippers. They also help to expedite shipments as they move through customs. Decisions on how to package perishables, proper labeling, rough ride considerations to minimize damage, custom considerations, package weight minimization, and the need for reverse logistics require proper planning by an exporting company or a selected third party.

A *shipping association* is a group of small exporters who join together to qualify for carrier rate discounts. A *ship broker* is an independent third party who brings exporters and ship operators together and finds ships that have space available to meet the exporter's shipping schedule.

A *ship agent* works for the carrier by arranging arrival berthing, loading and unloading, fee payments, and requesting ship clearance. They acknowledge cargo receipts from domestic carriers by issuing *dock receipts* as well as preparing a *ship manifest* showing the pickup location, the cargo placed in the vessel, and the delivery location based on the delivered *bill of lading* (B/L).

The import/export process involves a number of different documents and each one plays a unique role. A *certificate of origin* identifies the originating location of the manufactured product. The duty percentage can be waived or reduced based on that location. A buyer or seller will obtain a *certificate of insurance* to verify that insurance coverage exists during transportation in order to protect against cargo loss.

The *ATA Carnet* is an international custom document that permits tax free and duty-free admission of goods, under certain conditions, as it moves across different countries until it arrives at its final destination. The document simplifies custom formalities for the temporary importing of goods. For example, materials used for demonstration purposes at trade shows are exempt from custom duties.

Global Trade Management (GTM) traditionally focused on helping companies comply with the various country regulations governing cross-border product movement. Today, while compliance remains critical, it now includes validating how and where products were manufactured, assembled, packaged, and shipped from. Companies try to optimize these shipments across international borders with a goal of reducing costs, improving velocity, streamlining trade and custom regulation compliance, and supporting documentation, tariffs, and custom regulations.

An *ATR certificate* enables imported or exported goods to qualify for a duty reduction waiver if they originate between European Union (EU) members and Turkey.

A product can require an *export license* to authorize the exporting of cargo. One form is the *general export license*. This is used with merchandise that has no restrictions. The second form is a *validation export license*. This limits the export of selected strategic items such as military hardware, computer chips, and other sensitive materials.

The *B/L* is a document issued by a carrier to the shipper as a contract of carriage which covers the transportation of materials between the shipping and delivery destinations. It becomes a *goods receipt* upon delivery. A B/L is used to record damaged, late, or missing packages to support a claim against the carrier. A *clean B/L* is issued if the delivery arrives undamaged at its destination. An *ocean B/L* governs the port to port movement of the shipment. An *export B/L* tracks the carriage movement from the exporters' docks to the delivery countries' ports. An *order B/L* provides evidence of ownership, is negotiable, and permits a title to be transferred to an unknown third party during transit. A *straight B/L* is not negotiable and the delivery goes straight to the named consignee.

A pro forma invoice serves as a price quote and is used as supporting documentation for the *letter of credit* (L/C). It is similar to the regular commercial invoice, except it's issued in advance of the sale. A *commercial invoice* states the value of its shipped cargo. It serves as the buyer's and seller's transaction invoice. A commercial invoice is used along with an L/C, which requires the value of the shipment to be specified. An L/C applies when the exporter is unwilling to extend credit terms for ordered merchandise. A bank acts as an intermediary between all parties to guarantee contract obligation payment. A carrier's B/L confirms material receipt at the customer's designated location. This document is sent to the bank as proof of delivery by the seller requesting invoice payment. The bank then processes payment to the supplier. *Contract payment terms* and conditions must be met before the bank can execute the payment process. The bank doesn't assume any responsibility for the quality of goods, genuineness of documents, or any other provisions specified in the contract of sale.

The *consular invoice* is required by the receiving country for incoming shipments and must be written in that country's language. It contains information required by customs in the importer's country and is used to compile trade statistics.

Currency hedging eliminates risk resulting from using different currencies between different countries when purchasing a product or service. An example is a buyer using U.S. dollars and the seller in France using Euros. A company can buy or sell a specified currency amount at a fixed price on a fixed date to protect against currency exchange risk. Currency hedging prevents future currency gains or losses upon payment. The Certified Supply Chain Professional (CSCP) Learning System also shows different forms of financial instruments called derivatives. Examples are *forward contracts*, *futures*, *swaps*, and *options*. These are used along with hedging to determine future currency value on the payment due date.

GLOBAL ORDER FLOW AIR PARTICIPANTS

The import processes over water and air are very similar. However, a few differences do exist. The consolidator, freight forwarder, NVOCC, and the port aren't part of the air process. The consolidator/*airfreight forwarder* performs this function. A good example of an airfreight forwarder is Federal Express—who picks up freight, consolidates shipments, and prepares the *standard air waybill* (AWB) shipping document. The AWB is used in place of a B/L. It allows air carriers to facilitate shipments and customs' processing. The AWB is a non-negotiable document that doesn't provide title to the shipped goods, but instead only shows shipment receipt. After paperwork, the cargo is taken to an airport where it's flown to its destination and the shipment then gets delivered directly to the consignee.

IMPORT/EXPORT FINANCIAL CONSIDERATION TERMS

The *harmonized system classification codes* are a multipurpose international product nomenclature that provides a product description and classification. A *harmonized tariff schedule* (HTS) code is six digits that specify a general category. Countries are permitted to add an additional four digits for their internal classification and tracking. The total length of the HTS code can be expanded to 10 characters and is maintained by the *World Customs Organization* (WCO). Countries use the HTS code to identify applicable tariffs on imported merchandise. In the United States, the code (https://hts.usitc.gov/?query=wine) for wine in containers holding two liters or less is 2204.10.00 and the code for containers holding more than two liters but not more than 10 liters is 2204.22. The exporter specifies the code on export documents, which customs then uses to collect tariff payments. The *tariff* is a form of tax charged to the importer. Customs holds the importer responsible for assuring that the correct code has been applied.

A *free trade zone* or *foreign trade zone* (FTZ) is an area within a country where tariffs and trade barriers have been reduced or eliminated. The goal of an FTZ is to encourage international trade participation. In an FTZ, a company is permitted to import materials, as well as store, inspect, manufacture, assemble, repackage, repair, etc., without having to pay any duty upon material receipt. This permits companies to avoid quotas, import duty, duty drawback, inverted duty payments, and it can lower freight costs. Duty and taxes are deferred until the product leaves the FTZ for use in the received country, or they're eliminated if the product is exported. The FTZ location is considered to be outside of a country, and retail trade isn't permitted.

Declared value is the shipment value specified by the shipper that becomes the basis for calculating duties and taxes on imports. *Import duty* is a tax charged on imported merchandise based on the HTS. It factors in a percentage of the cost of the materials being shipped plus insurance and freight charges. A *quota* is a limit on how much material can be imported. If the quota is exceeded, an additional import duty will be charged. A *duty drawback* is a rebate on a tariff or duty that was previously paid by a company upon receipt of imported goods. The drawback refunds the tariffs paid by the importing company if the goods are used to produce goods that are subsequently exported. *Inverted duties* occur when imported components have a higher taxable rate than an imported finished product. A company can petition for a rebate to have the duty lowered to the imported component level to protect local manufacturers against foreign-based importers. *Value-added tax* (VAT) is a type of consumption tax that is assessed on the value added at each production stage and at final sale. The CSCP Learning System describes VAT as being assessed on the *Incoterms cost, insurance, and freight* (CIF) or *free on board* (FOB) plus import duties.

A *trading bloc* (or *trade bloc*) is an agreement between multiple countries who work together to reduce or eliminate trade barriers and duties between themselves. Members gain an economic advantage and receive preferential treatment over non-members by encouraging trade among members. Imports from a non-member country end up costing more. There are a number of different types of trading blocs, including *customs unions*, FTZ, *economic unions*, *common markets*, *preferential trade agreements* (PTAs), *customs and monetary unions*, and *economic and monetary unions*. A few examples of the different trading blocs are the *North American Free Trade Agreement* (NAFTA) which is an example of a PTA, and the Andean Community, which is a custom union that includes Bolivia, Colombia, Ecuador, Peru, and Venezuela. The EU, consisting of 28 independent European countries, is also an example of a custom union.

NAFTA is a trilateral North American trade bloc. It consists of the United States, Mexico, and Canada, and its objective is to eliminate or reduce most tariffs between the countries. *Maquiladora* is the name of foreign-owned, low labor cost manufacturing operations located in Mexico. It's here that materials can be imported and processed, and then exported back to the United States duty free.

Incoterms are established and regulated by the *International Chamber of Commerce* (ICC). They provide a common understanding of the obligations of sellers and buyers from the standpoint of risks, costs, and documents for the delivery of goods under a sale's contract. These standard rules are recognized throughout the world and help to reduce the uncertainty caused by international trade practices. Incoterms aren't legally binding until specified in a contract of sale. A list of Incoterms, their groups, and where they apply can be found in Table 5.1.

Table 5.1   Incoterms

Term Acronym	Term	Incoterm Group
Terms for any mode of transport		
FCA	Free carrier	F
CPT	Carriage paid to	C
CIP	Carriage and insurance paid	C
EXW	Ex works	E
DAT	Delivered at terminal	D
DAP	Delivered at place	D
Maritime (sea) and inland waterway transport		
FAS	Free alongside ship	F
FOB	Free on board	F
CFR	Cost and freight	C
CIF	Cost, insurance, and freight	C

There are different meanings behind each group. Group E is where the goods are made available to the buyer at the seller's premises. Group F is where the seller must deliver the goods to a carrier appointed by the buyer. Group C is where the seller must contract for the carriage of goods without assuming the risk of loss, damage to the goods, or additional costs due to events occurring after shipment. Group D is where the seller has to bear all costs and risks required to bring the goods to the place of destination.

Exercise 5.1 will test your knowledge and understanding of the various Incoterms. Read each question and write in all answers that apply. The answers to the exercise are available from the Web Added Value™ Download Resource Center at www.jrosspub.com.

Exercise 5.1   Understanding Incoterms

Question	Answer
1. Which term has the seller price including the cost of the goods, the freight or transport costs, and the costs of marine insurance?	
2. Which term has the passing of risk occurring when the goods have been delivered into the custody of the first carrier?	
3. Which term has the seller paying for transportation of the goods to the port of shipment?	
4. Which of the following Incoterms is used only for sea and inland waterway transport: CIF, CIP, DAP, or DDP?	
5. Which term only applies for shipments moving from an ocean port to an ocean port by vessel?	
6. Which term has the seller paying for the freight to the named point of destination and the buyer paying for insurance?	
7. Which term has the buyer paying all transportation costs and bearing all risks for transporting the goods to their final destination?	
8. Which term has the seller paying for costs and freight of the goods to the named destination port?	
9. Which term has the seller delivering the goods to the buyer who assumes responsibility for their unloading at a named destination?	
10. Which group has the responsibility for defining Incoterms?	
11. Which term has the seller delivering the goods into the carrier custody and the buyer paying only for the transportation from the place named in the Incoterm?	
12. Which term has the seller paying for all transportation costs and duties, plus bearing all risks until the goods have been delivered?	
13. Which terms generally have import duties assessed as a percentage of the shipment value?	

MULTICOUNTRY STRATEGY

A *multicountry strategy* is when the supplier develops products to meet self-contained, local market needs, and then those products are sold within that market. An example of this is a U.S. company selling an international variant of a laptop computer in China where the keyboard has Chinese characters and a different power supply. *Glocalization* combines globalization and localization to form a new term. It refers to the development of a product to meet the needs of each locality or culture. For example, Starbucks serves green and aromatic teas along with coffee in China. The term *reverse innovation* is used to describe a product that has been developed for a local foreign market that is later marketed and sold in the host company's market. An example of this is a company developing and selling a low cost, low-fat dried noodle for rural India that is later marketed in its host country. This is in contrast to the past, when innovations were made in the host country and were later used in another country's local market.

Every company has its own unique culture that is based on attitudes, values, and beliefs. *Multinational corporations* often try to instill their home values in their foreign location to determine policies and to create or change local culture. Substantial differences between local culture and corporate culture regarding standards of conduct, social structure, religion, language, regulatory requirements, education, and work ethic can influence business conduct and lead to organizational and marketplace problems. *Culture* is the beliefs and customs of a particular country, social group, or religion, which impacts businesses and people throughout the world. Socialization is the process where people learn about one another and their cultures. *Ringi* is the cultural Japanese decision-making process of building consensus from the ground up. *Hofstede's cultural dimension study* analyzes the influence of four workplace values; they include masculinity/femininity, power distance, individualism/collectivism, and uncertainty avoidance.

INTELLECTUAL PROPERTY, SOFTWARE, AND TECHNOLOGY LICENSING

Companies that are selling internationally need to seek out local representation and file quick international patent applications in order to protect their *intellectual property* (IP). IP is anything a company or person creates that needs protection—such as an invention, a branded product, or a software application. IP enforcement differs from country to country, and companies must be prepared against litigation by *patent assertion entities* (PAE) or *patent trolls* who are third parties that file aggressive litigation claiming patent infringement. *Software licensing* can be difficult to obtain due to its complexity. Licensees are responsible for compliance and they need to perform periodic compliance audits. *Technology licensing* permits a company to earn royalty payments from international licensing agreements. However, export restrictions and export license requirements can restrict what kinds of technology can be exported. Royalty and repatriation laws can also limit payment amounts.

Protection is required against *counterfeit goods or services* which can be placed within a supply chain. Companies need to be prepared to protect their IP and need to be alert for third parties who are selling *grey market* products. Grey market products are items such as video games and cameras that are bought and sold outside of authorized trading channels.

KEY TERMINOLOGY

Understanding key terms and the concepts they represent is crucial to passing the CSCP exam. In this chapter, the important terms are identified in Table 5.2.

Table 5.2   Import/export logistics provider participants key terminology

Airfreight forwarder
ATA carnet
ATR certificate
Bill of lading (B/L)
Certificate of insurance
Certificate of origin
Clean bill of lading

Continued

Commercial invoice
Common markets
Consolidator
Consular invoice
Contract payment terms
Cost, insurance, and freight (CIF)
Counterfeit goods or services
Culture
Currency hedging
Customshouse broker
Customs union
Declared value
Derivates
Dock receipts
Duty drawback
Economic unions
European Union (EU)
Export
Export bill of lading
Export license
Export management company (EMC)
Export packaging company
Export trading company (ETC)
Foreign trade zone (FTZ)
Forward contracts
Free on board (FOB)
Free trade zones (FTZ)*
Freight forwarder
Futures
General export license
General trading company
Global trade management (GTM)
Glocalization*
Goods receipt
Grey market
Harmonized system classification codes*
Harmonized Tariff Schedule (HTS)
Hofstede's cultural dimension study
Import duty
Importer

Continued

Incoterms*
Intellectual property (IP)
International Chamber of Commerce (ICC)
Inverted duty
Letter of credit (L/C)
Maquiladora
Monetary unions
Motor carriers (trucks)
Multicountry strategy*
Multinational companies (MNC)
Non-vessel operating common carrier
North American Free Trade Agreement (NAFTA)
Ocean bill of lading
Options
Order bill of lading
Patent Assertion Entities (PAE)
Patent trolls
Pipeline
Planes
Preferential trade agreement (PTA)
Reverse innovation
Ringi
Ship agent
Ship broker
Ship manifest
Shipping association
Ships
Software licensing
Sogo shosha
Standard air waybill (AWB)
Straight bill of lading
Swaps
Tariff*
Technology licensing
Trade bloc*
Trading bloc*
Trains
Validation export license
Value-added tax (VAT)
World customs organization (WCO)

*Key term found in the CSCP ECM

CSCP EXAM PRACTICE QUESTIONS ON IMPORT/EXPORT LOGISTICS

The questions presented in Table 5.3a cover the concepts presented in this chapter on import/export logistics. They are examples of what to expect on the actual exam.

Table 5.3a   Import/export logistics practice questions

No.	Questions
1	The European Union (EU) is best defined as a: a) Customs union b) Free trade zone (FTZ) c) Economic union d) Common market
2	Which is used to compile U.S. trade statistics: a) ATA carnet b) Export license c) Commercial invoice d) Electronic export information
3	Where do companies typically go to legally protect their intellectual property (IP)? a) World court b) Court systems c) Supreme court d) Better business bureau (BBB)
4	What type of strategy is a company using when it produces and sells a self-contained product locally, and a different but similar self-contained product in another country? a) Business strategy b) Marketing strategy c) Supply chain strategy d) Multicountry strategy
5	Which participant only handles the shipment to the port for later placement on a ship? a) Freight forwarders b) Shipping associations c) Export management companies (EMCs) d) Non-vessel operating common carriers (NVOCCs)
6	Which isn't a function of a freight forwarder? a) Obtaining insurance b) Quoting carrier rates c) Arranging inland transportation d) Buying and reselling carrier space
7	A country may impose what type of fee on imported or exported goods? a) Tariff b) Sales tax c) Duty drawback d) Value-added tax
8	All of the following are functions performed by a consolidator except for: a) Combining small shipments b) Obtaining discounts for combining small shipments c) Arranging for transportation to a freight forwarder d) Collaborating with a non-vessel operating common carrier (NVOCC)

Continued

9	Who pays all import custom duties upon material receipt at the dock? a) Ship agent b) Overseas carrier c) Customshouse broker d) Non-vessel operating common carrier (NVOCC)
10	Who acts as a consultant to an exporter to simplify the export process? a) Importer b) Export trading company (ETC) c) Export packing company (EPC) d) Export management company (EMC)
11	Which company is also known as a general trading company? a) Export trading company (ETC) b) Export packing company (EPC) c) Export shipping company (ESC) d) Export management company (EMC)
12	All of the following are responsibilities of a ship agent except for: a) Working for a carrier b) Arranging for ocean transport c) Providing ship docking information d) Arranging for custom fee payments
13	A seller using a letter of credit will ask their banker for payment when the seller can provide what document? a) Invoice b) ATA carnet c) Export license d) Carrier's bill of lading (B/L)
14	The primary purpose of the harmonized coding system is to: a) Avoid confusion b) Charge correct duty c) Compile export statistics d) Standardize the description of goods
15	A tariff rebated to a company upon re-exporting a product is best called: a) Rebate b) Tax refund c) Duty drawback d) Inverted duties
16	Which document constitutes the seller's and buyer's invoice for the transaction? a) Export invoice b) Consular invoice c) Commercial invoice d) Pro forma commercial invoice
17	Which document is written in the language of the importing country and contains information needed for customs in the importer's country? a) Export invoice b) Consular invoice c) Commercial invoice d) Pro forma commercial invoice

Continued

18	Which bill of lading (B/L) document is nonnegotiable and governs cargo that must be delivered to the named consignee? a) Clean B/L b) Order B/L c) Export B/L d) Straight B/L
19	Who issues a dock receipt at the port? a) Carrier b) Importer c) Ship agent d) Ship broker
20	What would be the duty on the cargo if the product cost was $70,000, insurance was $10,000, freight was $20,000, sales tax was $4,000, and the delivery charge to the customer was $1,000? The cargo is also subject to a 5% tariff. a) $3,500 b) $4,000 c) $5,000 d) $5,250
21	The MIP Company developed an innovative, low-cost product to meet the specific needs and budget requirements of customers in a local market. This is an example of: a) Localization b) Glocalization c) Globalization d) Reverse innovation
22	Culture is learned through a process of: a) Ringi b) Socialization c) Globalization d) Trial and error
23	Which free on board (FOB) term will best impact the customer cash flow? a) FOB origin b) FOB destination c) FOB destination, freight prepaid d) FOB origin, freight prepaid and charged back

ANSWERS TO CSCP EXAM PRACTICE QUESTIONS ON IMPORT/EXPORT LOGISTICS

The answers to the practice questions on import/export logistics are shown in Table 5.3b. Any question you answer incorrectly indicates a gap in your body of knowledge and encourages the need for additional study time.

Table 5.3b   Answers to CSCP exam practice questions on import/export logistics

No.	Answers
1	Answer: C The European Union (EU) is an economic union of 28 member states acting as a single market.
2	Answer: D In the U.S., electronic export information serves the purpose of compiling trade statistics as it electronically collects and compiles data.
3	Answer: B Companies typically go to the court system in local countries to legally try to protect their intellectual property.
4	Answer: D The key words in this question are *self-contained* and *locally*, which best describe a multicountry strategy.
5	Answer: D Handling the shipment to a port for later placement on a ship is the role of a non-vessel operating common carrier (NVOCC). A freight forwarder consolidates collected cartons and skids and delivers them over land to the NVOCC. The shipping association purchases space and the export management company (EMC) works with companies who want to export their products.
6	Answer: D The buying and reselling of carrier space is the role of the non-vessel operating common carrier (NVOCC). A freight forwarder moves freight over land to the NVOCC. Answers A, B, and C are also duties that the freight forwarder performs.
7	Answer: A This question requires knowledge of the APICS Dictionary definition of tariffs. A tariff is a tax imposed on imported or exported goods charged by a country.
8	Answer: D The consolidator uses a freight forwarder or motor carrier to arrange transportation. They have no direct interaction with the non-vessel operating common carrier (NVOCC).
9	Answer: C The key word in this question is *dock*. A customshouse broker, under power of attorney received from the importer, pays the duty before the materials leave customs. However, liability for unpaid or incorrect duties remains the responsibility of the importer, not the broker.
10	Answer: D An export management company (EMC) acts as a consultant to an exporting company. Generally, the EMC doesn't handle exporting by itself.
11	Answer: A An export trading company (ETC) is also known as a general trading company or a sogo shosha in Japan.
12	Answer: D The customshouse broker pays custom fees. It isn't a responsibility of the ship agent. Answers A, B, and C are all performed by the ship agent.

Continued

13	Answer: D A carrier's bill of lading (B/L) confirms material receipt at the customer's designated location. This document is then sent to the bank as proof of delivery by the seller requesting invoice payment. An ATA Carnet is a customs' document that permits goods to enter or pass through a country without having to pay any duty. An export license permits a company to sell materials to a different country.
14	Answer: D The primary purpose of the harmonized code is to provide an internationally standardized description of goods. The code uses a system of numbers to provide increasingly detailed classifications and descriptions.
15	Answer: C This question requires knowledge of the APICS Dictionary definition of duty drawback. A duty drawback refunds previously paid duties on imported materials if the product is later exported.
16	Answer: C A commercial invoice constitutes a seller's and buyer's invoice for a transaction.
17	Answer: B A consular invoice is written in the language of the importing country and it contains information required by customs.
18	Answer: D This question requires knowledge of the APICS Dictionary definition of a straight bill of lading (B/L). An order B/L is negotiable. A clean B/L certifies that the goods have arrived at the ship undamaged. The export B/L is used for exporting.
19	Answer: C A dock receipt is issued by a ship agent to signify that cargo was received from the domestic carrier at the port.
20	Answer: C Import duties are assessed as a percentage of cost, insurance, and freight (CIF). The calculation totals these costs and multiples it by the import duty tariff rate ($70,000 + $10,000 + $20,000 = $100,000 * 5% = $5,000). The delivery charge isn't subject to a duty, as it's incurred after the shipment is received.
21	Answer: B Glocalization is the process of adapting an existing product to satisfy local market product tastes.
22	Answer: B Socialization is how people learn about one another and their cultures. Ringi is a Japanese decision-making process of building consensus from the ground up.
23	Answer: C Free on board (FOB) destination, freight prepaid means that the customer doesn't initially pay for delivered products and shipping costs. Payment is deferred until the supplier prepares and submits an invoice to the customer. Answers A, B, and D all require earlier payment.

This book has free material available for download from the
Web Added Value™ resource center at *www.jrosspub.com*

6

SUSTAINABILITY, REGULATORY, AND SECURITY PROCEDURES

This chapter focuses on the importance of sustainability. It examines the various organizations and initiatives that have been put into place to improve the environment, sustainability and regulatory reporting requirements, and supply chain security initiatives.

SUSTAINABILITY

Sustainability has many different definitions. It ranges from focusing on protecting the environment, conserving natural resources, supporting long-term ecological balance, doing more with less, and encouraging behavioral change, to creating more sustainable processes for present and future generations.

The *triple bottom line* (TBL) consists of three pillars of sustainability—social, economic, and environmental practices. The social pillar consists of child labor, security, diversity, bribery, and corruption. The economic pillar consists of suppliers, customers, employees, and financial reporting. The environmental pillar consists of water, energy, emissions, and the concept of waste. These pillars link a firm's ability to operate successfully and profitably in a sustainable manner with a strong commitment to *corporate social responsibility* (CSR) and sustainability. The TBL concept became the foundation for CSR, the *United Nations Global Compact* (UNGC), the *Organization for Economic Co-operation and Development* (OECD), the *Global Reporting Initiative* (GRI), and the International Organization for Standardization (ISO) 26000 (social responsibility).

CSR looks at how companies voluntarily integrate social and environmental concerns in their business operations and in their interaction with their stakeholders. CSR considers labor practices, human rights, the environment, and anticorruption.

The UNGC is a voluntary corporate responsibility initiative. It's a practical framework for the development, implementation, and disclosure of sustainability policies and practices. UNGC is also a strategic policy initiative committed to helping businesses align their operations and strategies. It has ten universally accepted principles that were designed to advance sustainable business practices. The 10 principles break down into the same four general categories as CSR.

The OECD is an organization that creates a comprehensive set of government-backed guidelines, voluntary principles, and standards for responsible business conduct for *multinational enterprises* (MNE).

An MNE is a company that operates globally in numerous countries but has its base of operations in one country. The OECD encourages and maximizes the positive impact that MNEs can make on sustainable development and social progress.

The GRI is a program that is voluntarily used by companies to promote and track their economic, environmental, and social sustainability performances in a single report. The use of a common reporting framework helps to better measure, understand, and communicate sustainability performance. The GRI provides a comprehensive sustainability reporting framework that consists of metrics and key performance indicators (KPIs) to monitor performance. It works in cooperation with the UNGC and ISO 26000 (social responsibility) as it attempts to make the TBL operational. The GRI G4 Sustainability Reporting Guidelines are used to prepare sustainability reports. The GRI Standards will supersede the G4 Guidelines as of July 1, 2018.

Green supply chain management (GSCM) is defined as integrating environmental thinking into supply chain management including product design, material sourcing, selection, manufacturing processes, and product delivery as well as end-of-life product management. It's described as an expansion of the traditional supply chain focus and it includes environmental performances as well as cost, quality, and service. Companies use GSCM due to government and regulatory pressures to gain a competitive advantage through innovation and economic benefits from increased efficiency. They also hope to improve their public opinion and reputation.

Life-cycle assessment (LCA) reviews a product's life-cycle (PLC) environmental impact. It begins with the extraction of raw materials throughout the manufacturing process, distribution, usage, repair, and finally disposal at the end of its product life.

A company desiring to have a socially and environmentally responsible supply chain needs to address how it can best achieve this goal by incorporating responsible manufacturing and sensitive engineering into its operations. An *environmentally responsible business* focuses on reducing its adverse impact on the environment while maximizing resource efficiency. An example of this is a company that produces environmentally friendly products in a sustainable building while using renewable energy throughout that building. *Environmentally responsible manufacturing* focuses on using sustainable manufacturing practices throughout the design, operation, supply chain, and procurement areas. An example of this is a company that has improved its manufacturing practices by using less material; reducing waste, energy, and water; and delivering products via electric trucks. *Environmentally sensitive engineering* focuses on designing products that eliminate raw materials or components that can be hazardous to the environment. It also strives to reduce packaging materials or use materials that can be recycled at the end of their product life. An example of this is a company that has designed its products in a way that reduces its carbon footprint or is compliant with *Restrictions on Hazardous Substances* (RoHS).

Regulatory compliance requires companies to conform to various rules, policies, standards, regulations, and laws to help protect the environment. Companies collect, monitor, and report their data in a single, consolidated format to avoid data duplication to various government and regulatory agencies. The benefit of this approach is that it leads to better risk management and public disclosure.

RoHS restricts the use of six heavy metal substances such as lead or mercury in electrical and electronic products and metal and plastic products in the European Union (EU).

Waste electrical and electronic equipment (WEEE) is designed to prevent waste disposal and encourage the reuse and recycling of recovered materials in the EU. Equipment manufacturers are required to take back electrical and electronic equipment at the end of their economic life for recycling. WEEE's goal is to reduce the use of natural resources and to protect air and water quality.

Dangerous goods or *hazardous materials* (Hazmat) requires safety precautions and special handling during the transportation, usage, storage, or disposal of specified materials that could adversely affect the safety of the public, workers, or the environment.

The Globally Harmonized System of Classification and Labeling of Chemicals (GHS) is an international standard adapted by the United Nations. It includes criteria for the classification of health, physical, and environmental hazards as well as specifying what information should be included on the labels of hazardous chemicals and on the material *safety data sheets* (SDS).

A *carbon footprint analysis* monitors and reports the quantity of greenhouse gases such as carbon dioxide that are emitted during the manufacturing and transportation processes.

Leadership in Energy and Environmental Design (LEED) is a voluntary standard for measuring a building's *green* sustainability practices. Their first goal is to have a building designed, constructed, maintained, and operated using environmentally friendly materials and practices. LEED's second goal is to incorporate reusable, clean energy in order to reduce the building's impact on the environment.

Conflict minerals refer to minerals that are being mined where armed conflict and human rights' violations exist. These minerals are sold by armed groups to support their cause. In the United States, the Dodd-Frank Act of 2010 requires companies to verify that they don't purchase these minerals.

SECURITY

Customs-Trade Partnership Against Terrorism (C-TPAT) is a joint, voluntary initiative that establishes importing guideline requirements between the United States and any business that imports goods to them. Companies must agree with security procedures, training, and factory access control guidelines by validating the integrity of their security practices within their supply chain. C-TPAT's goal is to create a more secure and expedient supply chain. The benefits of C-TPAT are that shipments move quickly through port and have fewer delays due to inspection and material damage. A company who fails to comply with these guidelines loses the ability to continue to participate in the C-TPAT program.

Every country is allowed to prohibit certain goods, suppliers, individuals, or entities from importing or exporting goods. The governments of these countries can maintain a list of *prohibited goods* for security, health, safety, or trade protection. Countries can also have product *labeling and documentation regulations* pertaining to the importing and exporting of goods. These regulations can cover labeling language, ingredients, health, size, and environmental and *country of origin* compliance.

RISK STANDARDS

Corporate governance is the goal of the *Sarbanes-Oxley Act* (SOX). The U.S. Congress passed this legislation in 2002 to protect the public from fraudulent corporation accounting activities. It requires companies to implement strict financial controls and requires timely information disclosure.

Two frameworks address and use standards to monitor and control risk. They are the *Committee of Sponsoring Organizations of the Treadway Commission* (COSO) and the *governance, risk, and compliance* (GRC) tool.

COSO establishes an internal control/integrated framework called *enterprise risk management* (ERM). ERM helps management to establish and set a risk strategy, identify risk events, and manage internal controls as a means to manage risk. This concept has been incorporated into organizations' policies, rules, and regulations to better control companies' risk activities. ERM also provides a common language and clear direction to help manage risk. It expands internal controls which provide a more robust and extensive focus on the broader subject of risk management. Its goal isn't to replace any company's existing internal control framework, but rather to incorporate the ERM framework within it. Companies need to look at the ERM framework to move toward a detailed risk management process. There are eight components of ERM that need to be tightly integrated with management processes, as shown in Table 6.1.

Table 6.1 The COSO ERM framework components

Component	Response
Control activities	Policies and procedures are defined, implemented, monitored, and controlled to help ensure that proper action is taken.
Event identification	Risk, threats, and opportunities in internal and external events which can impact a company's objectives are identified. Opportunities need to be channeled back to the management strategy and its objective-setting processes.
Information and communication	Information is identified, captured, and communicated in a timely manner up and across the organization.
Internal environment	This encompasses the organization's tone and establishes how risk is viewed and addressed. It includes risk management philosophy, risk appetite, ethical values, and integrity.
Monitoring	A continuously improving ERM process is consistently reviewed.
Objective setting	Management needs to define objectives that align with the mission and risk appetite.
Risk assessment	This requires risks to be analyzed to determine the likelihood that they will occur and to determine how to properly manage a response.
Risk response	Management determines a proper risk response (avoid, accept, reduce, or risk sharing), which aligns each risk to match the organization's risk tolerance and risk appetite.

A GRC framework needs to be in place for an organization to have overall effectiveness and be balanced. GRC refers to an organization's coordinated strategy that manages corporate governance, ERM, and corporate compliance in regard to regulatory standards and requirements. Governance is a decision-making hierarchy for an effective, ethical management corporate approach at all executive and managerial levels. Risk management is an effective and cost-efficient approach to mitigate risks that might prevent a company from being competitive in the marketplace. Compliance is achieving defined requirements and conforming to applicable laws, regulatory requirements, and contractual requirements.

INTERNATIONAL ORGANIZATION FOR STANDARDIZATION

ISO is the world's largest developer of voluntary, market-driven international standards. These global consensus standards help break down international trade barriers. They serve to safeguard users and consumers and to make trade between countries easier and fairer by providing governments with a base for health, safety, and environmental legislation. ISO aids in the transfer of technology to developing countries, which makes the manufacturing and supply of products and services more efficient, safer, and cleaner. ISO's standards are used to provide tools for tackling challenges in the TBL. They also collaborate with the UN to establish harmonized regulations and public policies.

There are numerous ISO standards used by companies to improve their processes. There is an easy way to help distinguish the various components. Any standard ending in *000* is the high-level principle or foundation, *001* is a planning of the process or implementation, and *004* is the implementation activity.

ISO 9000 addresses quality management. It provides guidance and tools for companies that want to ensure that their products and services consistently meet customers' requirements, and that quality is consistently improved. *ISO 9001:2015* is one of the standards that specify requirements for a quality management system (QMS) within an organization.

ISO 14000 Series Standards consists of a family of standards related to *environmental management systems* (EMS). EMS standards provide a framework that companies use to validate compliance with applicable laws, regulations, and other environmental requirements. The goal of ISO 14000 is to continually improve the environment. ISO 14000 is further broken-down into ISO 14001 and ISO 14004.

ISO 14001 helps an organization better plan and manage environmental activities and demonstrate sound environmental management practices. It specifies a generic and holistic framework for them. ISO 14001 requires the development of policies, plans, and actions to prepare to implement ISO 14000. *ISO 14004* is the development and implementation of EMS and their principles as defined in ISO 14001.

ANSI Z.10 is a voluntary consensus standard on occupational health and safety management systems. It is a management tool that focuses on reducing the risk of occupational safety and health issues. ANSI Z.10 is designed to be compatible with ISO 9000 (quality) and ISO 14000 (environment). The current version of the standard is ANSI Z.10-2012.

ISO 26000 provides guidance, rather than certifiable requirements, on how an organization should operate in a socially responsible manner. It's intended to clarify what social responsibility is all about in order to give companies steps they can work toward. *ISO 26000:2010* was released in 2010 and was intended to assist organizations and stakeholders in contributing to sustainable development. It measures how the organization operates and its impact on the environment. Unlike other ISO standards, ISO 26000 is strictly a guideline, and there is no certification required.

Social accountability international SA8000 is a standard for managing human rights in the workplace. Its framework is based on a universal code of labor practices and is applied to all industries. Social accountability permits consumers to validate that manufactured or assembled products are produced in accordance with the nine principles found in the standard. They are child labor, forced or compulsory labor, health and safety, freedom of association and the right to collective bargaining, discrimination, disciplinary practices, working hours, remuneration, and management systems.

ISO 28000 Security Management System is a standard for managing security risks within a supply chain. It includes high-risk concerns pertaining to theft, damage, and vandalism.

ISO 31000 refers to a family of risk management standards. These standards help a company to better manage risks by protecting against potential threats. A threat is anything that could harm, prevent, or delay the supply chain. ISO 31000 identifies various risks by conducting three steps. They are placing risks in an appropriate context, assessing the risks (including identifying the risks, analyzing risks, and assessing the risk levels), and determining the risk response.

ISO Guide 73 and *ISO Guide 73:2009* provide a basic, common understanding of risk management vocabulary.

All of these ISOs are voluntary, internal management tools. ISO certifications are administered by third-party organizations and require an organization to be audited and re-certified by a third party every three years.

Exercise 6.1 will test your knowledge and understanding of both ISO and non-ISO standards and guidelines. Read each question and write in all answers that apply. The answers to the exercise are available from the Web Added Value™ Download Resource Center at www.jrosspub.com.

Exercise 6.1 Understanding various ISO and non-ISO standards and guidelines

Question	Answer
1. What is the name of the security management system that is a standard for managing security risks within a supply chain?	
2. What is the name of the worldwide federation that developed voluntary market-driven international standards?	
3. Which ISO documents show a glossary of risk management vocabulary?	
4. Which ISO documents provide guidance for social responsibility?	
5. Which ISO document is a set of principles to help manage risk in any type of organization?	
6. Which ISO document is a set of requirements for implementing a quality management system (QMS)?	
7. Which ISO document offers a framework for a strategic, holistic approach to an organization's environmental policy, plans, and actions?	
8. Which ISO document provides a general/generic guideline for an environmental management system (EMS)?	
9. Which ISO document provides a guideline to explain the specific elements of an EMS and its implementation, and discusses the principle issues involved?	
10. Which ISO document provides a QMS guideline?	
11. Which ISO document provides specifications that regulate classification and the use of seals on shipping containers?	
12. Which ISO document provides the requirements for an EMS?	
13. Which ISO document refers to a series of EMS standards?	
14. Which ISO document refers to installing approved seals on shipping containers?	
15. Which ISO document starts with an executive-level mandate and commitment toward risk management?	
16. Which ISO document will help all organizations talk about risk in the same manner?	
17. Which ISO family standard strives to help minimize harmful environmental effects?	
18. Which ISO standard is designed to manage human rights in the workplace?	

SUSTAINABILITY AND REGULATORY COMPLIANCE

Sustainability programs can be voluntary, mandatory, or corporate initiatives. An organization needs to weigh the costs of compliance such as lawsuits, non-compliance fines, and legal liability. It must also think about the loss of reputation versus potential benefits. Examples of this are an improved reputation, goodwill, and a possible income stream. *Voluntary program compliance* initiatives include material and product recycling, product recovery at the end of its life, GRI material content reporting, and carbon reduction. *Mandatory program compliance* initiatives can include RoHS and WEEE, which are both EU programs.

Wood pallets are monitored by the International Standards for Phytosanitary Measures (*ISPM 15*) regulations covering phytosanitary compliance. They require wood pallets to undergo heat treatment or fumigation to kill nesting, wood-boring insects and mold infestations. The three countries with restrictions and reporting requirements to ISPM 15 are China, the EU, and the U.S. *Slip sheets* that are made from plastic or corrugated paper can be used instead of wood pallets.

The U.S. *Food and Drug Administration* (FDA), or the United Kingdom's Medicines and Healthcare Products Regulatory Agency, establishes regulations pertaining to thorough documentation of the chain of custody, product and raw material traceability, material content, and the pedigree of pharmaceuticals and foods throughout the supply chain. A *pedigree* is a term used to track the movement of a product. An example of this is a prescription drug moving throughout the pharmaceutical supply chain. A pedigree's purpose is to validate the drug source and to protect customers from counterfeit drugs. *Material content* is the amount of a specified material found in a product. A *chain of custody* is used to validate and document a product's movement from raw materials, through its transformation to a product, its storage, and finally its distribution to an end customer. *Product traceability* or *traceability* is the ability to quickly and accurately identify the documented chain of custody of a raw material, component, end product, or associated process source across the value chain by country, production facility, distribution center, and manufacturing batch/lot to the end customer. The pharmaceutical, food, aerospace, and defense industries are required to track their materials and process chain of custody throughout their supply chains. In addition, it's often a requirement for a product label to indicate its manufacturing source, to show a country of origin, or to provide evidence that conflict minerals weren't improperly sourced. For example, a shirt may show a label *Made in the USA* or a company may file a due diligence conflict minerals report.

KEY TERMINOLOGY

Understanding key terms and the concepts they represent is crucial to passing the Certified Supply Chain Professional (CSCP) exam. In this chapter, the important terms are identified in Table 6.2.

Table 6.2   Sustainability, regulatory, and security procedures key terminology

ANSI Z.10
Carbon footprint analysis
Chain of custody
Conflict minerals
Corporate social responsibility (CSR)
Country of origin

Continued

Customs-Trade Partnership Against Terrorism (C-TPAT)
Dangerous goods
Enterprise risk management
Environmental management systems (EMS)
Environmental Protection Agency (EPA)
Environmentally responsible business*
Environmentally responsible manufacturing (ERM)*
Environmentally sensitive engineering*
Food and Drug Administration (FDA)
Global Reporting Initiative (GRI)*
Globally Harmonized System of Classification and Labeling of Chemicals (GHS)
Green supply chain management (GSCM)
Hazardous materials (Hazmat)
International Organization for Standardization (ISO)
International Standards for Phytosanitary Measures (ISPM 15)
Inventory compliance
ISO 14000 Series Standards*
ISO 14001
ISO 14004
ISO 26000*
ISO 26000:2010
ISO 28000
ISO 31000*
ISO 73
ISO 9000
ISO 9001:2015
ISO Guide 73:2009
Labeling dock relations
Leadership in Energy and Environmental Design (LEED)
Life-cycle assessment (LCA)
Mandatory program compliance
Material content
Multinational enterprises (MNE)
Organization for Economic Co-operation and Development (OECD)
Pedigree
Product traceability
Prohibited goods
Restrictions on hazardous substances (RoHS)
Safety data sheet (SDS)
Sarbanes-Oxley (SOX)

Continued

| Slip sheet |
| Social accountability (SA8000) |
| Sustainability |
| The Committee of Sponsoring Organizations of the Treadway Commission (COSO) |
| Traceability |
| Triple bottom line (TBL)* |
| United Nations Global Compact (UNGC) |
| Voluntary program compliance |
| Waste electrical and electronic equipment (WEEE) |

*Key term found in the CSCP ECM

CSCP EXAM PRACTICE QUESTIONS ON SUSTAINABILITY, REGULATORY, AND SECURITY PROCEDURES

The questions presented in Table 6.3a cover the concepts presented in this chapter on sustainability, regulatory, and security procedures. They are examples of what to expect on the actual exam.

Table 6.3a   Sustainability, regulatory, and security procedures practice questions

No.	Questions
1	Supply chain management has become greener by the addition of what focus? a) Jidoka b) Service c) Product returns d) Environmental performance
2	Environmental and economic are two of the three components of sustainability. What is the third component? a) Labor b) Social c) Human rights d) Anticorruption
3	The Global Reporting Initiative (GRI) has a strategic partnership with all of the following organizations except for: a) United Nations (UN) b) International Organization for Standardization (ISO) c) Waste Electrical and Electronic Equipment (WEEE) d) Office for Economic Co-Operation and Development (OECD)
4	Which organization is helping business develop reverse logistics key performance indicators (KPIs) to improve their environmental performance? a) European Union (EU) b) Object Naming Service (ONS) c) Global Reporting Initiative (GRI) d) World Trade Organization (WTO)
5	Which ISO standard provides a set of requirements for implementing a quality management system (QMS)? a) ISO 9000 b) ISO 14000 c) ISO 9001:2015 d) ISO 14001:2004

ANSWERS TO CSCP EXAM PRACTICE QUESTIONS ON SUSTAINABILITY, REGULATORY, AND SECURITY PROCEDURES

The answers to the practice questions on sustainability, regulatory, and security procedures are shown in Table 6.3b. Any question you answer incorrectly indicates a gap in your body of knowledge and encourages the need for additional study time.

Table 6.3b Answers to CSCP exam practice questions on sustainability, regulatory, and security procedures

No.	Answers
1	Answer: D Green supply chain management (GSCM) is described as an expansion of the traditional supply chain focus. It includes environmental performance as well as cost, quality, and service.
2	Answer: B Social, environmental, and economics are the three components of sustainability.
3	Answer: C The Global Reporting Initiative (GRI) is a network-based organization composed of several hundred stakeholders that disseminate globally applicable sustainability guidelines for voluntary use. They include the United Nations (UN), the International Organization for Standardization (ISO), and the Office for Economic Co-operation and Development (OECD). Waste Electrical and Electronic Equipment (WEEE) pertains to the return of equipment at the end of a product's life back to the manufacturer.
4	Answer: C The Global Reporting Initiative (GRI) establishes globally applicable sustainability guidelines for voluntary use including key performance indicators (KPIs). GRI has helped to standardize and quantify reporting to assist companies in improving their environmental performance.
5	Answer: C This question requires knowledge of the ISO standards. The key word in the question is *requirements*. ISO 9001:2015 refers to a set of standards for implementing a quality management system. ISO 9000 is the high-level generic standard, which isn't a set of requirements. ISO 14000 and ISO 14001 apply to the environment.

This book has free material available for download from the
Web Added Value™ resource center at *www.jrosspub.com*

7

MARKETING

This chapter focuses on the marketing process. It examines the marketing and business plans, the four Ps (4 Ps), customer segments, and measuring customer service. It also explores the importance of the voice of the customer and the communication process.

MARKETING

Marketing is a business activity designed to communicate information regarding a company's products and services to potential or existing customers. It promotes and positions them to various market segments based on the business plan that meets defined business goals and objectives. A *segment* breaks down marketing groups into smaller ones. For example, soda can be broken-down into regular, diet, or caffeine-free segments.

Marketing is integral to the success of any business. It identifies customer market and customer segment requirements. Marketing decisions to satisfy customer requirements are based on four variables called the *4 Ps*. They are products (what you plan to sell), price (how much you plan to charge), promotion (how you plan to communicate), and placement (where you purchase a product or service). The 4 Ps are referred to as the *marketing mix* and it supports making products and services winners in the marketplace. It also dictates where buyers and sellers interact with each other to obtain desired goods or services. This concept applies whether it's a physical store or an electronic website. A *marketplace* is a place where businesses or customers buy or sell goods and services. *Demand shaping* uses the 4 Ps to influence and better match demand against supply. For example, a sales promotion generates additional demand for a slow-moving product. Marketing and sales data is fed into a customer relationship management (CRM) system to enhance the marketing process. Exercise 7.1 will help reinforce the 4 P concepts. Place an "X" in the column that best reflects the 4 P attribute. The answers to the exercise are available from the Web Added Value™ Download Resource Center at www.jrosspub.com.

Exercise 7.1   Understanding the 4 P attributes

4 P Attributes	Product	Price	Promotion	Placement
Advertising				
Brand				
Chat room				
Contact channels				
Credit terms				
Customer segments				
Discounts				
Inventory				
Locations				
Logo				
Package				
Payment period				
Public relations				
Segmentation				
Sizes				
Variety				
Website				

BUSINESS PLAN

A *business plan* is prepared by upper management to identify long-term operational and financial objectives. It serves as a blueprint for guiding the direction of a firm's policies and strategies. The business then has the responsibility to follow and execute its defined plan.

A business plan is aligned with marketing, financial, engineering, logistics, and operational areas to establish a single, company-wide, unified plan. This plan includes information gained from a SWOT (strengths, weaknesses, opportunities, and threats) analysis, strategic goals, corporate strategies, and management controls, plus market and consumer research. Management uses *environmental scanning* to help identify and evaluate external opportunities and threats. It collects this information in order to understand its competition and marketplace trends. The information is later used to help improve the company's strengths and reduce its weaknesses. It's then further broken-down into tactical and operational plans. A company develops it's financial and marketing plans based on their business plan, which includes a *pro forma* balance sheet, income statement, and a statement of cash flow. A cash flow statement displays the actual or anticipated cash inflow or outflow position in future financial statements.

The business plan drives the development of the marketing plan. The *market plan* drives the development of the business, family/group, and item forecasts. These forecasts are inputs to the business plan, sales and operations plan (S&OP), and the master scheduling processes.

SUPPLY CHAIN NETWORK MODELING

Supply chain network modeling, also called network design, is a tool used to optimize the supply chain network. The process creates a mathematical model that helps supply chain managers select between different options. It analyzes many factors including manufacturing, transportation, distribution costs, location placements, inventory levels, and transportation routes in order to minimize costs and maximize flow.

The supply chain model design needs to consider infrastructure and develop a network based on locations (number and capacity), cost structure (storage and logistics), support services (seaports, rail, pipeline, airports, roads), and inventory levels (stock levels and lead times). It also needs to consider accessibility (access to transportation and customers), network configuration (levels and linkage), support processes (third-parties and services), and technology (system and equipment support).

Finally, the supply chain design and network configuration must consider the strategic objectives of an organization. *Supply chain design* refers to structuring the supply chain in terms of the type and number of manufacturing facilities and warehouses. *Network configuration* refers to the setup and location placement of manufacturing and storage facilities. Other factors to be considered are stocking levels versus customer service, where to use information technology, and support systems versus cost versus velocity. All of this requires additional decisions to be made on how to address balancing efficiency with responsiveness, determining the optimal product mix, and how to best transport inventory to customers.

OPERATIONS RESEARCH

Operations (or operational) *research* is the discipline that deals with the application of advanced analytical methods to solve problems. It attempts to maximize profit or performance while minimizing cost or risks, and it uses network modeling techniques to help solve problems and make process improvements. Tools include mathematical modeling, statistical analysis, simulations, economic methods, queuing theory, and decision analysis.

IDENTIFICATION OF SEGMENTS

Marketing *disaggregates* customer data into distinct segments to break down current and prospective customer information. It then further disaggregates data based on *customer value*, customer need, or preferred distribution or communication channels. Customer value is defined by the customer. It's their perception of received value before, during, or after purchasing a good or service.

Segmentation is the process of dividing a marketplace into subgroups of customers who desire product variety. The main motivation for segmentation is when the sales force requests product proliferation to expand the total market or to meet customer requests. Traditional segmentation focuses on identifying customer groups based on demographics and attributes such as attitude and psychological profiles. Today, market segmentation helps to identify lifetime customers who purchase a variety of products that best meet their needs. Examples of segmentation are automobile manufacturers that provide customers with a large number of choices such as sedans, SUVs, convertibles, or luxury cars. This helps them retain these customers for life.

Market segments are based on customer demographics such as age, gender, culture, race, income, zip code, or channel. The company can further target customer segments based on niches, mass marketing, or mass customization marketing. A *niche* is a market subset or segment where a product appeals to a smaller group based on attributes such as price, size, or flavor. Examples of a niche market are a unique ice cream flavor or big and tall clothing.

Market share is the percentage of a company's total sales volume for a product in a marketplace. It's calculated by dividing a company's total sales by the industry's total sales for a specified time frame. For example, a computer company has total sales of $10,000,000 and the industry had total sales of $100,000,000 during the past year. The company determines its market share by dividing $10,000,000 by $100,000,000 to determine that its market share is 10%. *Mass marketing* is a traditional approach that only sells products to the total marketplace. This approach is also known as undifferentiated marketing. An example is a $5.00 lunch promotion featured at a fast food restaurant chain to generate demand. A marketing or distribution channel is how the products or services are sold and how they move from the supplier, through intermediaries, to the customer. A sales or distribution channel can be a single channel, which goes directly from a supplier to a customer, or a multichannel that is interconnected to intermediaries and then to various retailers, wholesalers, outlets, or distributors. An example of a channel is selling products or services to domestic and international markets. *Channel stuffing* is when a supplier sends more inventory than can be used to distributors to temporarily boost sales. Marketing management identifies the criteria for order qualifiers and winners, which helps to define and make marketing strategy decisions, as shown in Exhibit 7.1.

Exhibit 7.1   Marketing management

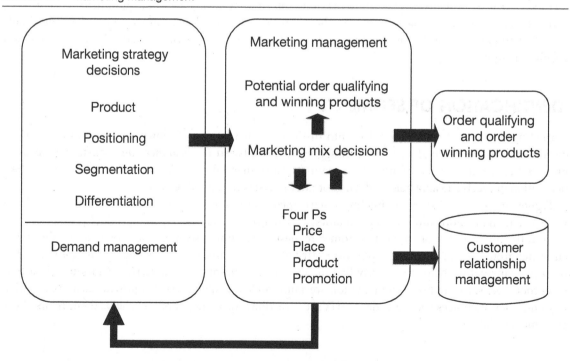

VOICE OF THE CUSTOMER

The *voice of the customer* (VOC) is used by companies to hear customer feedback, which leads to the overall improvement of the customer experience. Feedback can come from customer interviews, complaints, suggestions, surveys, focus groups, and repair or service field reports. The collected data leads to the improvement or development of existing products and services. This will be explained later in the process design section on how the VOC becomes the input into the *quality function deployment* (QFD) design process. QFD translates customer segment demand data requirements (VOC comments) into technical design requirements as process inputs and then into product specifications that can be produced.

COMMUNICATION

The purpose of *communication* is to influence various stakeholder opinions and decision making by creating, sending, and receiving messages. In order to be effective, communication must be two-way and use different types of media or technology to get its point across. It has to be collected throughout supply chains, analyzed, turned into useful information, and distributed.

The communications process has a number of key elements, which are shown in Exhibit 7.2. They include:

- *Sender*—person conveying the message
- *Message*—the subject matter in a written, verbal, or nonverbal form
- *Medium*—how the message is sent
- *Receiver*—intended audience
- *Filters*—influencing factors such as feelings or emotional states
- *Noise*—message distortion
- *Acknowledge*—knowing that the message has been received
- *Feedback*—reply to the sender that the message was received

Communication consists of a number of different formats that can impact or distort a message. They include:

- *Official/nonofficial*—on or off the record
- *Formal/informal*—documented and sanctioned or open and casual
- *Vertical/horizontal*—across or up and down the organization
- *Internal/external*—within or outside the organization
- *Written and voice/nonverbal*—with or without words to convey a message

A project manager has many things to consider when conveying a message. They include physical constraints, urgency, cost, security/privacy, preferences, message importance, and the need for feedback. Deciding between fax, phone, voicemail, e-mail, mail, internet, group meetings, or one-on-one face-to-face meetings depends on the urgency of the message being communicated.

A *communication management plan* is an effective and efficient tool for defining project roles and responsibilities and for showing how specific information will be disseminated to various stakeholders. The first step is to define whom you plan to communicate with (target audience) and then identify the

Exhibit 7.2   Communications process

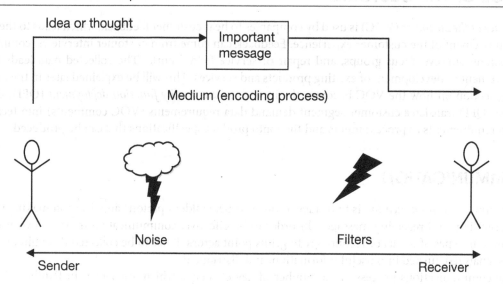

types of information required, media formats, timing, message importance, milestones, responsibilities, and incorporating a feedback process. *Stakeholder relations management* develops, manages, and controls communications between stakeholders. It helps to keep a project focused on what is important, minimizes *project scope creep* (uncontrolled expansion of a project), cost overruns, and changes to the project completion date. Proper control minimizes risk and issues that could delay the project.

Communication channels are how verbal, nonverbal, and written messages get transmitted to various project stakeholders within or outside of an organization. The formula to calculate the number of project *communication channels* is (n(n − 1) ÷ 2), with n being equal to the number of stakeholders. The greater the number of direct stakeholders, the harder the line of communication becomes. A large number increases complexity and the time needed to spend communicating. For example, if a project has six stakeholders, you have 15 possible communication channels (6(6 − 1) ÷ 2 = 6(5) ÷ 2 = 30 ÷ 2 = 15 channels). However, if the number of project stakeholders increases from six to 21, you increase the number of communication channels to 210 (21(21 − 1) ÷ 2 = 21(20) ÷ 2 = 420 ÷ 2 = 210 channels). This can make the communication process more dysfunctional. The increased number of channels equates to more risk. Complexity leads to message distortion, higher costs, and reduced productivity.

MEASURING CUSTOMER SERVICE

Companies must learn the importance of measuring the effectiveness and satisfaction of customer service—for example, whether on-time delivery or the ability to respond quickly to customer *rush* orders leads to satisfied customers. Companies can use a combination of customer-facing metrics, key performance indicators (KPIs), and operational metrics to measure and track customer satisfaction and determine if customer needs are being met. Companies benchmark internal measurements against competition improvement opportunities because they realize that satisfied customers often become lifetime customers; this results in increased sales and profits.

KEY TERMINOLOGY

Understanding key terms and the concepts they represent is crucial to passing the Certified Supply Chain Professional (CSCP) exam. In this chapter, the important terms are identified in Table 7.1.

Table 7.1   Marketing key terminology

Acknowledge
Business plan
Channel
Channel stuffing
Communication channels
Communication management plan
Communications
Customer value
Customer-facing metrics
Data warehouse*
Demand shaping*
Disaggregate
Environmental scanning
Feedback
Filters
Formal/informal
Four Ps (4 Ps)
Internal/external
Market plan
Market segments
Market share*
Marketing
Marketing mix
Marketplace
Mass marketing
Medium
Message

Continued

Network configuration
Niche
Noise
Official/nonofficial
Pro forma
Project scope creep
Quality function deployment (QFD)*
Receiver
Segment
Segmentation
Sender
Stakeholder relations management
Supply chain design
Vertical/horizontal
Voice of the customer (VOC)
Written and voice/nonverbal

*Key term found in the CSCP ECM

CSCP EXAM PRACTICE QUESTIONS ON MARKETING

The questions presented in Table 7.2a cover the concepts presented in this chapter on marketing. They are examples of what to expect on the actual exam.

Table 7.2a   Marketing practice questions

No.	Questions
1	What type of marketing is appropriate for a stable product which has broad market appeal? a) Mass b) Niche c) Low-cost d) Multicountry
2	Which of the following most likely will increase demand in the short term? a) Disasters b) Advertising c) Promotions d) No-interest financing
3	The starting point of the quality function deployment (QFD) process is called the: a) Voice of the customer (VOC) b) Product design activity c) Product planning activity d) Customer wants and needs

Continued

4	Communication flowing from the supply chain manager to all stakeholders is most likely using which communication dimension type? a) Lateral b) Vertical c) Written d) Informal
5	A supply chain manager that holds a weekly scheduled meeting to discuss metrics with his/her direct reports is most likely engaging in all of the following communication dimension forms except for: a) Voice b) Official c) Informal d) External
6	A company seeking to gain a competitive supply-chain advantage will best need to focus on: a) Cost reduction b) Velocity reduction c) Internet purchasing d) Communication improvements
7	A repository of data that has been specially prepared to support decision-making applications is called? a) Datamart b) Data mine c) Data warehouse d) Groupware database
8	A company will best use environmental scanning to: a) Understand the competition b) Understand marketplace trends c) Identify strengths and weaknesses d) Identify external opportunities and threats
9	All of the following tools can be used to help develop the most efficient and effective supply chain strategic plan except for: a) Network design b) Network modeling c) Operational design d) Operational research
10	The communication process consists of multiple elements. The pathway through which the message is sent is found in which element? a) Medium b) Receiver c) Feedback d) Acknowledge
11	Which of the following is the first step in a communication management plan? a) Define responsibilities b) Perform due diligence c) Define the target audience d) Define communication needs
12	A company currently has seven stakeholders and 21 communication channels. The company plans to increase the number of stakeholders to 15. What will be the new number of communication channels after they make this change? a) 105 b) 113 (rounded up) c) 147 d) 210

Continued

13	What is aligned with business strategy and market requirements? a) Business plan b) Corporate strategy c) Operations strategy d) Supply chain strategy
14	Intentionally selling too much inventory to a distributor is best called: a) Sales quotas b) Incentive selling c) Channel stuffing d) Promotional selling
15	A multinational company desiring to ship products from Europe to the United States has to be concerned with what type of infrastructure consideration? a) Rail lines b) Port facilities c) Highway conditions d) Warehouse locations
16	What does traditional segmentation focus on? a) Identifying demographics b) Identifying customer value c) Identifying customer groups d) Identifying customer attributes
17	How does segmentation help benefit a company and a preferred customer group? a) Creates mutual dependency b) Creates customer dependency c) Creates a special interest group d) Creates a customer-driven business
18	A company focusing on customer value includes all of the following except for: a) Low product cost b) Product innovation c) Value-added services d) Large product selection
19	Product proliferation is most likely dependent upon the: a) Nucleus firm b) Supplier base c) Sales channel d) Online retailer
20	The information system architecture arrangement of hardware, operating systems, application software, and networks is best called: a) Virtual network b) Distributed processing c) Configuration (network) d) Customization (network)
21	What is the input to the quality function deployment (QFD) process? a) Product required targets b) Technical design requirements c) Customer requirement ranking d) Customer segment demand data

Continued

22	All of the following are tangible quality function deployment (QFD) benefits except for: a) Enhanced design reliability b) Development time reduction c) Engineering change reduction d) Increased customer satisfaction
23	The differentiator between order winners and losers in today's business world is best defined as: a) Designing a better product b) Tailoring to customer needs c) Quickly responding to change d) Immediate delivery of inventory
24	Which of the 4 Ps focuses on perceived value and brand identity? a) Price b) Product c) Program d) Promotion
25	A voice of the customer (VOC) initiative is best used within customer relationship management (CRM) to permit a business: a) To hear their customers b) To gain customer insight c) To know their customers d) To respond to their customers
26	What does the lifeblood of a partner organization revolve around? a) Quality b) Profitability c) Communications d) Information flow
27	A company sells a high-volume, low-variety product that has broad appeal across many market segments. The product is designed for what type of market? a) Niche b) Mass market c) Trade exchange d) Commodity market
28	Which of the following business strategies aren't in conflict? a) Low-cost and high-quality b) Responsiveness and low-cost c) Responsiveness and product differentiation d) Product differentiation and niche marketing

ANSWERS TO CSCP EXAM PRACTICE QUESTIONS ON MARKETING

The answers to the practice questions on marketing are shown in Table 7.2b. Any question you answer incorrectly indicates a gap in your body of knowledge and encourages the need for additional study time.

Table 7.2b   Answers to CSCP exam practice questions on marketing

No.	Answers
1	Answer: A This question requires knowledge of the APICS Dictionary definition of *mass marketing*. Mass marketing is a strategy that sends the same message to all customers promoting a product or service.
2	Answer: C Promotions will increase demand in the short term. An example is an item that is advertised at 40% off. Advertising and no-interest financing are both forms of promotions. Disasters may or may not increase demand.
3	Answer: A The quality function deployment process begins with input from customers. This input represents the voice of the customer (VOC).
4	Answer: C Communications are usually written or verbal. When sending a message to all stakeholders, it is normally written. Lateral (across) and vertical (up and down) aren't forms of communicating. Informal communications aren't the best way to communicate with stakeholders.
5	Answer: D The meeting is scheduled, so it's official. It's verbal, since the manager will be talking, and it may or may not be informal. Since it's with just direct reports, however, it has to be internal—not external.
6	Answer: D Communication provides information that permits a company to react faster to customer wants and needs, and gives it a competitive edge. A company will want to increase velocity (speed), not reduce it, and cost reduction may or may not lead to a competitive advantage, so this can't be true 100% of the time. Internet purchasing doesn't apply to every company.
7	Answer: C This question requires knowledge of the APICS Dictionary definition of a *data warehouse*. A data warehouse is an integrated data repository that has been specially prepared to support decision-making applications.
8	Answer: D Environmental scanning by definition is a process that is used to identify external opportunities and threats. It collects information to understand its competition and marketplace trends. The information is later used to help improve the company's strengths and reduce its weaknesses.
9	Answer: C Operational design is a made-up term and must be the correct answer. Network design and network modeling are one and the same.
10	Answer: A The message pathway sent is found in the medium.
11	Answer: C The first thing you do in a communication management plan is define who you plan to communicate with (target audience).

Continued

12	Answer: A
	The formula to calculate the number of stakeholders in the communication channels is $(n(n-1)) \div 2$. In the equation, n represents the number of communication channels, which in the question is 15. The calculation process is $(15(15 - 1)) \div 2 = (15 * 14) \div 2 = 210 \div 2 = 105$ communication channels.
13	Answer: A
	A business plan provides a framework for an organization's performance objectives that are tied to their business strategy and market requirements.
14	Answer: C
	This question requires knowledge of the APICS Dictionary definition of *channel stuffing*. Channel stuffing occurs when a supplier sends more inventory than can be used to distributors to temporarily boost sales.
15	Answer: B
	A product going from Europe to the United States is shipped via ship or air. This question is referring to the port infrastructure that exports the product. Regardless of how a product is being shipped, it needs to be moved over a highway or via rail to a warehouse at a port.
16	Answer: C
	Traditional segmentation focuses on identifying customer groups based on demographics and attributes such as attitude and psychological profiles.
17	Answer: A
	A lifetime customer and the company create a mutual dependency on each other. Segmentation helps to identify this group.
18	Answer: A
	Not all customers value low product cost. Customers do value a large product selection (variety), new products (innovation), and value-added services, as they seek out companies who offer them.
19	Answer: C
	The sales channel will request product proliferation to meet customer requests. The nucleus firm and online retailers are subsets of the sales channel. The supplier base has very little to do with this decision unless components are in short supply.
20	Answer: C
	This question requires knowledge of the APICS Dictionary definition of *configuration of a network*. Configuration is the setup of the hardware, operating systems, application software, and networks, as defined in the company's information system architecture.
21	Answer: D
	The quality function deployment process translates customer segment demand data requirements (voice of the customers' comments) into technical design requirements as process inputs. Answers A, B, and C are all outputs.
22	Answer: D
	The key word in this question is *tangible*. Tangible benefits can be measured. Increased customer satisfaction is considered an intangible benefit, which cannot be easily measured.
23	Answer: C
	The ability to quickly respond to change satisfies key customer wants and needs. This ability is a key differentiator and it makes a company an order winner. Tailoring a product to meet a customer need is part of designing a better product. Immediate delivery of inventory doesn't meet the needs of all customers, and as such, isn't considered an order winner for everyone.
24	Answer: A
	Pricing is a strategic decision in which perceived value, competition, and brand identity are all considered. Promotion focuses more on strategy, advertising and brand image, logo, and name. Products meet customer needs by providing desired features, variety, and services. Program isn't one of the 4 Ps. The fourth P—not shown here—is placement.

Continued

25	Answer: A A business needs to hear what their customers have to say. A customer relationship management system provides a mechanism to transmit customer wants back to the business. Answers B, C, and D occur after the customer has been heard.
26	Answer: C Communications among partners is the lifeblood to make any partnership or relationship a success.
27	Answer: B Mass market is focused on selling high-volume, low-variety products which have a broad appeal across many market segments.
28	Answer: D Product differentiation and niche marketing go hand in hand and aren't in conflict.

8

DEMAND MANAGEMENT

This chapter focuses on demand and the forecasting process. It examines demand management and planning, demand data, qualitative and quantitative forecasting methods, seasonality, forecast error methods, tracking signals, and the role of the demand manager.

DEMAND

Demand management is the process of overseeing demand planning, which controls customer orders and assigns order priority. It strives to satisfy demand by balancing forecasts and customer orders against internal and external supply chain capabilities. Demand management examines time to market to determine if sufficient capacity exists to achieve predefined strategic goals. It influences and prioritizes product demand while coordinating demand-side activities to improve visibility and overall customer service levels and acts as an interface between different internal and external functional participants. For example, demand management serves as an intermediary between the customer and internal functional areas. It encompasses product development, marketing, and sales and operations to communicate customer wants, needs, and priorities. Workflow management provides the framework to quickly establish, execute, and evaluate the processes needed for a company to move toward having a customer-driven demand management system. Demand management is also a component of master planning.

Demand planning is used to develop business, family, and product *forecasts*. The process requires actual demand data to be obtained from historical records and demand input to be taken from marketing and sales. Demand planning starts with the review of forecasts and customer orders, evaluates collected data, projects future demand, and then assigns projected delivery schedules based on internal and external resource capabilities.

Demand planning requires knowledge of *forecasting principles*. Forecasting principles state that collected demand data is more accurate for product families (groups), for shorter time periods, rarely accurate 100% over time, must reflect the strategic plan, and should consist of a forecast and an estimate of error. A *product family* is an aggregate product grouping. An example of this is a wagon whose product family can be based on different manufacturing processes such as plastic, metal, or wood products. A *mix forecast* is based on the proportional makeup of different products within a family forecast. Poor product family forecasting will result in product shortages for the individual items within the family.

FORECAST INFORMATION

Forecasting starts with the *decomposition* of historical demand data and breaks apart this data into trend, cycle, seasonal, and random data components. A *trend* component reflects a gradual, upward, downward, or flat-line movement. A good example of a trend is a product whose sales increased 10% for the past five years. A *cycle* component represents up and down demand movement over multiple years. For example, demand fluctuates during periods of economic growth or decline, which can last for a number of years. A *seasonal* component represents a repeating demand pattern occurring during a period of time that is a year or less. This time period could be days, weeks, months, quarters, or a full year. An example of this is holiday sales that increase at the same time period every year. A *random* component has movements with no real patterns or logic. A good example of this is an unexplained large order from a customer who never previously ordered that item.

FORECAST PROCESS

The forecasting process requires an understanding of its intended purpose. For example, it must be understood that the forecast is going to be used to project manufacturing or purchasing requirements, capacity targets, financial budgets, or to determine needed staff. After this is determined, historical data is collected, cleansed, and then aggregated into family or business units. A time frame is specified and data is decomposed to determine if trends, seasonality, or randomness exists. The quantitative or qualitative method is selected and is used to develop a preliminary forecast. The results are tested and the preliminary forecast is then adjusted by management. The approved forecast is passed over to the sales and operations planning (S&OP) process team where it's validated against available resources. Finally, the forecast is monitored, the error level determined, and the process reviewed and adjusted.

Demand forecasting uses three methods to develop a forecast: qualitative, quantitative, and a combination of the two. *Qualitative* techniques are based on human judgment, intuition, opinion, informed decisions, and sometimes using a crystal ball. The results of this method lead to a very subjective forecast since it's not based on any historical information. Demand forecasting is used to forecast new products where historical data doesn't exist or to validate quantitative forecasts. Three types of qualitative techniques are covered in the Certified Supply Chain Professional (CSCP) Learning System. They are the Delphi method, judgmental method (expert judgment forecasting), and estimated average method.

The *Delphi method* develops a consensus forecast. It starts with a questionnaire being sent to a sales and marketing group requesting their product projections. The group gives anonymous responses that are aggregated into a group response and then shared within the group. The individuals within the group adjust their projections and the collection and aggregation process repeats through a number of rounds until a final consensus opinion can be agreed upon. The final consensus document becomes the forecast. The *judgmental method* is a guessing technique based on input from the sales force, market analysts, and management. This group uses its detailed knowledge of customers and products to appropriate a new product forecast whenever historical data is unavailable, or to modify a calculated forecast. The *estimated average method* is a judgmental method that tries to avoid bias by asking estimators for three estimates—pessimistic, most likely, and optimistic. An example of this is the most likely number being multiplied by four to give this estimate more weight, and the other two estimates are multiplied by one (2,000 + (7,000 * 4) + 12,000 = 42,000). The results are then divided by six (42,000 ÷ 6) to obtain an estimate of 7,000.

The *quantitative* forecasting technique uses historical demand data to perform *time-series* computations and to run mathematical or simulation models. Time-series computations are based on demand data that has been collected at regular time intervals (hourly, daily, weekly, or monthly). The technique uses intrinsic or extrinsic forecast analysis to project future demand. The quantitative forecasting process assumes that the future will look like the past and that a relationship exists between different variables. The *extrinsic method* assumes a relationship between demand and an external factor that will continue to occur in the future. A few good examples include forecasting products based on birth rate, car sales, interest rates, sales of luxury goods, or the economy. The *intrinsic method* is based on internal factors that are influenced by past sales. For example, an adjustment to demand data is required if an internal price increase artificially inflates sales just before a price change goes into effect. Another example is a product entering into the decline phase of the product life cycle (PLC) that will be shortly replaced by a new product. The intrinsic method requires historical demand data to be modified, either upward or downward, to eliminate bias.

BASIC TIME-SERIES FORECASTING METHODS

The time-series selected method begins with *visualizing* data, which makes it easy to spot trend movement and to identify seasonality. After visualizing the data, the next step is to deseasonalize it, which removes seasonality and generates a seasonal index.

The CSCP Learning System covers four quantitative forecasting methods—naïve, three-month moving average, weighted moving average, and exponential smoothing. The forecast calculation for each method will be based on historical actual sales data as shown in Table 8.1. M1 refers to the most recent month/period prior to the forecast period, M2 is two months/periods before the forecast period, and M3 is three months/periods before the forecast period. Please refer back to it when reviewing the upcoming formulas.

Table 8.1 Historical sales data

Month	Actual
January (M6)	284
February (M5)	305
March (M4)	314
April (M3)	328
May (M2)	424
June (M1)	440
July	???

Naïve forecasting is a very simplistic approach to forecasting. The belief is that reviewing prior demand data adds little value. The naïve forecast is based on the prior period's actual sales. The current demand is projected as the next period's forecast. For example, during the month of June, a company sold 440 units. Since the naïve forecast is based on the prior sales, the forecast for July becomes 440 units.

The simple *moving average* method is used when it's believed that prior demand data adds value. This method gives equal weight to all selected periods and removes randomness by smoothing the demand data. The larger the number of periods, the less weight that is given to each period; the smaller the number of periods, the more weight that is given to them. Two limitations of this method are that periods outside of the selected range don't get included in the calculation, and that the forecast lags actual demand during periods of rising demand or is higher during periods of falling demand. The *three-month moving average* forecast is calculated by summing the actual sales for the most recent three months, and then dividing by three (the number of months). For example, the July forecast is calculated by adding up the actual sales data for June, May, and April. Using the data from Table 8.1, this would be 440 plus 424 plus 328—for a total of 1,192 units—which is then is divided by three. The projected July forecast is 398, rounded up.

An extension of the moving average method is the *weighted moving average* method which places more emphasis on recent periods. It's a little more sophisticated than the naïve or moving average methods. The weighted moving average method has the same two limitations as the three-month moving average in that periods outside of the selected range don't get included in the calculation. The forecast also lags actual demand during periods of rising demand or is higher during periods of falling demand.

The weighted (three-month) moving average forecast is calculated as: ((3 * actual sales for M1) + (2 * actual sales for M2) + (1 * actual sales for M3)) ÷ 6, where 6 is the sum of the weighted number of periods (3 + 2 + 1 = 6). The calculation process assigns a multiplying factor of three to the first period (most recent), two to the second period, and one to the third period. The actual sales from the most recent period (M1) are multiplied by three, the prior period (M2) is multiplied by two, and the last period (M3) is multiplied by one. You then sum the calculated period value and divide by the weighted value of the assigned periods to obtain a weighted moving average value of 416 (M1 = 440 * 3 = 1,320; M2 = 424 * 2 = 848; M3 = 328 * 1 = 328; M1 + M2 + M3 = 2,496 ÷ 6 = 416).

The *exponential smoothing* formula requires the forecaster to select an *alpha factor* or *smoothing factor*. The factor can range between zero and one. The alpha factor determines the importance of the current data. The closer the factor is to zero, the greater the emphasis is on the old forecast. The closer the factor is to one, the greater the emphasis is on the most recent actual demand. The calculation process uses the prior forecast and compares it against actual demand to develop a new forecast. The formula is the:

New forecast = to the old forecast + alpha factor * (last month actual − old forecast)

For example, if the old forecast consisted of 400 units, last month's sales were 440 units, and the alpha factor was 0.2, the new forecast can be calculated as follows:

New forecast = 400 + .2 (440 − 400)
New forecast = 400 + (.2 * 40)
New forecast = 400 + 8
New forecast = 408

Note the difference between naïve, three-month moving average, weighted moving average, and exponential smoothing totals (440, 398, 416, and 408) in projecting the July forecast. The naïve method always places the greatest emphasis on the last actual period, followed by weighted moving average, moving average, and exponential smoothing if the alpha factor has a low number. However, if the alpha factor is equal to one, then exponential smoothing can match the naïve method.

The best forecasts use a combination of both quantitative and qualitative techniques. The initial forecasts are usually calculated using quantitative techniques. They are then reviewed, and if needed, modified upward or downward by qualitative techniques.

SIMPLE REGRESSION

Simple regression, also called *linear regression*, is used to show a mathematical relationship between one variable and another. If the relationship between two variables is linear, it is described by the equation y = a + bx. The "y" is the *dependent variable*, which describes the outcome. The "a" (*alpha*) is the *intercept*, which displays where the line crosses the vertical axis when "x" equals "0" on the chart. The "b" (*beta*) is the slope of the line and is used as a multiplier to find the correct placement when predicting forecasted results. The "x" is the *independent variable*, which is a single measure *predictor*. This concept is called *simple* because it uses only one predictor variable, while multiple linear regression uses more than one predictor.

In forecasting, simple regression is used as a method to project future demand. For example, the dependent variable "y" is demand, and the independent variable "x" is a factor that impacts demand (promotional activity). The relationship between demand and promotional pricing is shown in Exhibit 8.1.

Exhibit 8.1 Simple regression

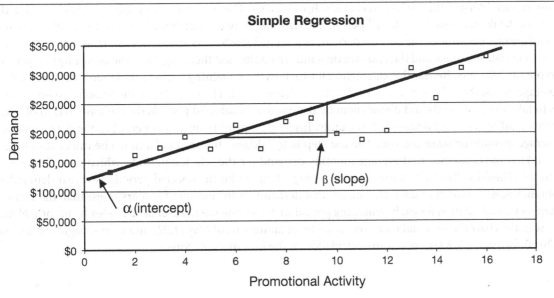

The *coefficient of correlation* (r) determines if a relationship exists between the independent and dependent variables. It measures the linear relationship strength between these variables and the range is between −1.00 to +1.00. A positive correlation, such as +0.70, means an increase in the independent variable will result in an increase in the dependent variable. A negative correlation, such as −0.70, shows an inverse relationship. This means that a decrease in the independent variable will mean an increase in the dependent variable.

A coefficient of correlation of +0.7 or −0.7 indicates that a strong correlation exists between the independent and dependent variables. A number such as +0.25 or −0.25 indicates that a weak correlation exists. A number of 0.0 indicates that no positive or negative correlation exists. The closer a number is to 1.0, the stronger the linear relationship is between the variables. For example, 0.7 is better than 0.6. A weak number, such as 0.25 indicates that the predictor needs to be changed.

MULTIPLE REGRESSION

Multiple regression is a more powerful version of simple regression. It uses two or more independent predictive variables and demand may be modified based on several independent variables. Examples of this are promotional pricing and tax refund spending. This process is more complex than simple regression and normally requires the use of a computer.

SEASONAL INDEX

Seasonality is when business activity is observed in a predictable and repeatable pattern. This seasonal pattern can be displayed as a day, week, month, or quarter. The *seasonal index* process begins by taking the sum of the demand for the selected period and dividing it by the number of periods to calculate the *seasonal average demand for the selected periods*, as seen in Table 8.2. As an example, in January, take the year one demand, 300 units, and the year two demand, 284 units, add them together, and divide by two periods to obtain 292 units. Repeat this calculation for each of the remaining periods, and then total the seasonal average demand for the selected period column (2,106 units). The next step in the seasonal index process is to take the 2,106 units and divide them by the number of selected periods (in this case, six) to obtain a *deseasonalized monthly demand* of 351 units. Insert this quantity into each period in the deseasonalized *average monthly demand* column. The last step is to calculate the *seasonal index*. The calculation begins by taking the deseasonalized average monthly demand for the selected periods, which was 292 units in January, then dividing that by the seasonal average demand for the selected periods' two year demand, to obtain a seasonal index of 0.83. This means that demand for the month of January is less than the average. Repeat this calculation for each remaining period to determine the *reseasonalized* index by month. Notice how in the chart the seasonal index increases from January until May (1.24) and then it begins to decline. This information is later used in the calculation of the new monthly forecast.

Table 8.2 Seasonal index calculation data

Month	Sales demand (a) Year one	Sales demand (b) Year two	Seasonal average demand for the selected periods (c) (a + b) ÷ 2 = c Average of year one and two	Deseasonalized average monthly demand (d) (c ÷ 6)	Seasonal index (c ÷ d)
January	300	284	292	351	0.83
February	299	315	307	351	0.88
March	319	325	322	351	0.92
April	311	329	320	351	0.91
May	444	424	434	351	1.24
June	427	435	431	351	1.23
Total	2,100	2,112	2,106		

FORECAST ERROR MEASUREMENTS

Forecast error is measured by taking actual demand minus the forecast quantity to determine the difference. For example, if actual demand in January is 284, subtract the forecast quantity of 300 to obtain a deviation of −16. This means that the forecast was undersold, as shown in Table 8.3. However, remember that APICS calculates forecast error as an *absolute number*. In our example, the minus sign is dropped and the forecast error is shown as an absolute number of 16. APICS only measures the size of the error (quantity), not the direction (over or under).

Forecast error as a percentage is calculated by taking actual demand minus the forecast, dividing that by the actual demand, and multiplying the results by 100%. In this case, take 284 minus 300, divide that by 284, and then multiply the results by 100% to obtain a forecast error percentage of 5.6% for July. *Forecast accuracy* is 100% minus the forecast error of 5.6%. A forecast accuracy of 94.4% is then obtained.

Table 8.3 Mean absolute deviation calculation

Month	Forecast	Actual	Deviation	Absolute Deviation
July	300	284	−16	16
August	330	325	−5	5
September	330	344	14	14
October	400	402	2	2
November	400	424	24	24
December	415	450	35	35
Total	2,175	2,229	——	96

The measurement of *mean absolute deviation* (MAD) takes the sum of the absolute deviation and divides it by the number of periods. For example, using the data shown in Table 8.3, calculate the deviation and drop the sign to make it an absolute deviation. Add up the absolute deviation column to obtain 96, and divide by six periods to obtain a MAD of 16.0.

Exercise 8.1 will test your knowledge and understanding of the MAD calculation. Calculate the MAD based on the information shown. The answers to the exercise are available from the Web Added Value™ Download Resource Center at www.jrosspub.com.

Exercise 8.1   Mean absolute deviation calculation

Month	Forecast	Actual	Deviation
July	300	285	
August	300	305	
September	300	314	
October	300	328	
November	400	424	
December	400	440	
Total	2,000	2,096	

A *normal distribution* has a *bell-shaped* curve, as shown in Exhibit 8.2. The ranges within the curve have a predefined value percentage. The further to the right of the curve, the higher the customer service level percentage; the higher the percentage, the more inventory that has to be maintained to support the customer service objective. Companies often look to maintain at least a 95% customer service level. This is two *sigmas* from the mean. If a company wants to obtain a 99.74% customer service objective, the objective needs to be three sigmas from the mean.

Exhibit 8.2   Bell-shaped curve

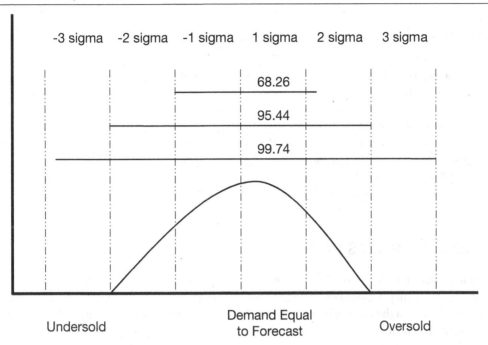

A MAD of 16.0 identifies the level of forecast variability. A high MAD indicates high forecast variability. A company desiring to protect itself from demand variability needs to maintain safety stock. A company will use a *safety factor table* (an example is provided in the CSCP Learning System) to select a customer service multiplier based on its desired service level. For example, a company wanting to have a 98% service level would multiply 16.0 times a MAD multiplier of 2.56. The company would need to maintain a safety stock of 41 pieces to achieve its desired customer service level.

A *tracking signal* (TS), also called cumulative sum of error, measures the accuracy of forecast predicting actual value movement. The TS formula is the algebraic sum of forecast errors divided by the MAD. A TS value over plus or minus four indicates high forecast bias. A tracking signal outside this defined limit indicates high forecast error, and the item requires reviewing. For example, if the algebraic sum of forecast errors is −4, and the MAD is 8.0, then the tracking signal is equal to −0.5, meaning that the forecast is within acceptable limits and requires no further review.

Mean square error (MSE) is the average of squared errors. It measures how closely the forecast matches product history. *Mean percentage error* (MPE) is the average of forecast percentage errors. *Mean absolute percentage error* (MAPE) is the average of the absolute values of the percentage errors of a forecast.

Exercise 8.2 will test your knowledge and understanding of the various forecast measurements. Identify the correct forecast error measurement and write in the correct answer. The answers to the exercise are available from the Web Added Value™ Download Resource Center at www.jrosspub.com.

Exercise 8.2   Understanding forecast measurements

Question	Answer
1. What best measures how closely the forecast matches history?	
2. What is absolute error divided by actual demand for a period?	
3. What is equal to the running sum of forecast errors divided by MAD?	
4. What best identifies variability of the forecast error?	
5. Which error measurement magnifies errors by squaring each one before adding them up and dividing by the number of periods?	
6. Which forecast error measurement predicts actual value movement?	
7. Which measurement uses the average of the absolute values of the percentage errors of a forecast?	
8. What is the best universal indicator of forecast error?	

DEMAND MANAGER'S ROLE

A *demand manager's* role is to oversee the demand planning process and partner with sales, marketing, product and brand managers, and key customers to develop a consensus demand plan. The demand manager then collaborates in the development, communication, and monitoring of the S&OP strategy to track demand against supply and identify any plan deficiencies. They also take corrective action and provide feedback on the demand plan effectiveness.

KEY TERMINOLOGY

Understanding key terms and the concepts they represent is crucial to passing the CSCP exam. In this chapter, the important terms are identified in Table 8.4.

Table 8.4   Demand key terminology

Absolute number
Alpha factor
Average monthly demand
Beta
Coefficient of correlation (*r*)
Cycle
Decomposition
Delphi method
Demand forecasting*
Demand generation
Demand management*

Continued

Demand manager
Demand planning*
Dependent variable
Deseasonalized average monthly demand
Estimated average method
Exponential smoothing
Extrinsic method
Forecast accuracy
Forecast error
Forecast error as a percentage
Forecasting principles
Forecasts
Independent variable
Intercept
Intrinsic method
Judgmental
Linear regression
Management estimate
Market research*
Mean absolute deviation (MAD)
Mean absolute percentage error (MAPE)
Mean percentage error (MPE)
Mean square error (MSE)
Mix forecast*
Moving average
Multiple regression
Naïve forecasting
Normal distribution
Predictor
Product family*
Qualitative
Quantitative
Random
Reseasonalized average monthly demand
Safety factor table
Seasonal
Seasonal average
Seasonal average demand for the selected periods

Continued

| Seasonal index |
| Seasonality* |
| Sigma |
| Simple regression |
| Smoothing factor |
| Three-month moving average |
| Time-series |
| Tracking signal (TS) |
| Trend |
| Visualizing |
| Weighted moving average |

*Key term found in the CSCP ECM

CSCP EXAM PRACTICE QUESTIONS ON DEMAND AND THE FORECASTING PROCESS

The questions presented in Table 8.5a cover the concepts presented in this chapter on demand and the forecasting process. They are examples of what to expect on the actual exam.

Table 8.5a   Demand and the forecasting process practice questions

No.	Questions
1	Which of the following forecasting methods isn't based on judgment and opinion? a) Qualitative b) Associated c) Delphi method d) Expert judgment
2	Calculate a three-month weighted moving average (rounded up) based on the following information. September = 105 October = 101 November = 99 December = 92 a) 96 b) 97 c) 99 d) 101
3	A company used simple regression to determine the relationship between sales and product pricing. Their study resulted in the following (y = 40,000 – 7,000x). This best implies that: a) A \$1.00 increase in product pricing resulted in a sales increase of \$7,000 b) A \$7.00 increase in product pricing resulted in a sales decrease of \$7,000 c) A \$1.00 increase in product pricing resulted in a sales decrease of \$7,000 d) A \$1.00 increase in product pricing resulted in a sales decrease of \$33,000

Continued

4	A demand planner was asked to find the predicted value of "y" using simple regression. The following equation was given to the planner y = 3.00 + 15x. Calculate the next period predicted value where x = 3. a) 15 b) 21 c) 48 d) 54
5	What is the valid range of numbers found in the correlation coefficient? a) −1.0 to +1.0 b) −0.01 to +0.01 c) −0.001 to +0.001 d) Must be above or below .01
6	What variable is being predicted in simple regression? a) Predictor b) Intercept c) Dependent d) Independent
7	A company projecting the demand for a product is best using: a) Demand forecasting b) Demand management c) Qualitative forecasting d) Quantitative forecasting
8	What term best describes the art of synchronizing supply and demand plans? a) Demand planning b) Sales management c) Production planning d) Demand management
9	Which of the following isn't one of the four elements of demand management? a) Planning demand b) Processing demand c) Influencing demand d) Managing and prioritizing demand
10	Who best serves as the communications' focal point between the supply and demand organizational areas? a) Master scheduler b) Demand manager c) Supply chain manager d) Highest ranking salesperson
11	Quantitative forecasting techniques include all of the following except for: a) Delphi method b) Moving average c) Naïve approach d) Exponential smoothing
12	What is the impact of including more periods in a moving average time series calculation? a) The more it corrects for chance variation b) The more it corrects for positive variation c) The forecast trend becomes positive d) The forecast trend becomes negative

Continued

13	Which forecasting technique is the most sophisticated? a) Moving average b) Naïve approach c) Exponential smoothing d) Weighted moving average
14	Calculate the seasonal index for Period XY based on the information provided below. Deseasonalized average demand = 675 Forecast error % = 18% Sum of seasonal average demand = 6,321 Mean absolute deviation = 130 Old forecast = 600 Seasonal average demand = 750 a) 0.03 b) 0.90 c) 1.11 d) 1.25
15	Which method is most likely used to calculate safety stock based on a customer service level? a) Tracking signal (TS) b) Mean squared errors (MSE) c) Mean absolute deviation (MAD) d) Mean absolute percentage of error (MAPE)
16	Mean squared errors are calculated by: a) Mean absolute deviation times 1.25 b) Add the errors regardless of sign and divide by the number of periods, then add up all of the errors and take the average c) Average the forecast errors for selected periods, then add up all the errors and take the average d) Take the sum of the errors for each period squared, divided by the number of periods
17	Which of the following activities isn't a key area within market research? a) Analyzing markets b) Refining product design c) Creating market demand d) Finding potential markets

ANSWERS TO CSCP EXAM PRACTICE QUESTIONS ON DEMAND AND THE FORECASTING PROCESS

The answers to the practice questions on demand and the forecasting process are shown in Table 8.5b. Any question you answer incorrectly indicates a gap in your body of knowledge and encourages the need for additional study time.

Table 8.5b Answers to CSCP exam practice questions on demand and the forecasting process

No.	Answers
1	Answer: B Associated forecasting, also called causal, correlation, explanatory, or extrinsic forecasting, is a quantitative method. The Delphi method and expert judgment are both found in qualitative forecasting.
2	Answer: A The calculation process for a three-month weighted average takes the last three months of actual demand and multiplies the last month by three, the next to last month by two, and the third month by one. The calculation is shown as $((92 * 3) + (99 * 2) + (101 * 1)) \div 6$ $= (276 + 198 + 101) \div 6 = 575 \div 6$ $= 96\ (95.8)$
3	Answer: C The study showed that for every $1.00 increase in product pricing, sales decreased by $7,000.
4	Answer: C The predicted value is 48 (3.00 + 45).
5	Answer: A The coefficient of correlation (r) determines if a relationship exists between the independent and dependent variables. It measures the linear relationship strength between these variables and the range is between −1.00 to +1.00.
6	Answer: C The dependent variable is the element being predicted in simple regression.
7	Answer: A This question requires knowledge of the APICS Dictionary definition of *demand forecasting*. Demand forecasting is the process of projecting product future demand.
8	Answer: D Synchronizing supply and demand plans is the role of demand management. Demand planning involves predicting demand (forecast).
9	Answer: B Processing demand isn't an element. The missing demand management element is communicating demand.
10	Answer: B The demand manager serves as the focal point between supply and demand areas. This person obtains or provides information to the master scheduler, supply chain manager, or the highest ranking salesperson.
11	Answer: A The Delphi method uses a panel of experts to give an opinion of what can happen to a product's demand. It is also a qualitative technique. A quantitative forecasting technique is based on a calculation.
12	Answer: A The more periods included in the average, the more it corrects for chance variation.

Continued

13	Answer: C Exponential smoothing is the most sophisticated forecasting technique because it considers trend and some seasonality.
14	Answer: C The seasonal index formula is seasonal average demand (750) divided by deseasonalized average demand (675). The seasonal index is 1.11.
15	Answer: C Mean absolute deviation is used to calculate safety stock based on a desired customer service level.
16	Answer: D The formula to calculate mean squared errors is to take the sum of errors for each period squared, divided by the number of periods.
17	Answer: C The market research function collects information about customer wants, needs, and preferences to identify current and future product demand. However, it doesn't create market demand for products or services. That is the role and responsibility of marketing and sales.

9

CUSTOMER RELATIONSHIP
MANAGEMENT STRATEGY

This chapter focuses on *customer relationship management* (CRM). It examines the need for companies to implement an enterprise business system, the four levels of CRM implementation, and the use of a plan-do-check-act model to continually improve the CRM process. It also explores the various customer types and how to effectively communicate with each one, the use of technology tools, the importance of obtaining and keeping lifetime customers, the differences between CRM and a company that focuses solely on sales, and the cultural issues impacting CRM and supplier relationship management (SRM).

CRM STRATEGY

The *traditional marketing strategy* and customer sales strategy is based on a short-term, transactional and price-driven, one-time sales effort. It's designed to generate high revenue for a company and it revolves around mass marketing. These strategies aren't designed to develop long-term customer relationships, nor focus on meeting their needs.

The purpose of a CRM strategy is to support a company's strategic, business, and financial goals. It strives to improve customer relationships by using information to quickly respond to customer wants and needs. CRM often means transforming the organization to become a customer-centric business. The company puts the customer first—they focus on doing what the customer wants and strive to create a positive customer experience throughout the entire sales and marketing process. This not only includes the experience before and during sales, but the post sales experience as well. In order to change its organizational attitude, a company must implement extensive organizational changes as it strives to become customer focused. This is accomplished by creating a customer segment map to define and group customers by their distinctive needs. Factors to be considered are product life-cycle (PLC) stages, customer profitability, and communication channels. The company monitors, measures, and reports results to management to sustain the customer-focused transformation. The differences between a transactional marketing strategy and CRM are displayed in Table 9.1.

Table 9.1   Differences between a transactional marketing strategy and CRM

Focus	Transactional marketing strategy	CRM
Goal	One-time sale	Retention
Time horizon	Short	Long
Metric	Margin	Lifetime value
Organization	Top down	Flat
Workers	Directed	Empowered
View	Product-oriented	Customer-oriented

CRM is an effective tool that draws customers into closer collaboration and subsequently entices them to become lifetime customers. An effective CRM program is the differentiator between order winners, order qualifiers, and order losers in the marketplace. An order winner is a company handling a process better than its competition. An example of this might be customers who join Amazon Prime and receive free shipping and other benefits as part of their paid membership. An *order qualifier* is what is required in order to be in a chosen business. An example is a florist needing to offer delivery services. An *order loser* is a company policy or process that drives business away—a restocking fee is an example of this.

Companies implement an *enterprise business system* (EBS) in conjunction with a CRM application, web systems, marketing, external data, and analytics, to collectively obtain a 360° view of the customer. EBS provides access to business and customer contact and sales information and increases employee productivity while minimizing manual data input.

EBS permits companies to better integrate business processes and information sharing to enhance their marketing and sales plans. These systems are linked to the web and aid in customer order processing. Marketing conveys product and service information to potential and actual customers to assist in their purchasing decisions. Processed externally sourced data that is placed in a data warehouse helps to link suppliers and customers in a collaborative environment. Analytics are used to identify hidden patterns in the collected data, which helps companies develop targeted marketing campaigns. CRM linkages to websites, e-mail, customer service, ordering and invoicing, and sales statistics all help to improve the overall customer experience. Providing after-the-sale service support can also help to improve the overall customer experience and resolve any product or service issues.

CRM IMPLEMENTATION PROCESS

One of the first steps in the CRM implementation process is to define the order process activity sequence needed to execute necessary marketing, sales, and customer service activities. The *PDCA (plan–do–check–action) model*, also known as the plan-do-check-act model, is a repetitive, four-step cycle used to make changes as part of a continuous process improvement (CPI) and effectiveness effort. The *plan* step defines what process needs improvement. The *do* step implements the plan and measures ongoing performance. The *check* step assesses whether desired results have been achieved. The *act* step identifies process modifications that need to be made in order to improve the process.

A company needs to develop a process to establish goals and metrics that can be used to enhance not only customer-driven and time-to-market activities, but profitability as well. One such metric is *supply chain lead time*, which is the time it takes to fill a customer order if inventory levels are at zero.

CRM STRATEGY BY CUSTOMER TYPE

A customer goes through four life-cycle stages. They start as a *prospective customer*—someone who isn't currently a customer but hopefully will become one. They then move on to become a vulnerable customer, a win-back customer, and finally, a loyal customer. Customers move from one stage to another throughout the life cycle, based on their customer lifetime value. CRM data helps to identify and classify customer life-cycle stages based on market segments and market channels. Marketing and sales will utilize tailored promotional activities to turn prospective customers into lifetime ones.

Vulnerable customers are those who may switch to a competitor to purchase products or services. The term used to describe this process is called *churn*. In order to retain customers who might switch, a company needs to target them as early as possible. Attracting new customers is very costly, and has a negative impact on profitability, so companies need to retain a high percentage of their customer base. Companies also need to develop a *win-back program* that focuses on their most valuable former customers. This effort requires rapid communication coupled with a reactivation special offer. *Loyal customers* are less likely to switch to a competitor and require less marketing, sales support, and costly win-back programs. It's in the best interest of companies to take the time and effort to develop a sustainable relationship with loyal customers. They are the ones who are more likely to purchase new products and services that offer additional sales opportunities for cross- and up-selling. An example of *cross-selling* is asking the customer if they would like a soda with their hamburger. *Up-selling* is selling a customer a more expensive product than the one they initially intended to buy. An example is a customer who desires to purchase a 19-inch television set but is enticed to buy a larger, more expensive one.

Exercise 9.1 will test your knowledge and understanding of CRM strategy by customer type. Read each question and write in all answers that apply. The answers to the exercise are available from the Web Added Value™ Download Resource Center at www.jrosspub.com.

Exercise 9.1 CRM strategy by customer type

Question	Answer
1. The goal of any CRM strategy is to increase the number of this customer type.	
2. This customer type is very receptive to cross-selling or up-selling.	
3. Which customer type requires the development of a promotional retention program?	
4. Which customer type requires early identification of customers who no longer purchase products?	
5. Which customer type must be contacted within the first week after customer service has been discontinued?	
6. Product pricing and audience segmentation is used in which customer type?	

CRM TECHNOLOGY TOOLS

Companies need to understand customer requirements and quickly respond to their requests, speed up marketing and sales efforts, improve overall efficiency, and lower sales and general administrative costs. In order to accomplish these tasks, a number of tools are used.

Account management (AM) manages customer information for the purposes of marketing and customer care. It provides detailed information about account data and sales activities. AM supports customer segmentation, sales promotions, and matches sales performance to customer attributes.

Sales force automation (SFA) is a software application that automates business tasks such as inventory control, sales order processing, contract management, and the tracking of customer interactions and sales performance. Some examples of SFA tools are: a to-do list, calendars, product configurators, and pipeline management.

Business intelligence (BI) uses software applications to perform analytical processing, which collects and studies internal and external product information and data transactions. It combines product information and technology to collect, store, analyze, identify, spot trends, and provide data access. Tools used in BI include: *decision support systems* (DSS), query reporting, statistical analysis, forecasting, and data mining. DSS are computer-based applications that gather, organize, analyze, and display business data, which helps to facilitate decision making at the strategic, tactical, and operational levels.

Marketing automation uses software to automate marketing processes. It makes existing and new processes faster and more efficient and is an integral component of CRM. *Enterprise marketing automation* (EMA) is an example of marketing automation that includes the direct marketing of special promotional events, loyalty campaigns, vulnerable customer campaigns, and different forms of media-based marketing. Marketing automation and EMA help companies target selected customer segments for unique marketing.

Exercise 9.2 will test your knowledge and understanding of CRM tools. Read each question and write in the best answer. The answers to the exercise are available from the Web Added Value™ Download Resource Center at www.jrosspub.com.

Exercise 9.2   CRM tools

Question	Answer
1. This tool can act like a person to answer a customer's question.	
2. This tool employs software to search a customer database to target customers for promotional activities.	
3. This tool collects customer information from transactions for use in a CRM.	
4. This tool utilizes EMA to reach customers to automatically send out a renewal notice.	
5. This tool helps a sales representative to better manage and use historical customer information for marketing.	
6. This tool uses a customer's product sales history for market segmentation and sales promotions.	
7. This tool utilizes an event management tool to establish a special loyalty program promotional event.	
8. This tool utilizes DSS and data mining tools to facilitate upper management strategic decision making.	

FOUR LEVELS OF CRM IMPLEMENTATION

CRM implementations are never as easy as they appear. The process often has unanticipated resource, hardware and software, training, integration, data integrity, and cultural issues that impact the implementation. Exhibit 9.1 shows the four levels of integration.

Exhibit 9.1   CRM levels of integration

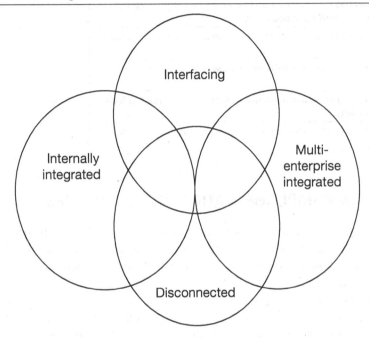

Disconnected technology has many stand-alone processes with a low degree of integration. Data isn't combined or shared. In this level, the company has a lack of clear, consistent supply chain management (SCM) processes—and they aren't aligned with strategic objectives.

Interfacing technology has various systems feeding each other with limited integration. It tries to optimize the supply chain planning process decisions across the internal supply chain between key suppliers and customers.

Internally integrated technology uses one integrated system to capture and store all information. Decisions are made based on the integration of key functional areas—including using a common forecast. Key measurements are shared among various departments.

Multi-enterprise technology uses one integrated system to capture all business lines and share data across the various enterprises. The involved supply chain partners act as a virtual corporation. All parties have extensive knowledge of the business environments because of shared data—and this helps everyone to focus on meeting strategic, service, and financial goals.

Exercise 9.3 will test your knowledge and understanding of the four levels of CRM implementation. Read each question and write in the answer that best describes the CRM implementation. The answers to the exercise are available from the Web Added Value™ Download Resource Center at www.jrosspub.com.

Exercise 9.3   Four levels of CRM implementation

Question	Answer
1. Which CRM level has only one system to capture and store customer sales information from multiple sources?	
2. Which CRM level stores data centrally and collects customer data from multiple sources?	
3. Which CRM level uses a non-interfacing database to store collected information?	
4. Which CRM level is just beginning to use stored customer data to feed other internal systems?	
5. Which CRM level utilizes cloud systems to capture and store external customer data?	

SUCCESSFUL CRM IMPLEMENTATION KEY ACTIVITIES

The success of any implementation requires a series of predefined activities to be performed. The project needs to define what is meant by success and it has to put people and processes first. The workforce has to be trained and educated on the new system and processes. Work plan activities must be monitored and compared against the budget.

The implementation team must collaborate and communicate to the executive sponsor and management team the project time-phased activity status on a regular basis. They must continually monitor and measure the implementation against the voice of the customer (VOC) defined requirements. Corrective action must be taken if resource or time frame problems exist. The implementation team, the executive sponsor, and the management team must all be actively involved to ensure a successful implementation.

CUSTOMER LIFETIME VALUE

Customer lifetime value (CLV) is a prediction of how much profit a company can obtain during its customer relationship. The concept changes the focus of a company from a one-time transactional sale to developing closer customer relationships. A company that retains its customer base doesn't have to spend excessive funds on marketing to obtain new customers. Lifetime customers lower total marketing costs and these customers are more willing to forgive customer service related issues. It's also easier to satisfy lifetime customers because of a company's deep knowledge of their buying patterns. Furthermore, greater lifetime opportunities exist for product and service cross-selling and up-selling.

The following is an example of calculating CLV. The longevity period for a phone customer is 20 years and they pay $100 a month for service. CLV can be calculated by multiplying $100 times 12 months times

20 years to obtain an expected revenue stream of $24,000. Subtract initial marketing and sales costs of $200, the cost of subsidized phones of $3,000, and operating expenses of $4,000. The remaining amount of $16,800 is the CLV.

CRM IMPLEMENTATION CHALLENGES

The main concern in implementing CRM is whether the company has the ability to make the necessary strategic changes at the macro level and at the micro organizational level. The success of the CRM implementation depends on the company's willingness to change. CRM requires a new corporate vision and mission statement, reengineering of the organization's structure, and the changing of the roles of the employees and culture of the organization. CRM also requires empowering employees, training employees, making hardware and software technology changes, and focusing on data integrity.

CULTURAL ISSUES IMPACTING CRM AND SRM

Companies and people throughout the world have different sets of values, attitudes, customs, beliefs, and behaviors. These cultural values differ by country or groups of people. Local culture often clashes with corporate culture and companies must be prepared to accept local beliefs. Data *dissemination* is the sharing of collected CRM customer information throughout a company. The sharing of data is a radical change for many companies. Understanding how this may impact communications, relationships, contract agreements, product use, timing, or laws is helpful. Also, note that there are times when local values may supersede corporate value standards. An example is when a local manager can purchase raw materials from a local supplier rather than using a corporate supplier.

KEY TERMINOLOGY

Understanding key terms and the concepts they represent is crucial to passing the Certified Supply Chain Professional (CSCP) exam. In this chapter, the important terms are identified in Table 9.2.

Table 9.2   CRM strategy key terminology

Account management (AM)
Business intelligence (BI)*
Churn
Cross-selling*
Customer lifetime value (CLV)
Customer relationship management (CRM)*
Data mining
Decision support systems (DSS)

Continued

Disconnected technology
Dissemination
Enterprise business system (EBS)
Enterprise marketing automation (EMA)
Interfacing technology
Internally integrated technology
Loyal customers
Marketing automation
Multi-enterprise technology
Order losers*
Order qualifiers*
Order winners*
Prospective customer
Sales force automation (SFA)
Supply chain lead time
Transaction marketing strategy
Up-selling
Vulnerable customers
Win-back program

*Key term found in the CSCP ECM

CSCP EXAM PRACTICE QUESTIONS ON CRM STRATEGY

The questions presented in Table 9.3a cover the concepts presented in this chapter on CRM strategy. They are examples of what to expect on the actual exam.

Table 9.3a   CRM strategy practice questions

No.	Questions
1	What could be better than having an excellent supply chain strategy in place? a) The ability to change the strategy b) The ability to create the strategy c) The ability to change the marketplace d) The ability to change the business direction
2	A high level of customer satisfaction and loyalty will have the lifetime customer focusing on: a) Cost b) Value c) Improved technology d) A sustained relationship

Continued

3	A company that increases the value of a single item purchase is most likely using what selling technique? a) Up-selling b) Cross-selling c) Down-selling d) Product-selling
4	Technology has allowed businesses to move from department-centric spheres of control to: a) Focusing on network optimization b) Enterprise resource planning (ERP) systems c) Focusing on internal supply chain business processes d) Focusing on supply chain extended business processes
5	What best provides a framework for a company moving toward a customer-driven demand management system? a) Sales force automation (SFA) b) Workflow management c) Enterprise resource planning (ERP) system d) Collaborative planning and forecast replenishment (CPFR)
6	A store asks a customer if they want batteries with their electronic device. This is an example of: a) Up-selling b) Promotions c) Cross-selling d) Bait and switch
7	A tool that can help an organization identify customers who are most likely to leave and then weigh the possible impact of using promotional efforts on those customers is: a) Business intelligence (BI) b) Sales force automation (SFA) c) Enterprise resource planning (ERP) d) Enterprise marketing automation (EMA)
8	The CRM technology integration touch points are designed to anticipate customer communication needs. This includes all of the following tools and systems except for: a) Call centers b) Online sales c) Voicemail messages d) Order/provisioning systems
9	In which CRM element is dissemination found? a) Analysis b) Collaboration c) Sales operations d) Customer information

ANSWERS TO CSCP EXAM PRACTICE QUESTIONS ON CRM STRATEGY

The answers to the practice questions on CRM strategy are shown in Table 9.3b. Any question you answer incorrectly indicates a gap in your body of knowledge and encourages the need for additional study time.

Table 9.3b Answers to CSCP exam practice questions on CRM strategy

No.	Answers
1	Answer: A The ability to change a strategy whenever the need arises is more important than having an excellent supply chain strategy in place.
2	Answer: D Lifetime customers focus on building sustained relationships. This helps to create a dependency where both parties need each other.
3	Answer: A Up-selling is getting the customer to purchase a more expensive and profitable item such as purchasing a computer with extra memory. Cross-selling is selling additional products such as software to go with the computer.
4	Answer: D The evolvement of technology has allowed businesses to focus on supply chain extended business processes and it permits the supply chain to be better connected. Answers A, B, and C either don't apply or don't show external movement.
5	Answer: B Workflow management provides the framework to quickly establish, execute, and evaluate the processes that are needed for a company to move toward having a customer-driven demand management system.
6	Answer: C This example is describing cross-selling.
7	Answer: D Enterprise marketing automation (EMA) is a tool that employs software applications to search, compile, and use customer databases to target customers who are likely to leave with a tailored marketing campaign.
8	Answer: C A voicemail system doesn't anticipate anything. It's used *after the fact* to record a message. Answers A, B, and D are used to anticipate and respond to customer wants and needs.
9	Answer: D Dissemination is found in the customer relationship management (CRM) element. Dissemination means getting timely, focused customer information to the right group in the supply chain.

10

PRODUCT DESIGN

This chapter focuses on the impact of product design. It examines the various product design method types, component and product standardization, component commonality, universality, and modular design.

PRODUCT DESIGN IMPACT

Product design has a number of approaches that take into account the users, sustainability, cost, logistics, and standardization requirements that are needed in order to develop new or enhanced products. The design needs to meet customer-defined attributes including safety, quality, and reliability.

The product design process lies between marketing and operations. Design decisions need to consider supply chain strategic goals and objectives, along with meeting customer requirements. The integration of product design with operations can lead to manufacturing issues that impact lead times, supply chain related costs, and engineering product changes. The Certified Supply Chain Professional (CSCP) courseware states that 5 to 15% of product cost expenses are related to design and 70% are related to delivery costs.

A dysfunctional product design method uses the *over-the-wall approach*. This approach has each functional area designing a product in a silo with limited communications or information sharing between functional areas or with the customer. When a group completes their portion of the design, it's forwarded to the next department for processing. If this department has a material or design concern, it returns the *design package* to the initiating department for rework. The two areas don't communicate with each other to explain and resolve the problem collectively. Both areas operate alone, which requires a longer development time, wasted effort, and has a much higher cost structure than the other approaches.

Companies often use the *informal collaboration approach* with suppliers and customers to discuss potential product design changes or to develop new products during casual conversations. They gain tacit as well as explicit knowledge of their wants and needs during these conversations. A better product design approach makes use of the integrated collaborative method, also called the *formal collaboration approach*. This approach involves listening to the voice of the customer (VOC) and obtaining input from customers and suppliers. Their expertise and product knowledge are used during the design process. Obtaining supplier and customer involvement in material selection, desired features, product assembly, product testing, and logistics is critical. *Collaborative information technology* permits the facilitation of communications and information sharing that provides visibility and velocity to help speed up product development. It results in improved customer satisfaction, operational efficiency, and productivity. It also delivers higher product quality for the price and results in fewer engineering changes and cost overruns.

Product life-cycle management (PLM) is a systematic approach to develop, use, and support products desired by customers. It manages the product from its design and development through the various *product life cycles* (PLCs) and its ultimate disposal. PLM is the corporate backbone that was designed to create and preserve product information.

Life-cycle analysis (LCA) is a quantitative forecasting technique that applies historical demand data patterns to each PLC stage (introduction, growth, maturity, and decline) against new products in order to project future demand. *Environment life-cycle analysis* examines the potential environmental impacts against each life-cycle stage. New product introduction needs to consider how to minimize customer service disruptions and streamline the material return process. *Maturity* focuses on product and component returns for repair, remanufacturing, or reuse. The decline stage considers product returns and disposal as part of an environmental friendly *end-of-life management* process.

Concurrent engineering (CE) shortens the design process by incorporating input from various stakeholders through simultaneous product development, rather than independent development. This speeds up the development process by helping to ensure that the product is designed correctly the first time, which results in less design changes, improved productivity, and reduced costs.

Exercise 10.1 will test your knowledge and understanding of the PLC stages. Read each question and write in the best answer. The answers to the exercise are available from the Web Added Value™ Download Resource Center at www.jrosspub.com.

Exercise 10.1   Product life-cycle stages

Question	Answer
1. In which stage are advertising costs the highest?	
2. In which stage are distribution costs the highest?	
3. In which stage can an opportunity to create customer ownership be found?	
4. In which stage can customer care promote lifetime customer development?	
5. In which stage do you generate the most profits?	
6. In which stage do you have rapid revenue growth?	
7. In which stage does a company entice its competitors' customers to switch?	
8. In which stage is customer care more critical than the other stages?	
9. In which stage is it essential to cultivate brand loyalty and development of lifetime customers?	
10. In which stage must customer care be sustained?	
11. In which stage must information be used to identify strong and weak customer segments?	
12. In which stage do competitors begin to enter the marketplace?	
13. What stage makes the best use of customer feedback data to identify new product ideas?	

Design for the supply chain utilizes product design for improving the sourcing, manufacturing, and distribution of products. It utilizes design to improve product standardization, simplification, sustainability, and quality. This helps to optimize the supplier-to-customer supply chain structure throughout the PLC, which results in improved transportation, reduced costs, and an increase in profitability.

Design for logistics (DFL) utilizes product design to minimize logistics costs. Logistics specialists become involved early in the design process and determine how to package, store, and transport finished goods easily and cost efficiently. Examples of this are stacking garbage pails inside one another, shipping bookcases disassembled and in a flat box, shipping square watermelons, and shipping wine in a 24,000 liter plastic bag to reduce shipping and custom duties.

Design for everything or design for X (DFX) designs a product to meet a company's strategic design considerations. This design is used to improve the probability that the collective efforts of all supply chain members will be successful. It incorporates concepts such as universality, *design for manufacture and assembly* (DFMA), quality function deployment (QFD), postponement, and reverse logistics into a product's design.

DFMA concurrently designs products and plans assembly processes by making the best use of lean production concepts and processes. Products are designed to limit the number of process touch points by limiting the number and variety of raw materials and components through the use of *off-the-shelf* standardized materials. Products utilize modular design to introduce product variety that will be incorporated at a later stage of production. *Design for manufacturability* simplifies the use of parts, products, and processes to enhance manufacturing flow.

Design for service or *design for maintainability* reduces the total cost of ownership by simplifying and streamlining the repair and replacement process. It improves the customer after-sale experience and it develops service scenarios to predefine the service and repair processes by preparing user-friendly service documentation, repair instructions, and required parts lists. An example of this is copiers using modular components that can be quickly removed and replaced with another modular unit to reduce downtime.

Design for quality looks to create new products with the customer in mind. The design focuses on aesthetics, cost, overall performance, and customer desired attributes.

Design for Six Sigma (DFSS) is an approach aimed at designing products and processes that can achieve Six Sigma quality levels of 3.4 defects per million opportunities.

Design for the environment (DFE) designs products that meet environmental, sustainability, safety, and corporate social responsibility attributes. DFE benefits include improved public opinion and reputation, reduced liability, less material usage, and minimized government regulations.

Design for reverse logistics considers how to process product returns for repairs, refurbishment, or component recovery. Its goal is to maximize material value recovery and reduce supply chain return costs.

Design for remanufacture designs the product to consider the return process and required effort to disassemble, clean, and examine parts for wear, breakage, and the rebuilding of products for later resale or reuse. In this case, the company is developing processes to convert returned parts back into the equivalent of a new part by considering total life-cycle costs into the design process, value recovery, and return supply chain costs.

Standardization promotes the use of common, *off-the-shelf* standard parts to speed up the conceptual design of products and material ordering across product families. Part standardization means that in conjunction with product design, companies can reduce PLC costs and part proliferation, as well as lower inventory levels and cost of goods sold.

PRODUCT DESIGN APPROACHES

Product design has a number of different approaches.

Component commonality replaces multiple raw materials and components with a single, common component used in the manufacturing or assembling of a higher-level end product. This process is called *integral design*, where all components can be interchangeable. Car companies use this technique to reduce supply chain ordering, processing, storing, and handling costs without any loss in product functionality. A disadvantage is that it can result in some loss of design flexibility, and a possible lowering of product quality as perceived by the customer. One example of component commonality is the use of a single bolt or electrical box rather than multiple parts with slightly different tolerances.

Universality designs one product with features and characteristics appealing to the global marketplace. It achieves economies of scale in design, procurement, production, and ongoing product support. A good example of universality is when Ford substantially reduced the number of car platforms while increasing the number of car models. The consolidation of these platforms permitted Ford to utilize the same ones on a global scale. Unfortunately, it also led to a loss of product uniqueness and customer loyalty.

Modular design strategy uses the same part or component, which permits the flexibility to produce a variety of product configurations. Companies use planning bills to plan standardized modular and subassembly units. Car and computer assembly factories use this technique.

Mass customization moves final product configurations closer to the customer and is also known as *delayed differentiation*. This process permits the customer to order a final product configuration that meets their unique specifications. The selected product is quickly built at a low cost from a set of components that remain in an undifferentiated form as long as possible. Some companies use this technique to sell customized candy, golf clubs, or personalized checks.

Postponement delays the differentiation of a product by postponing the assembly to the last supply chain location. It utilizes the push-pull strategy with final assembly being performed at a postponement center and/or a retail store. Postponement leads to a reduction in finished goods inventory, warehouse space, and product rework. It also improves customer service performance. Computer assemblers and food manufacturers who build or package-to-order (PTO) use this technique.

Simplification is the process of reducing complexity. It limits product variety and discourages unique tolerances, specifications, and other unique material attributes. Simplification strives to reduce the number of assembled components by simplifying the manufacturing and assembly operations. A good example of this is the elimination of computer cables by building functionality onto circuit boards to perform wireless printing. A second example is the use of quick disconnects rather than hard wiring electrical components. Simplification, standardization, and customization can all be used together in the manufacturing and assembly processes.

A *configuration management system* is used to identify and select product applications, features, and options for assemble-to-order (ATO) or engineer-to-order (ETO) products. Custom designed packaging equipment and airplane assemblies use this system.

Exercise 10.2 will test your knowledge and understanding of the various design processes. Read each question and write in all answers that apply. The answers to the exercise are available from the Web Added Value™ Download Resource Center at www.jrosspub.com.

Exercise 10.2 Understanding of the various design processes

Question	Answer
1. Which types move final assembly closer to the customer?	
2. Which type uses product design to manage logistics costs?	
3. Which types utilize a push-pull strategy with final assembly performed later?	
4. Which type is used to design a flat bookcase for stacking on a pallet?	
5. Which type designs a product so that assembly can be initiated upon receipt of an order?	
6. Which type designs a product from a customer's perspective?	
7. Which type of design limits the number of assembly process touch points?	
8. Which type looks at velocity, visibility, and cost improvement opportunities?	
9. Which type designs a product to achieve sustainability or meet regulatory requirements?	
10. Which type designs a product to improve the entire end-to-end supply chain?	
11. Which type prebuilds subassembly components for fabrication based on customer orders?	
12. Which type builds a unique product from raw materials upon receipt of a customer order?	
13. Which type transforms customer wants and needs into the design, based on quality, marketing, and manufacturing input?	
14. Which type designs a product so that it's easy to recover materials at the end of its product life?	
15. Which type replaces silo processes with parallel design and development?	
16. Which type designs one product with features and characteristics that appeal to all global markets?	
17. Which design concept helps to achieve economies of scale in design, procurement, production, and support?	
18. Which type preproduces and stores standardized subassembly units based on projected customer orders?	
19. Which type facilitates product and process design for ease of manufacturing, ease of use, and ease of service?	
20. Which type tries to maximize material value recovery and reduce logistics costs?	
21. Which type uses modular and lean assembly processes, and later introduces product variety during the production activity?	
22. Which type results in the loss of product uniqueness and customer loyalty?	
23. Which type replaces two or more parts with one standard part?	
24. Which type results in the loss of product flexibility and possible reduction in quality?	
25. Which type designs a product with all of the design considerations a company deems to be strategic?	
26. Which type develops scenarios to predefine the service process and project required repair parts?	
27. Which type helps to improve customer after-sale interaction and experience?	
28. Which type converts returned parts back into the equivalent of a new part?	

KEY TERMINOLOGY

Understanding key terms and the concepts they represent is crucial to passing the CSCP exam. In this chapter, the important terms are identified in Table 10.1.

Table 10.1   Product design key terminology

Collaborative information technology
Component commonality
Concurrent engineering (CE)
Configuration management system*
Design for everything (DFX)
Design for logistics (DFL)
Design for maintainability*
Design for manufacturability*
Design for manufacture and assembly (DFMA)*
Design for quality*
Design for remanufacture*
Design for reverse logistics
Design for service*
Design for Six Sigma (DFSS)*
Design for the environment (DFE)*
Design for the supply chain*
Design for X (DFX)
End-of-life management*
Environment life-cycle analysis
Formal collaboration
Informal collaboration
Integral design
Life-cycle analysis*
Mass customization
Maturity
Modular design strategy*
Over-the-wall approach
Product design
Product life cycle (PLC)
Product life-cycle management (PLM)*
Simplification
Standardization
Universality*

*Key term found in the CSCP ECM

CSCP EXAM PRACTICE QUESTIONS ON PRODUCT DESIGN

The questions presented in Table 10.2a cover the concepts presented in this chapter on product design. They are examples of what to expect on the actual exam.

Table 10.2a   Product design practice questions

No.	Questions
1	Collaborative information technology can best provide for increased: a) Value b) Velocity c) Volume d) Variability
2	What design method starts from the premise that the product design process can be shortened and simplified when stakeholders other than the engineers contribute design suggestions? a) Sustainability b) Customization c) Standardization d) Concurrent engineering
3	Life-cycle assessment best relates to which sustainability goal? a) Social b) Financial c) Environmental d) Employee relations
4	Design methods to enhance simplification include all of the following except for: a) Design for service b) Concurrent engineering c) Design for remanufacturing d) Design for manufacturing and assembly (DFMA)
5	What is the name of the concept in which all components are designed to be interchangeable in one specific product? a) Universality b) Integral design c) Modular design d) Standard design
6	Which of the following isn't a direct benefit of design collaboration? a) Fewer cost overruns b) Improved customer satisfaction c) Higher product quality for the price d) Increased marketability among ecology-minded consumers
7	In what stage of a product life cycle (PLC) does reverse logistics impact? a) Decline b) Maturity c) All stages d) Introduction
8	All of the following will occur if a company reduces the amount of plastic in a bottle by 20% except for: a) Reduced landfill costs b) Reduced raw material costs c) Reduced SKU shipping weights d) Reduced bottle inventory levels

ANSWERS TO CSCP EXAM PRACTICE QUESTIONS ON PRODUCT DESIGN

The answers to the practice questions on product design are shown in Table 10.2b. Any question you answer incorrectly indicates a gap in your body of knowledge and encourages the need for additional study time.

Table 10.2b   Answers to CSCP exam practice questions on product design

No.	Answers
1	Answer: B Collaborative information technology can provide visibility and velocity to help speed product development and allow for joint strategic sessions.
2	Answer: D This question refers to concurrent engineering, also called participative design, in which all functional areas simultaneously participate in the design process. Receiving input from these other areas helps to reduce and eliminate design errors and time-consuming engineering changes.
3	Answer: C Life-cycle assessment appraises the environmental impact on a company's product or service.
4	Answer: C Design for remanufacturing is used to enhance sustainability, not simplification. Answers A, B, and D all try to enhance simplification.
5	Answer: B Integral design is when all components can be interchangeable. Modular design is the planning of products with consideration for using existing components, rather than starting from nothing.
6	Answer: D The key words in this question are *direct benefit*. Increased marketability among ecology-minded consumers may occur, but it's not a direct benefit.
7	Answer: C Reverse logistics affects all stages of the product life cycle. Products can be returned at any time, in any stage.
8	Answer: D Bottle inventory levels aren't impacted by a reduction in the amount of plastic used to produce the bottle.

11

MANUFACTURING PLANNING AND CONTROL, MASTER PLANNING, AND SALES AND OPERATIONS PLANNING

This chapter focuses on the manufacturing planning and control hierarchy. It examines the movement of data from business planning, master planning, sales and operations planning (S&OP), master scheduling, distribution requirements planning (DRP), material requirements planning (MRP), and the production activity control (PAC) levels. It also explores the impact of various manufacturing environments, the use of level and chase strategies, and the improvement of product delivery lead times.

MANUFACTURING PLANNING AND CONTROL

The *manufacturing planning and control* (MPC) hierarchy displays the various planning hierarchy levels; their inputs and outputs; the capacity validation process; where planning and execution activities begin and end; the short, intermediate, and long time frames; and the operational, tactical, and strategic organizational levels. An example of an MPC hierarchy is displayed in Exhibit 11.1.

Exhibit 11.1   MPC hierarchy

Planning—long-term strategic functions

Inputs	Levels	Outputs	Validation
• Vision • Mission • Business forecast	Business plan	• Goals • Objectives • Business, financial, inventory, asset plans	Resource planning

Planning—intermediate to long-term tactical functions

• Inventory • Group forecast • Bill of resources	Sales and operations planning	• Production plan (volume/ aggregate)	Resource planning

Planning—intermediate tactical functions

• Inventory • Item forecasts • Customer orders • Bill of resources • Distribution orders	Master scheduling	• Master production schedule (mix) • Inventory/backlog plan	Rough cut capacity planning

Planning—short-term operational functions

• Inventory
• Resources
• Bill of material
• Planning factors
	Material requirements planning	• Exception and action reports
		   • Changes
		   • Releases
		• Planning reports
			Capacity requirements planning

Execution—short-term operational functions

• Resources • Load/capacity • Work orders and operations status	Production activity control	• Daily schedule • Resource shortages • Priority assignment • Input/output control • Operation sequencing	Scheduling

MASTER PLANNING

The *master planning* process is initiated after the development of the business plan. It consists of three distinct integrated components—demand management, production and resource planning, and master scheduling. Its goal is to complement and support the development of a long-term resource plan, and the tactical S&OP process for stakeholders.

SALES AND OPERATIONS PLANNING

S&OP aligns and integrates supply, demand, and financial resources to achieve a business plan. The framework creates one uniform plan by linking together all business functions. S&OP breaks down functional silos by improving communications and synergies between the demand and supply organizations, addresses competitive pressures, and helps to shorten delivery cycle times.

S&OP is an enabling tool that transforms the organization and its business processes and practices. It creates, implements, monitors, and continuously identifies demand and supply improvements. S&OP aligns the demand side against the supply side as it attempts to balance aggregated demand against available resources while the company strives for operational excellence.

The S&OP process starts with *data gathering* of the prior month's demand history, competitive data, and market conditions. The collected data is first filtered and cleansed to remove demand randomness and inconsistencies. The cleansed data is integrated with customer orders, intrinsic and extrinsic data, new products and promotional data, and financial and inventory data. All of the data is aggregated into product families and/or groups and then adjusted for returns, cancellations, and product substitutions. Financial and operational results are compiled and measured to determine the effectiveness of the prior month's performance.

After data gathering, the demand planning preparation process starts with the demand manager gathering the previous month's performance results. A meeting is then scheduled to review demand plans and is chaired by the highest ranking *demand-side professional*—for example, the vice president of sales or marketing. The preliminary forecasts are prepared and issued to team members for their review and adjustments.

During the demand planning meeting, a review of the preliminary forecasts is conducted. The first step is an examination of the calculated, system generated, quantitative forecasts. The team begins to make qualitative adjustments based on new products or promotions plans and the inclusion of spare and repair parts. During the review and approval process, the participants validate whether or not the submitted preliminary forecasts meet strategic goals and objectives. If they don't, additional adjustments are made to the forecasts. The final version of the forecast must be approved by the team.

The approved group and family forecasts are delivered to the supply chain manager and the operations planning team, who then prepares a *preliminary production plan* based on the submitted forecast. They use resource planning to determine whether sufficient resources exist to achieve the plan. The operations planning team checks on possible labor, material, or equipment constraints. They also validate that internal efficiency and utilization operational goals can be achieved. If no constraints exist, the *operations planning* team passes the production plan to the pre-meeting team. A constraint or issue that cannot be resolved gets passed back to the demand planning team along with alternative recommendations. The demand planning team then has to decide if they are able to accept the alternative recommendations or resubmit their original plan for reconsideration. The two teams meet and try to resolve their differences. The results of the meeting will prepare one of four options to be passed to the pre-meeting team for their review and approval. These options are:

- Option one has the accepted production plan getting sent to the pre-meeting group for their review and approval.
- Option two has both teams (demand and operations) agreeing on a solution after negotiations, but requiring pre-meeting review and approval. An example of this is the supply planning team submitting a request for overtime authorization.
- Option three has both sides in partial disagreement. The original demand plan can't be achieved, but one alternate action plan has been prepared by both teams to support the submitted plan.

However, the revised plan can have a different time frame with additional internal and external costs. The pre-meeting team will review the submitted plan and decide on how to proceed.

- Option four has both sides in complete disagreement. The two teams prepare a presentation explaining why the demand request has to be either totally accepted or rejected, due to resource constraints. The pre-meeting team will consider the alternative plans and make a decision to take action, one way or the other.

The *pre-meeting* team consists of managers and directors from various operational, financial, marketing, and supply chain functional areas. Their first requirement is to conduct a review of the prior month's performance metrics. Next, they review the submitted production plan along with any unresolved issues or identified future constraints. The pre-meeting team has the power to authorize changes to the production plan. The group's final requirement is to prepare an executive presentation, which consists of the production plan, the prior month's performance metrics, relevant issues, possible risks, and recommendations for discussion at the executive meeting.

At the *executive meeting*, the attendees review and approve the submitted production plan and authorize action to resolve supply and demand unresolved issues, approve capital authorization, and (if required) authorize tactical and strategic inventory, resource, or financial plan adjustments. This meeting is chaired by the president or CEO. At the conclusion of this meeting, the production plan is approved. The S&OP process flow is shown in Exhibit 11.2.

Exhibit 11.2   S&OP process flow

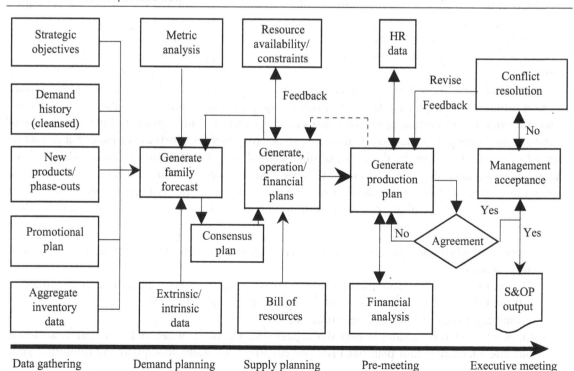

Exercise 11.1 will test your knowledge and understanding of the various S&OP process steps. Read each question and write in the best answer. The answers to the exercise are available from the Web Added Value™ Download Resource Center at www.jrosspub.com.

Exercise 11.1 S&OP process steps

Question	Answer
1. Which process activity identifies changes to the aggregate plan?	
2. Which process activity involves the participation of the CEO?	
3. Which process activity is attended by marketing and sales professionals to discuss their requirements?	
4. Which process activity reviews gaps between the demand plan and the business plan?	
5. Which process activity reviews the performance metrics in relation to demand and forecast accuracy?	
6. Which process activity requests an increase in available capacity by working overtime?	
7. Which process activity establishes the S&OP executive meeting agenda?	
8. Which process activity recommends how to resolve demand/supply mismatches?	

S&OP provides an organization with a number of improvement benefits. These include the establishment of a linkage between business planning and the tactics needed to implement it. It allows an organization to become more proactive in its processes, rather than reactive. S&OP is used to develop unified, cross-functional, short- to medium-term plans and processes throughout the organization. It's a bridge between customer values and supply chain efficiency, and it provides an incentive to engage in continuous process improvement (CPI). S&OP is a critical activity that permits the organization to move from stage two to stage three, as it becomes an internally integrated enterprise.

Exercise 11.2 will test your knowledge and understanding of the ownership of various S&OP processes. Read each question and write in the best answer. The answers to the exercise are available from the Web Added Value™ Download Resource Center at www.jrosspub.com.

Exercise 11.2 S&OP process ownership

Question	Answer
1. Who chairs the demand planning meeting?	
2. What is the output of the demand planning meeting?	
3. In which step is the production plan developed?	
4. In which step is the production plan consensus achieved?	
5. In which step does a discussion on forecast accuracy occur?	
6. What is the role of the demand manager in the demand planning meeting?	
7. In which step does cash flow and capital need to be reviewed?	
8. In which step does the authorization of additional resources take place to resolve supply/demand conflicts?	

AGGREGATE STRATEGIES

An *aggregate strategy* is the process of establishing, analyzing, and maintaining a preliminary production plan using the strategic objectives of an organization. The plan is based on the sales forecast, production capability, inventory goals, and customer orders. Its goal is to balance supply and demand at a minimum cost, meet operational efficiency and utilization objectives, and achieve strategic customer service goals. Aggregate strategy planning is performed in S&OP and uses an intermediate time frame that covers up to 18 months.

There are three aggregate strategies available for use by companies—level strategy, chase strategy, or a combination of the two.

A *level strategy* establishes a fixed, uniform production rate throughout the year. It will maintain a level work load and increase inventory levels when demand is low, and it will decrease inventory levels when demand exceeds production capability. Companies that manufacture seasonal products such as snow blowers or holiday candy use this strategy. A level strategy builds to an aggregate plan, which permits a company to produce the same output rate each period without increasing or decreasing its workforce. This occurs regardless of the rate of demand. A level strategy also allows a company to maintain a stable workforce and maximize its resources. However, a company incurs the added cost of carrying high inventory levels for part of the year. It also has the potential for a loss of sales and a lowering of customer service if inventory levels aren't sufficient to meet customer needs during periods of high demand.

The level production rate can be calculated by totaling up all of the forecasted demand for the selected periods and dividing the total by the number of periods. For example, if the aggregated, forecasted total of snow blowers is 46,000 for four quarters, then divide 46,000 by the four quarters to calculate a production rate of 11,500 per period.

A *chase strategy* matches the period rate of demand to the available capacity for a period. This requires a company to increase or decrease its workforce to meet varying production requirements period by period. An organization needs resource flexibility and agility in order to constantly adjust capacity levels to match the ever-changing demand. A chase strategy helps to maintain a very low level of inventory—usually retained in the form of safety stock—as a company builds a product *to order*. Examples of companies using the chase strategy are computer manufacturers, retail stores, or just-in-time (JIT) companies who manufacture assemble-to-order (ATO) products.

Some firms find it beneficial to utilize a combination of chase and level strategies at different times of the year. This is called a *hybrid strategy*. The combination helps a company to lower operational and inventory costs rather than using one of the other strategies by itself. Companies that manufacture a multi-seasonal product such as ice cream or holiday candy use this strategy. They produce holiday candy for half a year using the level strategy, and then switch to the chase strategy for the balance of the year as they produce to match customer orders. Table 11.1 demonstrates the calculation process for both the level and chase strategies.

Table 11.1   Level and chase calculation

Quarter	Aggregated Forecast	Planned Level Production	Ending Level Inventory	Planned Chase Production	Ending Chase Inventory
1	5,000	11,500	6,500	5,000	0
2	6,000	11,500	12,000	6,000	0
3	13,000	11,500	10,500	13,000	0
4	22,000	11,500	0	22,000	0
Total	46,000	46,000	————	46,000	————

S&OP COMMUNICATIONS PROCESS

Companies make a number of strategic, tactical, and operational decisions based on their selected manufacturing environment. There are four different kinds of manufacturing environments and each one has unique key attributes. Table 11.2 explores the differences in the various manufacturing environments.

Table 11.2   Manufacturing environments

Attribute	Engineering-to-order (ETO)	Make-to-order (MTO)	Assemble-to-order (ATO)	Make-to-stock (MTS)
Design	Build to customer specifications	Limited design	No changes	No changes
Inventory	None kept	Some raw materials	Modules	Finished goods
Initiate Manufacturing	After design approval and material ordering	Upon customer order receipt	Upon customer order receipt	Based on a forecast
Lead Time	Longest	Long	Short	Shortest
Design Changes	Extensive	Limited	None	None

DELIVERY LEAD TIME

Each manufacturing environment type has a different lead time based on its delivery activity. They range from immediate shipment upon customer order receipt, to waiting an extended period of time for the product to be designed, the materials to be ordered, the product to be assembled, and then shipment. Table 11.3 shows the four manufacturing environment types and their delivery activities.

Table 11.3   Manufacturing environment activity lead times

Type	Delivery Activity	Lead Time
Assemble-to-order (ATO)	Assemble and ship	Short
Engineer-to-order (ETO)	Design, purchase, make, assemble, and ship	Very long
Make-to-order (MTO)	Make, assemble, and ship	Long
Make-to-stock (MTS)	Ship from stock	Very short

KEY TERMINOLOGY

Understanding key terms and the concepts they represent is crucial to passing the Certified Supply Chain Professional (CSCP) exam. In this chapter, the following important terms are identified in Table 11.4.

Table 11.4   MPC, master planning, and S&OP key terminology

Chase strategy
Data gathering
Demand-side professional
Executive meeting
Hybrid strategy
Level strategy*
Manufacturing planning and control (MPC)
Master planning
Operations planning
Preliminary production plan
Pre-meeting
Production plan (PP)
Sales and operations planning (S&OP)*

*Key term found in the CSCP ECM

CSCP EXAM PRACTICE QUESTIONS ON MPC, MASTER PLANNING, AND S&OP

The questions presented in Table 11.5a cover the concepts presented in this chapter on MPC, master planning, and S&OP. They are examples of what to expect on the actual exam.

Table 11.5a   CSCP exam practice questions on MPC, master planning, and S&OP

No.	Questions
1	Where does internal supply and demand synchronization best take place? a) Master planning b) Resource planning (RP) c) Production planning d) Sales and operations planning (S&OP)
2	What is a direct input into the production plan? a) Business plan b) Financial plan c) Inventory plan d) Sales and operations plan (S&OP)

Continued

3	Which of the following is a direct input into sales and operations planning? a) Item forecasts b) Inventory levels c) Customer orders d) Distribution requirements planning (DRP) orders
4	In the manufacturing planning and control (MPC) hierarchy, where does execution and control begin? a) Shop floor control (SFC) b) Input/output control c) Production activity control (PAC) d) Capacity requirements planning (CRP)
5	The connecting point between material requirements planning (MRP) and distribution requirements planning (DRP) is the: a) Business plan b) Production plan c) Sales and operations plan d) Master scheduling process
6	A firm with excess worker capacity will typically be using a: a) Chase strategy b) Level strategy c) Hybrid strategy d) Tracking strategy
7	The chase strategy goal is best described as: a) Build only expected demand b) Match production to demand c) Maintain stable production rate d) Build the same product mix each period
8	The MIP Company has a backlog of 250 units, the forecast for the next period is 500 units, and production for the next period is 350 units. What is the supply demand strategy? a) Kanban b) Just-in-time (JIT) c) Make-to-order (MTO) d) Make-to-stock (MTS)
9	In an assemble-to-order (ATO) environment, master scheduling takes place at the: a) Option level b) Family level c) End item level d) Manufacturing level
10	Customer orders are addressed in what level of the manufacturing planning and control (MPC) hierarchy? a) Master scheduling (MS) b) Production activity control (PAC) c) Sales and operations planning (S&OP) d) Material requirements planning (MRP)
11	Interplant demand will best be processed into the: a) Production plan b) Master scheduling (MS) c) Material requirements planning (MRP) d) Distribution requirements planning (DRP)

Continued

12	The sum of the master production schedule (MPS) for the items within the product family must equal the: a) Inventory plan b) Production plan c) Capacity requirements plan (CRP) d) Material requirements plan (MRP)
13	Which of the following isn't a capacity communication tool? a) Dashboard b) Load profile c) Shop calendar d) Production plan
14	The demand review meeting held during the demand planning phase is best chaired by the: a) Product manager b) Demand manager c) Chief executive officer d) Vice president of sales
15	At which sales and operations planning (S&OP) process step does resource planning take place? a) Data gathering b) Supply planning c) Demand planning d) Pre-S&OP meeting
16	The best objective of the sales and operation planning (S&OP) meeting is to: a) Balance supply and demand b) Balance load input and output c) Authorize manufacturing output changes d) Authorize planning horizon changes
17	Which of the following isn't a sales and operations planning (S&OP) attribute? a) The link between business planning and tactics b) The incentive to engage in continuous process improvement (CPI) initiatives c) Unified, cross-functional plans and processes d) Bringing the planning group directly into the executive planning process
18	Who should chair the executive sales and operations planning (S&OP) meeting? a) Sales manager b) Master scheduler c) Operations manager d) Chief executive officer
19	At which step in the monthly sales and operations planning (S&OP) process do decisions regarding the financial impact of the balancing of supply and demand take place? a) Data gathering b) Supply planning c) Demand planning d) Pre-S&OP meeting

ANSWERS TO CSCP EXAM PRACTICE QUESTIONS ON MPC, MASTER PLANNING, AND S&OP

The answers to the practice questions on MPC, master planning, and S&OP are shown in Table 11.5b. Any question you answer incorrectly indicates a gap in your body of knowledge and encourages the need for additional study time.

Table 11.5b Answers to CSCP exam practice questions on MPC, master planning, and S&OP

No.	Answers
1	Answer: D Sales and operations planning (S&OP) is used to synchronize supply and demand. Resource planning validates the production plan. The production plan itself is the output of S&OP.
2	Answer: D Sales and operations planning (S&OP) is the direct input into the production plan. The business, financial, and inventory plan are inputs into the S&OP. The resource plan validates the strategic and S&OP plan (output). Knowledge of the manufacturing planning and control hierarchy chart will help to correctly answer this question.
3	Answer: B Inventory levels are used to plan a level strategy and to determine ending inventory levels in the sales and operations planning (S&OP) process. Item forecasts, customer orders, and distribution requirements planning (DRP) orders are all at the item level and are master scheduling inputs.
4	Answer: C Execution and control begins in production activity control. Refer to the manufacturing and planning control (MPC) hierarchy chart which displays the various MPC levels.
5	Answer: D Distribution requirements planning (DRP) orders (customer orders) go into the master scheduling process which passes data into material requirements planning (MRP). Refer to the manufacturing planning and control (MPC) hierarchy chart, which displays the various MPC levels.
6	Answer: C This question states that capacity won't be fully utilized for part of the year which refers to the hybrid strategy. Level and chase strategies have no excess worker capacity. Level has a level workforce and chase brings in workers as required. Hybrid is a combination of both the chase and level strategies which means that some full-time workers won't be fully utilized during part of the year.
7	Answer: B Chase aims to match production to demand for each period. It increases or decreases production based on daily customer order inflow.
8	Answer: C The key word in this question is backlog. Only make-to-order (MTO) has a backlog plan, while the other answers have inventory plans.
9	Answer: A Assemble-to-order (ATO) uses subassemblies/modules to produce a finished product based on customer selected options. These options (subassemblies or modules) are master scheduled, produced, and then placed in inventory for later use. The family level is performed at the sales and operations planning (S&OP) level. End item planning refers to make-to-stock (MTS) or make-to-order (MTO). The manufacturing level is not master scheduled, but rather produced based on the master schedule.

Continued

10	Answer: A Customer orders are part of the product mix that determines specific amounts of products, and they are inputted into master scheduling. Sales and operations planning (S&OP) is at a family and group level. Material requirements planning (MRP) performs material planning for dependent demand. Production activity control (PAC) executes the MRP plan.
11	Answer: B Interplant demands are requirements from an internal customer, and as such, will be processed into master scheduling. Answer A is families and not item level demand. Answer C is for dependent demand. Answer D can also be correct, but interplant demand is normally a request to produce something, which goes best into the master production schedule (MPS).
12	Answer: B The master production schedule (MPS) mix must equal the production plan (volume). The manufacturing planning and control (MPC) hierarchy chart indicates that the master scheduling process is for items and that the sales and operations planning (S&OP) process is for families and groups.
13	Answer: D The production plan reflects the need for demand. It doesn't communicate capacity. Answers A, B, and C all communicate the need for capacity.
14	Answer: D The highest-ranking demand-side professional should chair the demand review meeting. The product manager and demand manager both report to the vice president of sales. The chief executive officer chairs the sales and operations planning (S&OP) executive meeting.
15	Answer: B In supply planning, you validate the availability of resources, while in pre-sales and operations planning, you resolve the differences. In supply planning, you define requirements, but it's up to supply planning pre-sales and operations planning (S&OP) to determine if the plan can be achieved.
16	Answer: A The best objective of the sales and operation planning (S&OP) meeting is to balance supply and demand while meeting customer requirements.
17	Answer: D Sales and operation planning (S&OP) is meant to bring executives directly into the planning process, not the planning group.
18	Answer: D The executive sales and operations planning (S&OP) meeting is chaired by a decision maker such as the chief executive officer.
19	Answer: D In the pre-sales and operation planning (S&OP) meeting, plans are reviewed and discussed.

This book has free material available for download from the
Web Added Value™ resource center at *www.jrosspub.com*

12

STRATEGIC AND
BUSINESS PLANNING

This chapter focuses on why it's important to align a business strategy with an organizational and supply chain strategy, in order to meet corporate goals and objectives. Domestic and global competition among organizations requires companies to understand how to use their value and supply chains as competitive weapons.

STRATEGY

A *corporate strategy* defines and communicates how a company intends to compete and succeed against its competition in the global marketplace. It needs to link together the corporate mission and values while defining the operational, customer service, human resources, financial, and technological goals and objectives. The corporate strategy identifies how a company needs to move faster, deliver more value at less cost, and be more agile and flexible than competitors. A properly executed corporate strategy becomes a strategic supply chain resource and weapon that differentiates it in the marketplace. A multinational company's corporate strategy needs to be in sync with its *global strategy*. The global strategy must include growth objectives by country, product presence, expansion time frame, and customer requirements.

A company needs to align its business, organizational, and supply chain strategies so they can flow from one supply chain level to the next and be linked and dependent on each other to achieve corporate objectives. A *business strategy* is a long-range picture that establishes the direction of a company, defines how it intends to compete in the marketplace, leverages its core competencies, and depicts a future view. Least cost, differentiation, and focus are three generic business strategies that are used by companies to compete in the marketplace. An *organizational strategy* identifies how a company intends to evolve over time to achieve its long-term goals. It compares its current *as-is* organizational state to a proposed *to-be* state and identifies required changes that are needed to support the business strategy. These tend to pertain to cost, variety, quality, velocity, and flexibility. A *supply chain strategy* defines a game plan to help achieve strategic and organizational plans by evaluating the cost benefits and trade-offs of internal and external supply chain business decisions. A company needs to align its supply chain strategy with its organizational strategy. Strategies require *business rules* to define, control, constrain, or provide guidance to influence business behavior. Regulatory compliance, stocking levels, payment terms, or customer service objectives are examples of business rules that can be implemented at a company.

Business strategy change is never an easy task and requires the consideration of a number of factors. These include actual or anticipated marketplace changes, employee acceptance of the change, economic conditions, or a change in business direction. Change can be caused by disruptive technology, new product opportunities, declining sales of existing items, product life-cycle (PLC) stage changes, and business mergers. These all require the supply chain to be reconfigured. Organizations must be prepared to quickly spot and adapt to change in order to survive. Those who fail to recognize the need to change, who are slow to react, or have failed to react at all, pay a steep price in lost revenue and profits, or even survival. A few examples are online web-based companies that have impacted retail store sales, the use of technology to deliver music and videos, and the use of digital cameras that replaced the need for film.

Companies need to plan for the time when their strategic business direction may need to change. This requires them to consistently explore their strengths and weaknesses, and to identify the need to change, as well as where and when. Once the need to change is established, management has to create a future corporate vision. They need to begin to plan for the change and determine the costs and benefits of it versus the costs of not changing. The company then needs to build a consensus and obtain buy-in from all stakeholders in order to build enthusiasm for the change within the organization. When the company is ready to execute the change, it needs to follow its planned step-by-step approach. This requires the organizational structure to be reworked to implement the new vision and mission statement. It also leads to the redefinition of management and employee jobs. Change must be monitored in order to be effectively controlled. Feedback must be constantly given and reviewed to validate that the implemented changes are operating correctly and according to plan.

BALANCED SCORECARD™

Companies need a high-level business-related scorecard to track strategic performance and management planning. One such tool is the *Balanced Scorecard* (BSC) that was originated by Kaplan and Norton. It's used to align business activities to a company's vision, mission statement, and organizational strategy. The BSC helps to establish and monitor business performance against strategic goals. It's a strategic framework consisting of nonfinancial and traditional financial metrics, providing management with a balanced organizational performance view. The BSC tracks the organization's performance from four perspectives. They are financial, customer, business, and innovation and learning. The *financial perspective* tracks bottom-line results and future-oriented performance. The *customer perspective* tracks performance from the view of the customer as it assesses current and future business prospects. It selects metrics such as customer satisfaction or reliability. The *business process perspective* tracks how well the business runs and whether it meets customer expectations. It selects metrics such as flexible response, waste reduction, or productivity. Finally, the *innovation and learning perspective* tracks cultural attitudes toward continual learning and new product development. It selects metrics such as employee training hours or the number of new products or processes.

The benefits of the BSC are that it strives to clarify the strategic vision and the resource allocation process throughout the organization. It integrates the strategic planning and implementation processes that help to gain consensus and ownership of the defined key performance metrics. It also provides a framework to align the organization and improve management effectiveness by tying together decision-making strategies. The lack of communication and establishing too many metrics are key reasons for the failure of strategic performance and management planning.

BUSINESS STRATEGY TYPES

Today, rather than using mass marketing, companies can select one of five unique business strategies to distinguish themselves from their competition and achieve superior operational and financial results. This decision will drive the strategic supply chain and operation focus, and determine how it competes in the marketplace. The five basic competitive cost strategies are best-cost, low-cost, focused low-cost, broad differentiation, and focused differentiation (also known as product differentiation).

A *best-cost strategy* places an emphasis on enhanced functions, features, performances, quality, and service at a minimal cost. This strategy appeals to a broad market and creates a competitive advantage by giving customers more value for their money. An example of a best-cost strategy is the Lexus automobile, which offers more value at a lower price than its competitors.

A *low-cost strategy* places an emphasis on improving the value chain by finding ways to eliminate or reduce non-value activities. This strategy also appeals to a broad market and works best when competing companies sell similar products to customers who desire low prices. In this case, price is the only way for companies to differentiate themselves. Walmart, for example, is able to sell certain products at a lower cost than their competition due to their innovative supply chain.

A *focused low-cost strategy* places an emphasis on selling products to a target market niche. It differentiates itself by offering customers selected products at a price that is lower than competing rivals. This strategy works best in a narrow market where customers seek low cost and perceived product value. An example of a company using this strategy is a store selling all of their merchandise for a dollar.

Product differentiation is the process of offering a product with unique functions and features that make it stand out from anything else being sold in the market. A *broad differentiation strategy* places an emphasis on providing numerous products with features and characteristics that are distinct from its competitors. It differentiates itself by offering products that are considered to have value—people are more willing to pay a premium price for them and the company gains customer brand loyalty. An example of a company using this strategy is Whole Foods, which promotes itself as selling the highest quality natural and organic products.

A *focused differentiation strategy* is very similar to a broad differentiation strategy except that it focuses on a niche product. It, too, places an emphasis on providing exclusive features and characteristics that are very different from its competition. Products are unique and cherished by customers. They are considered to have great value and to be worth paying the premium prices. An example is Rolls Royce offering a car of unparalleled quality at a very high price to a very selective customer base.

Table 12.1 displays the five different competitive strategies and four attributes that distinguish one strategy from the other.

Table 12.1 Five competitive cost strategies

Attribute	Best-cost	Low-cost	Focused low-cost	Broad differentiation	Focused differentiation
Focus	Product value	Low price	Product value for the price	Product variety	Product uniqueness
Volume/ Variety	High/low	High/low	High/low	Low/high	Low/high
Supplier Objective	High product dependability	Low product cost	Fast product turn-over	Product quality	High product dependability
Market Segment	Customers looking for high value at a fair price	Customers looking for no frills and low prices	Customers looking for low prices/value	Customers looking for niche products at a fair price	Customers in a very small niche market looking for specialized products
Example	Lexus automobile	Walmart store	Family Dollar Store	Whole Foods store	Rolls Royce automobile

ORGANIZATIONAL STRATEGY

A company's organizational strategy is its action plan established to meet the wants and needs of its customer base, grow its business, compete against others, and develop new products and capabilities. A company that successfully implements its organizational strategy will achieve long-term financial and operational success. Together with business planning, an organizational strategy is used in the *strategic planning* process to develop the company's *strategic plan.*

There are four organizational strategy types. They are customer-focus and alignment, forecast-driven enterprise, demand-driven enterprise, and product type-driven. A company needs to select the organizational strategy that best meets their strategic goals and objectives.

A *customer-focus and alignment strategy* is used by companies who strive to meet and exceed customers' expectations. It places the customer's needs at the center of all business decisions. The strategy driver becomes: how to best service the customer from product design to product delivery. It achieves this by having the right product, at the right price, at the right time, in the right place, with the right attitude. These companies learn to balance quality, price, agility, service, and availability in order to make the customer experience a great one. They need to be highly effective and have high efficiency in order to thrive. A customer-focused and alignment strategy permits the company to quickly meet customer delivery dates and be a low-cost producer. By listening to the voice of the customer (VOC), companies are able to consistently outperform competitors who use other strategies. Customer focus and customer-focused strategy go hand in hand throughout the entire supply chain.

A *forecast-driven enterprise strategy* uses a demand forecast supplied by a *nucleus company* as its organizational strategy's starting point. The nucleus company, also known as a *channel master,* can be a supplier, manufacturer, or customer. It controls the entire supply chain and dictates that all participants meet its forecast. In a forecast-driven enterprise strategy, forecast and corresponding demand patterns can be quite volatile and act as a *push system* with inventory being pushed out to stocking locations. This creates a bullwhip effect as varying levels of inventory move throughout the supply chain due to lot sizing, seasonality, safety stock, and supplier forecasts. A push system produces inventory to a forecast without having any specific customer in mind. It pushes the inventory out to a stocking location regardless of the distribution center's need. For example, a company manufacturing a functional product such as soup or cereal typically produces to a forecast.

The *bullwhip effect* occurs when a small increase in demand at a downstream location distorts upstream material requirements due to forecasting and material ordering variability. This results in inventory placement orders at each level becoming larger than actual demand requirements. *Variability* refers to changes in demand from period to period, and it's impacted by trend, seasonality, promotional events, customer buying patterns, and competition. The further away from the upstream supply chain location, the greater the demand oscillation (swings). An example of this is when a downstream customer orders a shirt from a retailer. This requires the retailer to place an order for a case of shirts with their distributor. The distributor then has to turn around and place an order for a skid of shirts with their producer. The order breaks the producers order point system and they place an order for a partial truckload with the supplier. Finally, the supplier has to order a full truckload of various raw materials and components from their upstream supplier. At each step, the quantity becomes larger and larger which contributes to the bullwhip effect.

A *demand-driven enterprise strategy* reduces the bullwhip effect by eliminating the forecast and using actual customer orders to drive production and distribution. Companies produce only subassemblies and modules, and finished products are delayed until receipt of the customer order. Products are built or assembled upon receipt of customer orders and component demand is then pulled throughout the supply chain. A demand-driven enterprise strategy permits companies to substitute real information in place of a forecast, and actual demand is shared throughout the supply chain. It allows all upstream participants to better anticipate incoming customer orders and it moves the *push-pull frontier* closer to the customer. This permits final product assembly to be performed at a postponement center.

A *product type-driven strategy* is used by companies who have multiple supply chains. Products can be classified as functional or innovative, and a company will select a functional supply chain, an innovative supply chain, or a combination of the two based on delivery speed and cost. The product type and its manufacturing and supply chain processes impact a company's strategy choice based on existing and future demand patterns. *Functional products* are basic staples such as bread, eggs, or milk. They have predictable demand patterns, low demand variability, long PLCs, low margins, and competition can be fierce. Customers seek out suppliers based on low price and fast, reliable delivery. An *innovative product* and service that *focuses on innovation* can better meet customer needs, have quicker time-to-market development, and be on the cutting edge of newly released product developments such as smartphones, clothing, or electronic toys. They have unpredictable demand patterns, high demand volatility and variability, very short PLCs, high margins, and limited competition in the early stages of their PLC. Customers also seek out suppliers based on product availability, with price being the secondary consideration. Functional and innovative products require setting up different supply chains, as the traditional one-size-fits-all approach no longer applies. Different supply chains are needed for staple, innovative, seasonal, and fashion products because speed, reliability, agility, cost, and quality differs based on the selected approach.

Table 12.2 compares the attributes of functional versus innovative products.

Table 12.2 Functional versus innovative products

Attribute	Functional Products	Innovative Products
Margins	Low	High
Product variety	Low	High
Plant utilization	High	Low
Product life cycle	Long	Short
Forecast accuracy	Predictable	Unpredictable
Delivery lead time	Short	Long
Supplier selection focus	Low price, reliability	Speed, flexibility

RELATIONSHIPS

Collaboration is a strategic alliance between companies that builds relationships in order to enhance their supply chains. The sharing of ideas and data help bonds to become stronger and makes firms more competitive—and can lead to the creation of a virtual organization. A *virtual organization* consists of two or more independent companies who integrate themselves, often for a short period of time, to jointly produce or sell a product or service, but their members still retain their own unique identities. An example is Amazon, which started as a virtual, web-based company without any physical structure. It provided a service that marketed and sold products that were manufactured and maintained by other companies. *Service industry* companies perform intangible functions such as warehousing, transportation, retail, banking, education, repair, and return logistics.

A number of success factors need to be considered when forming a collaborative supply chain strategy. These include a willingness to trust and commit, and the ability to integrate supply chain processes. Resources, technical strengths, rewards, risks, culture, values, information, expertise, and learning must all be shared. This will help to create a common vision and mindset that leads to strategic growth, improved market access, stronger operations, and profitability among all participants. Relationship building takes time, patience, and a commitment toward making it work.

A collaborative relationship has communications taking place on four different levels. Table 12.3 identifies the levels, their purposes, the degree of collaboration, and the time frame between transactional vendors, partners, strategic alliances, and backward integration (company takeover).

Table 12.3 Communication levels

Level	Purpose	Collaboration Degree	Time Frame
Transactional with information sharing	Informal and limited sharing of information	Limited to single data source (a purchase)	Medium term
Shared processes with partnership	Limited collaboration such as design and a few linked processes	Shared knowledge across a network	Longer term
Linked competitive vision and strategic alliance	Virtual entity—common strategic vision, trust, social, and cultural understanding	Some information sharing	Time frame can be for longer periods
Mergers and acquisitions (backward and forward integration)	Complete information sharing and process linkage	Complete	Permanent

A company can utilize five different buyer-supplier relationship types with their suppliers. They are: buy on the market, ongoing relationships, partnership, collaboration/strategic alliance, and mergers and acquisitions.

The *buy on the market*, also called *transactional* or *vendor purchase*, has a short-term time frame. Demand sharing and process integration doesn't occur. Customers and vendors don't work together. No relationship or visibility exists, other than what occurs at order placement time.

The time frame for an *ongoing relationship* is medium in length and is between one or more businesses. It's the traditional vendor approach with repeated purchase transactions and some medium-term contract interaction. Communications occur between designated suppliers and a customer contact with limited demand sharing and/or future visibility.

A *partnership* is a long-term, legal arrangement between two or more businesses. The partners work together as one to increase visibility and awareness of each other's cultures, to advance their common interests, and to have full sharing of goals and strategies. The relationship is built on trust, shared risks, and rewards. This leads to an increase in supply chain efficiency, value-added services, and competitive advantages.

A *joint venture (JV)* is an agreement between two organizations who are both legally independent companies and have limited liability in the newly created entity. They share revenue, earnings, resources, capabilities, and control. This method helps a company to quickly enter new markets by joining another existing company. For examples, Mitsubishi Heavy Industries (engineering) and Caterpillar Tractor (earthmoving equipment) started as separate companies and then came together as a JV.

The time frame for a *collaboration/strategic alliance* is long term. It allows for full demand and information sharing between two or more businesses along with process integration. It also permits alliance partners to collaborate and work together to gain supply visibility. Cultures get meshed together and each party contributes money, resources, and knowledge, which enhances the overall performance. The collaboration/strategic alliance is a process that is built on trust, shared risks, and rewards. It leads to an increase in supply chain efficiency and a competitive advantage, but it requires continual monitoring and attention in order to succeed. An example of a strategic alliance is Starbucks and PepsiCo, who jointly produce and market Frappacino.

The *mergers and acquisition's* time frame is a permanent relationship. It allows for full demand sharing, complete visibility, and process integration. Two separate businesses become one and cultures are joined together. The company becomes more vertically integrated, which improves their control and efficiency and results in competitive advantages.

ORGANIZATIONAL DESIGN AND SUPPLY CHAIN MANAGEMENT EVOLUTION

Organizational design improves the efficiency and effectiveness of a company's supply chain. It establishes a plan for how a company needs to function. Organizational design allows a company to work more efficiently (internally and externally) and help achieve company goals and objectives, while also establishing a structure.

Table 12.4 presents a view of the four organizational design stages and describes the various attributes that impact communications, training, continuous process improvement (CPI), and integration. It also demonstrates how a company can migrate from chaos within stage one, to external integration in stage four, thus leading to supply chain stability and higher levels of customer service.

Table 12.4   Stages of supply chain evolution

Attributes	Stage 1 Multiple Dysfunction	Stage 2 Semi-functional Enterprise	Stage 3 Integrated Enterprise	Stage 4 Extended Enterprise
Material Planning Tool	Material requirements planning	Manufacturing resource planning	Internally integrated enterprise resource planning	Externally integrated enterprise resource planning
Communications	Informal and poor communications with dysfunctional meetings	Informal and limited internal communications	Formal with internal sales and operations planning	Formal with shared data and information across the supply chain
Training	No training	Job enrichment and some soft skill training	Internal teams, coaches, and mentors	Cross-functional training across the supply chain
Continuous Process Improvement	None	Within some functional departments	Internal functional areas	Across the supply chain
Silos	Yes	Yes	Eliminated	Eliminated
Integration	None	Limited	Internal	External including technology
Teams	None	Within some departments	Internal cross-functional	External cross–functional with partners

STAGES OF SUPPLY CHAIN MANAGEMENT EVOLUTION

Supply chains have changed their structure over the years. Historically, they started in a *stable* environment before evolving from a very simple, silo-based structure to a fully integrated supply chain. Table 12.4 describes this evolution of stages and the differences between supply chains strategies.

Supply chains operate in many different modes based upon how they view and manage supply and demand. Global companies need to progress from being reactive, to becoming strategic drivers if they want to survive and grow in this new economy.

Table 12.5 shows the various supply chain strategies.

Table 12.5 Supply chain strategies

Attribute	Stable	Reactive	Reactive efficient	Proactive efficient	Strategic driver
Goal	Low-cost and product availability	Speed and fulfillment without regard to cost	Efficiency and cost management	Cost and complexity reduction	Demand and fulfillment integrated
Integration	Silos	Minimal connectivity and capital equipment	Connectivity (integration) and equipment focus for improved operational efficiency	Product and process design improvements System integration Information sharing with third parties	Real-time information sharing with third parties who are all trying to enhance the strategic value of their supply chain
Run Types	Long runs	Short runs	Short runs	Short runs	Customer orders

A company's business and supply chain strategy involves implementing a *sourcing strategy*. A sourcing strategy includes bottleneck, direct/core competency, commodity, and leverageable materials. It can be thought of as a rectangular box that is divided into four quadrants. The lower quadrants are a low sourcing risk and the least important from a strategic (profitability) point of view. The upper quadrants are the most important, strategic in nature, high-risk, bottleneck, and core competency materials. Upper quadrants are difficult and costly to obtain, cannot be substituted, and can only be sourced from a limited number of suppliers.

The focus of *bottleneck materials* is fulfillment. A company must obtain reliable delivery of these materials or production can suffer because of material shortages. Material is of low strategic importance with high strategic risk. With this in mind, suppliers know they have strong bargaining power and companies need to reduce their dependence through supplier diversification and product substitution. Examples of bottleneck materials are specialized shipping cartons or a basic, raw material like steel sheets. Both are easy to obtain, but certain products can't be manufactured without them.

The focus of *direct/core competency materials* is availability. Material is of high strategic importance with high strategic risk. It's critical to producing products and it has a high cost-of-goods impact on product costing. Suppliers are few and this results in limited competition and higher prices. The strategic goal is to draw suppliers into a relationship ensuring long-term supply and material availability. Examples of core materials are computer chips or stainless steel with a custom designed metallurgy.

The focus of *commodity materials* is cost reduction. Material is of low strategic importance with low strategic risk. Suppliers have limited bargaining power as numerous alternative suppliers and substitute materials exist. A company doesn't have a high need to establish a long-term relationship with any one supplier, as the material doesn't impact cost or performance. Examples of commodity materials are wire coils or salt.

The focus of *leverageable materials* is reliability. Material is of high strategic importance with low strategic risk. Competition between numerous suppliers exists and this helps companies to push for reduced prices and for preferential treatment that can help to boost profitability. Examples of leverageable materials are paint and automobile components.

Exercise 12.1 will test your knowledge and understanding of the four strategic material types. Write in the name of the material type that best answers the question. The answers to the exercise are available from the Web Added Value™ Download Resource Center at www.jrosspub.com.

Exercise 12.1   Understanding material types

Question	Material Type
1. Which type best focuses on material reliability?	
2. Which type best focuses on material availability?	
3. Which type best focuses on material fulfillment?	
4. Which type best focuses on material cost reduction?	
5. Which type limits the bargaining power of the supplier?	

KEY TERMINOLOGY

Understanding key terms and the concepts they represent is crucial to passing the Certified Supply Chain Professional (CSCP) exam. In this chapter, the following important terms are identified in Table 12.6.

Table 12.6   Strategic and business planning key terminology

Balanced Scorecard™ (BSC)*
Best-cost strategy
Bottleneck materials
Broad product differentiation strategy
Bullwhip effect
Business rules
Business strategy
Buy on the market
Channel master
Commodity materials
Corporate strategy
Customer-focus and alignment strategy

Continued

Customer-focused
Demand-driven enterprise strategy
Direct/core competency materials
Focus on innovation
Focused low-cost strategy
Focused product differentiation strategy
Forecast-driven enterprise strategy
Functional product
Global strategy*
Innovative product*
Joint venture (JV)*
Leverageable materials
Low-cost strategy
Mergers and acquisitions
Nucleus company
Ongoing relationships
Organizational design
Organizational strategy
Partnership*
Product differentiation*
Product type-driven strategy
Push system*
Push-pull frontier
Service industry*
Sourcing*
Sourcing strategy
Stable
Strategic alliance*
Strategic plan
Strategic planning*
Supply chain strategy
Transactional
Variability
Vendor purchase

*Key term found in the CSCP ECM

CSCP EXAM PRACTICE QUESTIONS ON STRATEGIC AND BUSINESS PLANNING

The questions presented in Table 12.7a cover the concepts presented in this chapter on strategic and business planning. They are examples of what to expect on the actual exam.

Table 12.7a   Strategic and business planning practice questions

No.	Questions
1	Which phrase best describes the new supply chain focus? a) Collaboration between partner organizations b) Collaboration between supplier organizations c) Collaboration between customer organizations d) Cost reduction between all involved organizations
2	Demand-side professionals can reduce the bullwhip effect by using all of the following techniques except for: a) Cross-docking b) Reducing quoted delivery times c) Stable product pricing d) Sales and operations planning (S&OP)
3	The MIP Company is in transition from a functional organization to one that is pursuing business process excellence. What would be considered its biggest challenge? a) Conducting a benchmark study b) Developing organizational learning to modify employee behavior c) Gaining upper management approval d) Implementing new roles related to specific function activities
4	A supply chain for an innovative product needs to best focus on: a) Low-cost b) Physical efficiency c) Demand forecasting d) Market responsiveness
5	A company with a vertically integrated supply chain is most likely focusing on: a) Efficiency b) Responsiveness c) Order fulfillment d) Customer experience
6	A company that allows cross-functional communications between manufacturing and other functional areas by using a manufacturing resource planning (MRP II) system is at what stage of supply chain management evolution? a) Extended enterprise b) Multiple dysfunction c) Integrated enterprise d) Semi-functional enterprise
7	What causes manufacturing companies to reduce supply chain costs? a) Supplier pressure b) Customer pressure c) Stakeholder pressure d) Increased competition

Continued

8	Who can best energize a company's supply chain? a) Supplier b) Customer c) Competitor d) Government
9	What is the most important traditional operating decision a company can make if it has a low profit margin? a) Reducing inventory levels b) Reducing product variety c) Cutting supply chain costs d) Selling only innovative products
10	What does a company need to balance in order to thrive? a) Low effectiveness, low efficiency b) High effectiveness, low efficiency c) Low effectiveness, high efficiency d) High effectiveness, high efficiency
11	A supplier selling a commodity-based product must best be prepared to compete on: a) Design b) Variety c) Quality d) Availability
12	Which inventory policy best impacts the bullwhip effect in a negative manner? a) Lot-for-lot policy b) Fixed-order policy c) Just-in-time policy d) Period-review policy
13	A company that is focusing on delivering prices that are hard to match is using what strategy variation? a) Low-cost b) Best-cost c) Target costing d) Focused low-cost
14	The process of designing a product to meet a specific cost objective is best called: a) Low-cost b) Best-cost c) Focused low-cost d) Target costing
15	A company that offers a variety of products with each one containing unique functions and features is most likely using what form of marketing? a) Modular design b) Mass customization c) Product differentiation d) Product responsiveness
16	The supply chain strategy that a company should use is the one that best conforms to the company's: a) Production plan b) Organizational strategy c) Channel master strategy d) Sales and operations plan (S&OP)

Continued

17	What is the most important consideration for a customer focus-driven supply chain? a) High flexibility b) Low product cost c) Predictable forecast demand d) Meeting customer delivery dates
18	In a demand-driven supply chain, the push/pull frontier moves the production decision to the: a) Factory b) Supplier c) Customer d) Distributor
19	The bullwhip effect is driven by: a) A demand forecast b) Actual demand information c) The master production schedule d) The sales and operations schedule
20	Which of the following isn't a typical characteristic of an innovative product? a) High profit margins b) Fast innovation speed c) Short product life cycle (PLC) d) Predictable product volume
21	Building a collaborative relationship requires a company to: a) Develop tracking metrics b) Listen to the channel master c) Achieve customer service goals d) Place the interests of the whole above local interests
22	A company making a critical component that has high strategic importance and high supply chain difficulty needs to best focus on: a) Cost reduction b) Cost savings and reliability c) Forming a strategic partnership d) Forming an on-going relationship
23	The degree of efficiency and effectiveness of a supply chain's function is most likely limited by: a) Variety of information b) Velocity of information c) Visibility of information d) Variability of information
24	A company desiring to move from supply chain development stage two to stage three will need to: a) Use e-commerce b) Use capable-to-promise c) Use available-to-promise d) Initiate informal demand planning
25	A company achieving low production costs will have what impact on the marketing and finance relationship? a) Low customer service/low inventory b) High customer service/high inventory c) High customer service/low inventory d) Low customer service/high inventory

ANSWERS TO CSCP EXAM PRACTICE QUESTIONS ON STRATEGIC AND BUSINESS PLANNING

The answers to the practice questions on strategic and business planning are shown in Table 12.7b. Any question you answer incorrectly indicates a gap in your body of knowledge and encourages the need for additional study time.

Table 12.7b Answers to CSCP exam practice questions on strategic and business planning

No.	Answers
1	Answer: A Today the focus is on collaboration between partner organizations. In the past, the focus was solely on cost reduction.
2	Answer: D Sales and operations planning (S&OP) has no direct impact on the bullwhip effect. A company using cross-docking and reducing quoted lead times will reduce demand variability. Stable product pricing also helps to flatten demand variability. Answers A, B, and C directly help to reduce the bullwhip effect.
3	Answer: B Changing employee behavior and gaining employee acceptance of a change is never an easy task. It's the biggest challenge at many companies. Conducting a benchmark study or gaining management approval comes before any change is made and therefore isn't a challenge in the time period stated in this question. Implementing new roles is also a challenge, but you first need to change employee behavior before the new role can be properly implemented.
4	Answer: D An innovative supply chain requires market responsiveness, including speed and flexibility, to support the ever-changing marketplace demand requirements for products.
5	Answer: B Vertical integration focuses on responsiveness. This equates to internal speed and control. Efficiency, order fulfillment, and customer experience may or may not improve with vertical integration.
6	Answer: C The key words in this question are *cross-functional* and *manufacturing* and other functional areas, not manufacturing resource planning II. This means the company has integrated itself internally, which identifies the answer as integrated enterprise. Semi-functional enterprise has no cross-functional communications. There is also no reference to any external functions, so extended enterprise can't be the correct answer.
7	Answer: D Competition is the major driver to reduce costs for companies if they want to retain their competitive advantage.
8	Answer: C Competition can threaten a supply chain, and as a result, help to energize it. An example of this is an online company that has changed the way non-online companies view their supply chains.
9	Answer: A Traditional cost cutting means spending less in one area, which then impacts others. Inventory is always one of the first areas to be reduced.
10	Answer: D A company needs to be highly effective and have high efficiency in order to thrive. This permits the company to quickly meet customer delivery dates and be a low-cost producer.
11	Answer: D A commodity product must be in stock as customers purchase these items based on availability and low cost.

Continued

12	Answer: D
	A period-review policy aggregates the demand requirements based on a selected number of periods. This results in the placement of a much larger order size. This policy builds up inventory, which impacts the bullwhip effect in a negative manner.
13	Answer: A
	A company focusing on delivering prices that are hard to match is using a low-cost approach. This pricing strategy offers low prices to stimulate demand in an attempt to gain market share.
14	Answer: D
	This question is defining the target costing method in which a final cost is determined after market analysis, and the product is designed to meet a specific customer cost objective.
15	Answer: C
	This question requires knowledge of the APICS Dictionary definition of *product differentiation*. Product differentiation is offering a product with unique functions and features that makes it stand out from anything else being sold in the market.
16	Answer: B
	A company needs to align its supply chain strategy with its organizational strategy.
17	Answer: D
	Customers want delivery when requested, so meeting customer delivery dates is critical to the success of any company.
18	Answer: A
	A demand-driven supply chain uses the push-pull concept. It moves the final assembly decision from the supplier to the factory based on the customer requirements. A distributor is also a customer, so it can't be the correct answer.
19	Answer: A
	A demand forecast (demand uncertainty) creates variability within the supply chain, which becomes more distorted as it moves through the supply chain.
20	Answer: D
	Innovative products focus on producing a high variety (mix). High, predictable volume doesn't occur until the product line becomes more stable or functional.
21	Answer: D
	Collaboration means working together. This requires both parties to first consider the goals and objectives of the relationship. Both companies need to make changes in how they operate and place the interest of the relationship before their own needs.
22	Answer: C
	A company making a critical component needs to form a strategic partnership with a supplier to ensure availability and reliability. Cost savings and cost reductions aren't as critical as delivery and quality.
23	Answer: B
	A supply chain is limited by the ease and speed of the velocity of information. Visibility is important, but if you can't quickly receive information, it does you no good. Information variability impacts data if the data has to be cleaned up and aggregated, which then reduces the speed of its availability (velocity).
24	Answer: C
	Available-to-promise (ATP) is found in stage three as it implies internal integration with an enterprise resource planning (ERP) system. Capable-to-promise (CTP) and e-commerce are found in stage four. Informal demand planning is found in stage two.
25	Answer: D
	A company achieving low production costs focuses on longer production runs with minimal setup changes. This causes inventory levels to increase. However, this action prevents the company from quickly responding to customer requests to produce other products, or to accept rush orders. This is due to the need to perform a new setup or to maintain higher inventory levels that increase costs. This lack of action impacts customer service in a negative way.

13

MASTER SCHEDULING

This chapter focuses on the *master scheduling* (MS) process. It examines the movement of data from sales and operations planning (S&OP) into MS, capacity validation, and then as an input into material requirements planning (MRP). MS explores the inputs, outputs, and the validation processes that are associated with the development of an approved *master production schedule* (MPS).

MS

The MS process is performed on a tactical level, focusing on an intermediate time frame. The *master schedule* itself is a required inventory quantity per period of independent demand. It specifies what an organization plans to produce or purchase in terms of what item, how much, and when it's required. The objectives of the MPS are to effectively plan and control resources; meet customer priorities; and produce the right products, for the right customers, in the right quantities, at the right time. The goal is to create a realistic MPS plan for each independent planned item. MS strives to balance customer demand against available resources, meet customer service objectives, and effectively utilize resources and maximize profits. The MPS plan is detailed, time-phased, believable, written, meets the production plan, and requires management approval. It also includes *interplant demand* from another facility within the same organization.

The MS process begins upon receiving the approved S&OP developed production plan (PP). A sample PP is displayed in Table 13.1.

Table 13.1 Sample production plan

Computer Family and Groups (Volume)			
Months	Jan	Feb	Mar	Apr
Days	21	19	23	20
Plan	21,000	19,000	23,000	20,000

The PP for the month of April is 20,000 units. During MPS development, the approved PP is disaggregated. *Disaggregation* is the process of breaking down the monthly product family and group quantity, found in the PP, into individual weekly master schedule product quantities. It breaks down the quantity from a full month to individual weeks. Table 13.2 shows where the PP quantity is disaggregated into weekly quantities for the month of April. For example, the 20,000 computers are broken down into red and black individual units that make up the family.

Table 13.2 Master schedule disaggregation

Disaggregation of the Master Schedule					
Week/Product	**1**	**2**	**3**	**4**	**Total**
Red computers	2,000	4,000	5,000	2,500	13,500
Black computers	3,000	1,000		2,500	6,500
Totals	5,000	5,000	5,000	5,000	20,000

The *master scheduler* is the person who is responsible for overseeing the disaggregation process, development of the master schedule, coordinating the approval of the master schedule, and monitoring its execution. The MS process requires data inputs from a number of sources. These include the disaggregated PP, item forecasts, customer orders, distribution requirements planning (DRP) orders, on-hand inventory, work and purchase orders, planning and modular bills of materials (BOMs), routing data, bills of resources (BORs), time fences, and safety stock requirements.

A relationship exists between S&OP and the MS process but Table 13.3 displays the major differences between the two applications.

Table 13.3 S&OP and MS differences

S&OP	MS
Volume (quantity)	Variety (mixture)
How much	What type
Family and groups	Individual items
Aggregate totals	Disaggregate items
Total production rates	Individual customer orders
Total resources	Bottlenecks (constraints) resources
Output = PP	Output = MPS
Validate = resource planning	Validate = RCCP (rough cut capacity planning)

TIME FENCES AND ZONES

Time fences restrict operational and supplier schedule changes and are classified as either *demand time fences* (DTFs) or as *planning time fences* (PTFs). Both the DTF and PTF are used in the MS and MRP calculation process as shown in Exhibit 13.1. A DTF is a designated time period in which the MPS is frozen and changes aren't permitted. In MRP, the time fence is set upon material receipt to limit changes. The PTF permits negotiated changes to capacity and material levels and it allows schedule tradeoffs of one item for another as defined in operating procedures. The PTF lies between the frozen zone and the liquid zone.

Exhibit 13.1   Time fences and zones

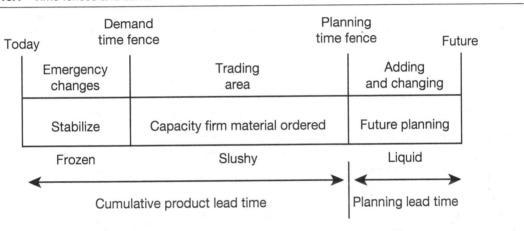

The *frozen zone* restricts material and capacity changes to the MPS unless upper management authorizes a change in order to minimize operational disruptions and cost overruns. The *slushy zone* permits negotiated changes to MPS quantities and required dates as defined in operating procedures. It authorizes suppliers to purchase raw materials and components, but the delivery schedule and quantity can be altered by either party. The *liquid zone* is for guidance only. It permits unlimited planning changes to be made to the MPS, as long as they conform to operating procedures. In the liquid zone, no authorization is given to purchase or manufacture any item.

COMMITMENT DECISION POINT

Buyers and suppliers become frustrated when demand data and plans are shared, but one party takes no action. For example, a supplier doesn't build to the submitted plan, and needed inventory is unavailable for customer delivery. On the reverse side, the supplier produced to the submitted plan, but the customer reschedules or refuses to take delivery. A lack of collaboration and communication caused this problem. The use of a *purchase commitment zone* (frozen) can prevent this from happening. The frozen zone treats requirements as being firm in terms of volume and timing. Both parties agree to a schedule, so the supplier produces to a plan and the customer must accept delivered materials.

MASTER PRODUCTION SCHEDULING PROJECTED AVAILABLE BALANCE CALCULATION

The MS planning time-phased record displays information required to properly develop the master schedule. Planning data resides on top of the record and displays information on the item being planned. This includes the part number, description, order policy, lot size, safety stock, time fences, inventory, and lead time. The total of all MPS time periods equates to the planning horizon. An example of MPS time periods is shown in Table 13.4, which displays five periods. The MPS planning horizon is how far out into the future it goes. A company often uses a three- to five-year time period for planning purposes.

Table 13.4   MS time-phased record

Item number: A
Description: red computers
Order policy/lot size: fixed/40 pieces
Safety stock: 0

Demand time fence: two weeks
Planning time fence: four weeks
Inventory: 50
Lead time: one week

Period		1	2	3	4	5
Forecast		20	20	20	25	25
Customer order		23	18	7	9	4
Project available balance (PAB)	50	27	9	29	4	19
Available-to-promise		9		24		36
Master production schedule				40		40

The MS calculation process begins with a review of the planning data as shown in Table 13.4. The current inventory quantity is posted to the right of the *projected available balance* (PAB) row. The PAB is a calculated inventory projection. Forecast and customer order data is entered into the top two rows. The PAB calculation begins with an understanding of the DTFs and PTFs. A DTF is used in the calculation of the PAB.

In Table 13.4, Period 1 shows the customer order quantity of 23 being subtracted from the inventory quantity of 50. The PAB is shown as 27 (50 – 23). Period 1 has sufficient inventory, so no further planning action is required. The DTF restricts production to actual customer orders, and the forecast is ignored in order to prevent the buildup of unwanted inventory.

In Period 2, the customer order quantity of 18 is subtracted from the Period 1 PAB quantity of 27. The PAB is shown as nine (27 – 18). The customer order quantity is used because it's within the DTF. Period 2 has sufficient inventory, so no further planning action is required.

In Period 3, the forecast quantity of 20 is subtracted from the Period 2 PAB quantity of nine. The forecast quantity is used because it's after the DTF, and it's higher than the customer order quantity. If the customer order quantity is higher, then it would be used. The calculated PAB is negative 11 (9 – 20). Sufficient inventory doesn't exist for this period, which now requires the creation of an MPS order. The MPS quantity is for 40 pieces, and it's based on the red computer order policy and lot size. The quantity of 40 is shown in the Period 3 MPS column, and it's added to the PAB quantity of nine (40 + 9 = 49). The forecast quantity is then subtracted (49 – 20) to arrive at a Period 3 PAB quantity of 29.

In Period 4, the forecast quantity of 25 is subtracted from the Period 3 PAB quantity of 29. The PAB is shown as four (29 – 25). The forecast quantity is used because it's after the DTF, and it's higher than the customer order quantity. Period 4 has sufficient inventory, so no further planning action is required.

In Period 5, the forecast order quantity of 25 is subtracted from the Period 4 PAB quantity of four. Sufficient inventory doesn't exist for this period. An MPS quantity of 40 is planned as specified by the fixed order quantity. The quantity of 40 is shown in the Period 5 MPS column, and it gets added to the PAB quantity of four (4 + 40), and then subtracted from the forecast quantity to obtain a PAB quantity of 19 (44 – 25). The forecast quantity is used because it's outside of the PTF, and it's higher than the displayed customer order. This same process is repeated for every MPS item. The preliminary MPS is developed when all items have been planned.

MASTER PRODUCTION SCHEDULING AVAILABLE-TO-PROMISE CALCULATION

Available-to-promise (ATP) is a critical MPS calculation. It represents the uncommitted inventory in a specified time period that can be used to promise customer delivery. The ATP calculation doesn't use time fences; instead, it uses beginning inventory, the PAB, customer orders, and planned MPS orders. Table 13.4 shows that Item A has a beginning inventory of 50 pieces. It also shows that the first planned MPS order is in Period 3 for 40 pieces, 23 customers orders are shown in Period 1, and another 18 orders are in Period 2. The ATP totals up all customer orders until the next planned MPS order. In this example, the customer order quantities of 23 and 18 are added together (41) and then subtracted from the beginning inventory of 50. This shows an ATP quantity of nine (50 – 41) in Period 1. The ATP quantity in Period 2 is blank, as the available inventory can be sold either in Period 1 or 2. The ATP calculation assumes that all inventories will be consumed by the end of Period 2. This means that in Period 3, the MPS quantity of 40 becomes the beginning inventory. ATP is calculated in Period 3 by adding the customer order quantities of seven plus nine together (16) and then subtracting them from the MPS planned quantity of 40. The ATP quantity in Period 3 is 24 (40 – 16). The ATP quantity in Period 4 is blank, as the available inventory can be sold either in Period 3 or 4. The ATP calculation assumes that all available inventories will be consumed by the end of Period 4. The process is repeated in Period 5 to obtain an ATP of 36 (40 – 4). Multiple versions of ATP exist in different enterprise resource planning (ERP) packages, but only this method is used in the Certified Supply Chain Professional (CSCP) Learning System.

Exercise 13.1 will test your knowledge and understanding of the PAB calculation. Calculate the PAB for each period and write in your answer. The answers to the exercise are available from the Web Added Value™ Download Resource Center at www.jrosspub.com.

Exercise 13.1 PAB calculation

Lot size = 30
Safety stock = 0
On-hand = 20

Demand time fence = three periods
Planning time fence = five periods
Lead time = one period

Periods	1	2	3	4	5	6
Forecast	5	5	5	5	5	5
Customer orders	5	3	2			
PAB | 20						
ATP						
MPS						

Exercise 13.2 will test your knowledge and understanding of the ATP calculation. Calculate the ATP for each period and write in your answer. The answers to the exercise are available from the Web Added Value™ Download Resource Center at www.jrosspub.com.

Exercise 13.2 ATP calculation

Lot size = 30
Safety stock = 0
On-hand = 20

Demand time fence = three periods
Planning time fence = five periods
Lead time = one period

Periods	1	2	3	4	5	6
Forecast	5	5	5	5	5	5
Customer orders	5	3	2			
PAB | 20						
ATP						
MPS						

ROUGH CUT CAPACITY PLANNING

Rough cut capacity planning (RCCP) is used to validate MPS feasibility or identify where the plan requires modification. RCCP converts the MPS into load requirements for each specified constraint work center. It compares the constraint work center load against available capacity to identify potential capacity issues or concerns. The master scheduler decides to increase or decrease capacity to support the preliminary MPS and resolve any RCCP identified constraints. The RCCP process flow is displayed in Exhibit 13.2.

Exhibit 13.2   RCCP process flow

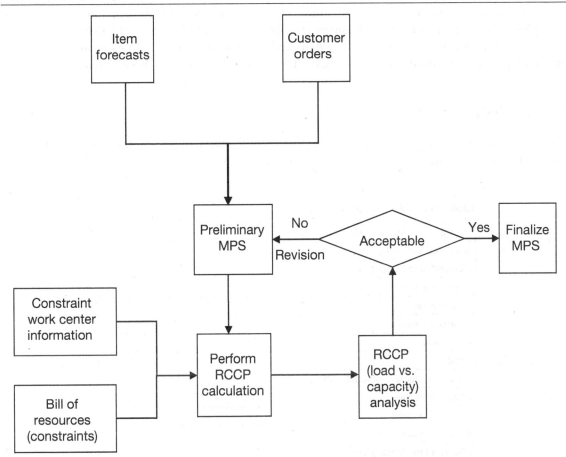

RCCP requires the identification of a constraint *work center*. The work center is an area within a facility where assigned machine or labor resources perform a function—such as fabricating, assembling, or packaging. Its capacity is determined by looking at the constraint machine or labor capability per hour and then computing the amount that can be produced in a day. For example, a work center with three machines running eight hours a day has 24 hours of capacity per day. A *BOR* is used to define an average run time for an average product based on historical production performance in order to produce an average family or group item. *Load* is the amount of output that can be produced based on the BOR average time multiplied by the master schedule quantity. The higher the machine load level, the longer the work center queues and lead times.

The work center load report per period is used to determine if sufficient resources exist. If they don't exist, the work center will need to add additional workers or work extensive overtime. If these recommendations are unacceptable to management, then the schedule must be revised downward. Load is calculated by taking the BOR average time of 20 minutes to assemble a typical product. An example of this is the red computers shown in Table 13.4 in Periods 3 and 5. The projected load for a future period is calculated by multiplying the MPS quantity times 20 minutes per unit. The calculation reveals 13.33 hours (800 minutes ÷ 60 minutes in an hour) of load for this item, and the process is repeated for every MPS item. Once the RCCP becomes approved, the MPS is finalized. It's then entered into the MRP system.

KEY TERMINOLOGY

Understanding key terms and the concepts they represent is crucial to passing the CSCP exam. In this chapter, the following important terms are identified in Table 13.5.

Table 13.5   MS key terminology

Available-to-promise (ATP)*
Bill of resource (BOR)
Demand time fence (DTF)
Disaggregation
Frozen zone
Interplant demand*
Liquid zone
Load
Master production schedule (MPS)*
Master schedule
Master scheduler
Master scheduling (MS)
Planning time fence (PTF)
Projected available balance (PAB)
Rough cut capacity planning (RCCP)
Slushy zone
Time fence (time fences)*
Work center

*Key term found in the CSCP ECM

CSCP EXAM PRACTICE QUESTIONS ON MS

The questions presented in Table 13.6a cover the concepts presented in this chapter on MS. They are examples of what to expect on the actual exam.

Table 13.6a   MS practice questions

No.	Questions
1	The material requirements planning (MRP) demand time fence (DTF) is usually set: a) Upon material receipt b) Upon ordering material c) Upon start of production d) Upon customer order receipt
2	All of the following tools assist the master scheduler to help balance supply and demand except for: a) Safety stock b) Safety capacity c) Safety lead time d) Demand time fence (DTF)
3	A company has the least planning flexibility: a) Within the demand time fence (DTF) b) Within the planning time fence (PTF) c) Outside the demand time fence (DTF) d) Outside the planning time fence (PTF)
4	The planning group uses a bill of resource (BOR) as an input to validate which level of capacity management? a) Input/output control b) Sales and operations planning (S&OP) c) Capacity requirements planning (CRP) d) Rough cut capacity planning (RCCP) requirements
5	A work center that doesn't produce to the material requirements planning (MRP) schedule may observe all of the following except for: a) Late deliveries b) Longer queues c) Overproduction d) Increased engineering change notices
6	Which of the following statements best describes disaggregation? a) Converts time frame from weeks to months b) Converts product families into end items c) Inputs the production plan into the master production schedule d) Moves data from lower to higher levels
7	Changes to the master schedule can best be limited if the company adopts a: a) Zero change policy b) No rush order policy c) Planning zone policy d) Demand time fence policy
8	In an assemble-to-order (ATO) environment, master scheduling (MS) takes place at the: a) Option level b) Family level c) End item level d) Manufacturing level

ANSWERS TO CSCP EXAM PRACTICE QUESTIONS ON MS

The answers to the practice questions on MS are shown in Table 13.6b. Any question you answer incorrectly indicates a gap in your body of knowledge and encourages the need for additional study time.

Table 13.6b Answers to CSCP exam practice questions on MS

No.	Answers
1	Answer: A Material requirements planning (MRP) demand time fences (DTF) are usually set upon material receipt. *Upon ordering materials* and *upon start of production* applies to the planning time fence (PTF). *Upon customer order receipt* applies to the master production schedule (MPS).
2	Answer: D The key word in this question is *balancing*. Demand time fences (DTFs) don't help to balance supply and demand. They restrict the addition of new orders. Answers A, B, and C can help to balance supply and demand.
3	Answer: A Within the demand time fence (DTF), no flexibility exists as the process focuses on only producing customer orders.
4	Answer: D The bill of resource (BOR) is used as an input in both resource planning and rough cut capacity planning (RCCP). It displays the average amount of time to perform a function such as a manufacturing or assembly activity at a family or group level.
5	Answer: D A work center that doesn't produce to the material requirements plan (MRP) won't be directly impacted by engineering change. Engineering change is impacted by a customer, marketing, and/or cost reduction change requests. Answers A, B, and C are all impacted by MRP.
6	Answer: B Disaggregation is the breaking apart of families into end items, from months to weeks, and from higher levels to lower levels. A production plan (PP) is input into the master scheduling process, and not the master production schedule (MPS) itself.
7	Answer: D A demand time fence (DTF) policy restricts master schedule changes. It requires upper management approval before it allows any changes.
8	Answer: A Assemble-to-order (ATO) uses subassemblies/modules to produce a finished product based on selected options. These options (subassemblies or modules) are master scheduled, produced, and then placed in inventory. The family level is performed at the sales and operations planning (S&OP) level. End item planning refers to make-to-stock (MTS) or make-to-order (MTO). The manufacturing level isn't master scheduled, but rather produces what is on the schedule.

14

MATERIAL REQUIREMENTS PLANNING AND DISTRIBUTION REQUIREMENTS PLANNING

This chapter focuses on the *material requirements planning* (MRP) and *distribution requirements planning* (DRP) applications. It explores inputs, outputs, and the validation processes associated with the development of MRP including the gross-to-net calculation and system nervousness. It also examines the movement of data from *bills of material* (BOM) to master scheduling (MS) and DRP, to MRP, with its outputs being passed to production activity control (PAC).

MRP

MRP is a computer-based application that focuses on material planning and inventory control. It's utilized on the operational level and has a short-to-intermediate time frame. MRP specifies what the organization needs to make or purchase for each dependent demand item in terms of how much and when. Its objectives are to effectively plan and manage inventory and resources, by having the right raw materials or components available to achieve the master schedule. MRP balances demand against supply to effectively utilize them while meeting desired inventory levels, and maximizing revenue. Its goal is to ensure a higher level of customer service.

BOM

A BOM, also called a *product structure*, is a list of raw materials and components, along with required quantities and units of measure, used in the manufacturing of a partially assembled product (subassembly) or a finished unit. BOMs, along with on-hand inventory, work and purchase orders (scheduled receipts), routing data (operation, set up, and run times), work center data (availability, efficiency, utilization, and rated and demonstrated capacity), and planning factors are entered into the MRP system. *Engineering change* can add or delete an item from a BOM, or it can change the quantity on it. These change suggestions are received from customers, marketing, and/or operations.

A *single-level BOM* depicts a parent-child/children relationship. The parent is on top, and the child/ children are underneath. The BOM displays the items and quantities required to produce the described item. Exhibit 14.1 displays a single-level BOM. In this exhibit, the parent is part number A (sheet metal box assembly). Part number B (sheet metal box), C (cover), and D (screw) are the children, which are displayed under the parent. The quantity shown in parentheses represents the number of required pieces that are needed in the manufacturing or assembly process. In this example, one sheet metal box, two covers, and two screws are required to produce a sheet metal box assembly.

Exhibit 14.1   Single-level BOM

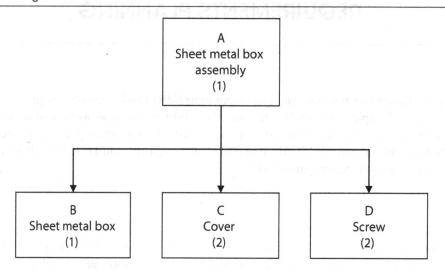

A *multi-level BOM* has more than one level of children. MRP uses a *low-level code* (LLC) to identify the lowest level where planning can occur. The MRP system assigns the proper LLC to each item. The highest level represents an LLC of zero, which indicates it's from the master production schedule (MPS). The level under it is called level one, which is the child of level zero. This level can contain multiple children. Level two will follow this same pattern, and so forth. There can be as many levels as required. In Exhibit 14.2, LLC one is linked directly to level zero, and LLC two is linked directly to level one. In this example, part A is a salable sheet metal box assembly, which is master scheduled. Part B is the sheet metal box, part C is the cover, and part D is the screw required to assemble part A. Please note that the multi-level BOM can have repeating components or raw materials existing on different levels, shown in our example as part E (cold roll steel (CRS) 14 gauge), which is used to make parts B and C.

An *indented BOM* starts with a parent item and then displays all subassemblies, raw materials, and components that are needed to produce it. The parent item appears on the top as level zero and is positioned furthest to the left. Underneath that and indented to the right one space, appear all level one raw materials, components, and subassemblies. A level one parent item has its children displayed under it, indented to the right one space, and these children are level two items. This process repeats itself until the complete hierarchical structure is displayed, and all materials are linked to each other.

Exhibit 14.2   Multi-level BOM

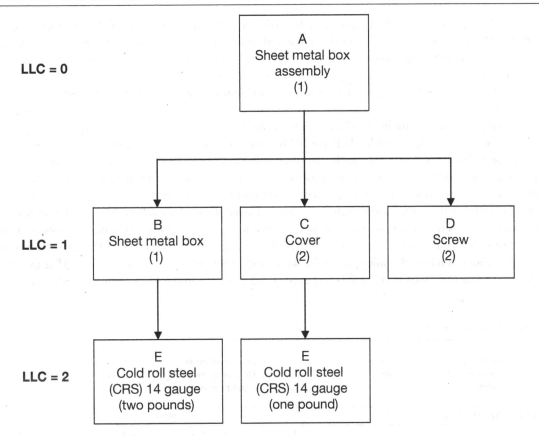

A *modular* or *planning BOM*, is structured to display the various modules or options that are used to produce an assemble-to-order (ATO) product. This example is about a car—where the car is the parent and beneath it are two components (children). One child is an automatic transmission with a historical usage rate of 70%. The other is a standard transmission with a historical usage rate of 30%. The use of these rates facilitates the forecasting, MPS, and material planning. It's easier to create one modular BOM rather than creating individual BOMs for every possible combination of the item being produced. Modular BOMs facilitate MS being performed at two levels—one is at the semi-finished level and the other is at the final assembly schedule (FAS) level.

Scheduled receipts are often displayed in the MRP basic time-phased record. If a quantity is shown then, it represents a placed work or purchase order. The scheduled receipt is based on the order due date. MRP treats all open orders as valid orders, regardless of the due date or remaining order quantity. For example, if the purchase order is for 100 tables, and 99 were received, MRP considers the remaining one table a valid open order. It will utilize this remaining quantity in the gross-to-net calculation to determine net requirements.

MRP CALCULATION PROCESS

Gross requirements represent the total materials needed for an item being planned. For example, requirements for a child's component will come from the higher-level parent planned order release. A *net requirement* states that insufficient inventory exists and the MRP system will generate a planned order receipt to resolve the imbalance.

The MRP *gross-to-net calculation* determines if sufficient inventory exists to meet requirements in a planned time period. It identifies the raw materials, components, and subassemblies that are needed to support a higher level assembly or MPS item requirements. Inventory, consisting of beginning inventory in period one or projected available balance (PAB) inventory beyond period one, is added to scheduled receipts for each time period. This total is then subtracted from gross requirements, allocations, and safety stock to determine whether sufficient inventory exists. It uses assigned planning factors such as lot-sizing, safety stock, and lead time. If the answer is yes and sufficient inventory exists, then the calculation process ends. If the answer is no, then a net requirement is displayed for planner action. MRP performs the same calculation process for each remaining period. These materials are subtracted from the opening inventory balance during the MRP calculation in period one. *Allocations* are materials that are assigned to a work order, but not released (pulled) from the stockroom. Table 14.1 demonstrates the MRP gross-to-net calculation process for part number B (sheet metal box) as shown in the MRP basic time-phased record.

Table 14.1   MRP calculation

Technique	Fixed		Low-level code	1
Order quantity	40		Beginning inventory	35
Safety stock	25		Lead time (weeks)	2

Part number: B (sheet metal box)		Periods				
		1	2	3	4	5
Gross requirements				40		40
Scheduled receipts						
Projected available balance	35	35	35	35	35	25
Net requirements				30		30
Planned order receipt				40		30
Planned order release		40			30	

The MRP gross-to-net calculation example begins with the receipt of MPS period requirements (as previously shown in Table 13.2). In our example, the MPS for part number A is 40 pieces in Period three and Period five. The BOM quantity is one piece, so the MPS quantity is exploded to generate component B (sheet metal box) gross requirements. Part number B requires 40 pieces in Periods three and five and it matches the MPS period requirements.

GROSS-TO-NET CALCULATION

The gross-to-net formula is: (projected on-hand + scheduled receipts) − (allocations + gross requirements + safety stock) = net requirements. The period-by-period calculation is displayed in Table 14.1.

Period one PAB = (beginning inventory of 35 pieces + zero scheduled receipts) − (zero allocations + zero gross requirements + 25 safety stock) = (35 + 0) − (0 + 0 + 25) = 10. The PAB quantity is sufficient to satisfy allocations, gross requirements, and safety stock so a net requirement is not required. The MRP planning function requires no further activity.

Period two PAB = (Period one PAB of 35 pieces + zero scheduled receipts) − (zero allocations + zero gross requirements + 25 safety stock) = (35 + 0) − (0 + 0 + 25) = 10. The PAB quantity is sufficient to satisfy allocations, gross requirements, and safety stock so a net requirement is not required. The MRP planning function requires no further activity.

Period three PAB = (Period two PAB of 35 pieces + zero scheduled receipts) − (zero allocations + 40 gross requirements + 25 safety stock) = (35 + 0) − (0 + 40 + 25) = −30. The PAB quantity is not sufficient to satisfy allocations, gross requirements, and safety stock so a net requirement of 30 (5 + 25) is shown. The net requirement for 30 pieces is increased to 40 pieces to match the displayed order quantity. The MRP system then generates a planned order (receipt) for 40 pieces in Period 3. The lead time is two periods, which offsets the planned order receipt, resulting in the placement of a planned order release for 40 pieces in Period one.

Period four PAB = (Period three PAB of 35 pieces + zero scheduled receipts) − (zero allocations + zero gross requirements + 25 safety stock) = (35 + 0) − (0 + 0 + 25) = 10. The PAB quantity is sufficient to satisfy allocations, gross requirements, and safety stock so a net requirement is not required. The MRP planning function requires no further activity.

Period five PAB = (Period four PAB of 35 pieces + zero scheduled receipts) − (zero allocations + 40 gross requirements + 25 safety stock) = (35 + 0) − (0 + 40 + 25) = −30. The PAB quantity is not sufficient to satisfy allocations, gross requirements, and safety stock so a net requirement of 30 (5 + 25) is shown. The net requirement for 30 pieces is required to be increased to 40 pieces to match the displayed order quantity and stated lead time. However, the supplier can only deliver 30 pieces due to a resource issue. The planner elects to override the system logic with a firm planned order which displays an order quantity of 30 with a one week lead time.

The quantity and order date of *planned orders* are automatically and continually modified by MRP logic until the planner authorizes the release of a work or purchase order. Planned order releases are used by MRP to determine lower level material gross requirements and to project future load. A *firm planned order* means that the due date, release date, or planned order quantity can't be altered by the MRP system. A quantity or lead-time offset that doesn't agree with MRP system logic is a firm planned order.

Table 14.2 is used to demonstrate the MRP calculation process for part number C (cover). This item has a scheduled receipt quantity of 80 in Period two. This item is an LLC one and can be observed by looking at Exhibit 14.2 BOM. The source of its gross requirements is part number A. It requires two covers, which doubles the part A planned order release quantity.

Table 14.2 MRP example part C

Technique	Fixed	Low-level code	2
Order quantity	80	Beginning inventory	170
Safety stock	50	Lead time (weeks)	2

Part number: C (sheet metal cover)		Periods				
		1	2	3	4	5
Gross requirements				80		80
Scheduled receipts			80			
Projected available balance	170	170	250	170	170	90
Net requirements						
Planned order receipt						
Planned order release						

Part number C has sufficient inventory and no further activity is required. Part D is shown in Table 14.3.

Table 14.3 MRP example part D

Technique	Fixed	Low-level code	1
Order quantity	200	Beginning inventory	200
Safety stock	50	Lead time (weeks)	2

Part number: D (screw)		Periods				
		1	2	3	4	5
Gross requirements				80	60	80
Scheduled receipts						
Projected available balance	200	200	200	120	60	180
Net requirements						70
Planned order receipt						200
Planned order release				200		

Part D is also sold as a spare part independent demand, with a requirement of 60 pieces as displayed in Period four. These requirements are combined with the planned order release needed to produce part A. The gross-to-net calculation follows the same calculation steps as previously shown for part B.

Part E, as shown in Table 14.4, is the lowest-level item being planned. This is the raw material needed to produce parts C and D. The planned order releases from these items are combined and are shown as gross requirements. The gross-to-net calculation follows the same calculation steps as previously shown for part B. The MRP process is now complete for part A, and all of its dependent demand parts and components.

Table 14.4 MRP example part E

Technique	Fixed	Low-level code	2
Order quantity	300	Beginning inventory	160
Safety stock	60	Lead time (weeks)	1

Part number: E (cold roll steel (CRS) 14 gauge)		Periods				
		1	2	3	4	5
Gross requirements		80			60	
Scheduled receipts						
Projected available balance	160	80	80	80	320	320
Net requirements					40	
Planned order receipt					300	
Planned order release				300		

Exercise 14.1 will test your knowledge and understanding of the MRP calculation process. The gross requirement for this part is 200 pieces per period. A total of 300 pieces are available. In addition, the company plans to donate an additional 50 pieces to charity in Period four. Perform the MRP calculation for part number A26557 and determine its net requirements, planned order receipts, and planned order releases for each period. The answers to the exercise are available from the Web Added Value™ Download Resource Center at www.jrosspub.com.

Exercise 14.1 MRP calculation

Technique	Fixed	Demand time fence (DTF)	2
Order quantity	600	Planning time fence (PTF)	5
Safety stock	50	Low-level code (LLC)	1
Lead time (weeks)	1	Beginning inventory	300

Part number: A26557 (Final Unit)		Periods					
		1	2	3	4	5	6
Gross requirements							
Scheduled receipts							
Projected available balance							
Net requirements							
Planned order receipt							
Planned order release							

Single-level pegging allows an MRP record to identify the source of its immediate higher level gross requirements. For example, Table 14.2, part C, shows a gross requirement of 80 pieces in Period one. This can be pegged back to the MPS quantity for part A. The requirement of 80 pieces in Period three can be pegged back to part B, which is a component of A. *Multi-level pegging* links a requirement back to its source. Pegging is extremely useful when material shortages exist and the master scheduler needs to establish an MPS order priority. A *where-used* report displays all items where a part is used, whether or not an open MPS or MRP requirement exists.

MRP CHANGES

The MRP calculation process will change upon receipt of new or altered MPS requirements, scheduled receipt quantities, date or lead-time changes, or an adjustment to inventory quantities. These changes impact the MRP calculation logic and a new planned order may have to be generated or an existing one changed. A small MPS lot size, date, or safety stock change can cause significant modifications in planned order release quantities. These types of changes, especially if they are frequent, will cause *system nervousness* and can require internal and external material expediting. System nervousness is when a small change in the MS or a higher level gross requirement causes a major change in required order need dates or quantities. *Expediting* is the process of requesting a supplier or work center to rush raw materials, components, or finished goods in a less-than-normal lead time. It can occur anywhere and at any time within the supply chain. Expediting can also occur due to material shortages, customer rush order requests, and demand variability.

Along with system nervousness, another concern is that MRP considers capacity to be *infinite* (unlimited). This is based on the assumption that manufacturing can achieve a plan regardless of available capacity. MRP expects the planner to either reschedule orders or find a different way to achieve the plan. This logic also applies to purchasing materials. MRP assumes that ordered materials will arrive as planned. It plans materials based on when they're required, rather than when the supplier can deliver. When this cannot happen as expected, components are delivered late, and it results in material shortages and delayed customer order shipments.

DISTRIBUTION PUSH AND PULL SYSTEMS

A *distribution push system* moves inventory to a central supply or to a warehouse, based on forecasted requirements. Inventory is built or purchased in anticipation of receiving customer orders. It gets pushed to a central supply location or to *distribution centers* (DCs), regardless of their need. The advantages of a distribution push system are that shipments to DCs can be synchronized, there is higher factory efficiency, and inventory is available for immediate delivery to customers. A disadvantage of this method is that it inflates inventory levels throughout the supply chain due to poor forecasting and variability in customer demand. A *centralized planning group* is responsible for managing the distribution push system.

The distribution network consists of push and/or pull distribution systems, the central supply, the DCs, and the manufacturing facilities. Disadvantages are that each DC orders materials independently of each other, requested quantities can be inflated because of lot sizing, and the supplying location has limited information on the individual DC's stocking situation. Customers also need to wait for delivery, backlogs can increase, and suppliers and operations can experience rush material requests. A *backlog* consists of all customer orders, including past due, current, and future not-yet-shipped orders.

A *distribution pull system* plans and replenishes inventory upon the receipt of customer orders. Each DC has a *decentralized planning group* that submits replenishment orders to a central supply location or directly to the factory. DCs retain the responsibility for their material ordering and stocking levels. Each DC determines its own order policies, safety stock levels, and calculates its own net requirements and planned orders. Manufacturing resupplies the central supply location or DCs only when requested. Advantages of this system are that inventory levels are kept very low, excess and obsolete inventory can be reduced, there is less need for storage space, and carrying costs are lower.

A *joint replenishment system* consists of a family of similarly planned items that are ready to be released. The item families are released together as if they are one. A joint replenishment system can be used with a distribution push or pull system.

DRP

DRP applies MRP principles and techniques to the distribution processes. It manages the downstream flow of finished goods between the manufacturing facility, central supply, DCs, and the customer. DRP is able to use customer orders, forecasts, DC orders, or central supply orders. The orders are aggregated to determine total demand requirements. DRP permits inventories to be either pushed or pulled. It monitors inventory levels to identify where and when a DC needs additional inventory.

Companies can derive a number of benefits from DRP—including improving customer service, better management of distribution inventory levels, providing a linkage between customers and suppliers, helping to drive inventory and transportation costs down, using less inventory due to improved information flow, and reducing the bullwhip effect.

DRP determines the need for time-phased, planned order receipts by performing a gross-to-net calculation. When the system determines an inventory replenishment need, it generates a planned order. This restores the PAB back to a positive number. As well as MRP, DRP uses time phasing, lead time offsetting, order planning, and safety stock to determine net requirements. An example is shown in Table 14.5.

Table 14.5 DRP calculation process

Technique	Fixed	Low-level code	· 1
Order quantity	40	Beginning inventory	35
Safety stock	10	Lead time (weeks)	1

DC A—part number: 123		Periods				
		1	2	3	4	5
Gross requirements		20	20	20	20	20
Scheduled receipts						
Projected available balance	35	15	35	15	35	15
Net requirements			15		15	
Planned order receipt			40		40	
Planned order release		40		40		

DC A identified its need for two replenishment orders from central supply for part number 123. Planned order releases need to be shipped in Period one for 40 pieces, and a second shipment in Period three for the same quantity in order to satisfy net requirements.

DC B needs to receive two replenishment orders from central supply for part number 123. Planned order releases need to be shipped in Period one for 60 pieces, and a second shipment in Period three for the same quantity as shown in Table 14.6.

Table 14.6 DRP part 123 example for DC B

Technique	Fixed	Low-level code	1
Order quantity	60	Beginning inventory	85
Safety stock	15	Lead time (weeks)	2

DC B—part number: 123		Periods				
		1	2	3	4	5
Gross requirements		35	35	35	25	25
Scheduled receipts						
Projected available balance	85	50	15	40	15	50
Net requirements				35		25
Planned order receipt				60		60
Planned order release		60		60		

DC C needs to receive one replenishment order from central supply for part number 123. A planned order release must be shipped in Period two for 30 pieces to satisfy this request as shown in Table 14.7.

Table 14.7   DRP part 123 example for DC C

Technique	Fixed	Low-level code	1
Order quantity	30	Beginning inventory	60
Safety stock	5	Lead time (weeks)	1

DC C—part number: 123		Periods				
		1	2	3	4	5
Gross requirements		20	20	20	20	5
Scheduled receipts						
Projected available balance	60	40	20	30	10	5
Net requirements				5		
Planned order receipt				30		
Planned order release			30			

In our example, central supply received replenishment orders from the three DCs. These orders are aggregated and processed into central supply as gross requirements. They appear as 100 units in Period one (40 from DC A and 60 from DC B), 30 units in Period two (from DC C), and 100 units in Period three (40 from DC A and 60 from DC B). Central supply has sufficient inventory to cover the planned order receipts in Periods one and two. However, in Period three, insufficient inventory exists due to safety stock requirements. The requirements of all three DCs generate 370 pieces of excess inventory to satisfy safety stock requirements. DRP is planning an order release for 250 pieces for the manufacturing facility in Period two as shown in Table 14.8.

Table 14.8   DRP example central supply

Technique	Fixed	Low-level code	1
Order quantity	250	Beginning inventory	250
Safety stock	25	Lead time (weeks)	1

Central supply part number: 123		Periods				
		1	2	3	4	5
Gross requirements		100	30	100		
Scheduled receipts						
Projected available balance	250	150	120	270	270	270
Net requirements				5		
Planned order receipt				250		
Planned order release			250			

Manufacturing needs to produce part number 123 in a batch of 1,000 pieces due to lot sizing and the need to satisfy safety stock. This inventory buildup is an example of how the bullwhip effect operates. Planned order releases by period (required date) from each DC are passed to the central supply for replenishment. For example, DC A has a planned order release for 40 pieces in Period one, and DC B has a planned order release for 60 pieces in Period one. These two planned orders are aggregated into a gross requirement at the central supply for 100 pieces in Period one. This same process is repeated for every period. The central supply will perform a gross-to-net calculation by period to determine if sufficient inventory exists to supply all DCs. If the answer is yes, then the available inventory is shipped to the requesting DCs. If sufficient inventory doesn't exist for any period, then a net requirement is shown. The net requirement will be converted into a planned order based on the designated order policy as displayed in Table 14.9.

Table 14.9   Factory

Technique	Fixed	Low-level code	1
Order quantity	1,000	Beginning inventory	260
Safety stock	150	Lead time (weeks)	1

Part number: 123		Periods				
		1	**2**	**3**	**4**	**5**
Gross requirements			250			
Scheduled receipts						
Projected available balance	260		1,010	1,010	1,010	1,010
Net requirements			140			
Planned order receipt			1,000			
Planned order release		1,000				

KEY TERMINOLOGY

Understanding key terms and the concepts they represent is crucial to passing the Certified Supply Chain Professional (CSCP) exam. In this chapter, the important terms are identified in Table 14.10.

Table 14.10 MRP and DRP key terminology

Allocation
Backlog
Bill of materials (BOM)
Centralized planning group
Decentralized planning group
Distribution center (DC)
Distribution pull systems
Distribution push systems
Distribution requirements planning (DRP)*
Engineering change
Expediting
Firm planned order
Gross-to-net calculation
Indented bill of material
Infinite
Joint replenishment system*
Low-level code (LLC)
Material requirements planning (MRP)*
Modular bill of material
Multi-level bill of material
Multi-level pegging
Net requirements
Planned order
Planning bill of material
Product structure
Purchase commitment zone
Scheduled receipts
Single-level bill of material
Single-level pegging
System nervousness
Where-used report

*Key term found in the CSCP ECM

CSCP EXAM PRACTICE QUESTIONS ON MRP AND DRP

The questions presented in Table 14.11a cover the concepts presented in this chapter on MRP and DRP. They are examples of what to expect on the actual exam.

Table 14.11a   MRP and DRP practice questions

No.	Questions
1	System nervousness attributed to supply variability can be controlled through the use of all of the following except for: a) Allocation of supply b) Rush order restrictions c) Use of a planning time fence (PTF) d) Infrequent production changes
2	A backlog best represents: a) Future customer orders not shipped b) Unshipped supply orders c) Past due customer orders not shipped d) Past due, current, and future customer orders not shipped
3	A manufacturing company implements a postponement strategy. In which environment can master scheduling best be performed at two different levels? a) Make-to-stock (MTS) b) Make-to-order (MTO) c) Assemble-to-order (ATO) d) Mass customization
4	Material requirements planning (MRP) logic will permit order quantity changes for all of the following except for: a) Scheduled receipt quantity b) Planned order receipt quantity c) Planned order release quantity d) Bill of material effective date or quantity changes

Continued

5	The scheduling process to have components with different lead times arrive simultaneously at a work center is called: a) Pegging b) Planning c) Heijunka d) Offsetting
6	A planner will most likely use which report to identify a gross requirement higher level source? a) Action b) Pegging c) Exception d) Where-used
7	What strategy does a company utilize when distribution is performed based on a fixed schedule? a) Pull b) Push c) Push-pull d) Pull-push
8	Which of these is best associated with a distribution requirements planning (DRP) planned order? a) Freeze order processing b) Scheduled receipt delivery c) Requirements can be changed d) Requirements can't be changed
9	A company replaced an order point system with distribution requirements planning (DRP); however, the planning horizon was set too short. What will the impact be on planning? a) Orders will be placed too late b) Orders will be received too early c) Order quantities will be set too low d) Order quantities will be set too high
10	All of the following are examples of how to use a planning bill except for: a) Planning product options b) Planning an average end item c) Representing a buildable product d) Planning a percentage split between components

ANSWERS TO CSCP EXAM PRACTICE QUESTIONS ON MRP AND DRP

The answers to the practice questions on MRP and DRP are shown in Table 14.11b. Any question you answer incorrectly indicates a gap in your body of knowledge and encourages the need for additional study time.

Table 14.11b Answers to CSCP exam practice questions on MRP and DRP

No.	Answers
1	Answer: C The demand time fence (DTF) controls supply as it restricts change but the planning time fence (PTF) doesn't. Answers A, B, and D are used to minimize change, which reduces system nervousness.
2	Answer: D A backlog includes all unshipped customer orders including past due, current, and future orders not shipped.
3	Answer: C Master scheduling can be performed at a semi-finished and at a final assembly level in the assemble-to-order (ATO) environment. Make-to-order (MTO) and make-to-stock (MTS) performs master scheduling at end items only. Mass customization may or may not be performed at two levels.
4	Answer: A Scheduled receipt orders are outside of the control of the material requirements planning (MRP) system. Only the planner can change the date or quantity on an open work or purchase order.
5	Answer: D This question requires knowledge of the APICS Dictionary definition of *offsetting*. Offsetting determines the difference between a planned order released and planned order receipt lead time to aid in the simultaneous arrival of material.
6	Answer: B This question requires knowledge of the APICS Dictionary definition of *pegging*. Pegging allows material requirements planning (MRP) users to trace an item's gross requirements back to its higher level source.
7	Answer: B A fixed schedule implies that the company is building to a forecast and pushing products to the distribution centers on a fixed schedule.
8	Answer: C Distribution requirements planning (DRP) system logic permits planned order changes to be automatically altered by the system.
9	Answer: A Orders with long lead times won't be planned properly. Insufficient lead time will cause materials to be ordered late—causing material shortages. Answer C may also be correct, but it's a result of placing late orders.
10	Answer: C A planning bill of material (BOM) is an artificial grouping of items in a BOM format. It's not a buildable product.

15

PRODUCTION ACTIVITY CONTROL AND CAPACITY MANAGEMENT

This chapter focuses on production activity control and the three levels of capacity management, along with input/output control, and the various capacity-related calculations to determine if products can be delivered as promised. It examines the execution phase of the manufacturing planning and control hierarchy, load versus capacity, overcoming capacity-related issues, capacity planning, the validation process, and the importance of defining and meeting capacity strategic objectives.

PRODUCTION ACTIVITY CONTROL

Production activity control (PAC) is a short-term activity used to determine the feasibility, control, and tracking of a work center schedule. It begins by reviewing all open and scheduled work orders. A work center load and capacity profile report is developed for every work center and is displayed by period. A scheduler uses this report to review capacity work center requirements against scheduled load to establish a work order priority. The execution of the work order priority is then tracked.

CAPACITY MANAGEMENT

The goal of *capacity management* is to compare resources against scheduled load in an attempt to achieve a balanced capacity plan. This requires *capacity* to be measured, monitored, controlled, and if necessary, adjusted to achieve a plan in a timely and cost-effective manner. *Capacity planning* identifies the overall planning method and the required resources needed to achieve desired business goals and objectives at the strategic, tactical, and operational levels. Decisions made at each level impact production velocity, visibility, competitiveness, and cost. *Capacity control* establishes an *order priority* sequence. This process resolves load imbalances based on work order *input/output* control sequencing. Exhibit 15.1 shows the capacity management hierarchy.

Exhibit 15.1   Capacity management hierarchy

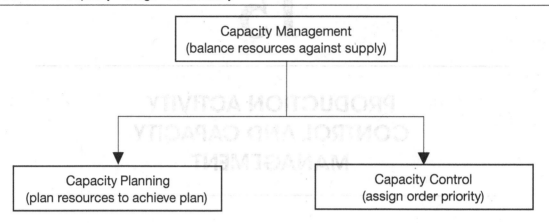

Capacity management attributes are shown in Table 15.1. Capacity management validates the feasibility of capacity plans at all three hierarchy levels. Business, sales and operations planning (S&OP), and master scheduling (MS) are validated by *resource planning* (RP), rough cut capacity planning (RCCP), and capacity requirements planning (CRP).

Table 15.1   Capacity management attributes

Hierarchy Level	Validate Plan	Forecast	Time Frame	Horizon	Unit of Measure
Strategic/ business planning	RP	Market direction	Quarters to years	Three to ten years (investment decisions)	Dollars
S&OP	RP	Product groups and families	Months	Six months to three years (resource projections)	Dollars/units
MS	RCCP	End items and subassemblies	Weeks	One month to two years (longest cumulative lead time)	Units

RP validates the medium- to long-term feasibility of the business, sales and operations plans against strategic goals and objectives, and operational and customer demand requirements. The process provides management with the capacity and load projections needed to determine if adequate resources exist to meet strategic, tactical, and operational plans. If not, capacity or load must be adjusted by increasing or decreasing resource capability. The RP process is shown in Exhibit 15.2.

Exhibit 15.2 RP process

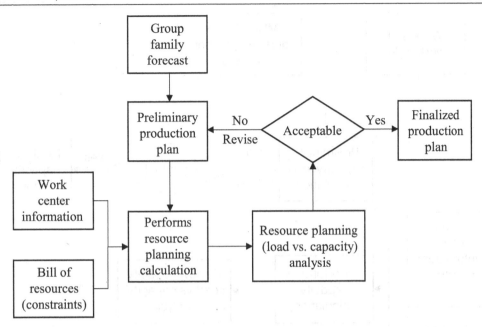

RP is used by upper management to project future capital, equipment, material, or labor resource requirements. The process begins with the strategic or group/family forecasts that create a preliminary business or production plan (PP). These plans are exploded against a bill of resource (BOR) to calculate a resource load for constraint facilities or constraint resources. The available capacity at a work center is calculated based on current labor or equipment. The calculated load is compared against work center available capacity to determine where any resource issues exist. For example, a company assembles computers and its BOR reveals that it takes 16 minutes to assemble a typical unit. The PP requires 400 family units to be produced per period for the entire year. The projected load can be calculated by multiplying 400 family units per period by 16 minutes. This equates to a projected load of 107 hours per period (week). If the work center has three workers, working 37.5 hours each week, it can then be validated that sufficient resources exist to meet this plan. However, if demand increases to 600 units per period in the following year, there is a need for two additional workers. The process is repeated for every item shown on the PP to determine the number of resources needed to achieve the necessary production amount. RP allows management to have sufficient time to properly plan future requirements.

CRP is used to validate material requirements planning (MRP). MRP requirements are then exploded to determine planned period requirements, by item, by period. This data is used to schedule receipts (work or purchase orders) and firm planned orders to project capacity load by period, by work center. Work center load is then compared against available capacity to determine if sufficient capacity exists to achieve the plan. If it doesn't, then additional resources are required or planned, and firm or work orders have to be revised to make sure that the MRP is feasible. The CRP process is shown in Exhibit 15.3.

Exhibit 15.3   CRP process

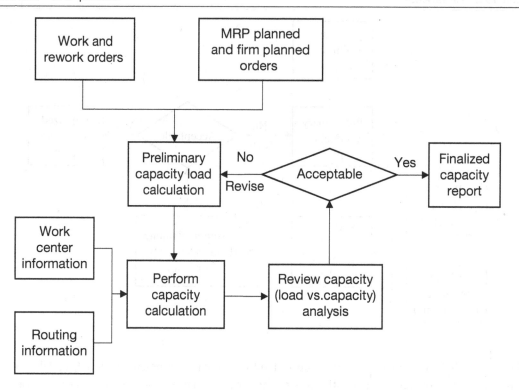

Table 15.2 displays how the horizon time frame and the capacity validation method apply to each capacity planning hierarchy level.

Table 15.2   Capacity validation methods

Horizon Time Frame	Level	Capacity Validation Method
Longer-term	Strategic	RP
Long-term	S&OP	RP
Intermediate (tactical)	MS	RCCP
Short-term (operational)	MRP	CRP
Daily/weekly	Production activity control	Purchase order scheduling Work order scheduling Priority assignment Input/output control

CAPACITY STRATEGIC OBJECTIVES

Capacity decisions are linked to strategic objectives. A company needs to consider anticipated growth, cost of expansion, and ongoing operational costs. These then need to be compared against future demand to determine where and when to use each one of the following four strategic methods to modify capacity.

One-step lead strategy is a very aggressive strategy to expand capacity in anticipation of future customer need. For example, a new warehouse is built to support product growth based on future forecast projections. This strategy reduces the risk of not having sufficient capacity, but it increases short-term operating costs until all capacity can be utilized.

Stepwise lead strategy expands capacity incrementally, which provides a cushion of extra capacity in anticipation of future demand. The company expands capacity in various stages over time in anticipation of a real need. This strategy considers the cost of a stockout to be higher than the cost to maintain excess capacity. *Stepwise lag strategy* delays adding additional capacity until customer demand exceeds current capability. A company utilizes alternative capacity methods such as overtime or subcontractors to satisfy existing customer requirements. This permits the company to lower risk by postponing capital investments. The *stepwise overlapping strategy* is the most conservative and risk-averse approach in which a company moves in a gradual manner to increase capacity. It's a combination of lead, adding capacity in small increments, and lag, delaying adding capacity; for example, a company delays ramping-up its internal capacity through overtime or subcontracting. The company only makes incremental changes to capacity when marketplace conditions can no longer be financially justified using the lag strategy, making it become more efficient to perform the function in-house.

INPUT/OUTPUT CONTROL

The input/output control process can be visualized by picturing a funnel as shown in Exhibit 15.4. It represents how a company manages load or capacity. Imagine pouring water into a funnel, which represents the work order load. If the neck of the funnel, which represents capacity, is too small, then water backs up and lead time gets longer. The more water you pour into the funnel, the more the water backs up, and the longer the lead time becomes. The only way to reduce load is to stop pouring water into the funnel and delay future pouring. This represents holding off adding any new work orders to the work center. A company can also choose to increase the neck of the funnel which represents adding capacity. Table 15.3 compares the various capacity planning types.

Exhibit 15.4   Capacity funnel

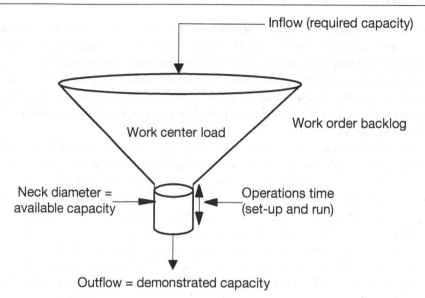

Table 15.3   Capacity planning types

Planning	RP	RCCP	CRP	Input/output control
Time frame	Long	Medium	Short	Immediate
Frequency	Yearly/quarterly/ monthly	Monthly	Weekly/daily	Daily
Horizon	Long	Medium	Short	Immediate
Focus	High-level resources	Bottlenecks/ constraints	All work centers	Work center priority
Validate	Strategic/production plan	Master production schedule	Material requirements planning	Work center/department

A *load profile* is a report that shows past due, current, and future projected load for a number of specified periods for each work center against available capacity. It includes all planned, firm, and scheduled work orders, and it displays *overload* and *underload* periods where analysis may be required. A work center is overloaded when load exceeds capacity and it's underloaded when capacity exceeds load. Load shown in a past due period must be added to the first period—which can cause an overload condition. Overloads are caused when the schedule is *front-loaded*. Front-loading places a heavy work order load in the beginning of the month which overloads work centers.

A load profile report is used to analyze capacity and take corrective action if necessary. Exhibit 15.5 shows an example that indicates that the work center has a past due load of 20 hours. There are 50 hours in Period one and 40 hours in Period two. Period one has a total load of 70 hours (20 + 50) but the work center capacity is only 40 hours. This indicates that the work center has a capacity issue and corrective action must be taken to address the capacity out-of-balance condition. The work center needs to work overtime or work orders need to be scheduled out into the future to resolve the problem.

Exhibit 15.5 Load profile

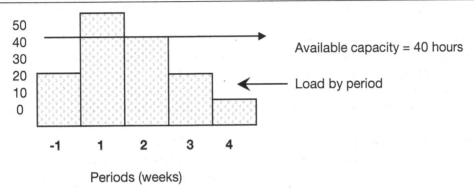

Exhibit 15.6 shows a work center capacity versus load report, which indicates a weekly view of capacity and load as a percentage. A scheduler uses this report to indicate if any overload/underload conditions exist. If they do exist, then corrective action needs to be taken. However, the overload in Period one, or the underload in Period three, cannot be moved in or out without researching how a change will impact other orders or the master schedule.

Exhibit 15.6 Work center capacity versus load report

Work center capacity   = 180 hours

Work center number	1001
Description	Drill
Labor capacity	180 hrs/period
Machine capacity	200 hrs/period

	Periods						
	1	**2**	**3**	**4**	**5**	**6**	**Total**
Released load hours	195	145	160	40	30	70	640
Planned load hours	0	20	40	80	200	30	370
Total load (hours)*	195	165	200	120	230	100	1,010
Available over/under hours**	−15	15	−20	60	−50	80	
Cumulative available hours	−15	0	−20	40	−10	70	
Cumulative available by period percent capacity***	108%	92%	111%	67%	128%	56%	

*Total load (hours) = Released load hours plus planned load hours
**Available over/under hours = work center capacity – total load
***Percent capacity = (total load/work center capacity) * 100

CAPACITY CORRECTIVE ACTION

Building operational flexibility within existing factories permits more efficient and effective operations. The use of a *flexible factory* permits a company to manufacture products demanded by their customers quickly and at a low-cost. A flexible factory is a production facility that manufactures a variety of products on the same production line with very short changeover times. Ford and Honda are good examples of companies using this technique.

There are a number of methods dealing with out-of-balance conditions. A company can increase or decrease capacity, reduce or increase load, or they can rebalance it. They often accomplish this task by moving up or pushing back customer orders from one period to another. This decision can impact efficiency due to setup changes or can create extra work to prepare for the order movement. Margins will suffer because of the extra required labor and discounts may have to be offered to entice the customer to accept an early shipment.

Exercise 15.1 will test your knowledge of how to best take corrective action. Place an X in the column that demonstrates the impact on capacity or load and how to best address the attribute. The answers to the exercise are available from the Web Added Value™ Download Resource Center at www.jrosspub.com.

Exercise 15.1   Capacity attributes

Attribute	Increase capacity	Decrease capacity	Increase load	Decrease load	Redistribute load
Add resources					
Cut lot size in half					
Early work order release					
Eliminate second shift					
Hold orders in planning					
Increase lot size					
Increase the master production schedule (MPS)					
Manufacture previously purchased items					
Reduce the master production schedule (MPS)					
Reduce setup times					
Split orders					
Subcontract work out					

CAPACITY CALCULATION

Available time is the theoretical or maximum amount of available capacity if everything operates as planned. It is calculated by taking the number of days per week, times the number of hours per day, times the number of shifts worked per day, times labor or machine hours. For example, the available time for a work center that operates five days a week for eight hours per shift with two shifts and four machines, can be calculated by taking the five days times eight hours per day, times the two shifts, times four machines, to determine that 320 machine hours are available in the selected week.

Utilization measures scheduled time against actual scheduled hours. A work center plans to operate 37.5 hours, but it actually worked only 30 hours due to a machine malfunction. Utilization is calculated by dividing 37.5 hours into 30 hours times 100% to obtain a utilization factor of 80%. *Efficiency* measures actual output performance against planned output. For example, a work center has a standard to produce 120 units but the workers produced 125 units. Efficiency is calculated by dividing 120 into 125 units times 100% to obtain an efficiency factor of 104.2%. A utilization percentage can never be over 100% but a highly efficient work center can exceed 100%.

Rated capacity is the expected internal output of a work center that can be demonstrated based on actual operational conditions. It's calculated by taking available time multiplied by utilization time's efficiency. For example, we can take the work center available time of 320 hours and multiply it by the utilization percentage of 80%, and then multiply that by the efficiency factor of 104.2%. This will calculate a rated capacity of 256.7 hours.

Demonstrated capacity is based on prior work-order production performance. It provides an average demonstrated production output based on this information. Demonstrated capacity is calculated by adding up standard hours or units for a selected number of periods, then dividing by the selected number of past periods. For example, for the prior four work orders, the output of work center 100 was 130, 135, 129, and 134 units. The demonstrated capacity of the work center can be calculated by adding up the four work orders to obtain 528 units and then dividing by four. The work center demonstrated that, on average, 132 units were produced each week.

KEY TERMINOLOGY

Understanding key terms and the concepts they represent is crucial to passing the Certified Supply Chain Professional (CSCP) exam. In this chapter, the important terms are identified in Table 15.4.

Table 15.4   PAC and capacity management key terminology

Available time
Capacity
Capacity control
Capacity management
Capacity planning
Capacity requirements planning (CRP)
Demonstrated capacity

Continued

Efficiency
Flexible factory
Input/output
Load profile
One-step lead strategy
Order priority
Production activity control (PAC)
Rated capacity
Resource planning (RP)
Rough cut capacity planning (RCCP)
Stepwise lag strategy
Stepwise lead strategy
Stepwise overlapping strategy
Utilization

*Key term found in the CSCP ECM

CSCP EXAM PRACTICE QUESTIONS ON PAC AND CAPACITY MANAGEMENT

The questions shown in Table 15.5a cover the concepts presented in this chapter on PAC and capacity management. They are examples of what to expect on the actual exam.

Table 15.5a   PAC and capacity management practice questions

No.	Questions
1	What is the primary output of rough cut capacity planning (RCCP)? a) Finite schedule b) Load profile report c) Work center leveling report d) Revised planned order schedule
2	The best short-term solution to resolve a capacity underload situation most likely will be to: a) Lay off workers b) Outsource work c) Build up inventory d) Drop a second shift
3	A strategy that expands in various steps to follow demand is best called: a) Stepwise lag strategy b) One-step lead strategy c) Stepwise lead strategy d) Stepwise overlapping strategy
4	A front-loaded schedule represents: a) Customers seeking early deliveries b) A way to avoid the end of month shipping surge c) Overloaded conditions in the beginning of the month d) Underloaded conditions in the beginning of the month

Continued

5	A work center supervisor notices that a machine load is approaching 98%. The supervisor should expect: a) Short queues and short lead times simultaneously b) Long queues and short lead times simultaneously c) Short queues and long lead times simultaneously d) Long queues and long lead times simultaneously
6	The MIP Company has five machines running eight hours per day, for five days per week, staffed by four employees per week. The utilization rate is 90%. What are the available machine hours? a) 144 b) 160 c) 180 d) 200
7	A work center produces 95 standard hours of work in a defined period. The hours available in the work center are 80 hours. The work center actually works 75 hours. What is the utilization percentage? a) 78.9% b) 87.5% c) 93.8% d) 106.7%
8	Work center 200 has a theoretical capacity of 500 units per week for part number 12345. It takes .2 standard hours to produce one unit. In the month of May, they produced the following units: week 35 = 420, week 36 = 450, week 37 = 395, and week 38 = 410 units. Calculate the demonstrated capacity in units for the last three weeks. a) 418.3 units b) 418.8 units c) 421.7 units d) 558.3 units
9	A consumer product company noticed a shift in consumer preferences away from carbonated drinks to noncarbonated drinks and from bottles to cans. These new products are being produced in a limited number of factories, resulting in half of the factories operating at full capacity, and leading to service problems. How should the company best plan in order to prepare to address these capacity problems? a) Eliminate a factory b) Develop a flexible factory c) Outsource some production d) Add manufacturing capacity
10	Which of the following best describes the resource planning (RP) process? a) Calculates detailed load b) Evaluates the consensus plan c) Evaluates the production plan (PP) d) Evaluates the master production schedule (MPS)
11	A company decides to move up customer orders from May to the last week in April. This decision will most likely cause the following problems except for: a) Lower margins b) Improved efficiency c) Month-end capacity crunch d) Discounts may be promised
12	If demand increases significantly, which of these manufacturing objectives would suffer most when production levels are held constant? a) Efficient plant operation b) Maximum customer service c) Minimum inventory investment d) Maximum inventory investment

ANSWERS TO CSCP EXAM PRACTICE QUESTIONS ON PAC AND CAPACITY MANAGEMENT

The answers to the practice questions on PAC and capacity management are shown in Table 15.5b. Any question you answer incorrectly indicates a gap in your body of knowledge and encourages the need for additional study time.

Table 15.5b Answers to CSCP exam practice questions on PAC and capacity management

No.	Answers
1	Answer: B A load profile is a graphic comparison of each work center load by period against capacity. This is the primary output of rough cut capacity planning (RCCP). A finite schedule, work center load report, and revised planned order schedule are more detailed and are the output of material requirements planning (MRP).
2	Answer: C The key word is *short-term*. The company needs to find additional work to resolve the underload condition. A planned buildup of inventory will increase load in the short term. Answers A, B, and D aren't short-term solutions, but rather longer term solutions.
3	Answer: A This question is describing the stepwise lag strategy. This method changes capacity to catch up with demand. It takes small steps to increase capacity after identifying the need (lag).
4	Answer: C A front-loaded schedule places a heavy load in the beginning of the month, which overloads work centers.
5	Answer: D The more load there is in a work center, the longer the queue. This means there will be longer lead times.
6	Answer: D The formula used to determine available capacity is the number of machines (or labor) times the number of hours times the number of days. The calculation is (five machines * eight hours * five days) = 200 machine hours per week.
7	Answer: C The formula used to calculate utilization is standard hours of work performed (or pieces) divided by hours available (or pieces) times 100%. The answer is then calculated as: (75 ÷ 80) * 100% = 93.75%.
8	Answer: A Demonstrated capacity is using the last three periods. The weekly production is displayed in units, so a unit calculation isn't necessary. Simply total up the last three lots and divide the total by three (410 + 395 + 450 = 1255 ÷ 3) to obtain 418.3 units. Capacity information is a distractor.
9	Answer: B Building flexibility within existing facilities allows for a more efficient and effective operation. This will permit all of a company's factories to manufacture all of their products.
10	Answer: C Resource planning (RP) is used to evaluate the business and production plan.
11	Answer: B Efficiency can suffer due to setup changes and extra work to prepare for the order movement. Margins will suffer because of the extra required labor. Discounts may have to be offered to entice the customer to accept an early shipment.
12	Answer: B If demand increases significantly, customer service will suffer the most if production levels are held constant. While demand has increased, supply hasn't, which means that materials won't be available to meet customer order requirements.

16

CONTINUOUS PROCESS IMPROVEMENT

This chapter focuses on waste reduction, which leads to improved velocity and visibility while reducing process and supply chain inefficiencies and costs. It examines a number of methodologies and tools that are used in this process.

CONTINUOUS PROCESS IMPROVEMENT CONCEPTS

Continuous process improvement (CPI) is a never-ending effort used to expose and eliminate root causes of problems and is a central theme found among the various improvement philosophies. These philosophies include lean, just-in-time (JIT), Six Sigma, Theory of Constraints (TOC), total quality management (TQM), and total productive maintenance (TPM). CPI states that companies should take small steps as opposed to big ones. It focuses on identifying and eliminating forms of waste including overproduction, overprocessing, unnecessary transportation, inventory, motion, waiting, defects, and unused people skills (talent). CPI does this by first performing *process analysis* of the business operation, activities, and tasks to determine their productivity and efficiency. They also look for non-value functions which can be eliminated. CPI believes that change is a friend that needs to be embraced by all company employees. It should start at the top, but be implemented from the bottom.

LEAN

Lean objectives strive to do more and more with less and less. They work to reduce cost, inventory, and lead time while improving quality, focusing on products and their value stream, and promoting value through waste elimination. Lean accomplishes all of this by using five core principles.

The first lean principle is identifying all *value-added* and *non-value activities* across the value stream itself. The second principle is eliminating non-value activities, which are defined and perceived by the customer. The third principle is *pull*, which starts with the customer order initiating material and product flow across the value stream and ends with the production and delivery of the customer's requested material or service. The fourth principle is *value flow*, which moves production, one item at a time, so the process flows steadily across all value chain activities. The final lean principle is striving for *perfection* to continuously reduce all non-value activities from the value stream.

Companies need to be aware that when lean is first implemented, profits appear lower. This is because the factory's utilization goes down as existing inventory is consumed. Overhead absorption is required which temporarily causes a higher cost of goods sold (COGS).

JUST-IN-TIME PHILOSOPHY

JIT is a manufacturing philosophy that aims to continuously reduce or eliminate all forms of waste. *Waste* is anything that doesn't add value to a product, process, or service from a customer's point of view. It can also be a process by-product. An example is a chemical residue that must be processed for disposal. The *Toyota Production System* (TPS), lean manufacturing, and the JIT philosophy have all identified seven forms of waste—process, excess inventory, movement, waiting time delays, overproduction, motion, and process defects. These concepts apply to manufacturing and service environments and encompass all activities from design to delivery (and beyond) as part of a continuous improvement effort. JIT's main components are takt time, one-piece flow, and the use of a pull system. *One-piece flow* refers to moving one component at a time between operations within a work area. Each item is pulled only when requested.

TOYOTA PRODUCTION SYSTEM

The TPS and the *House of Toyota* are both part of an integrated, customer-oriented philosophy developed by Toyota that comprises its management philosophy and practices. It focuses on eliminating all forms of waste through employee participation as shown in the House of Toyota which consists of three pillars— just-in-time, jidoka, and culture of continuous improvement. The three pillars lay on a foundation called operational stability and have a roof that locks the pillars together in an attempt to eliminate waste.

Jidoka is a Japanese term that means automation with *human* touch or intelligence. It's often associated with an andon device, such as a flashing red light. This alerts an operator of a problem upon detecting an abnormal condition and stops the line until the problem is resolved. *Autonomation* is a process or system that is used to detect abnormal conditions in the production process, and it sends a signal to stop the machine.

5S is used to develop and organize a lean business work area through the implementation of standards and disciplines. Its goal is to create a clean, organized, efficient, and safe work environment while enhancing productivity using visual management techniques and standard work activity processes. This effort sends a strong and visual message of improvement to the workforce. The five components of 5S are:

- *Seiri*—sort out, separate, and organize
- *Seiton*—straighten and become orderly
- *Seiso*—clean and shine
- *Seiketsu*—revisit and standardize the first three S's
- *Shitsuke*—sustain and maintain the standards, discipline, and work to continuously improve the process

Level production, also know as *heijunka* or *production smoothing*, means leveling the work flow. It begins by putting together and sequencing work order progression. The process focuses on removing *mura* (unevenness) and *muri* (overburdening). Its goal is to produce small production batches at a constant and predictable rate that match customer demand (takt time).

Takt time is the drumbeat that synchronizes the production flow rate to meet customer demand. It's calculated by taking net available time to work and dividing it by customer demand. For example, a company has net available time to work of 480 minutes per day (one eight hour shift times 60 minutes) and a customer order entry rate of 48 orders per day. Divide net available time by customer demand to obtain a takt time of ten minutes per item (480 minutes ÷ 48 customer orders). A unit is then scheduled to be produced every ten minutes. If the order entry rate increases to 50 units the following day, then the takt rate changes to produce a unit every 9.6 minutes. The production line either speeds up or slows down to match the order entry rate.

Exercise 16.1 will test your knowledge and understanding of takt time. Read the question and perform the calculation. The answers to the exercise are available from the Web Added Value™ Download Resource Center at www.jrosspub.com.

Exercise 16.1 Takt time calculation

A car company works five days a week, two shifts per day, and eight hours per shift. Demand is 240 cars per day. Calculate the takt time per day.

Kaizen is a Japanese term for continuous improvement, and it requires complete employee involvement and participation at all levels. In kaizen, a process is taken apart, the quality or process inefficiencies are identified along with improvement ideas, and then the ideas are implemented. A *kaizen event* is when a group of individuals are assigned to examine a process, identify quality concerns or process inefficiencies, and come up with improvement ideas. Those ideas are quickly implemented. A *kaizen blitz* is an overpowering, short-term rapid improvement effort to identify and remove waste from a particular process. It's performed by a team of people with the right skill set to quickly take a process apart, and then restructure it to make it better. *Mistake-proofing*, also known as *poka-yoke* or a *fail-safe mechanism*, is designing a process that performs 100% product validation in support of jidoka. This prevents an error from occurring rather than performing a manual inspection (detection) after the fact. For example, a bottling line can have a light sensor to monitor its liquid fill line compliance. A bottle that fails to comply will be *booted* off the line, and if two bottles in a row fail, the line stops until corrective action is taken.

Operation stability is the capability to produce consistent results over time in production methods and tasks, equipment, workplace organization, and output of work. It uses heijunka, standard work, TPM, and kaizen to reduce process instability by focusing on the removal of operational variability.

A *pull system* uses customer or work orders to initiate product flow across the value stream. The activity doesn't initiate until a *demand pull* request is received from a downstream operation or customer. It uses a *visual system*, such as a kanban signaling device—for example, an empty square on the floor or a flashing light to signal the start of a work request. A *kanban* is a request to either issue or produce a standard container with a predefined quantity.

Standard work consists of takt time, standard work sequencing, and standard in-process inventory. It's used to measure operational performance and continuously improve the *flow*. *Standard in-process inventory* includes raw materials, components, and partially built units located in the work area that are required to keep the operation running smoothly. *Standard work sequence* is the operation sequence in which an operator performs functions in a balanced and efficient manner. Each operational step is broken down into sequenced steps, timed, and repeated in the same way.

SIX SIGMA, DMAIC, AND DMADV

Six Sigma is a methodology that strives to improve business processes and quality by reducing process variations (defects). A *defect* is anything that doesn't conform to a customer-defined quality attribute or level of expectation. A *defect opportunity* is anything that impacts the quality of a product or service. For example, entering a customer order can have multiple defect opportunities including product pricing, quantity, required date, and ship to address. This means that four defect opportunities exist, one for each activity. Six Sigma accomplishes this by using statistical tools and techniques to improve performance. It strives for *zero defects* with a stated goal of tolerating 3.4 defects per million. *Statistical process control* (SPC) is a quality control tool that uses statistical methods for material sampling to monitor and control a process. The *define, measure, analyze, improve, and control* (DMAIC) process is a Six Sigma, continuous improvement, problem-solving approach that focuses on improving existing processes. It consists of five phases:

1. **Define** a problem
2. **Measure** problem causes and benchmark against competition
3. **Analyze** information to gauge processes and identify root causes
4. **Improve** processes by implementing upgrades
5. **Control** key process variables to maintain consistency and monitor progress

The *define, measure, analyze, design,* and *verify* (DMADV) process is used to guide the creation of new processes to determine if Six Sigma quality has been achieved. It consists of five phases:

1. **Define** goals and customer deliverables
2. **Measure** customer needs and specifications
3. **Analyze** the process to determine if it meets customer needs
4. **Design** the process to meet customer needs
5. **Verify** if the design meets customer needs

TOC

TOC is a methodology that believes that processes are inherently simple but contain at least one constraint (weak link) that limits it from maximizing its output. An improvement to any process before or after this constraint has no value, as throughput won't be improved. TOC stresses that the organizational focus must solely be on improving the constraint. In order to achieve this, it uses a continuous improvement program to enhance throughput and profitability by focusing on five repeatable steps. They are: identify the constraint, exploit the constraint, subordinate other processes to the constraint, elevate the constraint, and repeat the cycle. *Drum, buffer, rope* (DBR) is also part of TOC. The drum is the physical constraint of the work center that limits the work pace. The buffer is a stockpile of inventory that is used to protect the drum from interruption so that material can always flow. The rope is the order release mechanism that pulls material based on the speed of the constraint.

TQM

TQM is a comprehensive and structured approach that improves quality through continuous customer feedback. This approach is driven by top management's commitment with total employee involvement. It's considered a strategic initiative that focuses on managing process-centered, integrated systems with two-way communications. TQM divides all customer-focused activities into four sequential categories (plan-do-check-act) as part of its continuous improvement initiative. It looks at quality from a customer-focused point of view, with an internal focus on achieving long-term customer satisfaction.

TPM

TPM is a maintenance philosophy requiring the participation of the entire work force as part of a company-wide initiative to monitor and maintain operating equipment. Its goal is to reduce downtime and maximize overall equipment effectiveness, reliability, productivity, flexibility, and maintainability, by having operators assume equipment ownership. Equipment operators are responsible for performing routine maintenance which permits designated maintenance personnel to perform the more complicated setups and handle equipment repairs.

IMPROVEMENT TOOLS

The *seven basic tools* are a toolkit used for process improvement, and they easily help solve process and quality-related issues.

The use of a *process map* is the first step a company needs to undertake in order to improve a process. A diagram is drawn to display the flow of process activities and tasks and is shown as a series of boxes connected by arrows. The diagram is first used to illustrate the current *as-is* flow, which documents process discrepancies and variability patterns. It's then used to analyze the process that leads to the development of a conceptual process *to-be* improvement model.

A *control chart* is a visual tool that displays plotted process value changes (variability) over time. It displays the differences between target and actual performance values. The chart has a center line to show the target value, an upper line to show the *upper control limit* (UCL), and a lower line to show the *lower control limit* (LCL). When plotted values fall between the UCL and LCL, the process is considered to be stable or under control. If they fall outside the limits, the process is considered to be unstable or out of control.

A *cause and effect diagram*, also known as a *fishbone* or *Ishikawa diagram*, is a visualization, pictorial, and brainstorming tool used to identify, sort, and display problem causes. It shows the relationship between the factors causing the problem and the effects they create by drilling down to determine its root cause.

A *check sheet* is a simple form used to record data occurrences in a format that facilitates collection and analysis. Columns and rows are labeled with classification criteria such as types of occurrences, variability, speed, or error types. A check mark is entered in the designated columns based on what is needed to be analyzed. The check sheet provides a quick and simple visual overview of problem areas based on the number of check marks. A check sheet is the starting point that allows data to be further explored using the other CPI tools.

A *scatter diagram*, also called an X-Y graph or a scatter plot, displays a relationship between two different data variable occurrences as a two-dimensional graph. One set of data is shown on the X horizontal axis and another set of data on the Y vertical axis. Each data point is plotted to determine its relationship strength and whether a correlation exists between displayed variables.

A *histogram* shows the distribution frequency of collected data variables. It displays the activity in a bar chart but doesn't take into account changes over time. A histogram has a greater visual impact for displaying information than a check sheet.

A *Pareto chart* is a type of a histogram that displays data frequency by groups in a bar format. The bars help to prioritize the relative importance of each group. The longest bar symbolizes the most significant group, and the shortest bar, the least significant. A Pareto chart is used to identify which groups require immediate review and possible corrective action.

SEVEN NEW TOOLS

The *seven new tools* (N7) are an additional set of tools used to help promote innovation, complete project tasks, aid in the dissemination and exchange of project information, and reduce project failures.

Tree diagrams are used when the need exists to organize, visualize, and delineate tasks and activities in event sequence. They start with displaying the discrepancy, and then break it apart into specific and finer details. Those details are branched off and then further broken down into more detailed branches. The discrepancy can be easily analyzed in picture form as a whole or in individual parts that help to meet a specific goal.

A *matrix diagram* is a graphical tool used to compare and rank groups of information. It's made up of rows and columns that graphically help to organize data. The matrix diagram displays the relationship between data sets and shows strengths. It permits users to methodically identify, analyze, and evaluate the relationship within entered data found in the matrix.

A *matrix data analysis chart* (MDAC) arranges multiple groups of related data that contain large amounts of information. The chart is structured to analyze data to determine where, and if, a common relationship exists within a larger group. The results are displayed in a visual format that allows for easy comprehension. An MDAC is similar to the matrix diagram, but it displays information in greater detail.

An *affinity diagram* is a visual tool designed to help organize large amounts of dissimilar and unstructured information that is generated during a problem-focused team brainstorming session. The team makes note of ideas, issues, and observations which are then written on sticky notes and randomly posted on the wall. The next step is the creation of affinity cards (headers) with brief statements. The ideas are then grouped under each affinity header that applies to them, and once completed, they are used to help find a solution to the stated problem.

A *relationship diagram* is a graphical interrelationship picture used to explain a complex situation along with its causes and effects. It looks at various factors that lead to decisions derived from multiple data entities and displays its findings from a top-down viewpoint. The process begins with a written problem statement that is placed at the top of a white board. The team brainstorms the issue and uses sticky notes to describe problem causes. They place the notes that are directly related to the problem statement on the white board beneath the statement. They then subsequently place additional sticky notes under those since they are a contributing factor. The team later draws arrows to connect the various sticky notes to indicate whether it's a cause or influencing factor. The arrow will go from one sticky note to the problem statement if it's a root cause. The arrow will go from one sticky note to another one, if it's an influencing factor. The process is repeated until all sticky notes are posted and all arrows are drawn—revealing the relationship diagram.

An *activity network diagram* displays project activities, tasks, and the interdependencies between activities and tasks. The diagram uses arrows and boxes (nodes) to display predecessor and successor relationships along with known and projected time estimates for each activity. This permits for the calculation of start and end dates along with a developed *critical path*. A critical path is the sequence that best identifies the shortest project completion time frame.

A *process decision program chart* (PDPC) provides a systematic means of anticipating errors. It displays plan activities as they are being created to identify optimum project solutions. A PDPC maps out possible positive or negative alternative path outcomes for each planned activity so that preventive or countermeasures can be developed. This allows problems to be avoided or a contingency plan to be put into place should an error occur.

COST OF QUALITY

Cost of quality impacts the COGS, profits, and customer service. It's associated with products or services that don't conform to customer specifications. These include prevention and appraisal costs as well as internal and external failure costs.

Prevention costs are the costs incurred in avoiding poor quality in the production of products or delivering of a service that doesn't conform to specifications. A few examples of this are education and team training on quality techniques and the implementation of an operator SPC program to minimize process variability. *Appraisal costs* are the costs incurred in detecting anything that doesn't conform to specifications. A few examples of this are inspection or test equipment costs.

Internal failure costs are costs incurred by a nonconforming product that are detected before it's shipped to customers—for example, a soda bottle that requires rework to replace an upside-down label.

External failure costs are costs incurred by a nonconforming product that are detected after it's shipped to customers—for example, a recall of an automobile for defective air bags.

Exercise 16.2 will test your knowledge and understanding of the various quality type costs. Read each question and write in all answers that best apply. The answers to the exercise are available from the Web Added Value™ Download Resource Center at www.jrosspub.com.

Exercise 16.2   Understanding quality type costs

Question	Answer
1. A customer product recall is what type of quality type cost?	
2. A line defect is what type of quality type cost?	
3. A poka-yoke device is what type of quality type cost?	
4. A visual product inspection is what type of quality type cost?	
5. The salary of a quality control inspector is what type of quality type cost?	
6. Which quality type cost is always the overall lowest cost?	
7. Which quality type cost is the highest overall cost?	

KEY TERMINOLOGY

Understanding key terms and the concepts they represent is crucial to passing the Certified Supply Chain Professional (CSCP) exam. In this chapter, the following important terms are identified in Table 16.1.

Table 16.1   CPI key terminology

5S
Activity network diagram
Affinity diagram
Appraisal costs
Autonomation
Cause and effect diagram
Check sheet
Continuous process improvement (CPI)
Control chart
Cost of quality*
Critical path
Defect
Defect opportunity
Define, measure, analyze, design, verify (DMADV) process
Define, measure, analyze, improve, control (DMAIC)* process

Continued

Demand pull*
Drum, buffer, rope (DBR)
External failure costs
Fail-safe mechanism
Fishbone
Flow
Heijunka
Histogram
House of Toyota
Jidoka
Just-in-time (JIT)
Kaizen*
Kaizen blitz
Kaizen event*
Kanban*
Lean
Level production
Lower control limit (LCL)
Matrix data analysis chart
Mura
One-piece flow
Pareto chart
Perfection
Plan–do–check–act (PDCA)*
Poka-yoke
Prevention costs
Process analysis
Process decision program chart (PDPC)
Process map
Production smoothing
Pull
Pull system*
Relationship diagram
Scatter diagram
Seiketsu
Seiri
Seiso
Seiton
Seven basic tools (B7)

Continued

Seven new tools (N7)
Shitsuke
Six Sigma
Standard in-process inventory
Standard work
Standard work sequence
Statistical process control (SPC)
Takt time
Theory of constraints (TOC)
Total productive maintenance (TPM)
Total quality management (TQM)
Toyota production system (TPS)
Tree diagram
Upper control limit (UCL)
Value activities
Value flow
Value-added*
Visual signal
Waste*
Zero defects

*Key term found in the CSCP ECM

CSCP EXAM PRACTICE QUESTIONS ON CPI

The questions shown in Table 16.2a cover the concepts presented in this chapter on CPI. They are examples of what to expect on the actual exam.

Table 16.2a   CPI practice questions

No.	Questions
1	Which of the following relates to pull concepts? a) Demand on central supply centers determined by the branch warehouses b) Demand on supply center driven by material requirements planning (MRP) signals c) Distribution quantities determined by the central supply center d) Workers are empowered to pull the trigger to stop production
2	A company using demand pull is best: a) Avoiding a channel conflict b) Waiting for a customer order to begin production c) Waiting for a pull signal to begin production d) Waiting for a push signal to begin production

Continued

3	Which of the following is a signal device used to withdraw parts in a pull system? a) Kaizen b) Kanban c) Kaizen blitz d) Shop order pick list
4	What system assumes that the delivery frequency will provide a steady material flow while minimizing the need for buffer stock? a) Push b) Kanban c) Material requirements planning (MRP) d) Distribution requirements planning (DRP)
5	Which of the following isn't a pillar in the House of Toyota? a) Jidoka b) Just-in-Time (JIT) c) Operational stability d) Culture of continuous improvement
6	What typically occurs to the financials when lean is first implemented? a) Profits appear lower b) Profits appear higher c) Cash flow deteriorates d) Work center efficiency improves
7	What is best used to convert customer demand to a production rate? a) Lead time b) Takt time c) Cycle time d) Throughput time
8	A company produces electrical boxes. The plant operates 240 days a year and produces 57,600 units per year. It operates two eight-hour shifts per day. Demonstrated capacity on work center 100 is 900 minutes per day. The work center performs 30 minutes of preventative maintenance at the end of each shift. Calculate the takt time in seconds. a) 217.5 seconds b) 225.0 seconds c) 240.0 seconds d) 245.0 seconds
9	Automation with a human touch is best described by the term: a) Jidoka b) Keiretsu c) Heijunka d) Maquiladora
10	Poka-yoke is a tool used to best support: a) Jidoka b) Kaizen c) Heijunka d) Optimization
11	The ability to automatically stop the production line in the event of a problem is best described by the term: a) Mura b) Heijunka c) Poka-yoke d) Autonomation

Continued

12	Workers in a production cell initiate a short-term process improvement effort in their machine shop. This effort is best described by the term: a) Kaizen b) 5S c) Kaizen blitz d) Lean kaizen
13	Which of the following would most likely impede a lean organization? a) Mura b) Heijunka c) Tolerances d) Standardization
14	Which statement best describes Six Sigma: a) Increased productivity and profitability b) Enhanced process variability c) Detecting and correcting defects d) Specific methods to prevent defects from occurring
15	You have been assigned to a Six Sigma team investigating a process problem. You have implemented a number of process countermeasures to prevent a problem from recurring. What DMAIC step are you using? a) Do b) Control c) Monitor d) Improve
16	A non-constraint work center has to operate at less than full speed in the Theory of Constraints. This is an example of what step? a) Exploit the constraint b) Elevate the constraint c) Identify the constraint d) Subordinate a non-constraint
17	A drill department has limited capacity to meet master schedule load projections. The load imbalance can best be described in the Theory of Constraints as a: a) Buffer b) Constraint c) Pull signal d) Underload
18	Which of the following isn't one of the seven basic tools of quality? a) Process map b) Scatter chart c) Affinity diagram d) Cause-and-effect diagram
19	What is the first order of business that a company needs to undertake to improve a process? a) Create a process map b) Create a business map c) Create a process model d) Identify the value stream
20	The application of statistical methods to monitor and adjust an operation is best called: a) Statistical control b) Statistical thinking c) Statistical quality control d) Statistical process control (SPC)

Continued

21	What is the next step after using a process map to completely describe a process? a) Create a histogram b) Track process errors c) Initiate a kaizen blitz d) Identify variability patterns
22	A cause and effect diagram is best used to: a) Find the effect b) Find the problem c) Find the root cause of the problem d) Bring a process into conformance with the Six Sigma limit
23	A company is trying to determine the number of warehouses it requires to meet customer service objectives. It's reviewing all possible tasks and activities during its analysis. What tool might management use to help identify the best option? a) Matrix chart b) Tree diagram c) Arrow diagram d) Process decision program chart (PDPC)
24	What tool is used to show alternate paths to achieve a given goal? a) Tree diagram b) Arrow diagram c) Interrelationship diagram d) Process decision program chart (PDPC)
25	Total quality management (TQM) is: a) Focused on cost reduction b) Another name for just-in-time (JIT) c) Focused on resolving customer issues d) Focused on customer satisfaction
26	The MIP Company is interested in improving its operations. What is the initial step it should use in its supply chain continuous process improvement (CPI) effort? a) Process analysis b) Process benchmarking c) Creating a value stream map d) Establishing a total quality management team
27	A company should focus a supply chain improvement effort on which poor quality cost: a) Appraisal costs b) Prevention costs c) Internal failure costs d) External failure costs
28	Once a manufacturing error is detected, control charts track: a) Cost b) Cause c) Variability d) Root cause
29	Which strategy is the least desirable for a company focusing on lean manufacturing? a) Shitsuke b) Insourcing c) Low inventory levels d) Employee involvement

Continued

30	Which of the following applications doesn't support the sales and marketing area? a) Takt time b) Jidoka management c) Customer history tracking d) Field sales communications
31	Which of the following techniques wouldn't directly improve velocity? a) Lean b) Six Sigma c) Theory of Constraints (TOC) d) Total quality management (TQM)

ANSWERS TO CSCP EXAM PRACTICE QUESTIONS ON CPI

The answers to the practice questions on CPI are shown in Table 16.2b. Any question you answer incorrectly indicates a gap in your body of knowledge and encourages the need for additional study time.

Table 16.2b Answers to CSCP exam practice questions on CPI

No.	Answers
1	Answer: A The pull concept requires a downstream location to request materials. The downstream branch warehouse is asking the central supply location for materials. This request is a pull signal.
2	Answer: C Demand pull uses a visual (pull) signal to begin production. A customer order is also partially correct as it's a form of a pull signal, but it goes into answer C.
3	Answer: B A kanban is a signal device such as a returnable container. The empty container itself is a signal that materials need to be withdrawn from a sending location and delivered to the requesting location.
4	Answer: B A kanban signals the need for more parts to be received just-in-time (JIT) which minimizes the need for safety stock. Material requirements planning (MRP), distribution requirements planning (DRP), and push systems all use safety stock.
5	Answer: C The House of Toyota consists of three pillars—just-in-time, jidoka, and a culture of continuous improvement. The three pillars lay on a foundation called operational stability.
6	Answer: A Profits appear lower because the factory's utilization goes down as it uses up existing inventory. This reduces overhead absorption which temporarily causes higher cost of goods sold (COGS).
7	Answer: B The best way is to use takt time, which sets the pace of production to match the rate of customer demand. Answers A, C, and D are forms of lead time.
8	Answer: C The takt time formula is available production time divided by customer demand (900 minutes ÷ 240 units per day) = (3.75 minutes * 60 seconds = 225 seconds). Preventative maintenance has already been included in demonstrated capacity.

Continued

9	Answer: A
	Automation with a human touch is the Japanese translation of Jidoka.
10	Answer: A
	Jidoka means automation with a human touch which facilitates line stoppage. This prevents mistakes from happening. Poka-yoke means mistake proofing.
11	Answer: D
	This question requires knowledge of the APICS Dictionary definition of *autonomation*. Autonomation detects abnormal conditions in the production process and sends a signal to stop the machine.
12	Answer: C
	The key to this answer is *short-term*, which refers to a kaizen blitz effort. Kaizen is a continuous effort and lean kaizen is a made-up term. 5S is a tool used in the improvement effort.
13	Answer: A
	A lean organization is impeded by process unevenness, irregularity, and variability. This describes mura. Tolerances by themselves don't impede anything. It's only when they're not achieved and it results in process variability is lean impacted. Heijunka is used to level the workload and help improve the manufacturing process. Standardization helps to make the manufacturing process more efficient.
14	Answer: D
	The goal of Six Sigma is to reduce variability which prevents defects from occurring.
15	Answer: D
	DMAIC stands for define, measure, analyze, improve, and control. Implementation is part of the improvement process.
16	Answer: D
	In the Theory of Constraints, a non-constraint work center operates at less than full speed because it's limited by the constraint work center.
17	Answer: B
	In the Theory of Constraints, a load imbalance is called a constraint.
18	Answer: C
	The affinity diagram is one of the seven new management and planning tools.
19	Answer: A
	The first step is to document the process by creating a process map to understand what needs to be improved. Answers B, C, and D follow later.
20	Answer: D
	This question requires knowledge of the APICS Dictionary definition of *statistical process control* (SPC). SPC uses material sampling to monitor and adjust an operation.
21	Answer: D
	A process map displays a picture of process activities and tasks. It's used to first identify process discrepancies and variability patterns within a process. Once identified, the process can begin to be improved.
22	Answer: C
	A cause and effect diagram is a visualization pictorial tool used to identify a problem and then drill down to determine its root cause.
23	Answer: B
	A tree diagram delineates tasks and activities and increases finer details in order to meet a specific goal. The process decision program chart is partially correct, but it's used to identify what might go wrong, not to meet an objective.
24	Answer: D
	This question requires knowledge of the APICS Dictionary definition of a *process decision program chart*. This chart displays what might go wrong and show alternate paths to resolve the problem.

Continued

25	Answer: D
	This question requires knowledge of the APICS Dictionary definition of *total quality management* (TQM). TQM is a management approach to long-term success through customer satisfaction.
26	Answer: A
	It needs to begin by taking a hard look at its supply chain processes before doing anything else.
27	Answer: B
	The goal of any company is to prevent a problem from occurring in the first place. Answers A, C, and D incur costs that can be prevented if the supply chain stops the issue from ever happening.
28	Answer: C
	A control chart provides a visual method for tracking process variability (variances) in a product's performance.
29	Answer: C
	Low inventory strategy can lead to the disaster of inventory not being available to meet customer demand. Shitsuke means sustain in 5S. Insourcing is using internal resources to provide goods.
30	Answer: B
	Jidoka means automation with a human touch and is a pillar in the House of Toyota. It's used in the manufacturing area, not in the sales and marketing area.
31	Answer: D
	The key word in this question is *directly* and you must have an understanding of the word *velocity* (speed). Total quality management (TQM) is an integrative philosophy for continuously improving the quality of products. It doesn't directly impact speed, while answers A, B, and C have a direct impact.

17

SUPPLIER RELATIONSHIP MANAGEMENT AND PURCHASING

This chapter focuses on supplier relationship management (SRM) and purchasing. It explores landed and total ownership costs, how to perform a make-versus-buy cost analysis, and the differences between offshoring, insourcing, and outsourcing. It examines the purchasing process and the required functional steps to obtain a product or service while also examining the seven purchasing process steps, the different types of purchase orders, supplier certifications, supplier scorecards, and supplier colocations. It also explores buyer-supplier relationship types, traditional-versus-strategic sourcing, single-versus-sole sourcing, supplier selection strategies, negotiations, developing and implementing SRM strategies, alliance development steps, portals, trade exchanges, auctions, and how to measure supplier performance.

SRM STRATEGY

The purpose of an SRM strategy is to support a company's strategic, operational, and financial goals. These goals assist in the ordering of products and services, the interaction between suppliers and customers, and they improve communications to better the organization's overall performance. SRM tracks and monitors supplier performance capabilities against agreed-upon requirements. It assists a company in managing costs, risks, negotiations, contract development, purchasing, communications, collaboration, and order delivery. SRM improves interaction and feedback throughout the purchasing and delivery cycle. Customer relationship management (CRM) and SRM systems work hand in hand to support supplier and customer functions as they both focus on developing long-term relationships.

A landed cost is the traditional cost measurement that companies use to compare against internal manufacturing costs to perform a *make-versus-buy cost analysis*.

PURCHASING

The Certified Supply Chain Professional (CSCP) Learning System identifies seven *purchasing* functions. These functions are shown in Table 17.1, along with who has the responsibility to perform each one. It's important to understand that the purchasing manager is responsible for the strategic functions while the purchasing agent/planner is responsible for the tactical ones. For purposes of the exam, you should understand the duties and responsibilities as defined by APICS, and not your specific company.

Table 17.1 Purchasing functions

Function Number	Functions	Responsibility
1	Supplier selection	Purchasing manager
2	Negotiations	Purchasing manager
3	Order placement	Purchasing agent/planner
4	Supplier follow-up	Purchasing agent/planner
5	Supplier performance measurements and control	Purchasing agent/planner
6	Value analysis	Purchasing manager
7	Evaluation of new materials and processes	Purchasing manager

A *purchase order* is a legal commitment to buy a product or service from a supplier with a one-time delivery date for a specified quantity of items. A number of different purchase order types are used by customers and each one has their own unique attributes. For example, a purchase order is placed with a supplier to buy 100 blankets at $10.00 each, to be delivered on October 15. A *blanket purchase order* is similar to a purchase order, but instead of one delivery date, it has multiple ones, each with a specified quantity of items. For example, a blanket purchase order is placed with a supplier to buy 500 blankets at $10.00 each. Five shipments of 100 blankets will be delivered on the first day of the next five months. All purchase orders incorporate *terms and conditions* to define the responsibilities of the various participants. These statements form an integral part of the ordering process and include wording on pricing, delivery, performance, ownership transfer, language, currency, and legal authority, among other things.

A *contract* is a written or oral agreement between two or more parties for a product or service. An *annualized contract* is a longer-term negotiated agreement that defines pricing and estimated quantities. An example of an annualized contract is buying heating oil. Two parties agree that the supplier will sell up to a million gallons of oil at a fixed price of $2.00 a gallon. The customer will create purchase orders for their desired quantity and then reference the contract. The customer isn't legally obligated to purchase the oil, but the price and quantity are locked into place. The supplier agrees to sell this material regardless of the customer's actual demand need and therefore has the greatest risk. A *bilateral contract* is an agreement that one party makes to another party to perform a service. A *trading partner agreement* describes a relationship between trading partners. A *contract for the international sale of goods* (CISG) governs the sale of goods in an international environment.

Incentive arrangements and contracts are useful CRM and SRM tools. They identify the level and amount of financial risk, cost structure, and profit and margin expectations that each party is willing to accept. CRM and SRM establish reasonable and attainable targets, help to motivate participants, and discourage inefficiency and wasteful activities. *Incentive contracts* are used when uncertainty exists, in the development of new technology, or in the building of a unique product for the first time. The contract defines a target cost, maximum price, and profit percentage. Savings and overruns are shared, up to the maximum price. The intent is to discourage inefficiencies and waste. *Incentive arrangements* are designed to share costs between contract participants. The arrangement defines a target cost, target profit, and the sharing agreement terms. It also specifies objectives such as on-time or improved delivery, quality, or achieving a customer satisfaction level. If achieved, the arrangement specifies additional payments. An example of an incentive arrangement is completing a project early that results in a bonus. A *fixed-price-incentive-fee contract* is a fixed-price contract that pays the seller a specified amount. Payment is increased if specified conditions are exceeded, such as completing the project early.

All contracts have a degree of risk because of their long time span and market uncertainty. Suppliers and customers negotiate risk ownership which is then reflected in customer order pricing and in the supplier profit levels to better manage and control uncertainty. *Contract deployment* is the process of releasing a portion or all of a specified material to a requesting customer. It's used to ensure a smooth contract transition between all parties and successful adoption across the organization. Companies utilize a *service level agreement* (SLA) to document performance expectations between customers and suppliers on an on-going basis. It specifies how to measure performance and it outlines whether there are any defined penalties should the agreed-upon metrics not be achieved.

DEVELOPING SUPPLY PLANS

It's important for a company to properly plan to identify and manage suppliers in its supply network. Management needs to answer questions pertaining to the company regarding centralized or decentralized global sourcing, procuring from local sources, having the cheapest source regardless of location, the use of sole or single source suppliers, developing and maintaining contingency plans to minimize supply risks, and performing strategic-versus-nonstrategic material sourcing.

Supply plans need to be constantly validated and refined to consider ever-changing market conditions. The supply process starts with a corporate strategy alignment to help accomplish defined goals and objectives. It needs to consider how to achieve the corporate mission and whether the organizational local culture needs to be aligned as it pertains to its corporate social responsibility (CSR) policy. This might include the local community overriding corporate sourcing decisions in order to mitigate local risk, to meet government regulations regarding local content, and to provide local community benefits. The organization needs to perform an ongoing risk assessment to validate whether supply plans are in compliance. In addition, other decisions to consider are the selection of centralized or autonomous sourcing. Finally, management must consider how to identify and implement additional change opportunities to improve customer service, capacity, and costs to help ensure future growth.

MAKE-VERSUS-BUY COST ANALYSIS

A company performs a value chain and value stream analysis to decide if it's better to fully or partially make a product in-house, or purchase via subcontracting a completely manufactured product from a third party. *Subcontracting* is sending production work that is normally performed internally to a third-party manufacturer. Companies perform a financial analysis by examining both fixed and variable costs in order to decide how to best maximize the use of resources and assets. It examines the company's manufacturing and assembly capabilities, and it then considers patent protection, process expertise and reliability, short- and long-term capacity, equipment utilization, and the impact on internal overhead costs. The company determines if a buy decision will provide expected cost benefits. A decision on whether to be horizontally (buy) or vertically (make) integrated is a strategic one. A buy decision means that the company has decided to focus on its internal core competencies and outsource everything else. Once a company completes its analysis, it can make a decision based on collected data and decide whether to make or buy the analyzed item. Benefits of buying include internal risk reduction by transferring the risk to third parties, increased capital for investment as the supplier has the responsibility to purchase the latest equipment and technology, access to the newest supplier's technologies and products, and faster development times by using the supplier's technical expertise.

It's important to note that the make-versus-buy cost analysis can be a political decision that creates turf battles between different internal functional departments, management, and/or unions and workers. It can also distract management during the decision-making process.

Total cost of ownership (TCO) is the sum of landed costs, ongoing maintenance, and durability life-cycle costs. The product purchase cost is often only a small portion of the TCO and must be closely monitored and controlled, as seen in Exhibit 17.1. TCO includes all other related acquisition costs (transportation, custom-related expenses, and duties), regular recurring operating storage costs (facility, insurance, utilities, systems, and support staff) and other related personnel costs (administrative and support staffing). Its intent is to have supply chain decision makers consider improvement activities to be an investment in capabilities, rather than an expense to be minimized.

Exhibit 17.1   TCO

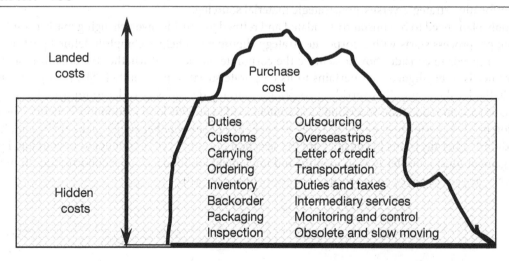

OFFSHORING

Offshoring is the process of relocating the manufacturing process to a location other than the company's original country. The first consideration for anyone considering offshoring is to identify what is best for the organization itself. This often includes cost reduction, improving organizational efficiency, and gaining new global markets. An example of this is a company based in Ohio that moves a manufacturing process from the United States to China to take advantage of lower labor costs and to seek out new markets for its products. Landed cost is the traditional measurement used to justify outsourcing. TCO is the new way of looking at costs before deciding to outsource. *Insourcing* is using the company's internal resources to produce a product or service. Outsourcing also has a supplier producing an item or service that was previously performed internally.

BUYER-SUPPLIER RELATIONSHIP TYPES

Table 17.2 shows the five different buyer-supplier relationships. It describes the time frame, integration with competitors, visibility, and cultural differences.

Table 17.2   Buyer-supplier relationship types

Attributes				
Relationships	**Time Frames**	**Integration with Competitors**	**Visibility**	**Culture**
Buy on the market	Short one-time purchase	A lot/batch	Limited to purchase order placement	Separate cultures
Ongoing relationship	Medium-term	Some	Some visibility	Some cultural sharing
Partnership	Medium- to long-term	Limited	Partial demand sharing	Cultural awareness
Collaboration/strategic alliance	Long-term	Limited to none	Full demand sharing	Cultures meshing
Mergers/acquisitions	Internal ownership	None	Complete demand sharing	One integrated culture

TACTICAL AND STRATEGIC SOURCING

Tactical buying is placing short-term, nonstrategic, reactive, and transactional-based purchase orders. It involves making isolated decisions with limited vendor communications and management involvement. Companies use this technique to place purchase orders for functional, noncritical routine materials with no quality or reliability issues. It quite often uses a reactive approach to purchase materials and services. The process consists of simplistic administrative duties such as obtaining a vendor quote, order placement, order follow-up, expediting, invoice matching, and order close-out.

Strategic sourcing is the process of establishing a long-term, proactive, global, holistic, and collaborative relationship with an alliance partner to acquire strategic materials and services. It has strong, top management involvement and communications between all involved organizations. Strategic sourcing involves more than just placing purchase orders. The process examines supply chain costs and works closely with local and global suppliers to find continuous process improvement (CPI) methods that lead to improved quality, reliability, and delivery performance. It also focuses on reducing TCO and supply chain risk. Global strategic alliances and sourcing need to overcome cultural differences, different legal systems, contrasting values and goals, and currency fluctuations in order to be successful.

There are seven differences between tactical buying and strategic sourcing. Table 17.3 lists them.

Table 17.3 Tactical buying and strategic sourcing

Attributes	Tactical buying	Strategic sourcing
Connection	All vendors	Strategic suppliers
Cost	Purchase price	TCO
Visibility	Internal	Entire supply chain
Focus	Lower prices	Value analysis
Process	Transaction	Collaborative
Boundary	Never crosses	Integrated supply chain
Relationship	Short-term	Long-term

SINGLE, SOLE, AND MULTISOURCING

A *single-source supplier* means that a customer decides to purchase a particular raw material or component from one supplier while other suppliers exist. For example, they decide to purchase all of their threaded rods from one supplier while other suppliers exist who can also provide them. A *sole-source supplier* means that the customer must purchase a raw material or component from one supplier because no other supplier is permitted to sell the item due to patents or brand names. For example, a company can only purchase a seventh generation *Core* i7 module processor from Intel. *Multisourcing* means that a company purchases similar materials from many different sources. For example, they decide to purchase a portion of their computer chip requirements from Advanced Micro Devices (AMD) and/or Nvidia.

Global sourcing is a procurement strategy in which a company obtains products or services from anywhere in the world in the most cost and labor efficient and effective manner. This process is similar to outsourcing but it occurs in another country. It has the same overall objective of being a reduction in labor, material, and transportation costs and fees. Problems related to quality, longer lead times, and control issues exist. Examples of global sourcing include establishing call centers, performing computer programming, and conducting design work.

Exercise 17.1 will test your knowledge and understanding of single, sole, and multisourcing suppliers. Read each question and write in the answer that best applies. The answers to the exercise are available from the Web Added Value™ Download Resource Center at www.jrosspub.com.

Exercise 17.1 Understanding single, sole, and multisourcing suppliers

Question	Answer
1. The customer consolidates all requirements for a commodity item and places it with one suppler.	
2. The customer places all orders with one suppler in order to gain a volume discount on a supplier customized designed product.	
3. The customer places an order with the only supplier who can produce the desired part.	
4. The customer purchases similar goods from more than one supplier.	
5. The customer selects one supplier even if others suppliers exist.	

SUPPLIER SELECTION STRATEGY

A company uses various supplier selection tools as part of its qualification criteria. Examples include approved vendor lists, referrals, prior relationships, *request for quotations* (RFQ), *invitations to tender* (ITT), and *Internet-enabled sourcing* methods. These methods have SRM features such as spend analysis, contract management, and procurement. It's important for a company to find strategic suppliers with whom they can develop a long-term relationship, learn to communicate, and share data. Alliances and partnerships need to be profitable for all involved parties in order to drive down the TCO.

NEGOTIATIONS

Negotiations take place between two or more independent parties who have different needs and goals but work together to find a mutually acceptable and beneficial outcome. This often involves both parties making concessions to reach an acceptable agreement. Informal negotiations are the best way a company can avoid arbitration or involvement of the court system. It requires both parties to have an open attitude of wanting to understand the other party's point of view to resolve an issue. An example is having two company presidents playing golf periodically to discuss and resolve open issues and concerns.

A *trading partner agreement* (TPA) describes a contract type between two parties. The agreement addresses issues such as responsibilities, duties, liabilities, and terms and conditions. It's used to prevent disputes since the terms of trade have been outlined and agreed upon in the TPA.

Hard negotiation occurs when one or both parties apply pressure and are reluctant to alter their position in any way. They mistrust the other side, demand concessions, and propose nothing in return. Victory is seen as the ultimate negotiation goal. *Soft negotiation* occurs when one or both parties are prepared to make concessions in order to cultivate the business relationship. They see agreement as the goal and are willing to trust the other side. They are also willing to concede to pressure and accept a one-sided agreement.

It's beneficial to learn how to identify if a customer or supplier is taking a hard or soft negotiation stand. Table 17.4 is a good study tool to help you determine the relationship.

Table 17.4 Hard and soft negotiations

Negotiation Style	Supplier (hard)	Customer (hard)	Supplier (soft)	Customer (soft)
Win-lose		X	X	
Lose-win	X			X
Win-win			X	X

SRM BENEFITS

Implementing SRM creates a simplified purchasing process. It leads to reduced costs, cycle time, and inventory levels, along with improved efficiency and effectiveness. SRM improves two-way communications, visibility, and implicit product knowledge. It also helps a company gain a competitive advantage. *Cycle time* measures the total time from the start of a process or operation until the end of it. The calculation of the average actual cycle time takes the sum of actual cycle times for all orders delivered and divides it by the total number of orders delivered. An example of this is taking 300 days divided by 100 customer orders—which equals three days of average actual cycle time. *Supply chain cycle time* measures the replacement time it takes to fill a customer order if inventory is at zero. It tracks the overall efficiency of the supply chain.

SRM COMPONENTS

SRM system components can be found in transactional or analytic systems and they use a number of tools that collect, monitor, and track supplier performances, which leads to better sourcing decisions. Examples of these tools are supplier master file databases, requests for information (RFI) and quotations, and catalog and content management applications. A *content management application* (CMA) is the front-end component of a content management system (CMS). It collects and stores data in a data warehouse repository for later access by web services to perform supplier scheduling, electronic funds transfer (EFT), CRM, and catalog processing.

CREATING ALLIANCES WITH SUPPLIERS

There are many reasons why a company would want to form an alliance with other companies. They include the need for a company to enter new markets, strengthen a non-core competency area, reduce risk, improve profitability and efficiency, learn new capabilities, hedge against uncertainty, and improve key capabilities.

ALLIANCE DEVELOPMENT STEPS

Alliance development strengthens the abilities and capabilities of key SRM suppliers. There are ten steps needed to develop and maintain a strategic alliance:

Step 1:   *Align internally*—This step requires a company to align itself internally in order to get its house in order and to avoid later surprises. The alignment begins by identifying important issues and decisions involving key stakeholders, looking at information technology (IT), data sharing, and determining the flexibility of existing processes. Aligning internally results in fewer surprises and gains user acceptance.

Step 2:   *Selection*—This step requires the proper selection of partners, which means looking beyond a strategic and financial fit. A company needs to consider its corporate culture, vision, operating style, and business practices. Negotiations with third parties must be based on mutual trust and respect. Selection requires both parties to have a willingness to assist each other in order to gain market share and profitability.

Step 3:   *Negotiate*—This step requires both parties to negotiate a win-win relationship. It means that both sides need to gain from the alliance or benefit from avoiding future conflicts.

Step 4:   *Ground rules*—This step requires the establishment of alliance ground rules. Both parties need to decide how to work together and resolve conflicts. It also requires the development of clear and flexible alliance guidelines, processes, and protocols.

Step 5:   *Alliance manager*—This step requires the appointment of a dedicated alliance manager to oversee the relationship and who will have real power and influence to make the alliance a success. This person's role is to promote partner relationships and to build joint initiatives to grow both businesses financially.

Step 6:   *Collaborate*—This step requires the alliance partners to develop problem and conflict resolution skills in order to learn how to better collaborate among themselves.

Step 7:   *Collaborative corporate mindset*—This step engages the alliance partners in a collaborative corporate mindset to focus on joint goals and learn how to think in terms of the alliance rather than the channel master.

Step 8:   *Multifaceted relationship*—This step develops a multifaceted relationship in which partners consist of competitors, customers, or suppliers. An example is that Apple and Microsoft are competitors, yet they purchase each other's products and work together to develop new ones. They interact with each other in a very complex relationship with everyone working together for the common good.

Step 9:   *Pulse check*—This step performs an alliance pulse check by auditing and assessing the health of the working relationship. The audit determines and validates if the alliance has effective two-way communication opportunities where everyone works together to create collaborative solutions.

Step 10:   *Plan for change*—This step anticipates and plans for change. Incidents will occur, and a process must be in place to have partners working and communicating together for the alliance to succeed.

Exhibit 17.2 shows the traditional purchaser-supplier as a *butterfly shape* with a single point of contact between the buyer and customer. The strategic alliance is shown as a *diamond shape* that has multiple functional points of contact.

Exhibit 17.2   Relationship point of contact

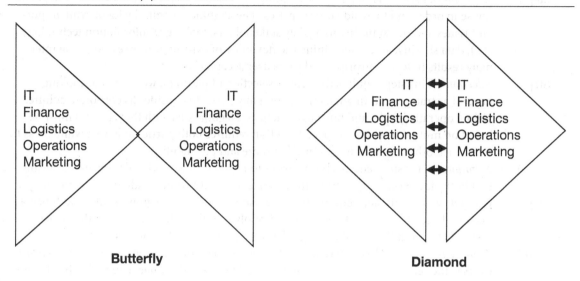

IT
Finance
Logistics
Operations
Marketing

IT
Finance
Logistics
Operations
Marketing

Butterfly

IT
Finance
Logistics
Operations
Marketing

IT
Finance
Logistics
Operations
Marketing

Diamond

SUPPLIER CERTIFICATION

A *supplier certification* program verifies that a supplier's products are manufactured according to specified requirements. The customer and supplier reach an agreement based on agreed-upon performance levels and on-site facility, manufacturing, and quality process evaluations. The performance requirements include attributes such as cost, technology, sustainability, responsiveness, quality, delivery, and flexibility. Performance is tracked during supplier analysis and communicated to the supplier periodically with areas of concern discussed and corrective actions suggested. Consistent internal processes must be in place before a supplier certification program can be implemented and successful.

A number of other certifications are sometimes required by customers and government agencies. These can include the International Standards Organization, Restriction of Hazardous Substances, the Food and Drug Administration, the Global Reporting Initiative, carbon credits, and the Occupational Safety and Health Administration.

CERTIFICATION PROCESS

A company or government agency can require a supplier to become certified. This certification indicates that a consistent process is in place. In order to have a successful certification process, both parties need to know and understand the process and its requirements. APICS has identified nine supplier certification process steps that must be followed. Numerous parties have the responsibility of performing each step and sometimes a third party will be involved to test or audit the process. The first certification step involves identifying key players and their roles, the need to establish metrics, and the creation of procedures and documents to validate that the processes are followed correctly. The nine certification process steps are displayed in Table 17.5.

Table 17.5 Certification process steps

Process Steps	Certification Process Steps
1	Define requirements, processes, and roles
2	Evaluate alternative suppliers
3	Select suppliers
4	Conduct joint quality planning
5	Cooperate and build partnerships with suppliers
6	Conduct measurements
7	Certify suppliers
8	Conduct quality improvement programs
9	Create and use supplier quality ratings

A company can share its supplier performance with various stakeholders using a number of different methods. One such method is using a *supplier scorecard* to gather supplier related data that measures and rates their performance. The scorecard uses a weighted point scale to monitor performance across various categories. Each category is assigned a different weight based on its importance. The rating is multiplied against the weight to determine a value. The values for all categories are summed up to determine a score, and this is used to identify improvement areas. A second method for sharing supplier performance is a *performance alert* that sends a message to a supplier alerting them of a pending issue or concern. A third method is a *survey* that is periodically sent to supply chain personnel in order to gather qualitative performance data. The results are summarized to determine the supplier's effectiveness.

Supplier colocation means that a third-party supplier, or a representative from one, works within the customer's facility. This supplier acts as a planner or buyer and performs functions such as forecasting, planning, purchasing, inventory management, or assembling a unit at a customer's location. Their role results in having improved communications and collaboration that quickly addresses quality or inventory issues and enhances the new product introduction process.

PORTALS

Portals are the gateway to the web and they provide a consistent look and feel. They are a search engine for researching Internet content. Examples of portals include Yahoo, Microsoft, and Google. These are all interactive web browsers that permit fast system interaction that helps to bring information together from diverse sources. A portal can be designed for either a consumer or a business.

TRADE EXCHANGES

The use of *trade exchanges* provides access to a global market connecting suppliers and customers in a dynamic, real-time environment. They lower transaction processing costs more quickly and efficiently than the traditional purchasing products and services method. A number of exchanges can require membership and precertification as a condition to participate.

There are four types of exchange models. They are the *independent public trade exchange* (ITX), *private trade exchange* (PTX), *consortia trade exchange* (CTX), and a *virtual trading exchange* (VTE). Each one has its own unique attributes.

The ITX is a public site that is owned by a third party that attracts many buyers and sellers. The focus of it is on price, variety, and wide access. The best example of an ITX is eBay. eBay has multiple sellers and buyers and charges the seller a transaction fee.

The PTX is established by a dominant buyer or seller who sponsors the exchange. They don't compete on price alone, nor do they charge a fee to participate. They do require membership, as it's a members' only site. The goal of the PTX is to reduce transaction costs, prequalify members, and improve visibility, efficiencies, and security. An example of this is Walmart, which requires its suppliers to sell merchandise to them through the exchange. Another example is IBM, which sells used equipment through its exchange.

The CTX is owned and operated by a third-party intermediary and has a limited number of participating buyers and sellers. Members use it to consolidate buying power through group purchases and to lower transaction processing costs. They also frequently trade excess inventory or capacity. A good example of CTX is Covisint, which is used by a number of automobile manufacturers.

The VTE is a network of legally and economically independent companies that are trading with each other. Companies work together as one competitive supply chain entity by sharing information and resources. A prime example of this is Amazon, which began as a virtual bookstore.

HORIZONTAL MARKETPLACE

A *horizontal marketplace* is an electronic trading exchange where buyers and sellers perform procurement activities across different industry segments. This leads to lower transactional costs and expanded global market reach. An example of a horizontal marketplace is W.W. Grainger's online exchange called *OrderZone.com*, which provides customer access to a number of different maintenance, repair, and operating supplies (MRO) providers.

AUCTIONS

Auctions use a process of competitive and open bidding to establish a selling or purchase price, rather than using negotiations. There are many auction types and each has their own advantages, disadvantages, bidding processes, works, and number of participants.

The *classic* or *forward auction* has one seller and multiple buyers looking to purchase assorted goods. The participant offers a higher price (bid) if they desire to purchase the offered item. The highest bid wins the auction.

The *reverse auction* has multiple sellers and one buyer looking to purchase assorted goods or services. The buyer is indifferent as to from whom they purchase the material or goods. Items being sold usually have a higher value and limited variety. Sellers continue to lower their prices until the buyer agrees to purchase the product or service. Examples of materials being sold at a reverse auction are excess or obsolete inventory from a company.

The *Dutch auction* has one seller and multiple buyers looking to purchase assorted goods. The seller sets a high seeking price. A buyer either accepts the price or waits to purchase the item. The selling price continues to drop until one buyer accepts the offered price. A buyer who delays making an offer may lose the opportunity to purchase the item to another bidder.

The *demand auction* has multiple sellers and buyers looking to buy or sell a time-sensitive product, such as a hotel room or airline ticket. A buyer offers a specified dollar amount and a seller either accepts or rejects the bid.

The *stock market-style auction* has multiple sellers and buyers who are looking to buy or sell finite quantities of the same item using dynamic pricing. The items have high demand variations and can be subject to shortages. A buyer offers to purchase a specified quantity at a set price and a seller can either accept or reject the offer. The auction ends when a buyer and seller agree on a price. In Exercise 17.2, identify the attribute which best describes the auction type. Fill in each column with your answer. The answers to the exercise are available from the Web Added Value™ Download Resource Center at www.jrosspub.com.

Exercise 17.2   Auction attributes

Auction Type	Number of sellers (one or multiple)	Number of buyers (one or multiple)	Bid (up, down, ask)	Winning bid (highest, lowest, negotiated dynamic)
Classic or forward				
Reverse				
Dutch				
Demand				
Stock market				

MEASURING SUPPLIERS

Measuring suppliers is more than monitoring a few metrics. Today's trend is to monitor a supplier's overall performance. A customer analyzes and tracks two-way communications, collaboration, quality, supply chain responsiveness, along with price and on-time delivery performance. Companies use APICS SCOR and other best-in-class metrics to accomplish the measuring process. They use an internal supplier rating system to track performances through the use of *scorecards*, *performance alerts*, and *surveys*.

KEY TERMINOLOGY

Understanding key terms and the concepts they represent is crucial to passing the CSCP exam. In this chapter, the important terms are identified in Table 17.6.

Table 17.6 SRM and purchasing key terminology

Alliance development*
Annualized contract
Auctions
Bilateral contract
Blanket purchase order*
Butterfly shape
Classic auction
Consortia trade exchange (CTX)*
Content management application (CMA)*
Contract
Contract deployment
Contract for the international sale of goods (CISG)
Cycle time*
Demand auction
Diamond shape
Dutch auction
Fixed-price-incentive-fee contract
Forward auction
Hard negotiation
Horizontal marketplace*
Incentive arrangements
Incentive contract
Independent public trade exchange (ITX)
Insourcing
Internet-enabled sourcing
Invitations to tender (ITT)
Make-versus-buy cost analysis
Multisourcing*
Negotiations
Offshoring
Performance alert
Pilot program

Continued

Portal*
Private trade exchange (PTX)
Private trading exchange (PTX)*
Purchase order
Purchasing
Request for quotations (RFQ)
Reverse auction*
Scorecards
Service level agreement
Single-source supplier*
Soft negotiation
Sole-source supplier*
Stock market-style auction
Strategic sourcing*
Subcontracting*
Supplier analysis
Supplier certification*
Supplier colocation
Supplier relationship management (SRM)*
Supplier scorecard
Supply chain cycle time
Survey
Tactical buying*
Terms and conditions
Total cost of ownership (TCO)*
Trade exchanges
Trading partner agreement (TPA)
Virtual trading exchange*

*Key term found in the CSCP ECM

CSCP EXAM PRACTICE QUESTIONS ON SRM AND PURCHASING

The questions presented in Table 17.7a cover the concepts presented in this chapter on SRM and purchasing. They are examples of what to expect on the actual exam.

Table 17.7a SRM and purchasing practice questions

No.	Questions
1	What is the best intent of total cost of ownership (TCO)? a) Reduce internal costs b) Reduce external costs c) Investment in capabilities d) Migrate to a vertical organization
2	All of the following are advantages of using supplier relationship management (SRM) software except for: a) Higher quality products b) It leads to lower production costs c) It leads to lower priced end products d) It leads to the implementation of a new enterprise resource planning (ERP) system
3	Global sourcing has had the following impacts except for: a) Increased quality issues b) Increased delivery lead times c) Decreased cost of goods sold d) Increased direct control over suppliers
4	What is the best way a company can avoid arbitration or involvement of the court system? a) File a lawsuit b) Formal negotiations c) Informal negotiations d) Stipulate ongoing contract negotiations
5	What must be in place before a supplier certification program can be implemented? a) Defined roles b) Process flow charts c) Consistent processes d) Orientation processes
6	The sum of the last 100 delivered customer orders was 300 days. Each of these orders waited in a queue for two days. The shipping time was also two days. Calculate the average actual cycle time for the delivered orders. a) Two days b) Three days c) Five days d) Seven days
7	What do we call the time it takes to make a product? a) Velocity b) Cycle time c) Standard time d) Customer order lead time
8	Who is responsible for adhering to the collaborative relationship? a) All parties b) Key managers c) Top management d) Sales and marketing

Continued

9	Traditional performance measurements include all of the following except for: a) Financially focused b) Focused on control c) Strategic goal focused d) Historically oriented
10	All of the following are reasons for global sourcing except for: a) Cost cutting b) Market growth c) Creating one culture d) Organizational efficiency
11	Which of the following best describes the term single-source supplier? a) No other suppliers exist b) Selected solely by the purchasing department c) Provided by more than one supplier d) Provided by one supplier but other suppliers exist
12	What is a key feature of a supplier evaluation program? a) SCOR metrics b) Reliability metrics c) Partnership agreement d) Supplier performance measurements
13	What is the first consideration for a company considering offshoring? a) Cost reduction b) Economies of scale c) Being closer to a customer d) Organizational needs
14	What is the traditional cost measurement used to justify outsourcing? a) Landed cost b) Cost of goods sold (COGS) c) Total cost of ownership (TCO) d) Total cost of manufacturing
15	What is the main purpose of contract deployment? a) Placing purchase orders b) Establishing clear performance expectations c) Monitoring supplier performance d) Smooth contract transition between all parties
16	A company may seek to form a strategic alliance for all of the following reasons except for: a) Gaining design input b) Sharing administrative costs c) Solving an immediate problem d) Having early supplier involvement
17	What shape best depicts a single point of interaction between a supplier and customer? a) Flower b) Butterfly c) Pyramid d) Diamond
18	A company needs to treat a strategic alliance like a/an: a) Event b) Process c) Merger d) Acquisition

Continued

19	What is the first required step in a successful alliance? a) Align internally b) Establish ground rules c) Select the proper partner d) Appoint a dedicated alliance manager
20	Which of the following isn't always used by a portal? a) Alerts b) Websites c) Search engines d) Shopping tools
21	In order to be successful, a business-to-business exchange must consider all of the following except for: a) Meeting customer needs b) Having a valid strategy c) Focusing solely on cost reduction d) Needing both buyers and sellers
22	Which auction method has one seller and multiple buyers with finite quantities of the same item for sale? a) Dutch b) Reverse c) Stock market type d) Demand
23	Which trade exchange is owned and operated by a third party? a) Hybrid trade exchange b) Private trade exchange (PTX) c) Vertical trade exchange (VTE) d) Consortia-based marketplace
24	Which auction type has multiple buyers and sellers? a) Dutch b) Classic c) Reverse d) Demand
25	A manufacturing company has a supplier performing an assembly operation on its shop floor. Which term best describes this practice? a) In-sourcing b) Team partnering c) Supplier colocation d) Integrated operation
26	Global alliances must overcome all of the following complexities except for: a) Cultural differences b) Currency fluctuations c) Different legal systems d) Component standardization
27	Web-enabled supplier relationship management (SRM) capabilities include all of the following except for: a) Internal interfaces b) Supplier certification c) External supplier interfaces d) SRM analytics

ANSWERS TO CSCP EXAM PRACTICE QUESTIONS ON SRM AND PURCHASING

The answers to the practice questions on SRM and purchasing are shown in Table 17.7b. Any question you answer incorrectly indicates a gap in your body of knowledge and encourages the need for additional study time.

Table 17.7b   Answers to CSCP exam practice questions on SRM and purchasing

No.	Answers
1	Answer: C The intent of total cost of ownership (TCO) is to have supply chain decision makers consider improvement activities to be an investment in capabilities rather than an expense to be minimized.
2	Answer: D The implementation of a new enterprise resources planning (ERP) system isn't a direct advantage of using supplier relationship management (SRM) software. SRM doesn't require ERP to be implemented as SRM can be a stand-alone system. Answers A, B, and C are all advantages of using SRM.
3	Answer: D Customers have less direct control over global suppliers. Answers A, B, and C impact global sourcing.
4	Answer: C Informal negotiations, with both parties having an open attitude of wanting to understand the other party's point of view, would be the best solution.
5	Answer: C Consistent processes must be in place before a supplier certification program can be implemented. Process flow charts and orientation processes are part of the consistent process. Answer A (defined roles) is partially correct, but it requires consistent processes to first be in place before they can be established.
6	Answer: B The calculation of the average actual cycle time takes the sum of actual cycle times for all orders delivered and divides it by the total number of orders delivered (300 days ÷ 100 customer orders = three days for the average actual cycle time).
7	Answer: B This question requires knowledge of the APICS Dictionary definition of *cycle time*. Cycle time is the time needed to manufacture or assemble a product from the beginning to the end of the process.
8	Answer: C Top management must stay involved and cannot abdicate their responsibility to lower-level management if they want a collaborative relationship to be a success.
9	Answer: C Traditional performance measurements look at historically oriented results, are focused on control, and have financially focused measurements. Strategic goal focus is the current supply chain-related measurement.
10	Answer: C Global sourcing has nothing to do with creating one culture. Creating one culture only comes with mergers and acquisitions.
11	Answer: D Having a single-source supplier means purchasing from one supplier when other suppliers exist (i.e., computer chips) while sole sourcing means only one supplier exists (i.e., Intel computer chips).

Continued

12	Answer: D Supplier performance measurements are critical in the success of any supplier relationship. The supply chain operations reference (SCOR) model and reliability metrics are part of supplier performance metrics, and the partnership agreement specifies what metric to use.
13	Answer: D The first consideration for anyone thinking about offshoring is to identify what is best for the organization itself. Answers A, B, and C occur after the decision is made.
14	Answer: A Landed cost is the traditional measurement used to justify outsourcing. Cost of goods sold (COGS) and total cost of manufacturing are internal manufacturing metrics. Total cost of ownership (TCO) is the new way of looking at costs before deciding to outsource.
15	Answer: D Contract deployment is used to ensure a smooth contract transition between all parties and successful adoption across the organization.
16	Answer: C Solving an immediate problem is a reactive solution, while answers A, B, and D are more proactive. Answers A, B, and D are ways companies form a strategic alliance.
17	Answer: B The butterfly shape depicts one point of contact (> <). The diamond shape depicts multiple points of contact, which is what companies desire for improved communications.
18	Answer: B An alliance is a process that requires continual monitoring and attention. A merger and/or acquisition is an event.
19	Answer: A A company needs to align itself internally before identifying key issues among stakeholders that may need correction. Aligning internally helps to avoid surprises during an alliance set up with selected partners.
20	Answer: D Portals are websites for customer interactions; these include e-mails, alerts, online shopping, product searching, and home pages. Shopping tools don't have to be in a portal. For example, a catalog, a flyer, or coupons are all shopping tools.
21	Answer: C A business-to-business exchange may see operational cost reduction as part of the implementation improvement process. However, it's only a starting point, not the sole focus.
22	Answer: A A Dutch auction has one seller and multiple buyers who are looking to purchase a finite amount of materials. Stock market type and demand both have multiple buyers and sellers. A reverse auction has multiple sellers and one buyer.
23	Answer: D A consortia-based marketplace is owned and operated by a third party.
24	Answer: D Demand and stock market-style auctions both have multiple buyers and sellers. A classic auction has one seller with multiple buyers.
25	Answer: C Supplier colocation has a supplier being located within a manufacturing plant.
26	Answer: D Component standardization is a problem that everyone has to overcome. It effects more than just global alliances.
27	Answer: B Supplier certification isn't part of supplier relationship management (SRM)—it's the result of SRM analysis.

18

SYNCHRONIZING DEMAND
AND SUPPLY

This chapter focuses on synchronizing both internal and external demand and supply and how its use can improve the supply chain. It also explores how inventory can be shared among partners within the supply chain. It examines distributor integration, quick response programs, continuous replenishment, vendor-managed inventory, consignment inventory, vendor-owned inventory, and collaborative planning, forecasting, and replenishment.

SYNCHRONIZATION

Synchronizing supply and demand requires the coordination of materials, products, and information flows throughout the supply chain. Internal supply and demand synchronization occurs during the sales and operations planning (S&OP) process. External supply and demand synchronization occurs between supply chain partners when they operate in a collaborative, flexible, and seamless manner to communicate and synchronize information. *Synchronization* requires all parties to have defined roles and responsibilities and to achieve expected results over short-, medium-, and long-term time periods. This leads to improved velocity and visibility, which results in enhanced customer service, delivery performance, effectiveness, efficiency, and inventory reduction. Collaboration between supply chain partners leads to the making and delivering of customer desired products and services within the marketplace.

PRINCIPLES

A successful collaborative supply chain relationship requires an organization to adhere to a number of principles. These include focusing on the most profitable partners, understanding their partners' needs, striving for flow, using supply chain assets collectively, monitoring performance, and continuously improving the process.

IMPLEMENTATION CHANGES

Companies may find it difficult to implement supply and demand synchronization across their supply chain. A number of challenges must be overcome before achieving implementation success. These challenges include incomplete or poorly designed specifications, resource and technology cost considerations, lack of integrated infrastructure, network and language barriers, software and hardware that doesn't meet business requirements, implemented software that can't deliver promised benefits, technology that is underpowered, overly complex or inadequately designed technologies, and internal and external members who fail to reach an agreement on their role or accept the guiding principles.

SUPPLY CHAIN INTEGRATION

Implementing a supply chain integration strategy is a five-step process.

The first step requires a supply chain network to designate a channel master to drive the implementation. The channel master is normally the largest organization within the supply chain, but any supply chain participant can assume this role. The channel master defines and leads the supply chain project, obtains agreement on goals and objectives, gains accord based on shared information, and strives to have everyone work together as peers. A good example is the channel master requiring all supply chain participants to use electronic funds transfer (EFT) or place radio frequency identification (RFID) tags on all shipped products.

The second step in a supply chain integration system is the channel master inviting supply chain partners to become members of a *cross-functional team*. The team responsibilities include conducting a process assessment, looking at best practices, and determining how the supply chain can be synchronized across the network.

The third step develops a supply chain integration and project plan, creates a budget, sets a time frame, and estimates required resources. This developed plan is presented to the various team members' management to obtain their feedback and approval.

The fourth step executes the developed plan, evaluates results against the plan, and is repeated until the plan becomes implemented. The team monitors the plan progress, makes resource and time frame adjustments, identifies how each supply chain partner will differentiate themselves, and keeps management informed of the plan status.

The fifth and final step in the supply chain integration process is the constant re-evaluation and innovation of the supply chain network and its existing alliances by the addition of partners and capabilities to the network. The supply chain integration process changes how a supply chain looks at performance measurements. It focuses on historically-oriented results, tight internal controls, and being financially focused. Synchronization success is defined when the supply chain achieves predefined goals that improve the efficiency of the supply chain network.

INVENTORY SYNCHRONIZATION BETWEEN TRADING PARTNERS

A *trading partner* consists of a customer and one or more participants (supplier, another customer, or another country) who have an ongoing business relationship.

Distributor integration (DI) permits a supplier and its distributors to integrate their systems with each other allowing all participants to share inventory stocking levels. This results in improved inventory control and enhanced customer service which then leads to lower overall inventory levels. Two potential obstacles with DI are the question of inventory ownership and the unwillingness of some participants to share information. New automobile dealerships use this technique to share new car and spare parts inventory availability.

A *quick response program* (QRP) is used by retail stores to quickly replace sold merchandise. Stores provide *point-of-sale* (POS) information electronically along with an order authorizing replenishment to their suppliers. A POS system electronically captures customer data, time and place, stock-keeping unit (SKU) information, and it updates the inventory status for each sale's transaction. This information is then passed to suppliers who can quickly issue replenishment materials. A QRP reduces lost sales and stockouts.

Continuous replenishment (CR), also known as *rapid replenishment*, is also used by retail stores. Stores electronically pass daily POS information to their suppliers and material replenishments are quickly issued without an order being placed. This technique lowers stockouts, inventory levels, and processing costs while improving customer service, material availability, and inventory turnover. The main difference between a QRP and CR is that in CR, materials are automatically replenished while a QRP requires a purchase order.

Vendor-managed inventory (VMI) is when the supplier maintains mutually agreed-upon inventory levels with the customer. Both parties jointly develop a forecast and decide on inventory levels and replenishment cycles. The supplier delivers and restocks inventory based on the agreement. The customer displays the inventory, processes sales and inventory transactions, and shares collected data with their suppliers. Inventory ownership is defined in the contract, and either party can have this responsibility. VMI lowers inventory levels for both parties, minimizes stockouts, and improves customer service and fill rates.

Consignment inventory, also known as *vendor-owned inventory* (VOI), places inventory at a customer location. The supplier retains title of the goods until sold, and ownership then transfers from the supplier to the customer. This technique helps to improve velocity, visibility, and customer service.

Collaborative planning, forecasting, and replenishment (CPFR) was developed by the Voluntary Interindustry Commerce Standards Association in 1998. It's used by a supplier and customer to create a combined plan with a goal of meeting customer demand and having an integrated supply chain network. CPFR integrates processes between both parties helping to synchronize actual demand, product forecasts, and production. It electronically exchanges POS data, schedules promotions, demand forecast, and inventory between both parties. This results in a reduction in the bullwhip effect, enhanced visibility and velocity, early problem detection, and improved overall customer satisfaction while driving supply chain inventory levels and costs downward. A few implementation and ongoing issues and challenges in CPFR are internal and external integration with trading partners, resistance to data sharing, partners learning how to speak with one voice, increased costs (especially during startup), and savings objectives not always being achieved.

Collaborative transportation management (CTM) is a holistic process that brings together supply chain trading partners to drive inefficiencies out of the transport, planning, and execution process. It's an outgrowth of CPFR, and it extends collaboration to include transportation carriers as strategic partners.

Exercise 18.1 will test your knowledge and understanding of the various trading partner types. Read each question and write in the correct answer. The answers to the exercise are available from the Web Added Value™ Download Resource Center at www.jrosspub.com.

Exercise 18.1   Understanding various trading partner types

Question	Answer
1. Which trading partner type best permits all participants to share their inventory stocking level balance?	
2. Which trading partner type creates a jointly developed plan to best satisfy customer demand?	
3. Which trading partner type defines inventory ownership in a formal contract?	
4. Which trading partner type focuses on retail sales and passes POS data to their suppliers without generating a purchase order?	
5. Which trading partner type jointly develops a forecast and then decides on inventory levels with the supplier assuming inventory replenishment responsibility?	
6. Which trading partner type shares POS data, production schedules, and inventory levels among all participants?	
7. Which trading partner type has the supplier retaining inventory ownership until a product is sold?	
8. Which trading partner type has to overcome an obstacle against sharing inventory information with others?	
9. Which trading partner type requires a purchase order to be generated to request material replenishment?	

KEY TERMINOLOGY

Understanding key terms and the concepts they represent is crucial to passing the Certified Supply Chain Professional (CSCP) exam. In this chapter, the important terms are identified in Table 18.1.

Table 18.1 Synchronizing demand and supply key terminology

Collaborative planning, forecasting, and replenishment (CPFR)*
Collaborative transportation management (CTM)
Consignment inventory
Continuous replenishment (CR)*
Cross-functional team
Distribution integration (DI)
Point-of-sale (POS)
Quick response program (QRP)*
Rapid replenishment*
Synchronization
Synchronizing supply and demand
Trading partner
Vendor-managed inventory (VMI)*
Vendor-owned inventory (VOI)

*Key term found in the CSCP ECM

CSCP EXAM PRACTICE QUESTIONS ON SYNCHRONIZING DEMAND AND SUPPLY

The questions shown in Table 18.2a cover the concepts presented in this chapter on synchronizing demand and supply. They are examples of what to expect on the actual exam.

Table 18.2a   Synchronizing demand and supply practice questions

No.	Questions
1	All of the following are reasons for distributor integration (DI) resistance except for: a) Loss of technical skills b) Fear of poor customer service c) Skepticism of financial benefits d) Long-term alliance involvement
2	What term best describes distributors who have the ability to view inventory levels at other distributors? a) Distributed processing b) Distributor integration (DI) c) Vendor-managed inventory (VMI) d) Distribution requirements planning (DRP)
3	A quick response program (QRP) can help to achieve all of the following benefits except for: a) Reduced lead times b) Reduced inventory levels c) Increased customer service d) Reduced income statement inventory assets
4	A supplier is currently being notified daily of warehouse shipments. They are committed to replenishing inventory without stockouts and without receiving replenishment orders. They will most likely be using what supplier-managed inventory model? a) Quick response program (QRP) b) Distributor integration (DI) c) Continuous replenishment (CR) d) Vendor-managed inventory (VMI)

Continued

5	All of the following are reasons for a customer to implement a vendor-managed inventory (VMI) program except for: a) Reduced overhead b) Decreased need for internal working capital c) Reduced total inventory dollars from the income statement d) Shifted responsibility for maintenance and replenishing inventory to the supplier
6	Vendor-managed inventory (VMI) benefits for the supplier include all of the following except for: a) Higher on-time deliveries b) Reduced delivery lead times c) Decreased inventory turns d) Reduced supply network inventory costs
7	What is the best purpose of collaborative planning forecasting and replenishment (CPFR)? a) Manage demand b) Create a value chain c) Increase discrepancies d) Eliminate redundancies
8	Which of the following is the key to collaborative planning, forecasting, and replenishment (CPFR) system success? a) The ability to automate the transfer of forecasting and historical data b) The willingness to work with technology c) The ability to automate the collaboration arrangement d) The willingness to work with shared data
9	What is the biggest impact when transportation delivery times decrease? a) Cash-to-cash days go up b) Transportation costs go down c) Customer service costs go down d) Inventory handling costs go up
10	A holistic process that brings together supply chain trading partners to drive inefficiencies out of the transport, planning, and execution process is best called: a) Collaborative intensity b) Collaborative relationship c) Collaborative transportation management (CTM) d) Collaborative planning, forecasting, and replenishment (CPFR)

ANSWERS TO CSCP EXAM PRACTICE QUESTIONS ON SYNCHRONIZING DEMAND AND SUPPLY

The answers to the practice questions on synchronizing demand and supply are shown in Table 18.2b. Any question you answer incorrectly indicates a gap in your body of knowledge and encourages the need for additional study time.

Table 18.2b Answers to CSCP exam practice questions on synchronizing demand and supply

No.	Answers
1	Answer: D Resistance is caused by the fear of losing something or by change itself. Distributors may not object to a long-term alliance, as this may not change anything. However, the other answers can impact participating companies, causing resistance.
2	Answer: B This question requires knowledge of the APICS Dictionary definition of *distributor integration*. In distributor integration, distributors are able to view inventory stocking levels (quantities) at the supplier location and at other distributors.
3	Answer: D Inventory dollars are displayed on the balance sheet, not the income statement.
4	Answer: C The key difference between continuous replenishment and vendor-managed inventory (VMI) is that VMI has data access and the supplier maintains the inventory, which isn't asked in the question. Both methods provide quick delivery. Quick response uses orders and the others methods don't.
5	Answer: C Total inventory dollars appear on the balance sheet. Answers A, B, and D are all true.
6	Answer: C A decrease in inventory turns isn't a benefit—it means that higher levels of inventory exist. A benefit of having higher turns is that inventory turns over more.
7	Answer: D Collaborative planning, forecasting, and replenishment (CPFR) helps to eliminate redundancies and discrepancies between companies.
8	Answer: D The key to collaborative planning, forecasting, and replenishment (CPFR) system success is the ability and willingness to work with shared data between all involved parties.
9	Answer: C Improved transportation will reduce overall customer service costs as there are fewer customer calls, expediting, and rush shipments.
10	Answer: C This question requires knowledge of the APICS Dictionary definition of *collaborative transportation management* (CTM). CTM is a holistic process that brings together supply chain trading partners to drive inefficiencies out of the transport planning and execution process.

19

INVENTORY MANAGEMENT

This chapter focuses on managing the inventory levels of raw materials, components, and finished goods. It examines order policies, the importance of safety stock and safety lead time, and echelon reduction. It further explores the ABC concept, inventory policies, storage locations, aggregate inventory management, inventory types, and inventory related costs.

INDEPENDENT AND DEPENDENT DEMAND

Independent demand is driven by forecasts and/or customer orders and it's not calculated from the demand of any other inventory item. It becomes a direct input to the master schedule (MS) without any calculations being performed. An MS displays the requirement and quantity needed to be produced or purchased, per period, for each independent demand item. A few examples of independent demand include orders received from customers, distribution requirements planning (DRP) orders, spare parts, or promotional items.

Dependent demand is derived from the demand of a higher level item. This type of demand isn't forecasted but rather calculated within material requirements planning (MRP). Examples of dependent demand include raw materials, components, and subassemblies.

ORDERING QUANTITIES AND SAFETY STOCK

The order quantity is the amount to be ordered or produced and retained in inventory. Quite a few different methods exist to tell a supply chain planner how much to order and whether or not they need to consider the economics of manufacturing or purchasing. Each method needs to provide sufficient inventory to balance supply and demand at the lowest total cost of ownership (TCO) and still achieve customer service objectives. No one method meets the needs of every organization, so multiple models exist. The three models covered in the Certified Supply Chain Professional (CSCP) Learning System are *lot-for-lot* (L4L), *fixed order quantity* (FOQ), and *economic order quantity* (EOQ).

The L4L technique places an order for the exact quantity that satisfies customer orders or MRP net requirements by period. It's frequently used for expensive items, or to satisfy variable, just-in-time (JIT) delivery requirements. For example, if period three has net requirements of five pieces, and period four needs seven pieces, L4L will order the exact specified quantity in each period.

FOQ is a predetermined fixed item quantity to be ordered. This means that regardless of the actual specified net requirement, an order will be placed for the FOQ. A company or supplier establishes an FOQ to meet a minimum carton requirement, number of units on a skid, or a manufacturing batch size. An example of this is a company wanting to order eight light bulbs, but the supplier only sells full cases of 24. The order is placed for 24 pieces regardless of the actual need. FOQ builds up inventory because it can exceed actual requirements.

EOQ is a calculation that determines the optimal order size while minimizing total inventory costs. The process compares the inventory order quantity to the inventory carrying cost to best determine the optimal quantity size. *Inventory carrying costs* include costs such as storage, labor, equipment, perishability, and insurance. The calculation formula is (average inventory times (capital costs plus storage costs plus risk costs)). An example of the calculation is ($500,000 * (9% + 5% + 6%)) or ($500,000 * 20%) = $100,000. The development of the optimal order size is shown in Exhibit 19.1.

Exhibit 19.1   EOQ

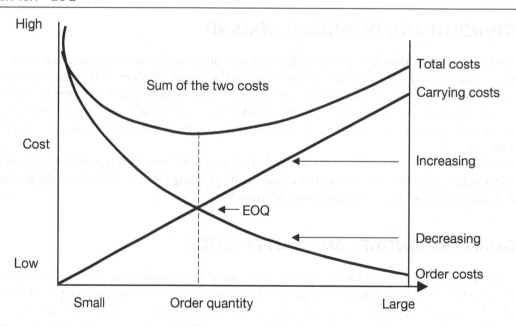

EOQ is based on a number of assumptions including demand and lead time being constant and known, orders being received on time, no quantity discounts being given, and stockouts never occurring if orders are placed on time.

The EOQ formula is the square root of two times the annual demand, times the setup cost (or order preparation cost), divided by the product of the annual carrying cost rate and the item cost. The following two examples demonstrate the calculation process based on the provided information:

A = Annual demand is 20,000 units

S = Setup cost or cost of order preparation is $10.00 per order (in dollars)

C = Item cost is $0.50 each (in dollars)

I = Annual carrying cost rate is 25% (expressed as a decimal)

EOQ = (2 * 20,000 * $10) ÷ ($0.50 * .25) then calculate the square root to derive at an answer of $1,789. A second calculation method is displayed in Table 19.1. EOQ is determined when the ordering cost and the carrying cost come closest to matching.

Table 19.1 EOQ calculation

Annual Demand (A)	Order Costs (S)	Order Quantity (Q)	Cost Per Unit (C)	Carrying Cost Rate (I)	Ordering Cost (AS/Q)	Carrying Cost (QCI/2)	Total Cost
20,000	$10.00	1,500	$0.50	.25	$133.33	$ 93.75	$227.08
20,000	$10.00	1,700	$0.50	.25	$117.64	$106.25	$223.89
20,000	$10.00	1,789	$0.50	.25	$111.79	$111.81	$223.60
20,000	$10.00	1,850	$0.50	.25	$108.11	$115.63	$223.74
20,000	$10.00	1,900	$0.50	.25	$105.26	$118.75	$224.01

There are two important points to remember about EOQ. The first is that the order quantity increases in geometric proportion to reductions in carrying cost and item cost. The second is that the order quantity also increases in geometric proportion to increases in annual usage and setup costs. Both of these points can be observed in Exercise 19.1. Determine the impact of an order quantity change in EOQ by showing if the order quantity is higher or lower. The answers to the exercise are available from the Web Added Value™ Download Resource Center at www.jrosspub.com.

Exercise 19.1 EOQ change

Question	Order Quantity Change (higher or lower)
1. Carrying cost increases	
2. Carrying cost decreases	
3. Demand quantity increases	
4. Demand quantity decreases	
5. Setup cost increases	
6. Setup cost decreases	
7. Item cost increases	
8. Item cost decreases	

SAFETY STOCK AND SAFETY LEAD TIME

Safety stock is a *buffer* of inventory that exceeds forecast or gross requirements and is used to protect against demand and lead time variability, late deliveries, scrap and yield requirements, unplanned usage, and quality related issues. The higher the safety stock service levels, the greater the inventory carrying costs. However, it reduces the possibility of a stockout.

Safety lead time is a form of safety stock that protects against late delivery uncertainty by building up extra inventory based on a period of time. For example, a company sells 100 units a week, but their supplier is always two weeks late. The company decides to establish a safety lead time quantity of 200 units to cover the delivery uncertainty period.

INVENTORY ORDERING SYSTEMS

Quite a few different methods exist to tell the planner or buyer how much to order. These methods attempt to provide sufficient inventory to balance supply and demand at the lowest TCO while still achieving customer service objectives. Three methods of ordering management are covered in the CSCP Learning System—reorder point (ROP) systems, periodic review systems, and min-max systems. No one method meets the needs of every organization.

A *reorder point system* considers the supplier lead time plus the expected usage quantity during the review time. The ROP formula is demand during lead time (DDLT) plus safety stock (SS). In order to perform this calculation, some basic order data is required. An example is a company that has a period demand of three units per period, a lead time of four periods, and an SS of five. This information is inserted into the formula and the following calculation can be performed:

ROP = DDLT plus SS
ROP = three units per period times four periods plus five units of SS
ROP = $(3 * 4) + 5 = 17$

A *periodic review system* is an independent inventory ordering method where inventory is validated and reordered at a set time *interval*. The review interval is fixed, but order placement quantities vary from period to period. A company establishes a maximum inventory target that can't be exceeded when new orders get placed for a variable order quantity.

For example, cardboard boxes are used to package finished products. Every week a planner checks the inventory levels and orders are then placed for this amount. The delivery lead time for boxes is three days, and the time interval between ordering is five days. The demand per day is ten boxes, but actual usage can vary. The company maintains a safety stock of five days, or 50 boxes, to protect against a stockout. The order quantity is calculated using the following formula: maximum inventory level is equal to demand times (order interval plus lead time) plus SS. A calculation example is shown below:

D = demand per unit of time
T = time interval between ordering in days
L = item lead time in days
SS = safety stock (D * number of days of safety stock)

Maximum inventory level = D (T + L) + SS
Maximum inventory level = 10 (5 + 3) + (5 * 10)
Maximum inventory level = 10 (8) + 50
Maximum inventory level = 80 + 50 = 130 maximum inventory needed

The maximum inventory quantity minus the on-hand inventory equals the target order amount. If a company has 20 pieces on-hand, this gets subtracted from the maximum inventory level of 130. The company then places an order for an additional 110 cardboard boxes.

INVENTORY LOCATIONS AND ECHELONS

A supply chain manages inventory at every movement *stage* from the supplier to the customer. Companies have a number of *nodes* (locations) at which inventory and information flow between them. Examples of nodes are a warehouse, a distribution center (DC), a central DC, a wholesaler, or retail stores. An echelon is a layer or layers in a supply chain where inventory is stored. It's placed between a supply chain and the end customer.

A *single-echelon*, or *tier*, has a single DC between the supplier and the customer. The supplier ships and stores inventory in the DC to support customers. Inventory and the DC are under the control of a single company, and this reduces customer delivery lead time. A *multi-echelon* has multiple DCs and other stocking locations between the supplier and the customer. Inventory and the various DCs and other stocking locations are under the control of multiple companies. Each echelon increases throughput time (lead time from one location to another) and delivery times, causes higher levels of inventory to be stocked at each level, and creates demand variability throughout the supply chain. The elimination of an echelon will reduce transportation times and overall customer service costs as there are fewer customer calls, expediting, and rush shipments. *Lead time* is the time difference between the start and end of a process.

DCs require SS to protect against demand variability and late deliveries. The total amount of SS will increase as more DCs are added to the network. The percent of the increase can be calculated by using the following formula: the square root of the ratio of total future DCs to current DCs. For example, the number of DCs is planned to increase from two to three. The current SS level is 5,000 units. The revised level of SS is calculated as the current SS level is multiplied by the percent increase which is 6,124 units $((5,000) * \sqrt{(3 \div 2)} = 5,000 * 1.2247)$.

Supply chain inventory management becomes very difficult when companies have hundreds or even thousands of products placed in different tiers or echelons throughout the world. Each tier impacts inventory visibility, velocity, and levels. It also impacts lead time, service levels, and costs. All of these together amplify the bullwhip effect. *Inventory visibility* is the process of how information is shared within a firm among echelons, partners, and customers. It can be quite challenging coordinating and managing multiple products and nodes while trying to minimize inventory and maximize customer service. Inventory management requires an understanding of the *three Vs* (visibility, velocity, and variability) along with volume and variety. They all have a major impact on inventory levels and lead times throughout the supply chain.

Joint store clustering is the process of blanketing an area with a number of retail stores. Examples of this are Starbucks or Staples being supported by one or more DCs.

Inventory optimization software is a computer-based program that uses advanced modeling techniques to help define an optimal, multi-echelon supply chain inventory strategy. The program helps lead to improved customer service, and lowers inventory and SS levels. This frees up working capital and reduces overall costs. *Optimization* is a strategy to find alternative, cost-effective, constraint driven methods that maximize operational performance. *Suboptimization* occurs when different units (work areas) develop a solution that is best for them, but not for the entire organization.

PARETO ANALYSIS

Pareto analysis, also known as the *80/20 rule* or *ABC analysis*, is a decision-making technique used to separate major causes from minor ones. It logically shows how a small number of events create the majority of critical activities and it helps to separate the costly few from the trivial many. This technique permits a user to prioritize and focus resources and some degree of control to the critical activities.
The ABC analysis percentages are defined as:

"A" items are 20% of the items which have 80% of total value.
"B" items are 30% of the items which have 15% of total value.
"C" items are 50% of the items which have 5% of total value.

INVENTORY POLICY

Inventory policies are guidelines and rules that help a company make informed and timely decisions about managing raw materials, components, work-in-process (WIP), and finished goods. There are many different decisions that need to be made in order to establish them.

A *planning horizon* requires a management decision about how far into the future a plan needs to extend. *Replenishment lead time* requires a decision about how often inventory stock replenishment needs to occur. It's calculated as the processing time from identification of the reorder need until the product is received and then placed on the shelf. *Product variety* requires a decision on stocking similar products and families. For example, classifying computers as desktops, laptops, or tablets creates three different product families. These computers are similar in nature but can be planned separately. *Inventory costs* require a decision about inventory ordering and carrying costs. *Customer service requirements* require a decision about stocking levels by item and location to achieve customer service objectives.

Companies have to manage *customer demand* regardless of demand variability caused by inaccurate forecasts or customer orders that exceed expectations. This requires companies to maintain SS to protect against variability due to poor forecasting.

INVENTORY ACCURACY

Inventory accuracy is measured by comparing the system quantity for an item against the physically counted quantity. It can be tracked by location, a total of all locations combined, or it can be measured by dollar value or aggregated total. Accounting is concerned about dollar values, while the planning group is concerned with item aggregate and accuracy.

The item count method by location is frequently used to track inventory accuracy. The process begins by counting all items in a particular inventory location. The count total is then compared against the inventory system record. The smaller count quantity is subtracted from the larger one. For example, if a system displays a quantity of 75 pieces, but the count quantity is 78, the count discrepancy is three units. The first step is to divide the subtracted quantity by the actual count (3 ÷ 78) times 100% equals 3.85% to show the item error rate. Next, subtract 3.85% from 100% to obtain 96.15% inventory accuracy.

Two methods are used to validate inventory accuracy. They are *periodic inventory* (also called the *physical inventory*) and *cycle counting*. Table 19.2 compares selected attributes in these two methods.

Table 19.2 Periodic inventory versus cycle counting

Attribute	Periodic Inventory	Cycle Counting
Timely detection of errors	No	Yes
Identification mistakes made during the counting process	Many	Few
Production time loss	Extensive (plant shutdown)	Minimal loss (plant operates)
Counters	Inexperienced and inefficient	Experienced and efficient
Safety stock	Requires higher levels	Requires lower levels
Year-end inventory adjustments	Required	Minimal
Items selected for counting	Everything	Small numbers of items
Inventory accuracy trend	Downward trend throughout year	Upward trend throughout year

AGGREGATE INVENTORY MANAGEMENT

Aggregate inventory management, or risk pooling, tracks cumulative performance by looking at total inventory requirements rather than individual items. This makes the risk to the aggregated total less than the sum of risk of the individual items. The aggregation process is a key component of business planning and sales and operations planning (S&OP). It's concerned with totaled raw materials, components, WIP, and finished goods inventory levels and costs. Aggregate inventory management assists a company in figuring out the purchase or production requirements needed to meet market demand and reduce medium- to long-term uncertainty. An example of aggregate inventory management is a company using a decentralized supply chain with multiple warehouses, each of which can maintain inventory and SS by item. If *warehouse A* has 300 units of inventory plus 100 units of SS, *warehouse B* has 450 units of inventory plus 125 units of SS, and *warehouse C* has 250 units of inventory plus 75 units of SS, then the total inventory for the item is 1,000 units plus 300 units of SS. Each warehouse in the decentralized supply chain amplifies the bullwhip effect and is subject to demand variability. This results in stockouts and a reduction in customer service. Inventory aggregation doesn't immediately reduce the bullwhip effect or SS levels. This comes later when demand variability swings are reduced.

A second type of aggregate inventory management occurs when a company decides to move to a centralized replenishment center. It consolidates inventory from multiple locations into one central location. This consolidation activity is called *risk pooling*.

The benefits of risk pooling and/or aggregate inventory management are reduced stockouts along with possible lower inventory levels, SS levels, and storage costs. Demand variability is reduced when aggregating demand across multiple locations causes high demand from one DC to be offset by low demand from a second one. The higher the market demand is, the greater the consolidation benefits. The disadvantages of risk pooling and aggregation are longer delivery times and increased transportation costs from the central site. This can lead to reduced customer service. This consolidation can have a positive or negative impact on performance metrics. *Positive correlation* occurs when two variables move in the same direction, and *negative correlation* happens when both variables move in different directions. For example, a positive correlation occurs when transportation delivery speed increases, resulting in an increase in customer service levels. A negative correlation occurs when a company has high inventory levels, which equates to lower profits and less cash-on-hand.

INVENTORY TYPES

The following terms describe the various inventory types. All of these terms are used to track inventory movement.

Raw materials are items directly used in the manufacturing transformation process. Examples include steel, chemicals, and flour.

Components are purchased or manufactured assemblies as well as spare parts, and semi-finished units and assemblies directly used in the manufacturing transformation process. These materials are called direct materials. Examples include a purchased power supply, bulk liquids, and an electrical harness.

WIP consists of an open work order when the manufacturing process has begun to transform raw materials and components into a higher level subassembly or finished good.

Finished goods are converted products available for sale, storage, or delivery. A good example is a make-to-stock (MTS) commodity product, such as a can of soup, that is available for immediate sale.

Maintenance, repair, and operating (MRO) *supplies* are inventory not used in the manufacturing process. These materials are considered indirect materials because they can't be traced back to a finished product and get expensed immediately upon receipt. Examples include work gloves, lubricants, sandpaper, and plastic wrap.

Returns are inventory being sent back from a customer for reprocessing, repair, evaluation, or disposal. For example, a customer returns an old car battery after purchasing a replacement one.

In transit, also called *pipeline inventory* or *distribution inventory*, is the amount of inventory being transported from a supplier to a customer stocking location. Global supply chain companies strive to reduce in transit inventory to lower inventory levels and costs. The formula for calculating in transit inventory is average annual inventory in transit divided by 365 days.

For example, a company has an annual demand of 100,000 units. The delivery from the supplier takes ten days. The annual demand is divided by 365 to obtain an in transit daily time of 274 units. The in transit time of ten days is then multiplied by 274 units to obtain the in transit inventory of 2,740 units. The calculation process can be used to determine the dollar amount by multiplying the number of units by its cost. It can also be used to determine the financial or quantity impact of reducing in transit lead times.

INVENTORY FUNCTIONAL TYPES

The following terms describe the various inventory functional types. All of these terms are used to manage inventory.

Anticipation inventory is the building up of inventory in anticipation of future demand. It helps to level production, and it reduces the cost of changing production rates for vacation down time, peak selling, promotions, or possible strikes.

SS inventory or *fluctuation inventory* is used to cover random, unpredictable oscillation fluctuations and swings in supply and demand. It provides protection against forecast variability and manufacturing or supplier disruptions. The word buffer and SS are often used interchangeably.

Decoupling inventory is extra inventory that needs to be held because of the difference in supply and demand orders or production batches. For example, a company produces a batch of 1,000 liters of a bulk solution, but it only plans to package 500 of the 1,000 liters based on current customer demand. The remaining inventory is retained for future use.

Lot size inventory is inventory that is purchased or manufactured in a quantity greater than immediate requirements in order to take advantage of quantity discounts, reduced shipping charges, reduced setup costs, or where actual demand requirements are decoupled from the production or purchase supply order batch size.

Cycle stock inventory is the portion of inventory that depletes gradually upon receipt of customer orders and is replenished cyclically upon receipt of supplier orders.

Hedge inventory is inventory purchased or manufactured to protect against supply disruption caused by material shortages, labor unrest, or price increases.

Buffer inventory is inventory consistently kept at a constraint work center or at a downstream work center to protect it from disruption due to material shortages from the feeding work center. The inventory buffer also acts as a cushion against an abrupt increase in short-term internal or external demand that exceeds production capacity.

Transportation inventory is the inventory required to cover the time period for moving products from the supplier to the customer.

Slow moving inventory is inventory that has a projected future usage that is less than existing inventory levels. *Obsolete inventory* or *obsolescence* is inventory that has no future projected usage and, as such, has no value.

Exercise 19.2 will test your knowledge and understanding of the various inventory functional types. Read each question and write in all answers that apply. The answers to the exercise are available from the Web Added Value™ Download Resource Center at www.jrosspub.com.

Exercise 19.2   Understanding various inventory functional types

Question	Answer
1. Which types best build inventory in excess of requirements?	
2. Which types best provide protection against supply and demand variability?	
3. Which type best breaks apart supply and demand?	
4. Which type best builds up inventory for a plant shutdown?	
5. Which type best maintains a material backlog kept behind a critical work center?	
6. Which type best manages event risk by buying extra inventory?	
7. Which type best provides protection for seasonal inventory?	
8. Which type best provides results in different lot-size work center quantities?	
9. Which type best replenishes cyclical inventory?	

INVENTORY-RELATED COSTS

The following terms are types of costs that relate to the process of acquiring, storing, using, and maintaining inventory over time.

- *Acquisition costs* are the costs that are needed to obtain a product or service. They are calculated by multiplying the purchased quantity against the unit cost and then adding the transportation costs.
- *Landed costs* for internally manufactured items include the sum of direct labor and material plus factory overhead costs. Externally sourced items include the sum of direct costs, transportation, customs, and insurance.
- *Carrying (holding) costs* are the costs of capital tied up in holding inventory. They are shown as a percentage of the total inventory dollar value over a time period. The percentage is based on the total storage, capital, risk, and insurance costs. Carrying costs vary inversely with ordering costs.
- *Ordering costs* are costs associated with placing, making or buying, receiving, inspecting, and putting away a purchase or shop order. Ordering costs vary inversely with carrying costs.
- *Storage costs* include the storage facility operating and labor costs, building and equipment depreciation, utilities, and insurance costs related to storing inventory.
- *Capital costs* are funds obtained from equity or financing to purchase one-time expenses such as buildings or equipment that are required in the production of goods and services.
- *Risk costs* are costs associated with the loss or damage of inventory from fire, theft, handling mishaps, and perishability.
- *Backorder* or *stockout costs* are costs associated with poor customer service due to late delivery. Two examples of this are customer chargeback costs or overnight premium freight costs.
- A *chargeback* is a service fee imposed by the customer against suppliers who don't meet a predefined and agreed-upon criteria. Examples include late deliveries or shipping the wrong materials.
- *Lost sale costs* are costs associated with poor customer service, as they lead to lost sales. An example is the freight and reprocessing costs of returning materials due to an order cancellation.

- *Lost customer costs* are costs associated with permanently losing a customer due to poor customer service. An example is the cost to acquire a new customer to replace the lost one.
- *Capacity variance costs* are costs associated with changing capacity levels. Examples of this are overtime, adding or ending a second shift, or closing a facility.
- *Opportunity costs* look at different investment alternatives to identify what must be given up if one option gets selected over the other. For example, a company is deciding to purchase either a new truck or a software system. It can select to spend money on either option. The company has to decide which option has the most value with the selected one becoming the opportunity cost.

STORAGE LOCATIONS

There are two types of storage locations. A *fixed location* keeps materials in a permanent site. The advantages of this type are that it makes it very easy for pickers to find materials in a warehouse, it reduces the amount of record-keeping, and it's easier to train workers to find the materials. The disadvantages of using a fixed location are that it has poor cube utilization and that it can require secondary storage locations. A *random location* can store materials in any open location. The advantages of this type are that it improves cube utilization, meets the need of controlling different material lots, and it permits first-in, first-out (FIFO) material storage. The disadvantages of the random location method are that it's difficult to find materials without having a computerized location system, it requires additional worker education and training, and it requires prior knowledge of where to find the previously put-away material.

KEY TERMINOLOGY

Understanding key terms and the concepts they represent is crucial to passing the CSCP exam. In this chapter, the important terms are identified in Table 19.3.

Table 19.3 Inventory management key terminology

80/20 rule
ABC analysis
Acquisition costs
Aggregate inventory management
Aggregate strategy
Anticipation inventory*
Backorder costs
Buffer*
Buffer inventory
Capacity variance costs
Capital costs

Continued

Carrying costs
Chargeback
Components
Customer demand
Customer service requirements
Cycle counting
Cycle stock inventory
Decouple
Decoupling inventory
Dependent demand
Distribution inventory*
Economic order quantity (EOQ)
Finished goods
Fixed location
Fixed order quantity (FOQ)
Fluctuation inventory
Hedge inventory
Holding costs
Independent demand*
Interval
In transit inventory
Inventory accuracy*
Inventory carrying costs
Inventory costs
Inventory optimization software*
Inventory visibility*
Joint store clustering
Landed costs*
Lead time
Lost customer costs
Lost sale costs
Lot size inventory
Lot-for-lot (L4L)
Maintenance, repair, and operating (MRO) supplies
Multi-echelon
Negative correlation

Continued

Nodes
Obsolescence*
Obsolete inventory
Opportunity costs
Optimization
Ordering costs*
Pareto analysis*
Periodic inventory
Periodic review system
Physical inventory
Pipeline inventory*
Planning horizon*
Positive correlation
Product variety
Random location
Raw materials
Reorder point
Replenishment lead time
Returns
Risk costs
Risk pooling*
Safety lead time*
Safety stock (SS)*
Single-echelon
Slow-moving inventory
Stage
Stockout costs
Storage costs
Suboptimization
Three V's (velocity, visibility, and variety)
Tier
Transportation inventory
Work-in-process (WIP)

*Key term found in the CSCP ECM

CSCP EXAM PRACTICE QUESTIONS ON INVENTORY MANAGEMENT

The questions shown in Table 19.4a cover the concepts presented in this chapter on inventory management. They are examples of what to expect on the actual exam.

Table 19.4a   Inventory management practice questions

No.	Questions
1	Which cost will typically increase when ordering a larger material quantity? a) Setup costs b) Ordering costs c) Carrying costs d) Transportation costs per hundred weight
2	A component assigned a unique and permanent location within a zoned warehouse for serial controlled materials is using what type of stock location system: a) Fixed b) Hybrid c) Random d) Floating
3	All of the following are sources of demand variability except for: a) Competition b) Forecast errors c) Seasonal effects d) Introduction of new products
4	What is the best goal of a supply chain implementation integration strategy? a) Create a flexible strategic plan b) Meet the needs of all participants c) Meet the needs of the channel master d) Meet the budget plan and time frame
5	What is the best advantage of using the Pareto diagram to identify process issues? a) Use it to resolve root causes b) Rank attributes by occurrences c) Eliminate the majority of problems by focusing on a small number of causes d) Eliminate major causes by focusing on a large number of problems
6	A company that has implemented a distribution center (DC) replacement collaboration program will do all of the following with its distribution partners except for: a) Joint forecasting b) Issue orders jointly c) Joint store clustering d) Mutually support order generation
7	What term refers to a solution to a problem that is best from a narrow point of view but not from a higher or overall company point of view? a) Optimization b) Suboptimization c) Over optimization d) Exception management

Continued

8	The extent to which inventory information is shared within a firm and with supply chain partners is called? a) Inventory velocity b) Inventory visibility c) Inventory optimization d) Inventory management
9	The MIP Company shipped a container of custom-made machine parts to South America. The average in-transit time is 20 days. The annual demand of this product is 12,000 units. What is the in-transit inventory? a) 61 units b) 200 units c) 329 units d) 658 units
10	Which of the following wouldn't be considered a stockout cost? a) Layoff costs b) Lost sale costs c) Price reduction costs d) Premium freight costs
11	What is most important to an integrated supply chain network? a) Information sharing b) Collaborative planning c) Joining forces with customers d) Enhanced product forecasting
12	Which type of inventory function is best for seasonal items? a) Mix inventory b) Pipeline inventory c) Fluctuation inventory d) Anticipation inventory
13	Creating independence between supply and material use is the function of: a) Safety stock b) Buffer stock c) Reserve stock d) Decoupling stock
14	A company is selling 20,000 units per year. The total cost to place an order is $50 per purchase order and the cost of carrying inventory is 25%. The standard cost of each unit is $10. Calculate the economic order quantity. a) 163 b) 400 c) 632 d) 894
15	A company that is looking to improve the effectiveness of its supply chain should consider eliminating: a) An echelon b) A factory c) A warehouse d) A retail store
16	A company decided to consolidate its inventory in a centralized warehouse instead of three stand-alone warehouses. What is the best reason for taking this action? a) Risk pooling b) Reduction of inventory c) Centralized inventory control d) Decentralized inventory control

Continued

17	What is the biggest overall impact if you reduce one partner from your supply chain network? a) Reduced logistics costs b) Reduced inventory levels c) Reduced delivery cycle time d) Reduced transportation costs
18	Inventory carrying costs include all of the following types except for: a) Pilferage b) Insurance c) Material costs d) Investment costs
19	Calculate the total cost of carrying inventory based on the following: average inventory is $300,000, capital costs are 9%, storage costs are 3%, risk costs are 4%, and interest rates are 7%. a) $40,000 b) $48,000 c) $51,000 d) $77,000
20	A retail company always orders a case lot of 24 pieces. What order quantity is being used? a) Fixed b) Lot-for-lot (L4L) c) Period supply d) Economic order quantity (EOQ)
21	Item A has a lead time of six weeks, average demand of 150 units per week, and safety stock (SS) of 300 units. The order quantity is 2,000 units, and it's purchased in boxes of 100 units. What is the reorder point? a) 300 b) 900 c) 1,200 d) 2,000
22	Safety stock (SS) is used for all of the following purposes except for: a) Protection against forecast errors b) Protection against shipping errors c) Protection against demand or supply fluctuations d) Protection against short-term backlog changes
23	A company seeking to develop an inventory solution to maximize customer service and return on investment (ROI) over several supply chain tiers is most likely using what type of software? a) Inventory optimization b) Inventory management c) Enterprise resource management (ERM) d) Customer relationship management (CRM)

ANSWERS TO CSCP EXAM PRACTICE QUESTIONS ON INVENTORY MANAGEMENT

The answers to the practice questions on inventory management are shown in Table 19.4b. Any question you answer incorrectly indicates a gap in your body of knowledge and encourages the need for additional study time.

Table 19.4b Answers to CSCP exam practice questions on inventory management

No.	Answers
1	Answer: C Carrying costs are variable costs that increase as the level of inventory increases.
2	Answer: A The key word in this question is *permanent*. A component placed in the same location every time is using a fixed location system.
3	Answer: B Forecast errors are used solely to measure and track demand variability and therefore aren't a source of it. Competition, seasonal effects, and the introduction of new products can cause variability by changing demand patterns.
4	Answer: B A supply chain implementation integration strategy must meet the needs of all participants in order to be successful. The strategic plan, budget, and time frame have to be developed before the implementation integration strategy. Meeting the needs of the channel master could be correct, but it's not the best goal.
5	Answer: B A Pareto analysis groups and ranks process issues by frequency of occurrences. A company can use this ranking to focus on making improvements on the largest groups of process issues first, and can therefore receive the greatest benefits.
6	Answer: C Joint store clustering is the process of blanketing an area with a number of retail stores. Examples of this are Starbucks and Dunkin Donuts. It is the store owner's responsibility to decide where to locate their stores. The store placement decision isn't directly linked to any collaboration program.
7	Answer: B This question requires knowledge of the APICS Dictionary definition of *suboptimization*. Suboptimization occurs when different units (work areas) develop a solution that is best for them, but not for the entire organization.
8	Answer: B This question requires knowledge of the APICS Dictionary definition of *inventory visibility*. Inventory visibility is the ability to see across the supply chain into a company's inventory position.
9	Answer: D In-transit inventory is calculated by taking the annual demand and dividing it by the number of days in a year and then multiplying that answer by the number of in transit days ((12,000 ÷ 365 = 32.877) * 20) to obtain 658 (657.54) units of in-transit inventory.
10	Answer: A Stockout costs mean that you don't have adequate resources (material, equipment, or people) to produce a product. Hiring might be considered a stockout cost in order to meet demand but not layoffs. Price reductions are used to make a customer happy (chargebacks or rebates) or costs may be incurred in premium freight to express ship a backorder.

Continued

11	Answer: B
	Collaborative planning leads to answers A, C, and D.
12	Answer: D
	This question requires knowledge of the APICS Dictionary definition of *anticipation inventory*. Anticipation inventory is used to build up inventory in advance of a peak selling season and to accommodate seasonal demand.
13	Answer: D
	This question requires knowledge of the APICS Dictionary definition of *decoupling*. Decoupling is creating independence between supply and material use. It breaks apart supply and demand due to material ordering, manufacturing, and material use patterns. Answers B and C are forms of safety stock.
14	Answer: D
	This question requires knowledge of the economic order quantity (EOQ) formula. The formula is the square root of 2AS ÷ IC. The calculation is shown as ((2 * 20,000 * $50) ÷ (0.25 * $10) = (2,000,000 ÷ 2.5)) = square root of 800,000 or 894.
15	Answer: A
	A company should look to eliminate an entire echelon (tier) in order to improve their supply chain effectiveness. It will reduce lead time, inventory, and costs.
16	Answer: A
	Risk pooling (consolidation) reduces storage, equipment, labor costs, and it lessens the possibility of stockouts resulting in less risk. Please note that this question doesn't mention reducing inventory, which is why B isn't the correct answer. It only states that inventory was consolidated, meaning the same amount of inventory was put into one location.
17	Answer: B
	The removal of one partner from the supply chain will directly reduce inventory levels. This is because the supply chain network has one less location requiring inventory to be stored. Answers A, C, and D may not see a direct reduction in inventory.
18	Answer: C
	Material costs are part of costs of goods sold (COGS). Answers A, B, and D are all included in carrying costs.
19	Answer: B
	The total cost of carry inventory formula is ((average inventory times (capital costs plus storage costs plus risk costs)). The calculation is (($300,000 * (9% + 3% + 4% = 16%) = $48,000).
20	Answer: A
	A fixed order quantity requires a minimal order quantity to be placed (i.e., 24 pieces).
21	Answer: C
	The reorder point formula is demand during lead time plus safety stock (DDLT + SS). The calculation is ((6 * 150) + 300 = 1,200).
22	Answer: B
	Safety stock (SS) won't provide protection against shipping errors. It's used to provide extra inventory for demand variability.
23	Answer: A
	This question requires knowledge of the APICS Dictionary definition of *inventory optimization*. Inventory optimization is the process of determining the right inventory levels across the supply chain while maximizing customer service and return on investment (ROI).

Web Added Value™

This book has free material available for download from the
Web Added Value™ resource center at *www.jrosspub.com*

20

FINANCIAL AND MANAGERIAL ACCOUNTING CONCEPTS

This chapter focuses on financial concepts, financial statements and reporting components, metrics, and calculations that are used to perform financial and managerial analysis. It also examines why it's important for a supply chain professional to understand financial and managerial concepts and their corresponding analysis.

FINANCIAL STATEMENTS

A supply chain professional needs to understand the following three financial statements which are prepared from *aggregated* financial data. They are the balance sheet, income statement, and a statement of cash flow. A *balance sheet* is a snapshot of the financial condition of a company at a given point in time, as shown in Table 20.1. It consists of *assets* (something of economic value), *liabilities* (a debt or financial obligation), and *stockholder equity* (invested capital). *Accruals* are short-term revenue or liabilities that a company expects to receive or spend in a future accounting reporting period.

Table 20.1   Balance sheet

Balance Sheet December 31, 2017		
Current assets		
Cash		$325,000
Accounts receivables		$320,000
Inventories		
Material	$120,000	
Work-in-process	$240,000	
Finished goods	$345,000	
Total inventory		$705,000
Gross fixed assets (at cost)		
Land and buildings		$900,000
Vehicles		$250,000
Machinery and equipment		$500,000
Total assets		$3,000,000
Current liabilities		
Accounts payable	$500,000	
Notes payable	$400,000	
Accruals	$100,000	
Total current liabilities		$1,000,000
Long-term debt		$900,000
Stockholder equity		
Common stock		$600,000
Retained earnings		$500,000
Total liabilities and stockholder equity		$3,000,000

An *income statement* reveals if a company has net income or loss during a specified period; it consists of *revenue, cost of goods sold* (COGS), and *operating expenses.* An income statement measures financial performances over a stated time period. Companies also like to track net income as a percentage of revenue. Table 20.2 indicates whether the company generated a net profit or loss. In this example, the company earned an operating income of $97,000.

Table 20.2   Income statement

Income Statement For the Period Ending December 31, 2017		
Sales revenue		$850,000
Cost of goods sold	$510,000	
Gross profit/loss on sales		$340,000
Selling, general, and administrative (SGA)	$243,000	
Operating income		$97,000
Net income as a % of revenue ($97,000 ÷ $850,000)		11.4%

FINANCIAL ANALYSIS

Supply chain improvements can reduce COGS through better management of resources. Any reduction in material, labor, and overhead can boost profitability. Table 20.3 displays a pro forma income statement showing the effect of a five percent reduction in each COGS area.

Table 20.3   Five percent reduction in COGS

Area	Before	After
Sales	$100.0	$100.0
COGS	—	—
Material	$30.00	$28.50
Labor	$13.00	$12.35
Overhead	$29.00	$27.55
	—	—
COGS total	$72.00	$68.40
	—	—
Gross profit	$28.00	$31.60

The COGS for each area displays the five percent reduction. A calculation of the reduction can now be determined from the before to the after. The before can be compared against the after to show the financial impact of the reduction effort. A five percent COGS reduction results in a 12.9% increase in profits (($31.60 − $28.00) ÷ $28.00).

A *cash flow statement* provides information on *spend management* regarding *cash inflow* (receipts) and *cash outflow* (payments) for a stated time. Cash inflow enters the business through the sale of products or services, and cash outflow is money leaving the business to pay for raw materials, components, labor, and overhead related expenses. A *positive cash flow* occurs when cash inflow exceeds cash outflow. This permits the business to pay invoices in a timely manner. A *negative cash flow* occurs when cash outflow exceeds cash inflow. A business has to then borrow money, pay invoices late, ask for extended terms, or use internal cash reserves to cover its cash shortfalls. A positive or negative cash flow indicates the financial health of a business.

A cash flow statement can be shown in two different ways. The first is the *direct method* which reports operating cash inflows (customer receipts) and cash outflows (supplier payments) in the operating activities section in the statement of cash flow report. The second is the *indirect method* which reports operating cash flows beginning with net income and adjusting for revenues and expenses that don't involve the receipt or payment of cash.

Financial accounting governs the preparation and reporting of corporate financial statements according to a common set of accounting principles, standards, and procedures. They simplify the recording and reporting of accounting information. *Generally Accepted Accounting Principles* (GAAP) is used only in the United States (U.S.), while the *International Financial Reporting Standards* (IFRS) is used everywhere else in the world. The objective of *managerial accounting* is to help management make informed financial decisions based on collected information.

Exercise 20.1 will test your knowledge and understanding of the impact of process changes on a company's financials. Read each question and write in whether the results go up or down. Also, write in why you think your response will occur. The answers to the exercise are available from the Web Added Value™ Download Resource Center at www.jrosspub.com.

Exercise 20.1   Impact of process changes on a company's financials

Question	Answer
1. The company produced more units than planned. What was the impact on gross profit?	
2. The company outsourced its warehousing operations. What will be the impact on cost of goods sold (COGS)?	
3. The company implemented a lean initiative. What will most likely be the impact on inventory levels?	
4. Management has implemented an overall 10% inventory reduction program to reduce inventory levels at year end. What will most likely be the impact on customer service?	
5. The company purchased an automatic storage and retrieval system (ASRS). What will the impact be on fixed assets on the income statement?	
6. The company increased its country-specific asset footprint. What is the impact on its transportation costs?	
7. The company decided to utilize a demand-shaping technique to move excess inventory. How will this action impact cash flow?	

FINANCIAL REPORT COMPONENTS

A *standard cost* is an estimated cost to produce a product or perform a service. This method uses predefined standard costs to project future product or service costs by totaling up *direct material costs* (materials used in the production process), *direct labor costs* (labor charged against a work order producing a product), and *overhead costs* (charges not directly assigned against a work order to produce a product, but rather allocated). The financial department in a company compares standard costs against actual costs to identify any discrepancies. Discrepancies are then analyzed to determine the reason for the differences, and corrective action is taken to resolve root causes.

The formula used to establish a standard cost is based on first determining the direct material, direct labor, and overhead rate per unit. These totals are then summed up in Table 20.4.

Table 20.4   Standard cost calculation

Type	Price	Calculation	Quantity (or hours)	Calculated Cost
Direct material	$6.50	Times	Two pounds	$13.00
Direct labor	$20.00	Times	One hour	$20.00
Overhead	$24.00	Times	One unit	$24.00
Total				$57.00

The calculated costs are added together ($13.00 + $20.00 + $24.00) to obtain a standard cost of $57.00 for this product.

OVERHEAD COSTS

Overhead costs aren't directly associated with a revenue-generating function. These costs include rent, utilities, warehousing, insurance, indirect labor and materials, and administrative and management expenses. They are often very substantial and require close monitoring, as they impact profitability. The overhead cost rate driver is calculated by dividing total overhead costs by the total cost driver. The calculated rate is then allocated against the completed work order. A cost driver can be labor, machine hours, or produced units.

For example, a factory's total overhead cost is projected to be $240,000 and its units (cost driver) are projected to be 24,000 units. The calculated overhead rate is determined to be $10.00 per charged unit ($240,000 ÷ 24,000 units). The company produced 1,900 units last month. The overhead cost is determined by taking the 1,900 units produced and multiplying them by $10.00 (direct labor hours) to calculate that $19,000 of overhead was earned. However, $20,000 was budgeted, so a variance exists. The variance is $19,000 minus $20,000 to show that a $1,000 negative variance exists (less cost than projected). The $1,000 variance directly impacts the bottom line by reducing profit. The opposite occurs when a company overbuilds since the company sees a positive impact on the bottom line.

COGS is a financial value that appears on an income statement. It's calculated for manufacturing products by taking the beginning inventory, adding COGS consisting of material, adding labor and allocated overhead, and subtracting ending inventory. The cost of COGS is calculated and tracked through the *periodic inventory method* to determine material cost. The periodic inventory method is an accounting method that is used to update inventory records at specified time periods. COGS knowledge can be a valuable analysis tool in understanding the operations and supply chain cost structure, and in helping to identify cost reduction opportunities. The manufacturing COGS calculation is the only method used in the Certified Supply Chain Professional (CSCP) Learning System. The retail and services' method isn't shown in the courseware.

Three *asset footprint* models impact organizational costs. They are *global* asset footprint, *regional* asset footprint, and *country-specific* asset footprint. A *global asset footprint* is when all production takes place at one manufacturing or distribution location. This permits economies of scale and lower costs due to greater use of capital-intensive equipment. A *regional asset footprint* is when production becomes localized by region. It's used when transportation costs or time is a significant consideration. A *country-specific asset footprint* is when production becomes localized by country. It's used when transportation costs, time requirements, and duties are extremely high, or when meeting local sourcing requirements.

Cost structures consist of fixed and variable incurred costs. Supply chain and organizational cost structures need to support each other. Customer service, sales channels, value systems, operating models, and asset footprints form the basis of a supply chain cost structure. The costs can differ significantly based on the selected manufacturing environment. These can include make-to-stock (MTS), make-to-order (MTO), assemble-to-order (ATO), package-to-order (PTO), configure-to-order (CTO), and engineer-to-order (ETO). The costs associated with each environment will differ based on inventory types, production processes, delivery speed, design differences, and whether products are manufactured in-house or subcontracted to a third party.

A company can use *first-in, first-out* (FIFO) or *last-in, first-out* (LIFO) to determine inventory value. *Inventory valuation* is calculated based on actual or market monetary value. Both of these methods are permitted by GAAP, but the IFRS only permits the use of the FIFO method. In FIFO, the COGS are based upon the cost of materials purchased first. The inventory cost is based on materials bought last. Inventory valuation is calculated at current replacement costs. During periods of inflation, FIFO shows lower COGS resulting in higher net income. In LIFO, the COGS are based upon the cost of materials purchased last. The inventory cost is based on materials bought last. Inventory valuation is calculated at the original purchase cost. During periods of inflation, LIFO shows higher COGS resulting in lower net income.

For example, a company purchased 200 bottles throughout the year. The first lot of 100 was at a cost of $30 and the last lot cost $32. The company has $5,000 in revenue. In FIFO, the bottle cost is based on its original purchase price of $30, and in LIFO, the bottle price is $32 based on the remaining inventory cost. Table 20.5 displays the differences in COGS and gross profit between the two methods for the first 100 bottles.

Table 20.5   FIFO and LIFO calculation

Information	FIFO	LIFO
Revenue	$5000	$5000
COGS	$3000 (100 * $30)	$3200 (100 * $32)
Gross profit	$2000	$1800

Table 20.6 displays the FIFO and LIFO impact on COGS, gross profit, taxes, inventory, and inventory turns.

Table 20.6 FIFO and LIFO impact

Impact	FIFO	LIFO
COGS	Lower	Higher
Gross profit	Higher	Lower
Taxes	Higher	Lower
Inventory (assets)	Higher	Lower
Turns	Lower	Higher

TAX IMPACT

A global tax-aligned supply chain can help to lower *corporate tax liability*. For example, a company operating in Ireland pays a much lower, flat corporate tax rate. A company operating in the U.S. pays a much higher rate. A U.S.-based company can decide to move its operations to another country in order to gain a substantial *tax savings*, which will result in higher corporate profits. *Tangible costs* are direct costs that can be easily identified, quantified, or measured, while *intangible costs* are very subjective, and can't be easily identified, quantified, or measured. An example of a tangible cost is purchasing a piece of equipment, while an intangible cost is labor hours spent improving productivity or efficiency.

FINANCIAL METRICS

Four ratios are used to determine the financial health of a customer or supplier. They are activity, liquidity, leverage, and profitability—and they're obtained from a company's financial statements.

Activity ratios measure how efficiently a company is using its resources. They monitor inventory turnover, inventory days or receivable, payables outstanding, and total assets. These metrics are discussed later in the book.

A *liquidity ratio* measures the ability of an organization to meet its short-term financial obligations when they become due. It's measured by calculating current assets less inventories, then dividing that by current liabilities. The results indicate the number of times short-term debt obligations are covered by liquid assets. A value greater than one indicates that short-term obligations are fully covered, while a value less than one indicates financial difficulties. For example, a company has current assets consisting of cash ($15,000), accounts receivables ($35,000), and inventory ($20,000). Its liabilities consist of accounts payable ($5,000) and a short-term bank loan ($15,000). The *quick ratio* can be calculated with the following formula: ((current assets – inventories) ÷ current liabilities). The calculation is (($70,000 – $20,000) ÷ $20,000 = 2.5). The quick ratio for the organization is 2.5. This means that for every $1.00 in current liabilities, it has $2.50 available in current assets. This indicates that sufficient assets exist to pay off their creditors.

Leverage ratios are used to track the amount of debt a company carries, and to determine if debt repayment can be met. Three common ratios are debt-to-equity ratio, debt ratio, and equity ratio. The higher the leverage ratios, the higher the investors' level of risk. When creditors own a majority of the company's assets, the company is considered highly leveraged. All of these measurements are important for investors to understand how risky the capital structure of a company is and if it's worth investing in.

The following is an example of a leverage ratio. A company has a $500,000 mortgage and a $200,000 bank revolving credit line. The business owners have $500,000 in equity. The formula to calculate the debt-to-equity ratio is current liabilities divided by total equity (($500,000 + $200,000) ÷ $500,000). The ratio is 1.4, which means that the company is highly leveraged. This can be a concern, as debt is being funded by the company's creditors.

A *profitability ratio* is used to assess a company's ability to generate earnings from its investments. *Net profit margin* is used by companies to track *return on investments* (ROI). It measures the amount of net income earned from each dollar of generated sales. The profitability ratio compares net income against a company's net sales. In other words, it determines the percentage of sales' profitability remaining after paying all business expenses. For example, a company had net sales of $1,000,000 and their net profit was $150,000 last year. The formula to calculate net profit margin is net profit divided by net sales. Net profit margin is calculated as 15% ($150,000 ÷ $1,000,000). This means that the company converted 15% of its sales into profits.

The profitability ratio shows if sufficient operational profits can be achieved from the investment. It's considered an efficiency ratio because it indicates how well assets are being used to generate profits. A low profitability ratio indicates that expenses may be too high and that they need to be reduced.

The Altman *Z-Score* is a statistical measurement tool that is used to predict an organization's solvency. The process uses four weighted financial ratios to identify firms with a high probability of going bankrupt. A public organization with a score of less than 1.8 or a private organization with a score of less than 1.1 is considered at risk.

The formula that public organizations use is ((working capital ÷ total assets) * 1.2) + ((retained earnings ÷ total assets) * 1.4) + ((earnings before interest and taxes (EBIT) ÷ total assets) * 3.3) + ((net worth ÷ total liability) * .6) + ((net sales ÷ total assets) * 1.0). The collected financial data is inserted into this formula and then processed to calculate a company's financial solvency ratio.

The Z-score assigns a green (safe), yellow (warning), and red (risk) rating to track solvency. A score of 3.0 or higher means the company is in a green zone, a yellow zone is 1.8 to 3.0, and a score of less than 1.8 means they're in a red zone. Non-manufacturing and private organizations use a slightly different formula with different percentages.

Operational metrics measures the day-to-day operational efficiency and effectiveness to determine the degree of value found in a company's operations. The operational metrics are broken down into quality, productivity, and asset/financial management.

Quality metrics are used to measure products against predefined quality standards. Examples include avoidance of damage to goods, warranty claims, or number of product or service defects. They also track customer order accuracy. Examples of this include order entry process errors, information accuracy, order and item picking, and invoice accuracy.

The *supplier performance index* (SPI) tracks the true cost of ownership and not just the original material purchase price. It calculates the nonconformance costs required to rectify any supplier-delivered product defects. The SPI takes the sum of the purchase material and all nonconforming costs and divides it by the cost of the materials. The formula is shown as (SPI = (material cost + nonconformance cost) ÷ material cost). For example, a supplier quoted the material cost for an item to be $200. The company determined, based on past performance, that nonconformance costs are $40. The SPI is calculated as ($200 + $40) ÷ $200 = 1.20. The total cost of ownership (TCO) is determined to be $240 ($200 * 1.20). The SPI is used to compare the true material costs from different suppliers and then supplier selection is based on real cost.

Asset management metrics measure asset usage. An asset can be inventory, equipment, or even manufacturing or warehouse capacity.

The *basic accounting equation* displays economic events that occur in an organization. It's shown as *assets equal liabilities plus owner's equity*. However, it's important to learn the other variations of this basic formula which are *liabilities equal assets minus owner's equity* and *owner's equity equals assets minus liabilities*, as they might appear on the exam.

The *basic income statement equation* displays the profitability of a business. It's used to analyze the business operation in the reported period to show profit earned or losses incurred. The basic income statement equation is *income equals revenue minus expenses*. However, you may also see it displayed as *revenue equals income plus expenses* or *expenses equal revenue minus income*.

Days payable outstanding (DPO) measures the number of days it takes for a company to pay its bills. The formula takes the average of gross accounts payable, divides it by cost of sales, and then multiplies the results by 365 days. The number indicates how many days on average it takes a company to pay its debts for ordered materials.

The following is an example of how to calculate DPO. A company has payables of $140,000 and cost of sales of $1,000,000. The DPO calculation is shown as:

$$DPO = (\$140,000 \div \$1,000,000) * 365$$
$$DPO = 0.14 * 365$$
$$DPO = 51.1 \text{ days}$$

Days receivable outstanding, or *days sales outstanding* (DSO), measures the liquidity of receivables or the time it takes from the sale of a product or service to receive customer payment. The formula takes the average of gross accounts receivables, divides it by annualized revenue, and then multiplies the results by 365 days. The results indicate the time frame that customers take to pay for a product or service. Slow-paying customers require the company to internally finance these purchases or to borrow funds until a customer payment is received.

The following is an example of how to calculate DSO. A company has outstanding gross accounts receivables of $100,000 and annualized revenue of $1,000,000. The DSO calculation is shown as:

$$DSO = (\$100,000 \div \$1,000,000) * 365$$
$$DSO = 0.10 * 365$$
$$DSO = 36.5 \text{ days}$$

Average inventory is calculated by taking the beginning inventory, plus the ending inventory, and dividing by two. For example, at the beginning of the month, a company has $1,200,000 worth of inventory, and at the end of the month, $800,000 remains. Add $1,200,000 to the remaining balance of $800,000, and then divide by two to calculate the average inventory of $1,000,000.

Inventory turnover (inventory turns or turns) measures inventory liquidity or the number of times inventory is sold during the year. A high turnover requires less cash to be tied up in inventory, and it demonstrates how efficiently inventory is being used to generate revenue. A high inventory turnover equates to a high inventory velocity. *Inventory velocity* is the speed or frequency at which inventory turns over during the year. There are three variations of the manufacturing inventory turnover formula. They are turns times average inventory, COGS divided by average inventory, and COGS divided by turns.

Option one is turns times average inventory to obtain COGS. An example takes inventory turns of two times the average inventory of $500 to obtain COGS of $1,000.

Option two is COGS divided by inventory turns to obtain average inventory. An example takes COGS of $1,000 divided by two turns to obtain average inventory of $500.

Option three is COGS divided by average inventory to obtain inventory turns. An example takes COGS of $1,000 divided by average inventory of $500 to obtain inventory turns of two.

Retail and non-manufacturing companies use different variations of the inventory turnover formula. They include generic inventory turnover, inventory turnover ratio for retail, and inventory turnover for commodity products. For example, if the COGS is unknown or not used, inventory turnover is calculated by dividing net sales by average inventory at cost (purchase price). If the average inventory at cost is also unknown, a company is able to use inventory at selling price (selling price less margin).

The *generic inventory turnover* (*turns*) formula determines the number of times that inventory generates sales. It reveals the relationship between sales and average inventory. This method is used by retail companies because it's easier to obtain sales information. For example, a store had sales of $20,000 last year, and its average inventory value was $4,000. Turns are calculated by taking sales and dividing it by the average inventory ($20,000 ÷ $4,000) to obtain a turn rate of five or 73 days (365 days ÷ five turns) of inventory. The higher the turn rate, the more it turns over in a store. This method permits a retail store to compare itself against its competitors to benchmark how well they are doing.

The *inventory turnover ratio for retail* formula determines the number of times inventory generates sales. It reveals the relationship between sales and average inventory at the selling price. The only difference between *inventory turnover for retail* and *generic inventory turnover* is the use of average inventory at selling price. This method is also used by retail companies because it's easy to obtain the sales information needed to compare one store against another. For example, a store had sales of $30,000 last year where it sold 15,000 units ($2.00 per unit). Its average inventory at selling price was $7,500. Turns are calculated by taking sales divided by average inventory by selling price ($30,000 ÷ $7,500) to obtain a turn rate of four or 91.25 days (365 days ÷ four turns) of inventory.

The *inventory turnover for commodity* products can have volatile swings in both demand and product pricing. The use of units sold is a better way to measure turns for this type of product. For example, a company sold 50,000 units last year and its average inventory was 5,000 units. Turns are calculated by taking units sold divided by average inventory in units (50,000 ÷ 5,000) to obtain a turn rate of ten or 36.5 days (365 days ÷ ten turns) of inventory.

Inventory *days of supply* measures the average time needed for a company to sell its existing inventory. The formula takes average inventory and divides it by COGS and then multiples it by 365 days.

In the following example, a manufacturing company has average inventory of $500,000 and COGS of $1,000,000. The inventory day's calculation is:

$$\text{Inventory days} = (\text{average inventory} \div \text{COGS}) * 365$$
$$\text{Inventory days} = (\$500,000 \div \$1,000,000) * 365$$
$$\text{Inventory days} = 0.5 * 365$$
$$\text{Inventory days} = 182.5 \text{ days}$$

The second method used to calculate average inventory uses a variation of the inventory turn formula. It takes COGS and divides it by inventory turns. In the following example, the company has COGS of $1,000,000 and it turns its inventory over two times a year:

$$\text{Average inventory} = \text{COGS} \div \text{turns}$$
$$\text{Average inventory} = \$1,000,000 \div 2$$
$$\text{Average inventory} = \$500,000$$

The *cash-to-cash cycle time* measures the number of days it takes to convert inventory into salable products, sell the products, and receive payment from the customer. The longer the time frame, the longer a company is deprived of cash, which may result in a negative cash flow. There are four versions of the cash-to-cash formula.

Version one is cash-to-cash cycle time = inventory days of supply + days sales outstanding – days payable outstanding. An example of version one is taking an average days of supply of 25 days plus DSO of 40 days and subtracting 30 days of DPO to calculate a cash-to-cash cycle time of 35 days (25 + 40 – 30).

Version two is days payable outstanding = days sales outstanding + inventory days of supply – cash-to-cash cycle time. An example of version two is taking average days of supply of 40 days plus DSO of 25 days and subtracting 35 days of DPO to calculate a cash-to-cash cycle time of 30 days (40 + 25 – 35).

Version three is inventory days of supply = cash-to-cash cycle time + days payable outstanding – days sales outstanding. An example of version three is taking average days of supply of 35 days plus DSO of 30 days and subtracting 40 days of DPO to calculate a cash-to-cash cycle time of 25 days (35 + 30 – 40).

Version four is days sales outstanding = cash-to-cash cycle time + days payable outstanding – inventory days of supply. An example of version four is taking average days of supply of 35 days plus DSO of 30 days and subtracting 25 days of DPO to calculate a cash-to-cash cycle time of 40 days (35 + 30 – 25).

An understanding of supplier capacity and supplier capability is required for a company that experiences significant demand variability and product growth. It needs to validate that its suppliers have the capability to meet current and future demand. Failure to do so is a potential risk and any doubts will leave the company seeking an alternate supplier. A key step in making the right decision is to determine if their existing supplier has sufficient capacity. The formula to perform this analysis is ((sales of products ÷ capacity utilization) * (1 – capacity utilization)) ÷ price per unit. For example, consider a company currently selling 1,000,000 units, at $7.00 per unit, with its capacity utilization rate at 98%. This information is inserted into the formula and processed ((1,000,000 ÷ 0.98) * (1 – 0.98)) ÷ $7.00 equates to ((1,020,408.16 * 0.02) ÷ $7.00)—to calculate the supplier capacity as 2,915 units. If the company projects the need for 4,500 units next year, discussions with the supplier must take place to determine how the supplier plans to meet this increased need.

Supply chain management costs (SCMC) include all direct and indirect expenses that are associated with the operation of the APICS Supply Chain Operations Reference (SCOR®) model business processes found across the supply chain. The formula is the sum of the cost to plan, plus cost to source, plus cost to deliver, plus cost to return. Please note that the cost to make isn't part of SCMC, but is captured within COGS. SCMC is used in the calculation of *return on supply chain fixed assets* (RSCFA) and return on working capital.

Supply chain revenue is a calculated metric that is shown as supply chain revenue minus COGS minus SCM costs. It shows the revenue being generated through the supply chain minus the total supply chain costs.

Return on assets (ROA) is a profitability ratio that indicates a company's efficiency in using resources (assets) to generate income during a financial year. The ratio determines if a company earned its desired return on each invested dollar. A company with an upward ratio reveals improving profitability, while a downward ratio indicates deteriorating profitability.

ROA is calculated by taking net profit margin times assets turnover. In order to calculate ROA, finance needs to determine a company's net profit margin. For example, net profit margin is calculated by dividing net profit of $15,000 by net sales of $60,000 times 100% to obtain a net profit margin of 25% (($15,000 ÷ $60,000) * 100%). Next, determine asset turnover by dividing net sales of $60,000 by total assets of $80,000 times 100% to obtain an asset turnover rate of 75% (($60,000 ÷ $80,000) * 100%). Finally, calculate ROA by dividing net profit margin by asset turnover times 100% to obtain an ROA of 18.75% (ROA = (25% * 75%) * 100%). This reveals that for every invested dollar, the company generated $0.19 in profits.

RSCFA measures the return that a company receives on every dollar invested in fixed assets such as its motor carrier fleet or warehouses. The RSCFA formula is *return on supply chain revenue* minus COGS, minus SCM costs, divided by supply chain fixed assets. A higher ratio implies that a company is obtaining a better return on fixed assets from each dollar invested. Selling a company's warehouses or its motor carrier fleet to a third party reduces the value of its fixed assets.

The supply chain fixed assets formula is return on supply chain revenue minus COGS, minus SCM costs, divided by supply chain fixed assets. For example, a company currently has supply chain revenue of $10,000,000, COGS of $6,500,000, SCM costs of $500,000, and supply chain fixed assets of $5,000,000:

$$RSCFA = (\$10,000,000 - \$6,500,000 - \$500,000) \div \$5,000,000 = 60\%$$

The company outsources and sells the warehouse and motor carrier fleet to a third party. This results in the total value of fixed assets dropping to $2,000,000. RSCFA can be recalculated to show the impact of a reduction in fixed assets. Notice the improvement on supply chain fixed assets:

$$RSCFA = (\$10,000,000 - \$6,500,000 - \$500,000) \div \$2,000,000 = 150\%.$$

Return on working capital (ROWC) is a financial metric which measures a company's investment against the revenue being generated from capital being invested. It provides an idea of whether capital is being used effectively, as a high number is preferred.

The ROWC formula is (supply chain revenue minus COGS minus SCMC) divided by (inventory plus accounts receivable minus accounts payable). The measurement shows if a company has a positive or negative cash flow and/or operating liquidity. Liquidity implies that assets, such as inventories or accounts receivables, can be quickly converted into cash. Accounts receivables have a negative impact on liquidity because they require an outflow of cash. A company needs positive working capital to efficiently manage its business.

The following example is provided for use in the calculation of ROWC. The supply chain revenue is $2,000,000, the COGS is $1,500,000, the SCM costs are $300,000, inventory is $500,000, accounts payable is $200,000, and accounts receivable is $200,000. The ROWC formula is equal to (supply chain revenue minus COGS minus SCM costs) divided by (inventory plus accounts receivable minus accounts payable).

$$ROWC = (\$2,000,000 - \$1,500,000 - \$300,000) \div (\$500,000 + \$200,000 - \$200,000)$$
$$RSCFA = \$200,000 \div \$500,000$$
$$RSCFA = 40\%$$

Benefit-cost analysis is used to evaluate a project by comparing benefits against activity costs. It's a simple method to evaluate a project and determine the financial benefits of accepting or rejecting it. It's important to use the same time frame for both benefits and costs in the calculation, and not compare projects of unequal service length. Table 20.7 is provided for use in the following calculation.

Table 20.7 Benefit-cost analysis

Type	Year One	Year Two	Year Three	Year Four
Benefits	$150,000	$150,000	$150,000	Unknown
Costs	$50,000	$50,000	$50,000	$50,000

According to Table 20.7, the expected total benefits are $150,000 a year for the next three years, and the total costs are $50,000 a year for the next four years. In the following example, the calculation time frame compares three years of benefits against three years of costs (three years times $50,000), rather than the four years shown in the table.

The benefit-cost analysis formula is total benefits divided by total costs for the identified time period:

$$Benefit\text{-}cost\ analysis = \$450,000 \div \$150,000$$
$$Benefit\text{-}cost\ analysis = 3$$

The benefit-cost analysis reveals that for each dollar invested, the company will see a return of $3.00. This appears to be an excellent investment.

ROI measures the relative return from an investment. It's calculated by taking total benefits minus total costs, dividing by total costs, and then multiplying by 100%. As with the benefit-cost analysis calculation, the CSCP exam can show a different time frame for total costs and total benefits.

The data provided in Table 20.7 is being used in the following calculation. The ROI formula is total benefits minus total costs divided by total costs for the identified time period times 100%:

$$ROI = (\$450,000 - \$150,000) \div \$150,000$$
$$ROI = \$300,000 \div \$150,000$$
$$ROI = 2 * 100\% = 200\%$$

The ROI reveals that for each dollar invested over the three year period, a 200% return will be realized. This appears to be an excellent investment.

Net present value (NPV) is a financial tool used in capital budgeting to analyze the profitability of a proposed project investment. It compares the present value of the expected future benefits against expected future project costs. A project with a positive number may be considered, while a negative number should be rejected. NPV considers that today's dollar is worth more than a future dollar, or a dollar earned in the future is worth less than a dollar being earned today. This is because today's dollar can be used to generate earnings elsewhere, and because of inflation decreasing the value of the dollar. For example, a company plans to invest $200,000 on a new packaging line, and they expect to earn $100,000 a year for the next three years on their investment. The discount rate is determined to be 12%, and the present-value factors are obtained from a standard table. The NPV of the project can be calculated by taking the project value benefits of $240,200 minus project value costs of $200,000 to obtain a value of $40,200 as shown in Table 20.8. This represents, on the surface, a good investment decision because it's a positive number. NPV must be equal to or greater than zero to be an acceptable project.

Table 20.8   Net present value calculation

Project ABC			
Cost	$200,000		
Expected future cash flow			
Year One	$100,000		
Year Two	$100,000		
Year Three	$100,000		
Year Four and beyond	$0		
Total	$300,000		
Discount rate	12%		

Year (n)	Cash Flow (CF)	Present Value Factor (PV) (Table)	Present Value of Benefits CF * PV
1	$100,000	0.893	$89,300
2	$100,000	0.797	$79,700
3	$100,000	0.712	$71,200
		Total Present Value of Benefits	$240,200

The discounted payback period is the time frame required to determine when the initial investment breaks even. It discounts future cash flows and it considers the time value of invested funds.

Economic value added (EVA) measures the profitability of a company's projects. It shows if the return is in excess of the invested cost of capital, from an investor's point of view. EVA lets investors know that management is making investments that create wealth for them.

EVA is calculated by taking the after-tax operating income minus the cost of capital invested. It forecasts expected cash flows, cost of capital, and return over time which can be used to compare different projects. For example, a company invested $750,000 in a project that generated an after-tax operating income of $1,000,000. The project generated a positive cash flow of $250,000. For this example, the cost of capital had a simple interest rate of 10% to borrow money ($750,000 * 10% = $75,000). This is a good investment as it more than covers the cost of capital. A positive number informs all stakeholders that a company has the ability to cover its cost of capital. A negative number reveals that the project didn't generate sufficient profit to cover the investment.

KEY TERMINOLOGY

Understanding key terms and the concepts they represent is crucial to passing the CSCP exam. In this chapter, the important terms are identified in Table 20.9.

Table 20.9   Financial and managerial accounting concepts key terminology

Accruals
Aggregated
Asset footprint
Assets
Average inventory
Balance sheet
Basic accounting equation
Basic income statement equation
Benefit-cost analysis
Cash flow statement
Cash inflow
Cash outflow
Cash-to-cash cycle time*
Corporate tax liability
Cost of goods sold (COGS)*
Country-specific asset footprint
Days of supply
Days payable outstanding (DPO)
Days receivable outstanding (DRO)
Days sales outstanding (DSO)
Direct labor costs
Direct material costs
Direct method
Downside supply chain adaptability

Continued

Economic value added (EVA)*
Financial accounting
First-in, first-out (FIFO)
Generally accepted accounting principles (GAAP)
Global asset footprint
Income statement
Indirect method
Intangible costs
International Financial Reporting Standards (IFRS)
Inventory turnover*
Inventory valuation*
Inventory velocity*
Last-in, first-out (LIFO)
Liabilities
Managerial accounting
Negative cash flow
Net present value (NPV)
Operating expenses
Overall value at risk (VaR)
Overhead costs
Periodic inventory method
Positive cash flow
Quick ratio
Regional asset footprint
Return on assets (ROA)*
Return on investment (ROI)*
Return on supply chain fixed assets (RSCFA)
Return on supply chain revenue
Return on working capital (ROWC)
Revenue
SCOR level 1 metrics
Spend management*
Standard cost
Stockholder equity
Supply chain agility
Supply chain management costs (SCMC)
Supply chain revenue
Tangible costs
Upside supply chain flexibility

*Key term found in the CSCP ECM

CSCP EXAM PRACTICE QUESTIONS ON FINANCIAL AND MANAGERIAL ACCOUNTING CONCEPTS

The questions shown in Table 20.10a cover the concepts presented in this chapter on financial and managerial accounting. They are examples of what to expect on the actual exam.

Table 20.10a   Financial and managerial accounting concepts practice questions

No.	Questions
1	Which financial statement informs investors if the company has made or lost money in a given period of time? a) Cash flow b) Gross profit c) Balance sheet d) Income statement
2	A company implementing a tax aligned supply chain looks to obtain all of the following long-term benefits except for: a) Reducing global tax liability b) Obtaining tax holiday savings c) Increasing earnings per share d) Increasing operating efficiency
3	What would be the immediate impact on inventory turns if the cost of goods sold (COGS) was reduced significantly? a) Turns would stabilize b) Turns would increase c) Turns would decrease d) No impact on turns would occur
4	What will the average inventory be if inventory turns are increased from four to six turns per year and the COGS remains the same. The company has COGS of $6,000,000, average inventory of $1,500,000, sales of $10,000,000, and profit of $1,000,000? a) $750,000 b) $1,000,000 c) $1,500,000 d) $1,666,666
5	A project to construct a new manufacturing facility most likely would be accepted by management if the net present value (NPV) is: a) Equal to zero b) Less than zero c) Greater than one d) Equal to or greater than zero
6	What metric is used by companies to measure its financial performance based on its residual wealth that's calculated by deducting the cost of capital from its after-tax operating income? a) Marginal analysis b) Net present value (NPV) c) Economic value added (EVA) d) Discounted payback period

Continued

7	In order to control external costs, it would be best for supply chain managers to use: a) Cost variance b) Standard costing c) Spend management d) Activity based costing (ABC)
8	A company that produces less than the production plan in the current period will have what impact on cost management? a) Inventory will be overstated b) Inventory will be understated c) Overhead will be over-absorbed d) Overhead will be under-absorbed
9	Which of the following is correct about overhead usage variance? a) Cost drivers generally pertain to fixed overhead costs b) Deviation of the actual consumption of materials as compared to the standard c) Volume variance pertains solely to variable overhead costs d) The difference between what has been budgeted for an activity and its actual costs
10	Reporting related revenues and expenses together in the period in which they were incurred is best called: a) Accruals b) Matching c) Bottom line d) Triple bottom line (TBL)
11	Raw material inventory is displayed on which financial report? a) Cash flow b) Fixed assets c) Balance sheet d) Income statement
12	What is the correct way to display the basic accounting equation? a) Assets = liabilities + owner's equity b) Assets = liabilities – owner's equity c) Owner's equity = revenue – liabilities d) Revenue = cost of goods sold (COGS) – expenses
13	A new packaging line will cost a total of $120,000 over three years. The line installation will save $75,000 for the next four years in headcount and overtime. What is the return on investment (ROI) percentage? a) 26% b) 53% c) 88% d) 1.04%
14	Which of the following wouldn't be a benefit to a winning supplier? a) Reduction in cash flow b) Reduction in inventory levels c) Reduction in transportation costs d) Reduction in replenishment lead time

ANSWERS TO CSCP EXAM PRACTICE QUESTIONS ON FINANCIAL AND MANAGERIAL ACCOUNTING CONCEPTS

The answers to the practice questions on financial and managerial accounting concepts are shown in Table 20.10b. Any question you answer incorrectly indicates a gap in your body of knowledge and encourages the need for additional study time.

Table 20.10b   Answers to CSCP exam practice questions on financial and managerial accounting concepts

No.	Answers
1	Answer: D The income statement displays revenue minus expenses, which tells investors the financial status of a company and whether the company had a profit or loss in a given period of time.
2	Answer: B The key word in this question is *long-term*. A tax holiday waves taxes for a temporary period, such as a week, and a week isn't long-term. Answers A, C, and D all represent long-term savings.
3	Answer: C Knowledge of the inventory turnover formula is required to answer this question. The formula is cost of goods sold (COGS) divided by average inventory. The best way to answer this question is to perform two calculations. The first is a standard calculation using a high COGS number ($1,000,000 ÷ $500,000 = 2) and the second is a calculation showing a reduced COGS number ($780,000 ÷ $500,000 = 1.56). You then compare the differences. This calculation reveals that a reduction in COGS decreases turns.
4	Answer: B In order to answer this question you need to know a variation of the basic inventory turnover formula. The question provides the number of turns and COGS sold. The revised formula is average inventory = COGS divided by inventory turns ($6,000,000 ÷ 6). Average inventory is then $1,000,000.
5	Answer: D Net present value (NPV) is a financial tool used in capital budgeting to analyze the profitability of a proposed project. The proposed project must be equal to or greater than zero to be accepted.
6	Answer: C This question requires knowledge of the APICS Dictionary definition of *economic value added* (EVA) and the formula described in the question. Economic value added is a measure of a company's financial performance.

Continued

7	Answer: C
	The key word in this question is *external*. Spend management controls external costs while answers A, B, and D are used to control internal costs.
8	Answer: D
	Overhead costs are under-absorbed if planned production levels cannot be achieved. This has a negative impact on profits.
9	Answer: B
	Usage variances refer to deviation of the actual consumption of materials, as compared to the standard.
10	Answer: A
	This question requires knowledge of the APICS Dictionary definition of *accrual*. Reporting revenues and expenses in the period in which they occur is tracked under accrual accounting.
11	Answer: C
	Raw materials, work-in-process, and finished goods are all assets. Assets are recorded on the balance sheet.
12	Answer: A
	The basic accounting equation is shown as assets = liabilities plus owners equity (not minus).
13	Answer: C
	The formula for return on investment (ROI) is ((total benefits minus total costs) divided by total costs). The calculation takes the $75,000 savings a year times three years less the packaging line cost of $120,000, which is then divided by the $120,000 cost (($225,000 − $120,000) ÷ $120,000 = 88%). Remember to use three years, not four, for the analysis.
14	Answer: A
	For a winning supplier, cash flow would improve, as they would be selling goods faster and receiving cash faster.

21

ECONOMICS

This chapter focuses on microeconomics and macroeconomics. It examines a number of economic concepts including the business cycle, price elasticity, marginal analysis, the aggregate demand-aggregate supply (AD-AS) model, gross domestic product, inflation, deflation, consumer price index, and a limited discussion of John Maynard Keynes' economic theory.

MICROECONOMICS AND MACROECONOMICS

Microeconomics examines the behavior of companies and households in order to understand their decision-making processes. It looks at individual supply and demand, rather than aggregate supply and demand. Microeconomics helps to explain what influences market decisions in product pricing, cost trends, product mixes, and the determination of future output levels.

Macroeconomics is the study of the aggregate behavior and performance of the overall economy as impacted by market forces over the long term. These forces include employment levels, *gross domestic product* (GDP), the global economy, the national debt, balance of payment between countries, business cycles, product pricing, inflation, and deflation. A supply chain manager needs to understand how economic fluctuations will impact supply and demand throughout the supply chain.

GDP measures the total dollar value of goods and services produced within a country in a given time period to reveal the current economic business cycle stage, as shown in Exhibit 21.1. When *expansion* occurs, it's an indication that the economy (real output) is growing rapidly. New innovative products can create increased demand, resulting in the creation of new employment opportunities. This helps to improve the economy and trigger a period of economic expansion. Market forces will reflect high GDP, output, and employment levels. Expansion is measured from the *trough* (bottom of a curve) to the *peak* (top of a curve). *Recession* is a period of general economic decline in GDP for two consecutive quarters that reflects declining income and higher unemployment levels. Recession occurs when a country's economy and manufacturing output declines (contracts) and consumers restrict their buying. It's measured from the peak (top of the expansion period) to the trough (bottom of the recession period). A *depression* is a severe, prolonged economic downturn lasting longer than two quarters.

Exhibit 21.1   Economic business cycle

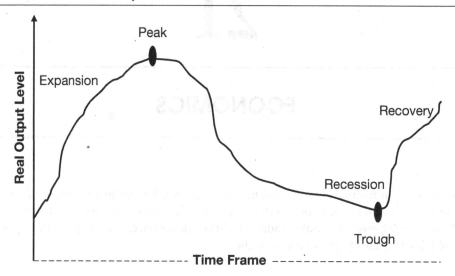

Two metrics help explain macroeconomic environments in different countries and economic regions. The first is the *consumer confidence index* (CCI), which measures consumer confidence. It's based on a random sample survey that is sent out each month to a different group of consumers. The CCI determines whether consumers are optimistic or pessimistic in regard to how they view making future purchases. Optimistic consumers spend more on goods and services, which helps to stimulate the economy, while pessimistic consumers spend less. The second CCI metric is the *producer price index* (PPI), which measures the average wholesale change in the manufacturer's selling price of consumer goods and capital equipment. An increase in the PPI is an indication of inflation, while a decrease reflects deflation. Both the CCI and PPI indexes reflect a future view of the economy. In addition, the World Bank, the International Monetary Fund (IMF), and the World Trade Organization (WTO) publish GDP and *gross national income* (GNI) to track global economic conditions. GNI is the sum of a country's GDP plus net income received from other countries. *Market demand* is the aggregate of all customer demands for a particular product over a specific time period in a given area.

AD-AS MODEL

John Maynard Keynes, a British economist, developed a theory in the 1930s that revolved around total aggregate demand spending. He stated that low market demand resulted in high unemployment due to a reduction in consumer spending, low capital investment by businesses, and diminished government spending. Keynes believed that government intervention was necessary to stimulate spending and felt that increased government spending would help the economy to grow. A good example of this theory is the $152,000,000,000 Economic Stimulus Act that was passed in 2008 to help the U.S. economy grow.

The *AD-AS model* is based on Keynes's theory and requires an understanding of two economic laws. The first is the *law of supply*, which states that as the price of goods or services increases, supply will increase—if all other factors are equal. Agriculture is a good example of this concept. If the price of corn or wheat increases, then farmers plant more to increase supply and earn more income. The second law is the *law of demand* which states that as the price of goods or services increases, demand will decrease—if all other factors are equal. Ticket sales for a sporting event are an example of this concept. If tickets are in great demand, then the price of tickets increases substantially, which limits future demand. Tickets to the NFL Super Bowl or the FIFA World Cup Final are good examples of the law of demand.

Exhibit 21.2 displays the AD-AS model. It shows price on the vertical axis, which indicates the value of average products sold (demand). The model displays output on the horizontal axis, indicating GDP based on the total value of goods and services produced in a country. Price ranges from low aggregate (bottom) to high aggregate (top) and output ranges from low (left side of the chart) to high (right side of the chart). The *aggregate demand* (AD) *curve* starts at the upper left-hand corner (high aggregate prices) and moves diagonally downward to the bottom right-hand side (high output). The short-term *aggregate supply* (AS) *curve* starts on the bottom left of the graph and moves upward as output and prices increase. The curve indicates that with high prices, there is high supply (companies will produce more as long as prices remain high), but only within constraints. It also indicates that with low prices, there is low supply (companies see no economic benefit to produce more or to invest in the business). The point at which the supply and demand curved lines intersect represents *equilibrium*. This is where prices and inventory quantities become equal.

Exhibit 21.2 AD-AS model

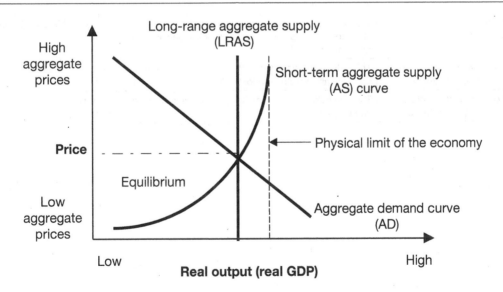

Long-range aggregate supply (LRAS) is shown in Exhibit 21.2 as a plotted vertical line. It indicates that a change in aggregate demand results in a change in supply. Specific short-term economic events such as government action on pricing and demand (tax cuts or stimulus spending) will impact the economy. This results in an improvement in demand as consumers and businesses have more money to spend. The opposite is true when taxes are raised or inflation occurs.

A company that anticipates higher future demand levels will need a plan to increase their capacity levels. This plan will require a monetary investment to increase inventory levels, purchase new equipment, and/or boost employment levels. The investment will cause the AD curve to shift to the right, resulting in more products being available for sale. A company will continue to make additional investments as long as demand and prices remain high. The oil industry is a good example of this concept. When prices and demand are high, companies invest in expanding capacity. When prices fall, companies cut back on their investments. Table 21.1 demonstrates the impact of change in microeconomics and macroeconomics.

Table 21.1   Microeconomics and macroeconomics

Action	Result	Curve Shift
If a company anticipates higher future demand levels	This will cause the company to increase capital spending to purchase new equipment resulting in additional capacity levels	It will cause the AS curve to shift to the right
If a company closes a factory	This will cause reduced capacity levels and production output	It will cause the AS curve to shift to the left
If a company's products generate high sales and profits	This will cause competition to enter the market, resulting in increased supply which makes the product less expensive	It will shift the AS curve initially to the right
If a country has full employment	This will increase labor costs, causing the economy to slow down by making products more expensive, thus reducing demand	It will shift the AD curve to the left
If prices increase substantially for a critical raw material	This will cause the price of the product to increase substantially, resulting in lost sales	It will cause the AD curve to shift to the left
If the government enacts a stimulus act or cuts taxes	This will help the economy to grow, leading to economic capacity expansion	It will shift the AS curve to the right

Exercise 21.1 will test your knowledge and understanding of the AD-AS curve shift. Read each question and write in whether the curve will shift to the right, left, or have no impact. The answers to the exercise are available from the Web Added Value™ Download Resource Center at www.jrosspub.com.

Exercise 21.1 Understanding AD-AS model curve shift

Question	Answer
1. A country has reached full employment. What will be the impact on the demand curve?	
2. A manufacturing company is notified that a critical raw material is going to increase in price by 33%. What will be the impact on the demand curve?	
3. A product reached equilibrium. What will be the impact on the supply curve?	
4. Technology has created a new improved phone. What will be the impact on the demand curve?	
5. What will be the impact on the demand curve if a country increases its duty on imports by 25%?	
6. What will be the impact on the supply curve if a country reduces its income tax rate by 20%?	
7. What will be the impact on the supply curve if the borrowing interest rate is increased?	
8. A manufacturing company can't find a sufficient number of skilled factory workers. What will be the impact on supply?	

ECONOMIC ATTRIBUTES

The *consumer price index* (CPI) measures the change in price (purchasing power) of a group of different consumer goods and services (market basket). *Inflation* occurs when prices increase and *deflation* occurs when prices decline. They are both measured by the CPI.

Price elasticity is an economic measure of how demand (quantity) for goods or services becomes responsive to a change in price. Prices are elastic if demand varies with price changes (goes up or down), and inelastic if demand doesn't change. Elastic products are items such as toilet paper and beer. They can also be service-oriented items such as telephone and cable utilities. Products or services that are elastic aren't one-of-a-kind; there are a variety of them to choose from, and an increase in price will cause consumers to switch. Inelastic products include food staples such as milk, salt, or flour and energy-related products such as gasoline for your car or oil to heat your home. No alternative products or services exist, and customers need to continue to purchase these items regardless of their price.

Suppliers are very price sensitive, and they attempt to shift consumer demand to products or services that have more elasticity in order to gain additional revenue and more profits. An example of this is a beer manufacturer trying to sell consumers high-priced premium or craft beers.

Price elasticity can be determined by performing a calculation to establish the relationship between the elasticity of a demand curve and its slope over its length. The slope is calculated by dividing a change in the price by a change in quantity. The slope will always be shown as a negative value.

After establishing the relationship, the next step is to determine the price change. For example, the price of a product increased from $12 to $14. The price percentage change calculation process begins by taking the difference between the new and old price. The result is then divided by the old price ($2 \div 12 = 0.167$) times 100%. You are left with a 16.7% change in price. Our example has management projecting that the price increase will result in a drop in demand from 150 units to 130 units or 20 less units ($150 - 130 = 20$). The percentage change is calculated by taking the old quantity and subtracting the new quantity, and then dividing it by the old quantity ($20 \div 150 = 0.133$) times 100%, to obtain a 13.3% change in quantity. The price elasticity of demand is determined by taking the percentage change in demand and dividing it by the percentage change in price ($13.3 \div 16.7 = 0.80$) to obtain the *coefficient of elasticity* (COE). COE is used to measure the responsiveness of elasticity. It projects the percentage change in demand (quantity) that will occur when one variable, such as price, changes one percent. Since the COE is less than one, it means the percentage change in quantity is less than the percentage change in price. Demand, in this case, is considered inelastic.

MARGINAL ANALYSIS

Marginal analysis is a management tool used to compare costs versus the benefits of increasing production against incurred additional costs. It does this by determining the incremental impact of the production change. This analysis is used to determine how and if a proposed small increase in production can be profitable for a company.

For example, a company manufactures 100 units of washing machines for a customer at a cost of $200,750. It sells them for $2,500 each, resulting in total revenue of $250,000. The customer then wants to place a new order for one additional unit. The company uses marginal analysis to determine if this request should be accepted or rejected. The new order will increase total revenue to $252,500 ($250,000 + $2,500) and its manufacturing costs will increase to $203,500. This includes an additional setup charge of $750. The marginal revenue (benefit) of the one extra unit is $2,500 ($252,500 – $250,000), and the marginal cost is $2,750 ($203,500 – $200,750). After performing marginal analysis, the company decides to reject it for financial considerations. While revenue would increase by $2,500 (benefit), overall costs would increase by $2,750. The $250 extra cost outweighs any additional revenue benefits gained from the sale of one additional unit. This extra cost is due to the need to perform a second setup. In addition, other extra cost charges to consider are overtime and purchasing additional raw materials, which might further increase the loss of producing the extra unit. Table 21.2 displays the marginal analysis cost calculation.

Table 21.2 Marginal analysis cost calculation

Quantity	Revenue	Total Revenue	Fixed and Variable Costs	Setup Cost	Total Costs	Total Revenue– Total Costs
1	$2,500	$2,500	$2,000	$750	$2,750	–$250
25	$2,500	$62,500	$2,000	$750	$50,750	$11,750
50	$2,500	$125,000	$2,000	$750	$100,750	$24,250
75	$2,500	$187,500	$2,000	$750	$150,750	$36,750
100	$2,500	$250,000	$2,000	$750	$200,750	$49,250
101	$2,500	$252,500	$2,000	$1,500	$203,500	$49,000

KEY TERMINOLOGY

Understanding key terms and the concepts they represent is crucial to passing the Certified Supply Chain Professional (CSCP) exam. In this chapter, the important terms are identified in Table 21.3.

Table 21.3 Microeconomics and macroeconomics key terminology

Aggregate demand (AD) curve
Aggregate demand-aggregate supply (AD-AS) model
Aggregate supply (AS) curve
Consumer confidence index (CCI)
Consumer price index (CPI)
Deflation
Depression
Elasticity coefficient
Equilibrium
Expansion
Gross domestic product (GDP)
Gross national income (GNI)
Inflation
Law of demand
Law of supply
Long-range aggregate supply (LRAS)
Macroeconomics
Marginal analysis
Market demand*
Microeconomics
Peak
Price elasticity
Producer price index (PPI)
Recession
Trough

*Key term found in the CSCP ECM

CSCP EXAM PRACTICE QUESTIONS ON ECONOMICS

The questions shown in Table 21.4a cover the concepts presented in this chapter on economics. They are examples of what to expect on the actual exam.

Table 21.4a   Microeconomics and macroeconomics practice questions

No.	Questions
1	What can help to trigger a period of economic expansion? a) Raising prices b) Political events c) Product scarcity d) Product innovation
2	In which economic cycle period does real gross domestic product (GDP) increase? a) Peak b) Trend c) Trough d) Expansion
3	Companies are facing a sharp increase in commodity prices. How does this impact the AD-AS model? a) AS curve has no movement b) AS curve shifts to the left, cost pushes inflation c) AS curve shifts downward d) AS curve shifts to the right, cost pushes inflation
4	All of the following would shift the long-range aggregate supply (LRAS) curve to the right except for: a) Decrease in price levels b) Improvement in technology c) Increase in international trade d) Increase in the supply of money
5	The price of Product A is reduced by 10% and the demand quantity increased from 20,000 units to 25,000 units. Calculate the elasticity of demand percentage. a) 2.5% b) 25.0% c) 40.0% d) 250.0%
6	A company has been asked to manufacture 3,000 additional units at a reduced cost by an existing high-volume customer. What should be the deciding factor to accept this order? a) The need to keep the factory busy b) If marginal revenue exceeds the marginal cost c) The desire to keep the customer happy d) If marginal cost exceeds the marginal utility
7	What will be the most likely impact if a manufacturer increases the price of an innovative product by 20%? a) Demand becomes elastic b) Demand becomes inelastic c) Demand increases sharply d) Law of supply and demand doesn't apply

ANSWERS TO CSCP EXAM PRACTICE QUESTIONS ON ECONOMICS

The answers to the practice questions on economics are shown in Table 21.4b. Any question you answer incorrectly indicates a gap in your body of knowledge and encourages the need for additional study time.

Table 21.4b   Answers to CSCP exam practice questions on microeconomics and macroeconomics

No.	Answers
1	Answer: D New innovative products can create increased demand resulting in the creation of new employment opportunities. This helps to improve the economy and trigger a period of economic expansion.
2	Answer: D Expansion means that the economy is growing. Gross domestic product (GDP) increases during the expansion period.
3	Answer: B Higher prices and lower supply will push prices to the left (upward) leading to inflation.
4	Answer: D An increase in the supply of money causes inflation which impacts demand. This causes the long-range aggregate supply curve to shift to the right.
5	Answer: D The formula for the elasticity of demand is change in quantity demand divided by change in price. The calculations are shown as change in quantity = ((25,000 − 20,000) ÷ 20,000) * 100% = 25% and then 25% ÷ 10% * 100 = 250%.
6	Answer: B If marginal revenue (extra usefulness gained from purchasing one extra unit) exceeds the marginal cost, then accepting the order is the correct answer.
7	Answer: A Demand becomes more elastic as innovative products will cause demand to rise and fall sharply based on pricing.

22

RISK MANAGEMENT

This chapter focuses on risk management and its relationship to a supply chain. It examines how to manage supply chain risk, risk probability and its impact, risk at various supply chain levels, how to develop a plan to reduce risk, the role of the risk manager, expected monetary value, sensitivity analysis, and simulation capability. It also explores how to set up a risk matrix.

RISK MANAGEMENT AND SUPPLY CHAIN OVERVIEW

Risk management consists of risk identification, risk exposure analysis, and risk assessment. Corporate management needs to plan for risk, and expect the unexpected. It's important for them to anticipate potential issues and understand how to mitigate end-to-end supply chain disruptions and damages before they occur. *Supply chain risk* is an event that has a negative impact on the supply chain that causes a loss of time, product, money, or resources. *Supply chain risk identification* serves as a tool for recognizing areas of an organization or processes in the organization that don't operate effectively, and therefore are more exposed to risk.

Every company looks at risk differently and has different levels of *risk tolerance* (acceptance levels) and *risk appetite* (amount and type of risk they are willing to accept). Companies need to establish an internal *risk threshold cutoff point* where risk is acceptable, but anything above that point would require a proactive response. Risk management strategies need to address vulnerabilities. A *vulnerability* is something that is susceptible to damage, temptation, harm, or criticism.

A *risk management plan* is a document used by companies to anticipate and proactively prepare for risk. It describes how to plan and structure risk in order to minimize potential problems. The plan identifies the various processes, tools required, team members, roles and responsibilities, internal and external data sources, duration, and budget. It also describes how the risk management plan is be integrated into an organization's overall *supply chain risk management* (SCRM) process. SCRM continuously identifies, detects, assesses, monitors, and mitigates threats to ensure supply chain continuity and profitability. Risk types found in SCRM can be classified as supply, demand, process, or environmental risks.

A good risk management plan needs to be cost effective, provide visibility, be timely, and cover how to address and resolve the various levels of risk. After the risk management plan is created, a company must manage its supply chain risk process to develop a risk response plan.

MANAGING THE SUPPLY CHAIN RISK PROCESS

An organization must learn to manage four supply chain processes in order to control risk. They are: identifying risks, assessing and classifying risks, developing a risk response plan, and executing the risk response plan.

Identifying risks is the first step in the supply chain process. In order to recognize existing and potential risks, a company will use *brainstorming* to identify threats and opportunities. This technique stimulates creative, group thinking to develop new ideas or to solve problems. A risk-related brainstorming session looks at strategic supply chain, supply and demand processes, technology, environment, hazards, security, finance, malfeasance (wrongdoing or misconduct), and legal, regulatory, and litigation risks. Each risk and its attributes are entered into a *risk register* for tracking purposes. A risk register is a summary report of identified risks and their associated details, as shown in Exhibit 22.1. It's used to track and address problems among project stakeholders.

Exhibit 22.1   Risk register

Risk Id #	Risk Title	Risk Desc.	Risk Status	Risk Owner	Risk Category	Probability Score	Impact Score	Total Score	Mitigation and Contingency Action

In step two, risks are assessed and classified by management and process owners who perform a qualitative risk assessment. Risk category codes are assigned to explain why a risk might occur, what might affect it, and what might be the initial cause. This step provides a structured approach to classify risks in order to improve the effectiveness of risk analysis. The key risk classification factors are probability and its financial impact, along with risk tolerance (time and cost) and any business constraints. This risk analysis is used to identify an initial *risk classification* to recognize those risks which require the greatest financial or resource support. Risk classification defines a risk as being internal, external, environmental, technical, or organizational. It also identifies a *time dimension*, which is a specific time horizon such as a day, month, quarter, or year.

Developing a *risk response plan* is the third step in the supply chain process, as is displayed in Exhibit 22.2. Each risk is documented in a standard format showing its root cause, the triggering event, the internal or external impact on the organization, and its overall effect throughout the supply chain. The risk response plan shows what action to take for each identified risk, assigns responsibility to an individual for turning a plan into action, and, if required, approval and funding. Examples of risks that require a risk response plan are a product recall or an on-site accident. *Risk response planning* is the process of deciding how to avoid or mitigate risks.

Exhibit 22.2   Risk response plan

Risk #	Risk Category	Risk Description	Risk Impact on the Organization (Cost and Time)	Risk Response (Action)	Risk Owner	Risk Response Tracking (Status)

A risk response plan is an ongoing living document that needs to be integrated into an organization's business process review cycle and should be constantly monitored. For example, company executives who travel to high-risk areas need to understand what should happen if they were to get kidnapped and held for ransom. They need to be informed that kidnap insurance exists and that they shouldn't try to escape or negotiate with their captors.

Once the risk response plan is developed and approved, it's ready to be executed. This can be performed on a schedule, or as a contingent response to a triggering event. The plan must be consistently monitored, measured, and updated to keep the risk register current by performing ongoing analysis, validating the budget and financial reserves, identifying new potential risks, and removing risks that no longer require action.

A channel master often requires supply chain partners to develop a risk response plan to prevent a disruption of material deliveries. A *risk manager* is assigned the responsibility to map the supply chain, identify supply chain failure points, identify and categorize risks, define risk parameters, create risk awareness, prepare and execute the risk management plan, and chair the risk management review meetings. Tools to aid in the response plan include interviews, a risk checklist, brainstorming, SWOT (strengths, weaknesses, opportunities, and threats) analysis, the Delphi technique, risk diagramming, root-cause analysis, and document and assumption reviews.

RISK PROBABILITY AND IMPACT ASSESSMENT

Probability refers to the likelihood of an event occurring, and is expressed as a percentage between zero and 100. The higher the risk percentage, the more likely it will occur; the lower the percentage, the less likely of an occurrence. Companies decide and assign probabilities based on internal discussions and assumptions. For example, they might determine that it's 60% likely that a dock strike will occur next week or that it's 10% likely that their manufacturing plant will be destroyed by a tsunami.

Impact refers to the projected magnitude of a loss or gain of an asset or process because of an unknown event. Examples of this are a natural disaster, strike, or industrial accident. Impact is expressed as a percentage between zero and 100. Companies decide and assign impact based on internal discussions and assumptions. For example, a tsunami will have an 80% financial impact on the organization.

Probability and impact can be used to plot and plan risks through the development of a risk rating calculation. It gives management a simple, clear way to measure potential risks. The calculation is used to provide a priority list as to where the company needs to focus its resources.

The risk rating calculation is based on the following equation: risk rating = probability * impact (10% * 80% = 8%). The results are classified and grouped into four risk categories: high probability, low impact; high probability, high impact; low probability, low impact; and low probability, high impact. These are all displayed in Table 22.1.

Table 22.1　Risk level categories

Probability of Occurrence	**High**	High probability, low impact (accept risk if it happens, but try to minimize impact)	High probability, high impact (of critical importance and requires immediate planning and action to avoid this risk at all costs)
	Low	Low probability, low impact (often ignore taking action)	Low probability, high impact (unlikely to occur but develop a contingency plan if it happens)
		Low	**High**
		Risk Impact	

Companies use a *suppliers'/customers'/products' risk rating* survey to show how effectively risks are identified and managed within the supply chain. They begin the survey by interviewing participants or by performing a self-assessment to determine potential risks. A numerical score is determined and normalized for analysis and comparison purposes. This score helps in the creation of a risk matrix for suppliers, customers, or product categories. The next step is creating a *probability and impact risk matrix* to display each listed risk scenario by category. The matrix displays defined impact and probability ratings to provide risk awareness and visibility. It's a simple yet very objective tool to aid in risk management decision making.

Risk urgency assessment is another tool that helps a company to identify those risks that require immediate or future action. *Data quality assessment* helps to determine if a risk is truly understood within the organization and defines those risks that require future review and action. Risk data requires *risk accuracy* and reliability, and users must have confidence in what is presented. This means that all data must be free from errors. *Data integrity* requires information to be complete and meaningful. Risk data must be properly entered, processed, and summarized in a timely manner. Data integrity also includes controlling the physical environment and restricting data access to authorized personnel. It's an ongoing process—requiring consistent review to re-evaluate each risk.

The *risk data gathering* process begins with interviewing people who are closest to the data collection point, and it's best performed by asking for three risk cost estimates. These estimates are: most likely, optimistic, and pessimistic. The collected costs are added together, and then divided by three to obtain a risk *simple average*. An example of this is taking $25,000 + $15,000 + $50,000, dividing the total by three, and then obtaining a risk simple average of $30,000. A risk *weighted average method* is a second form of data gathering. It's used when uncertainty exists and is based on the program evaluation and review technique (PERT). It places a higher weight on the most likely cost and a lower weight on the pessimistic cost. The most likely cost is multiplied by four, the optimistic and pessimistic costs are multiplied by one, the results are totaled, and then divided by six. An example of this is ((($25,000 * 4) + ($15,000 * 1) + ($50,000 * 1)) ÷ 6) to calculate a risk weighted average of $27,500. The collected and calculated data is then displayed in a *probability distribution* chart to show how actual results may differ from anticipated results.

A probability distribution is a statistical model used to create a scenario analysis that constructs numerous different and distinct outcome possibilities for a particular course of action. The risk cost estimate table helps management to visually project future results. Management then uses this data to prepare a distribution chart that displays probability on the vertical axis, possible results on the horizontal axis, and the statistically most likely results are shown at the peak of the chart.

For example, a business might create three scenarios: worst-case, likely, and best-case. The pessimistic (worst-case) would contain some value from the lower end of the probability distribution; the most likely scenario would contain a value toward the middle of the distribution; and the optimistic (best-case) scenario would contain a value in the upper end. A simple average and risk weighted average can also be determined, as seen in Exhibit 22.3.

Exhibit 22.3   Risk cost estimate table

Type	Risk Cost Estimate
Optimistic	$15,000
Most likely	$25,000
Pessimistic	$50,000
Simple average	$30,000
Risk (weighted average)	$27,500

Now that the company has additional calculated data, it can go back and modify its risk register with an updated priority ranking. The company then needs to reassess the cost of preparing and executing a response against expected benefits or losses that may be associated with each decision. The comparison can be expressed mathematically to show the expected best-cost outcome in order to identify possible risk vulnerabilities in its supply chain.

EXPECTED MONETARY VALUE

A company may use a technique called *expected monetary value* (EMV) to quantify risk and prioritize identified costs and benefits. It begins with a qualitative risk analysis to develop a risk list, assigns a risk probability for each item, determines the monetary value of the risk impact, and then defines its urgency. It compares and balances the cost of the risk response against the impact of the risk. The formula to calculate EMV is probability times impact. This is similar to the risk rating formula that was shown earlier in this section, but EMV displays risks with the greatest occurrence probability and highest monetary value. For EMV, impact is represented in dollars instead of percentages. The steps to calculate EMV are:

Step 1: Assign a risk probability of occurrence
Step 2: Assign a monetary value to the risk impact

Step 3: Multiply risk probability by risk impact
Step 4: Review the calculated EMV and take action

A risk result can be a positive risk, which is an opportunity—or a negative risk, which is a threat. A company needs to manage and address both scenarios. An example of a positive risk is looking at delaying raw material purchases in anticipation of a potential price reduction. Management projects the savings to be $100,000 and to have a probability rating of 75%. An example of a negative risk is the possibility of a dock strike impacting product delivery. Management projects the strike to last one week, cost the company $500,000, and have a probability rating of 10%. Table 22.2 displays an EMV calculation for each risk.

Table 22.2 Expected monetary value required budget amount

No.	Probability	Impact	EMV = (probability * impact)
1	75%	$100,000	(75% ÷ 100) * $100,000 = $75,000
2	10%	–$500,000	(10% ÷ 100) * –$500,000 = –$50,000

NET IMPACT EXPECTED MONETARY VALUE

Risk management projects often require up-front costs before they can begin. For example, the cost to enhance a company's existing legacy system to improve inventory tracking is $300,000. It has a risk probability factor of 50% to quickly gain $500,000 in inventory savings. The $300,000 to upgrade the system must now be included in the equation. The EMV total shows that the true cost is 0.5 * ($500,000 + –$300,000) = $100,000. This option results in $100,000 of potential inventory savings. The second option is to purchase a new system at a cost of $1,200,000 with a 70% chance of success to gain $2,500,000 in long-term inventory savings. EMV is calculated as 0.7 * ($2,500,000 + –$1,200,000) = $910,000. This option results in $910,000 of potential inventory savings, as shown in Table 22.3. A third option is to develop in-house a new system at a cost of $2,100,000 with a 90% chance of success to gain $2,500,000 in long-term inventory savings. EMV is calculated as 0.9 * ($2,500,000 + –$2,100,000) = $360,000. This option results in $360,000 of potential inventory savings, as shown in Table 22.3. EMV permits a company to view all options based on total costs, and this helps them to make informed decisions. In our example, the second option is the best choice resulting in net EMV of $910,000.

Table 22.3 Expected monetary value upgrade project

Option #	Option	Probability	Impact	Additional Costs	EMV = probability * (impact + cost)
1	Upgrade	0.5	$500,000	$300,000	$100,000
2	Purchase	0.7	$2,500,000	$1,200,000	$910,000
3	Develop	0.9	$2,500,000	$2,100,000	$360,000

EMV is used in conjunction with a *decision tree* to help decide multiple options. A decision tree is a graphical, tree-shaped diagram that displays the various paths, statistical probability, outcomes, and consequences of a decision, as shown in Exhibit 22.4. Each tree branch represents a possible decision, their course of action, statistical probability, and their possible consequences. It's used to manage uncertainties and to help management make informed decisions by quantifying those decisions and their consequences to determine the best action to take.

Exhibit 22.4   Decision tree

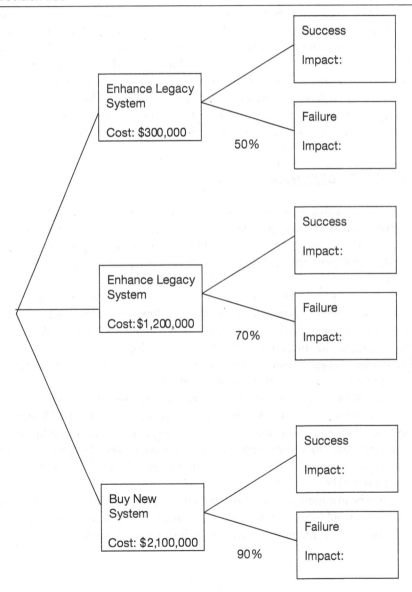

SENSITIVITY ANALYSIS AND SIMULATION

Companies often develop risk models to determine how risk can impact the supply chain. The two modeling tools often used by companies are sensitivity analysis and simulation.

Sensitivity analysis—also called what-ifs—are techniques that are used to determine an outcome based on a given set of variable input values. It demonstrates to management how changing one variable at a time impacts the outcome. An example of this technique is when management wants to determine the financial impact of a sales promotion on total product sales, and how a price change will impact transaction volume. The company sells a consumer electronic product for $100.00, and they sell 10,000 units in the last period. This generates revenue of $1,000,000. Management believes that each one percent decrease in price increases transaction volume by three percent. A financial model is developed to perform a sensitivity analysis showing different promotional scenarios to determine the best promotional price. Management then selects the best price that meets their financial and marketing goals.

Simulation is a tool used to project future performance based on mathematical or analytical means. It manipulates different conditions or parameters and observes how these changes impact performance. For example, a company can use this technique to test the impact of a 10% increase in the master production schedule to observe if sufficient resources exist, or what resources need to be added.

RISK RESPONSE PLANNING

Risk responses can be classified as *preventive action*—they block nonconformity issues from reoccurring by taking corrective action when an issue is discovered. An example of this is the utilization of an automated system that monitors liquid levels in bottles in order to discover filled bottle nonconformity. On the other hand, a *contingent action* along with a *contingency plan* is able to help a company quickly respond or recover from a malfunction problem like an unexpected dock strike. *Malfunction recovery* is the process of executing the plan to resolve the disruption. *Corrective actions* are actual activities that take place once nonconformity has been discovered in order to eliminate it. They permit the organization to quickly return to normal operations. For example, a critical component has been damaged in transit, or a key supplier goes bankrupt. The corrective action requires the supplier to be contacted and a replacement part immediately shipped via air. It also involves the development of sourcing processes within the contingency plan to determine how to quickly replace a supplier.

Companies use one of four *basic risk responses* to manage risk. They are: *avoid* (exploit), *accept* (allow), *transfer* (share), and *mitigate* (enhance). An example of this is a company that identifies the risk of not being able to meet a customer delivery commitment for a large, custom-built product and they have a financial penalty contract clause for late delivery. The company is concerned that they can't obtain sufficient component inventory being sourced from a sole supplier located in another country. They now have to choose which risk path to take.

The first option will be to completely avoid risk by not accepting the customer order, thus avoiding any financial penalties. They would choose this action in an attempt to eliminate any risk exposure or threat that can negatively impact their finances, reputation, or business operations.

Second, a company can accept risk by deciding that the risk level is low, and the risk avoidance cost is too high not to commit to the customer order. This path is taken knowing full well they might not meet their deadline and have to pay a contract penalty.

Third, a company can transfer the risk to a third party. For example, local third-party suppliers can be asked to maintain sufficient inventory to support a small distributor who needs fast and reliable product delivery.

The final option is to mitigate. An example of this is when a company decides to purchase critical raw materials from multiple suppliers to avoid any delivery disruption due to a possible labor strike at one supplier's location.

Exercise 22.1 will test your knowledge and understanding of the four basic risk response types. Read each question and write in all answers that apply. The answers to the exercise are available from the Web Added Value™ Download Resource Center at www.jrosspub.com.

Exercise 22.1   Four basic risk response types

Question	Answer
1. A company decided to remove all lead paint from toys being sold at children's stores.	
2. A company decided to purchase business interruption insurance to minimize the financial risk of a fire at its manufacturing location.	
3. A company with a low probability, low magnitude risk, will most likely utilize this type of risk response.	
4. A company decided to implement additional training on its product installation process. The goal is to prevent incorrect setup information from being given to customers looking for assistance.	
5. A company is concerned about pending government certificate of origin regulations. It decides to source components locally.	
6. A company elected to ignore the possibility that a foreign-based oil refinery and distribution system may be nationalized by the local oil-producing country's government.	
7. A company decided to hold inventory in local warehouses so it can quickly deliver raw materials to its key customers.	
8. A retail store implemented a vendor-managed inventory (VMI) program with its suppliers. The program made its suppliers responsible for maintaining adequate inventory levels at the store.	

SUPPLY CHAIN RISKS

A number of supply chain risk types exist. These include risk of loss of tangible assets (physical in nature) and intangible assets (not physical in nature). *Tangible assets* include buildings, land, inventory, and equipment. *Loss of goods* can occur due to theft, damage, fire, or vandalism. Loss can also occur from malfeasance, bribery, fraud, or corruption. These illegal activities can result in fines being assessed, goods seized, or the shutdown of a business. *Intangible assets* include intellectual property (IP) such as patents and copyrights, a company's reputation, brand recognition, and goodwill.

Other supply chain risk types are the *abduction* of key business leaders, which may require the payment of a ransom. *Bribery* is defined as offering something of value to a third party in order to gain an illicit advantage. It's classified as commercial bribery, bribery of public officials, or the bribery of foreign representatives. The offering of a bribe to a public official is considered a crime in the U.S., and the acceptance of a bribe is also illegal. *Fraud* is a criminal action taken with the intent to deceive others. *Corruption* is the abuse of power by a person in charge who performs a dishonest act for financial gain. *Loss of intellectual property* includes *product counterfeiting*. In the European Union (EU), companies report violations of their IP to the official customs department in any member state. Elsewhere, companies typically go to the local court system to try to protect their IP. Product counterfeiting is the production and distribution of inferior products by unauthorized third parties throughout the supply chain. Examples of this are drugs, watches, and clothing. Product counterfeiting can severely damage a company's reputation, especially when the third party has access to proprietary designs. *Losses from lawsuits* are another potential risk that companies must protect against. They need to be prepared to defend themselves against broken contracts, theft of trade secrets, product counterfeiting, and frivolous lawsuits.

BUSINESS CONTINUITY AND PLAN IMPLEMENTATION

A *business continuity management system* (BCMS), also known as *continuity planning and disaster planning*, is used to protect stakeholders by predefining actions to be taken if a disruptive incident occurs. This permits the organization to have a response structure in place to quickly implement a well-defined action plan. The BCMS includes a set of interrelated activities to establish, implement, operate, monitor, review, maintain, and improve internal business continuity capabilities. Continuity planning and disaster planning are similar, but differences do exist. Continuity planning is proactive and it anticipates and plans for problems before they occur. Disaster planning is reactive, and it develops and implements a plan after a problem occurs. For example, a company uses continuity planning to develop a strategy to protect internal resources (personnel and equipment) in the event that a disaster might occur and then plans how to quickly restore operations. Disaster planning, on the other hand, determines how to quickly recover the workplace to normal operations after a disruption happens.

Supply chain continuity works together with internal and external supply chain partners on a tactical and strategic level to plan, review, test, and execute joint disaster recovery plans. It decides how a supply chain can survive when a disruption occurs. Supply chain continuity is one aspect of SCRM that ensures supply chain resilience exists and can continue to function regardless of the situation.

ISO 22301 is a BCMS standard to ensure that business operations continue to function whenever a disruptive incident occurs. It pre-establishes contingency plans to be used to resolve and quickly restore operations to pre-issue levels.

KEY TERMINOLOGY

Understanding key terms and the concepts they represent is crucial to passing the Certified Supply Chain Professional (CSCP) exam. In this chapter, the important terms are identified in Table 22.4.

Table 22.4 Risk management key terminology

Abduction
Accept risk
Avoid risk
Basic risk responses
Brainstorming
Bribery
Business continuity management system (BCMS)
Contingency plan
Contingent action
Continuity planning
Corrective actions
Corruption
Data integrity
Data quality assessment
Decision tree
Disaster planning
Expected monetary value (EMV)
Fraud
Impact
Intangible assets
ISO 22301
Loss of goods
Loss of intellectual property
Losses from lawsuits
Malfunction recovery
Mitigate risk
Preventive action
Probability
Probability distribution
Probability and impact risk matrix

Continued

Product counterfeiting
Risk accuracy
Risk appetite
Risk data gathering
Risk management
Risk management plan
Risk manager
Risk register*
Risk response plan
Risk response planning
Risk threshold cutoff point
Risk tolerance
Risk urgency assessment
Sensitivity analysis
Simple average
Simulation
Statement of risk
Suppliers'/customers'/products' risk rating
Supply chain continuity
Supply chain risk
Supply chain risk identification
Supply chain risk management (SCRM)
Tangible assets
Time dimension
Transfer risk
Vulnerability
Weighted average method

*Key term found in the CSCP ECM

CSCP EXAM PRACTICE QUESTIONS ON RISK MANAGEMENT

The questions shown in Table 22.5a cover the concepts presented in this chapter on risk management. They are examples of what to expect on the actual exam.

Table 22.5a   Risk management practice questions

No.	Questions
1	A material planner has been asked to accept a rush customer order. What tool can this person use to best determine if adequate resources exist to accept this order? a) Simulation b) Diseconomies of scale c) Customer relationship management (CRM) d) Program evaluation and review technique (PERT)
2	Who is responsible to perform key duties involving methods to lessen risks, prioritize funds, and implement and analyze feedback? a) Risk manager b) Financial manager c) Operations manager d) Supply chain manager
3	What is the best method an organization can use to recognize and identify different forms of potential risks to their supply chain? a) Histogram b) Brainstorm c) Root-cause analysis d) Plan-do-check-act (PDCA)
4	All of the following are forms of risk tolerance except for: a) Hedging b) Avoidance c) Buffering d) Speculation
5	Which of the following isn't one of the four basic responses for any identified risk? a) Avoid b) Ignore c) Accept d) Mitigate
6	The MIP Company is concerned about the future loss of a key supplier. What action should the company take to minimize a potential issue as part of its contingency planning? a) Build up safety stock b) Find alternate suppliers c) Develop in-house capabilities d) Develop a sourcing process
7	The MIP Company has material and operational issues that prevent the company from meeting customer delivery requirements. What type of malfunction plan is needed? a) Contingency plan b) Replacement part plan c) Material substitution plan d) Alternate manufacturing site

ANSWERS TO CSCP EXAM PRACTICE QUESTIONS ON RISK MANAGEMENT

The answers to the practice questions on risk management are shown in Table 22.5b. Any question you answer incorrectly indicates a gap in your body of knowledge and encourages the need for additional study time.

Table 22.5b   Answers to CSCP exam practice questions on risk management

No.	Answers
1	Answer: A This question requires knowledge of the APICS Dictionary definition of *simulation*. Simulation is a tool that is used to test the behavior of a system based on different operating conditions to see how it responds. Diseconomies of scale occurs when more output is required than the factory can produce. Customer relationship management (CRM) is a marketing philosophy that puts the customer first. Program evaluation and review technique (PERT) is a project management tool.
2	Answer: A The risk manager is directly responsible to perform the duties being asked in this question. The others are involved in the process, but don't have direct responsibility for the entire process.
3	Answer: B The best method is to hold a brainstorming session. The process will help to identify and categorize potential issues requiring corrective action.
4	Answer: B Avoidance means avoiding all risks, and as such, a company won't tolerate any risk. The others will tolerate some risk by taking corrective actions such as building up inventory in anticipation of an issue.
5	Answer: B Ignore isn't one of the four basic responses. The four basic responses are avoid, accept, transfer, and mitigate.
6	Answer: D A sourcing process should be developed as part of a contingency plan to avoid the future loss of a key supplier. Answers A, B, and C should be part of the contingency plan.
7	Answer: A A company needs to develop a contingency plan to address malfunctions. Answers B, C, and D are forms of malfunctions.

23

TECHNOLOGY

This chapter focuses on how technology is altering the way *customers buy* and how *suppliers sell* in an ever-changing business environment. Technology speeds up the flow of information, lowers transaction costs, allows for improved communications, helps improve supplier-customer relationships, and encourages collaboration, efficiency, and productivity. Customers look for and demand speed, agility, global sourcing, and reliable communications when selecting a supplier. Suppliers have to be able to meet these customer demands. The Internet, cloud, big data, hardware, software, and related tools all play a critical technology role in managing the supply chain.

ARCHITECTURE

Technology requires information to be communicated and shared through the use of various types of hardware and software. *Information architecture* (IA) is the integration setup of the transmission, storage, processing, analysis, and reporting of information via technology. *Organizational architecture* is a high-level strategic approach that is used by a business to structure its supply chain strategy. It includes workers, their skills, and information systems that are needed to support customers and suppliers, and all components operate efficiently and effectively together. A company's IA needs to support its organizational architecture, and gaps must be identified and resolved to best meet business needs. *Information system architecture* provides the ability to integrate hardware and software together. *Software* are the programs or applications that computers use to perform a function. Examples include customer relationship management (CRM) and warehouse management systems (WMS). *Hardware* is a physical device, such as a computer or server that is used to run or display a software application.

A computer's *operating system* manages the execution and performance of hardware and software. Their location and placement, along with the computer's operating system and communication devices, determines the company's network configuration.

A *modular system* is composed of separate but connected hardware and/or software components. For example, an external hard drive, printer, and monitor can be added, deleted, or replaced without impacting the operation of the computer system.

Today, many companies use *cloud computing*, also called *software as a service* (SaaS) to run applications, store shared information, and communicate with other non-connected computers via the Internet. Data and software applications are stored off-site in servers found at third-party locations. This permits any authorized party to view or change stored data.

Database management systems (DBMS) store and maintain information in a database file. Data can be queried, retrieved, and developed into a report using a data manipulation language such as *structured query language* (SQL). Programs such as SQL require the use of a data dictionary to identify the database field names and the number of records. A *data dictionary* defines the database structure and format, and includes information on the format and size of each data field.

A hierarchical database is used to store and organize large amounts of raw data. It places data into folders (parents) and subfolders (children). A subfolder can also have extra subfolders linked to it. A parent folder can have more than one subfolder child, but a child can only be linked backed to one parent folder. A hierarchical database has a number of problems. First, the data has to be replicated in a number of different subfolders, which wastes space. Second, data inconsistencies can occur during transaction updates.

A *relational database* stores information in tables with rows and columns. Data can be easily retrieved in different ways without having to reorganize the tables. For example, a company has a database with a table showing suppliers' names and assigned numbers. It also has a separate table for item numbers and a third one for open purchase orders. Data in each table relates to the supplier number, which permits historical data on purchases to be easily extracted and reported. A *virtual private network* (VPN) uses a low-cost, Internet-based, secure transmission method that creates tunnels of encryption and secure data flows that transmit private data communications. A VPN permits secure data sharing between a company and invited third parties that are located over a geographically dispersed area.

A *computer network* consists of two or more computer systems, including peripherals and communication devices, that are linked together to exchange data. There are two main types of computer networks used throughout a supply chain. A *local area network* (LAN) has computers connected together in one location. A *wide area network* (WAN) has two or more computer systems connected together from widely dispersed geographic areas. Both of these networks use computers, servers, and other peripheral devices to pass data back and forth over the Internet, intranet, or extranet.

The *Internet* is a global network that provides direct connectivity for everyone. It allows for the exchange of information via an *Internet service provider* (ISP). An *intranet* is a private computer network, used internally by an organization, and secured behind a firewall. An *extranet* is a private computer network that uses a VPN to link intranets securely over the Internet. The Internet, intranets, and extranets all permit low-cost, efficient data sharing and communication among users. Web browsers—such as Internet Explorer®, Safari®, Chrome®, and Firefox®—display, request, retrieve, and transmit data over the *World Wide Web* (WWW).

Web services are program functions that don't require any special custom coding. They can use multiple operating systems and programming languages because of *Extensible Markup Language* (XML), open standards, and *service-oriented architecture* (SOA). An example of a web service is one computer making a request and receiving a response from another one.

XML was developed by the World Wide Web Consortium® (W3C). It's an open standard language designed to share and exchange data across the Internet. XML emphasizes simplicity and helps to make web applications smarter and more powerful by using building blocks to send requests and receive responses. This permits businesses to quickly and efficiently communicate with each other.

SOA manages services and uses common tools to design applications (open standards). A few examples of SOA are web development tools, credit checking, PayPal, and web catalogs and shopping carts. Both XML and SOA allow widespread and flexible code sharing (scalability). They permit simple substitution of code for the ease of developing new applications, which allows for loose coupling and modular design. *Loose coupling* permits incompatible network computers from different locations to join together to process transactions from SOA developed applications. An example of this is a customer wanting to find a specific product on a company website. Loose coupling allows the service (supplier) and the software code accessing the company's website (from the customer) to communicate with each other regardless of the hardware device being used. It also permits two systems to pass data back and forth. These technology components, applications, and tools add velocity, agility, and scalability throughout the supply chain.

MATERIAL REQUIREMENTS PLANNING SYSTEM EVOLUTION TO ENTERPRISE RESOURCE PLANNING

Material requirements planning (MRP) is a stand-alone, non-integrated, batch-oriented system with limited applications and functionality. It explodes a finished good's schedule against bills of materials to calculate desired raw material and component requirements. Purchased and manufactured requirements are then scheduled. The original system application of MRP was limited to bills of materials, production planning, and some purchasing and inventory control functionality.

MRP evolved into *closed-loop MRP* that added additional material planning applications such as aggregate production planning, master production scheduling, and capacity requirements planning (CRP). Closed-loop MRP is a semi-integrated system, primarily batch-oriented, which permits feedback to go from the execution area (shop floor) to the planning area. It includes a number of execution functionalities, such as input/output control and supplier scheduling, that allow a feedback loop to update schedule and order information.

Closed-loop MRP evolved into *manufacturing resource planning* (MRP II). MRP II adds even more applications and functionality, is more sophisticated, and performs business and sales planning. It also allows for production personnel to better plan material requirements.

MRP II systems were integrated into *enterprise resource planning* (ERP) which added software applications and functionality. These applications include CRM, supplier relationship management (SRM), supply chain management (SCM), a warehouse management system (WMS), a transportation management system (TMS), and the ability to integrate to an endless number of third-party applications. ERP also has a different system architecture that incorporates client/server technology, graphical user interfaces (GUI), communication interfaces, and relational databases. It became web-centric—which allows for e-business (electronic business). Today, ERP systems are migrating to cloud computing.

A *software package* is a set of software applications such as MRP, sales and operations planning (S&OP), master scheduling (MS), and financial programs all bundled together. An ERP software package provides a comprehensive business solution that offers better and tighter application integration. Companies select an ERP package to avoid having to integrate to other applications or to perform software code customization. Its advantages are that it uses one master file that supports all enterprise functions, has a larger development staff, has a single ERP contact to provide support and training, and has a lower total cost of ownership. On the other hand, a *best-of-breed* application can offer a better overall solution to meet a company's specialized business requirements. A good example is a sales and use tax compliance system, such as Vertex® or Avalara®. Although the best-of-breed application requires constant enhancements and updating, a third party will implement these changes into a company's existing ERP package. Other best-of-breed examples include forecasting, financial consolidation, a WMS, and advanced planning and scheduling systems. The best-of-breed applications offer more functionality and have better technology solutions than can be found in a single ERP package. However, these programs have more integration issues, high operating costs, and take longer to implement.

SOFTWARE SELECTION CONSIDERATIONS

A company needs to define strategic system objectives and requirements before making a software selection. They must then compare their requirements against available system capabilities.

A choice to upgrade to a new software release or install new application modules requires a company to make the decision to meet strategic objectives, gain new desired functionality, and resolve system bugs and/or other deficiencies. It can also happen when a software vendor decides to no longer provide maintenance to the current system. Examples of this are Microsoft® deciding to no longer support the Windows NT® operating system or SAP discontinuing support of R/3 4.6C. A company will often undertake a technology audit before making a decision to upgrade their systems. This audit will assess the current state of a company's technology including its hardware, software, databases, and security. The audit is best performed by an independent, unbiased third party, and its intended audience is someone in top management who is responsible for reviewing the findings and making a decision whether or not to upgrade.

OTHER SOFTWARE APPLICATIONS

An *advanced planning and scheduling* (APS) system is an application found within an ERP system. It can also be a best-of-breed application, but that requires integration into the ERP system. A stand-alone ERP system plans material and capacity separately, which often creates an unattainable, infinite capacity plan. APS uses advanced mathematical algorithms and modeling techniques to perform finite capacity scheduling, material sources, resource planning, and demand planning. The system then performs complex trade-off calculations between competing priorities in an attempt to balance internal constraints against limited resources. Its goal is to optimize plant material requirements, capacity, and resources while simultaneously balancing it against customer service, resource utilization, and profitability goals. The APS system performs synchronization planning decisions at the strategic, tactical, and operational levels. The benefits of APS are the optimization of materials, labor, facilities, and equipment resources.

The APS system receives demand, resource, and capacity input from one or more ERP systems. It begins its analysis by looking at customer information, customer orders, forecasts, promotional activities, and seasonality in the demand management module. It then prepares a supply chain and organizational demand projection that is passed over to the resource management module. The APS system evaluates the demand plan and compares capacity against constraints, supplier and manufacturing resources, and order priorities across the supply chain to define required resources. The output is then passed to the requirements optimization where demand and resources are analyzed. The system generates multiple planning options based on predefined customer service and operational priority rules in its attempt to select the best operational plan. The plan is then sent back to the ERP system so that it can be entered into the MRP application for execution in its master production schedule (MPS). The MPS provides sales and customer service with information on available-to-promise (ATP) which shows uncommitted inventory, *capable-to-promise* (CTP) which projects future material availability if needed to quote future delivery dates, and *profitable-to-promise* (PTP) which determines the profitability of a customer order.

In a warehouse, there is a need to keep track of material movement, storage identification, and transactional processing. Technology plays a major role in the storing and selecting of materials. For example, pick-to-light, conveyors, bar coding and scanners, and automated storage and retrieval systems (ASRS) are just a few technological items. A stand-alone WMS is a software application that controls the daily movement, storage, and tracking of materials within a warehouse. It performs activities such as receiving, put-away, picking, shipping, invoicing, cycle counting, physical inventory, location identification, slotting, cross-docking, and reverse logistics. A WMS uses capacity forecasting and planning to project future warehouse space and size requirements to store inventory. It also uses average inventory in an aggregate mode to determine maximum inventory levels and safety stock. The process looks at the number of projected pallets and bays needed to store inventory and multiplies it against an adjustment factor to project future space need, utilization percentage, and whether expansion is required.

A stand-alone TMS is a software application that focuses on logistics and material movement during the shipping process. The system attempts to maximize efficiency and reduce costs associated with shipping. Key processes include the use of planning and decision making to identify transportation costs and to select the fastest delivery type with the fewest stops. The transportation execution feature identifies and selects the best carrier, carrier rate, carrier dispatching, route optimization, and dock scheduling. The transport follow-up feature tracks shipments and assists in customs clearance, invoicing, and preparing all required shipping documentation and reporting. Other key TMS activities are picking, load consolidation, route planning, shipment planning, shipment tracking and settlement, load matching and optimization, transportation network design, load tendering and delivery, carrier selection, post-shipment analysis and auditing, manifesting, freight rating, and payment.

Supply chain event management (SCEM) is an automated, proactive function that provides *supply chain visibility* (SCV). It has the ability to flag supply chain events, which trigger an alert message, and then passes it off to another application by sending out a real-time alert or exception message. This informs the supply chain participants of an internal and/or external unexpected event. The message enables the supply chain participant to become aware of a shipment status, or quickly respond to changing conditions enabling all parties to take corrective action. An example of this is the automated FedEx shipment notification that e-mail customers receive, which leads to improved service.

Before the selection and implementation of any new system, a company has to consider if it can meet at least 80% of the defined system requirements. If it can't, then the company can perform system configurations or code customization to meet desired system capabilities. *Configuration* is the ability to adjust system parameters without reprogramming the software code. This permits quick and flexible changes to the program. *Customization* is the reprogramming of software code to get an application to execute a function that it wasn't originally designed to perform. This option is costly and limits the ability to perform future upgrades.

MIDDLEWARE

Middleware is software that interconnects two otherwise incompatible databases, software components, or applications. It lies between the operating system and the applications on each side of a distributed computer network, as shown in Exhibit 23.1. Typically, it supports complex, distributed business software applications, and permits data to be easily transmitted back and forth between them. *Data-oriented* and *process-oriented* (also known as *business process management* (BPM) *or smart middleware*) are types of middleware systems.

Exhibit 23.1   Middle ware illustration

Data-oriented middleware is used with *legacy systems* or ERP systems that require the development of custom linkage. It needs field-by-field data comparison, identification, mapping, and data conversion. An example of a legacy system is an unsupported, outdated computer application that needs to pass data to a corporate ERP system. Data-oriented middleware is costly, and developing this unique conversion linkage is time-consuming.

Process-oriented middleware focuses on shared processes. It minimizes ongoing costly and time-consuming customization for the initial system implementation. Process-oriented middleware adds flexibility by giving multiple systems a common communication method. This allows system upgrades to be quickly implemented because the software provider provides the data transfer linkage. For example, a smartphone can be integrated to an order entry system allowing a customer to order an item and later receive a system alert that provides delivery status.

Electronic data transfer (EDT) is the electronic passing of data based on defined standards. Companies use EDT to electronically exchange documents such as customer or purchase orders, invoices, and *advanced shipping notices* (ASN). These *electronic documents* can also be used in a printed format. Examples include graphs, spreadsheets, and electronic mail (e-mail). It's also used to send SCEM messages over the Internet and through secured wireless and cellular devices. *Electronic funds transfer* (EFT) is the sending of an electronic payment from one company to another in a paperless format.

Electronic data interchange (EDI) is a form of EDT that performs paperless, computer-to-computer communications. It uses a batch-process that groups numerous orders together and processes them as a single batch. EDI is a form of middleware that passes converted, electronic, standard formatted business data between users. It improves worker productivity by reducing or eliminating data entry errors. This results in improved velocity and visibility, and a reduction in operational costs and inventory. A *value-added network* (VAN) is a private network provider or hosting service that helps to simplify the communication process by providing additional services between companies.

Exercise 23.1 will test your knowledge and understanding of middleware. Read each question and write in the best answer. The answers to the exercise are available from the Web Added Value™ Download Resource Center at www.jrosspub.com.

Exercise 23.1 Understanding middleware

Question	Answer
1. What are five forms of middleware? (list their names)	
2. What are three reasons why a company might choose to use custom linkages rather than smart middleware?	
3. What is the best name of the software that interconnects two otherwise incompatible applications?	
4. What is the name of the electronic communication method used by middleware that provides standards for exchanging data via any electronic means?	
5. Which form of middleware focuses on shared processes?	
6. Which form of middleware passes converted, electronic, standard formatted business data between users?	
7. Which form of middleware requires field-by-field mapping?	
8. What is the most costly form of middleware?	

KEY TERMINOLOGY

Understanding key terms and the concepts they represent is crucial to passing the Certified Supply Chain Professional (CSCP) exam. In this chapter, the important terms are identified in Table 23.1.

Table 23.1 Technology key terminology

Advanced planning and scheduling (APS)*
Advanced shipping notices (ASN)
Best-of-breed
Business process management (BPM)*
Capable-to-promise (CTP)*
Closed-loop MRP
Cloud computing
Computer network
Configuration
Customization
Data dictionary
Database management systems (DBMS)*
Data-oriented middleware
Electronic data interchange (EDI)*
Electronic data transfer (EDT)
Electronic document*
Electronic funds transfer (EFT)
Enterprise resources planning (ERP)*
Extensible Markup Language (XML)
Extranet
Hardware
Hierarchical database
Information architecture (IA)
Information system architecture*
Internet
Internet service provider (ISP)
Intranet
Legacy system*
Local area network (LAN)
Loose coupling
Manufacturing resource planning (MRP II)
Middleware
Modular system*

Continued

Operating system (OS)
Organizational architecture
Process-oriented middleware
Profitable-to-promise (PTP)
Relational database
Service-oriented architecture (SOA)
Software
Software as a Service (SaaS)
Software package
Structured query language (SQL)
Supply chain event management (SCEM)*
Supply chain visibility (SCV)*
Technology
Transportation management system (TMS)*
Value-added network (VAN)*
Virtual private network (VPN)
Warehouse management system (WMS)*
Web services*
Wide area network (WAN)
World Wide Web (WWW)

*Key term found in the CSCP ECM

CSCP EXAM PRACTICE QUESTIONS ON TECHNOLOGY

The questions shown in Table 23.2a cover the concepts presented in this chapter on technology. They are examples of what to expect on the actual exam.

Table 23.2a   Technology practice questions

No.	Questions
1	Which advanced planning system (APS) module passes data to an enterprise resource planning (ERP) system for final processing? a) Demand planning b) Resource allocation c) Resource management d) Requirements management
2	Which form of middleware is most likely the most time-consuming and expensive? a) Endware b) Data-oriented c) Process-oriented d) Business process management (BPM)

Continued

3	What is an approach to software design architecture in which applications are assembled from reusable components? a) Web-services architecture b) Extensible markup language (XML) c) Service-oriented architecture (SOA) d) Information system architecture
4	What is the best name of a low-cost, Internet-based transmission method that allows secure communications within an organization called? a) Extranet b) Wide area network (WAN) c) Virtual private network (VPN) d) Datamart private network
5	Which of the following won't be an advantage of using a best-of-breed application? a) Niche market applications b) Targeted industry expertise c) Lower total cost of ownership d) Innovative functions and features
6	Reprogramming the enterprise resource planning (ERP) software code to have the system perform a function it wasn't originally designed to perform is best called: a) Enrichment b) Configuration c) Enhancements d) Customization
7	At the operational planning level, an advanced planning system (APS) creates all of the following except for: a) Demand plans b) Inventory plans c) Demand forecasts d) Daily production plans
8	An advanced planning system (APS) may not function best without being connected to one or more: a) Warehouse management systems (WMS) b) Supply chain management (SCM) systems c) Transportation management systems (TMS) d) Enterprise resource planning (ERP) systems
9	A company looking to support collaboration between its suppliers and customers will most likely need to make an information technology investment in which software application? a) Advanced planning system (APS) b) Enterprise resource planning (ERP) c) Business process management (BPM) d) Material requirements planning (MRP)

Continued

10	Which form of middleware is called smart middleware? a) Endware b) Data-oriented c) Custom linkage d) Process-oriented
11	A company that plans to send complex messages via supply chain event management (SCEM) would most likely not use this feature: a) Web services b) Electronic data interchange (EDI) c) Hypertext transfer protocol (HTTP) d) Extensible markup language (XML)
12	A relational database procedure that helps to minimize data duplication and protect the database from certain logical and structural anomalies when data is merged is best called? a) Data mining b) Data cleansing c) Data clustering d) Data normalization
13	Which of the following isn't true for a company using software as a service (SaaS)? a) Operates through a third party b) Is a web-native software application c) Best used for standardized applications d) Converts IT variable costs to fixed costs
14	A company is using manufacturing resource planning (MRP II). Which of the following applications won't be found in this system? a) Accounts payable (A/P) b) Capacity requirements planning (CRP) c) Material requirements planning (MRP) d) Customer relationship management (CRM)

ANSWERS TO CSCP EXAM PRACTICE QUESTIONS ON TECHNOLOGY

The answers to the practice questions on technology are shown in Table 23.2b. Any question you answer incorrectly indicates a gap in your body of knowledge and encourages the need for additional study time.

Table 23.2b   Answers to CSCP exam practice questions on technology

No.	Answers
1	Answer: B Resource allocation passes data to an enterprise resource planning (ERP) system after the optimization process has been completed. This is the final processing and planning execution step within the advanced planning system (APS).
2	Answer: B Data-oriented middleware is very time consuming. Each data field must be matched between both systems.

Continued

3	Answer: C This question requires knowledge of the APICS Dictionary definition of *service-oriented architecture* (SOA). SOA uses information-sharing technology to develop business applications. The applications are assembled from reusable components that communicate with other applications to perform a function such as credit card payment validation. Web services are functions that communicate over the Internet. Extensible markup language (XML) is a language rather than an application. Information system architecture applies to the creation of the system and it includes system business processes, rules, structures, and technical framework.
4	Answer: C This question requires knowledge of the APICS Dictionary definition of a *virtual private network* (VPN). A virtual private network creates an encrypted, secure connection within an organization.
5	Answer: C A best-of-breed application has higher total cost of ownership (TCO) because of additional data integration, user training, and software maintenance fees. Answers A, B, and D are advantages of the best-of-breed supplier.
6	Answer: D This question describes customization which is the process of reprogramming software code.
7	Answer: D The output of an advanced planning system (APS) is used to help optimize daily production schedules which later creates daily production plans to identify what has to be produced.
8	Answer: D Enterprise resource planning (ERP) systems and advanced planning systems (APS) are linked together. APS may be looking at more than one manufacturing location and each location may have its own ERP system. ERP passes calculated requirements to the APS which optimizes the where and when a finished product is to be produced.
9	Answer: C Business process management (BPM), also known as middleware, shares data between multiple external partners. Answers A, B, and D are all external.
10	Answer: D Process-oriented middleware is also called smart middleware. This is because it uses a process map to send information that can still be used even after a computer system upgrade.
11	Answer: B Electronic data interchange (EDI) is batch processed, time consuming, and expensive to implement. XML, web services, and HTTP are all used to transmit messages.
12	Answer: D This question requires knowledge of the APICS Dictionary definition of *data normalization*. Data normalization helps to minimize data duplication and protect the database from anomalies when merged with data from multiple files.
13	Answer: D Software as a service (SaaS) costs are variable based on usage, while purchasing software is more fixed.
14	Answer: D Customer relationship management (CRM) isn't part of manufacturing resource planning (MRP II). The other answers are part of MRP II.

24

DATA ACQUISITION, STORAGE, AND INTEGRITY

This chapter focuses on data acquisition, storage, and data integrity. It examines the timely capture of data, the importance of accuracy, how to cleanse and maintain data, data aggregation, and big data. It also explores the use of bar codes and scanners, automatic identification and data capture, and the various types of radio frequency identification (RFID) tags.

DATA ACQUISITION AND COMMUNICATION TOOLS

Transactional activity is constantly being generated throughout a company. Customer orders, purchase orders, factory work orders, cycle counting, receipts, and shipments all generate transactions. These transactions impact financial, demand data, operational, and supply chain related activities.

TIMELY AND ACCURATE DATA CAPTURE

Timely and cost-effective processes are required to quickly capture and immediately transmit and process accurate *real-time* transactions or collected *batch* data files. A fast and accurate process reduces a visibility gap which leads to enhanced supply chain integration. This is especially true when collecting data from multiple supply chain collection points and databases. The data capture process creates a seamless link between internal and external functional areas, resulting in improved planning, effectiveness, velocity, and visibility.

Tactical and operational processes are established to capture data at its source—and there are a number of specific factors regarding data capture. These factors include using partial data rather than having to delay the processing of transmitted data, and the need for data capture accuracy at the data entry source. In this process, timeliness is critical. A company needs to enhance its batch data collection through incremental data process improvements over time as part of a continuous process improvement (CPI) program.

One method that is used to improve data accuracy is employing *work cards* or *pictographic instructions* to overcome language or data entry training barriers. A good example is a fast food restaurant that uses pictures to speed up the entry of purchased products at the cash register. The use of an *automatic identification system* (AIS), or an *automatic identification data capture* (AIDC) device, permits hands-free scanning and faster data transmission to improve both speed and data accuracy.

STATIC AND DYNAMIC DATA

Captured data can either be static or dynamic. *Static data* doesn't change. The data is fixed and gets processed only once. Examples of static data include a warehouse name or location, a plant number, part numbers, or a supplier's name and number. *Dynamic* data is ever-changing. Examples of dynamic data include inventory movement transactions, new customer orders, monthly forecasts, and shipment transactions.

DATA ACCURACY

It's important for a company to have and maintain *data accuracy*. In order to accomplish this task, they need to create policies and procedures for adding, changing, or deleting data fields, establishing data ownership, and conducting periodic audits to validate accuracy. Collected data must be cleansed and normalized, and duplicate records must be eliminated to improve data accuracy and quality. A company also needs to establish an ongoing user education and CPI training program. This program should be established to identify and track data errors, determine root causes, and implement a data resolution method in order to improve data accuracy.

Data cleansing is the process of fixing or deleting corrupt, poorly formatted, duplicate, and incomplete data records. The process requires the establishment and use of formatting standards and controls. Data normalization (*normalized*) requires standardizing data record information to minimize any logical and structural anomalies when merging data from multiple data files. Its attributes demand that values must be single, have a unique name, and contain the same data type. A *duplicate record* is when more than one record for the same information exists in a file. For example, two customer order records contain exactly the same information for the same entered order.

Data aggregation, also called *pooling*, allows raw data to be viewed in a meaningful manner, reducing random variability and permitting it to be interpreted at the granular level. This permits aggregated data to be easily understood and allows raw data to become business information.

DATA COLLECTION, BIG DATA, AND DATA MINING

A *data warehouse* is a centralized *repository* of collected (big) data from internal customers and product transactional data, and from external customers and market data. *Big data* is the collection and storage of massive amounts of data in a data warehouse or repository. A *customer data warehouse* (CDW) is a subset of a data warehouse that contains stored files pertaining to customer transactional activity. *Data mining* extracts useful information from storage files based on a user-defined selection criteria. This collected customer and transactional data gets mined to develop a deeper understanding and discovery of unknown and hidden data relationships. Big data and data mining seek out relationships between variables, (inputs and outputs) leading to the discovery of hidden data patterns and current trends to help predict future trends. Big data proves to be very useful to marketing and sales professionals, and it leads to additional sales as well as providing a higher level of customer service. Exhibit 24.1 explores the flow of big data and how it's used in a customer relationship management (CRM) system.

Exhibit 24.1   CRM process flow

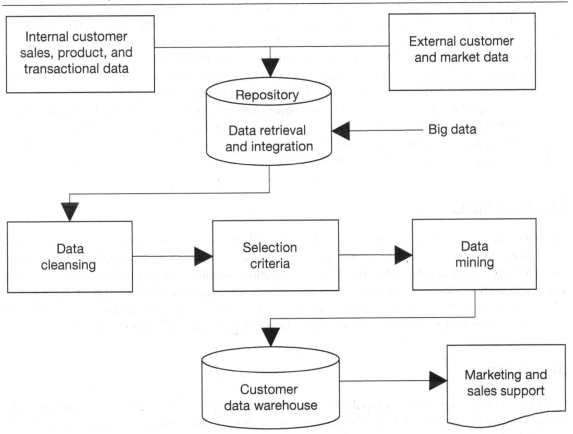

SCANNERS AND BAR CODES

The use of scanners and bar codes increases product velocity and visibility throughout a supply chain. A barcode *scanner* is a stationary or hand-held device that is used to capture and read *universal product code* (UPC) or *electronic product code* (EPC) information on products or packaged containers. Scanners quickly read bar codes as products or containers are picked or put away. Sorters, conveyors, or hand-held devices are used for scanning in order to quickly record movement activity with minimal worker involvement. Scanned data is passed to a computer for transaction processing.

Bar codes consist of a row of nine machine-readable black bars and white spaces representing 12 human-readable digits that identify a unique code. The code has intervening spaces with varying thicknesses to distinguish a product. The bars and digits both convey the same information.

GS1 is the organization responsible for maintaining the Object Naming Service (ONS). The ONS is an automated networking look-up service that routes computers to a website where they can obtain product and service information from the EPC. This code is designed to be a universal bar code identifier that is easily read by RFID and optical/vision systems. The code provides data about the manufacturer, stock-keeping units (SKU), product information, and serial number. A second bar code is the UPC. The UPC is a common bar code standard that identifies a product's manufacturer and SKU number.

The *quick response* (QR) *code* consists of black square dots arranged in a square grid on a white background. A smartphone or an imaging device can read the code and extract data to display product information. The code can be read and decoded at high speeds from any direction. The QR code also has a larger storage capacity than the UPC or EPC barcodes.

AIS AND AIDC

The automatic identification system or AIS (also called AIDC) device communicates real-time product transaction and customer information movement tracking. The AIS reduces manual data entry, leads to improved labor efficiency, improved inventory and location visibility, and reduced stockouts, inventory levels, and safety stock. The reduction in inventory offsets the required capital investment. Examples of AIS devices include vision systems, pick-to-light devices, RFID tags, smart cards, and magnetic strips. AIS and AIDC devices read, record, and process supply chain transactional data automatically into a computer.

RFID TAGS

RFID tags are tiny, wireless microchip devices that use electromagnetic fields to transmit electronic data signals. The tag is a type of AIDC device that has the capability to be configured to both read and write data. This allows the tag to communicate broadcasted data with a host device. The transmitted data is collected and stored by readers/interrogators, allowing companies to identify transaction movement activity and current storage locations. RFID helps to reduce manual data entry, improve labor efficiency, improve inventory and location visibility, and helps prevent product counterfeiting and theft.

There are three types of RFID tags. They are active, passive, and semi-passive. The *active* tag contains its own battery source and is self-powered. It constantly broadcasts electronic information that identifies the container or pallet location. A simple example of an active device is a wireless key fob that opens a car door. The *passive* tag doesn't broadcast any electronic information, nor does it contain a battery power source. It responds when queried by a reader, which then sends power to the tag. These devices are inexpensive chips that are often used by retail stores to tag merchandise. The reader device is a network connected device that sends a read command to the tag. It's usually found at the cash register or at the store's exit, and it captures and records product sale or movement transactions. A *semi-passive* tag contains a battery, but receives transmission power from a reader. The NJ E-ZPass®, an electronic toll collection device, is an example of a semi-passive tag.

Exercise 24.1 will test your knowledge and understanding of RFID tags. Read each question and write in the correct answer. The answers to the exercise are available from the Web Added Value™ Download Resource Center at www.jrosspub.com.

Exercise 24.1   Understanding RFID tags

Question	Answer
1. Which form of radio frequency identification (RFID) tag contains its own battery source and is self-powered?	
2. Which form of RFID doesn't broadcast any electronic information, nor does it contain a battery power source?	
3. What supply chain development stage will a company be at if they are using RFID?	
4. Which form of RFID obtains its transmission power from a reader?	
5. Which form of RFID responds when queried by a reader, and then sends power to read a device?	
6. Which form of RFID uses an electronic product code (EPC) tag that doesn't broadcast information or contain its own power source?	
7. Who or what most likely will drive an RFID implementation?	

KEY TERMINOLOGY

Understanding key terms and the concepts they represent is crucial to passing the Certified Supply Chain Professional (CSCP) exam. In this chapter, the important terms are identified in Table 24.1.

Table 24.1   Data acquisition, storage, and integrity key terminology

Active tag*
Automatic identification and data capture (AIDC)*
Automatic identification system (AIS)*
Bar codes
Batch
Big data
Cleansed
Customer data warehouse (CDW)
Data accuracy
Data aggregation
Data cleansing
Data scrubbing
Data standardization
Duplicate records
Dynamic data
Electronic product code (EPC)*
Normalized
Passive tag*
Pictographic instructions
Pooling
Quick response (QR) code
Radio frequency identification (RFID)*
Real-time
Scanners
Semi-passive tag*
Static data
Universal product code (UPC)
Work cards

*Key term found in the CSCP ECM

CSCP EXAM PRACTICE QUESTIONS ON DATA ACQUISITION, STORAGE, AND INTEGRITY

The questions shown in Table 24.2a cover the concepts presented in this chapter on data acquisition, storage, and integrity. They are examples of what to expect on the actual exam.

Table 24.2a   Data acquisition, storage, and integrity practice questions

No.	Questions
1	Which of the following isn't a direct benefit that a retailer using radio frequency identification (RFID) tags can expect to achieve? a) Inventory reduction b) Labor cost reduction c) Product mix reduction d) Out-of-stock reduction
2	Which of the following is the biggest problem with collected transaction data? a) Data clustering b) Velocity reduction c) Variability reduction d) Granular level interpretation
3	All of the following are key benefits of an automatic identification system (AIS) except for: a) Elimination of data entry b) Increased processing speed c) Faster information visibility d) Increased transaction accuracy
4	The group of black bars and white spaces on a bar code label best represents: a) Characters b) Part numbers c) Product codes d) Stock-keeping unit (SKU) numbers
5	A uniform product code (UPC) can identify all of the following information except for: a) Serial number b) Manufacturer c) 12-digit number d) Stock-keeping unit (SKU)
6	An electronic product code (EPC) tag that broadcasts information, contains its own power source, and harvests transmission power from the reader to extend its broadcast range is best called a/an: a) Active tag b) Passive tag c) Dynamic tag d) Semi-passive tag

ANSWERS TO CSCP EXAM PRACTICE QUESTIONS ON DATA ACQUISITION, STORAGE, AND INTEGRITY

The answers to the practice questions on data acquisition, storage, and integrity are shown in Table 24.2b. Any question you answer incorrectly indicates a gap in your body of knowledge and encourages the need for additional study time.

Table 24.2b   Answers to CSCP exam practice questions on data acquisition, storage, and integrity

No.	Answers
1	Answer: C Product mix is dependent on customer demand patterns. It receives no direct benefit from radio frequency identification (RFID) tags.
2	Answer: D The biggest problem with collected transaction data is that it's difficult to interpret at the granular level because of the massive amount of collected data.
3	Answer: A Data entry is reduced, not eliminated when using an automatic identification system (AIS). Some data, like quantities, still has to be entered.
4	Answer: A The black and white space represents a character which is a letter or number.
5	Answer: A The uniform product code (UPC) tracks information on the product stock-keeping unit (SKU), the code itself (digits), and the manufacturer, but it cannot identify a product by its serial number.
6	Answer: D A semi-passive tag broadcasts information about a product but receives transmission power from a reader. EZ Pass, used by a number of toll roads in the United States, is an example of a semi-passive tag. The tag broadcasts information about the car and payments. It's then viewed by a reader who records the transaction.

25

ELECTRONIC BUSINESS
AND COMMERCE

This chapter focuses on electronic businesses and commerce. It examines business-to-commerce, business-to-business, the buy and sell side of electronic commerce, virtual organizations, and the differences between a traditional and electronic business.

ELECTRONIC BUSINESS TYPES

Electronic commerce (*e-commerce*) is facilitating or processing business transactions electronically. It's generally considered to be the sales aspect of electronic business (e-business). E-commerce is more than buying and selling over the Internet. It also includes businesses that are buying or selling products and services over the telephone, telegraph, fax machine, or any other electronic method.

E-business uses information and communication technologies to support supplier and customer business activities that are needed to buy, sell, transfer, or exchange products or services over a wireless Internet network, which improves productivity and profitability. *Business-to-business* (B2B) *commerce* is a commerce transaction for a product or service that occurs between two businesses. *Business-to-consumer* (B2C) *sales* describe the exchange of products or services from a business to the end consumer. It focuses on creating customer value.

The *sell-side e-commerce* company sells products or services to a pool of potential customers, often through the use of an electronic catalog. An example of this is a major office supply store offering paper products for online sales to corporate clients. The *buy-side e-commerce* customer looks to purchase products and services from a pool of suppliers. An example of this is a customer participating in an online reverse auction to purchase materials at a low cost.

A *virtual organization* is an alliance between two or more independent organizations that temporarily join together and appear to be one company to address specific market opportunities. These organizations sell a product or service by pooling resources and sharing data, risks, costs, and profits. A good example of this is an online e-business such as Amazon, which initially outsourced all activities to third parties. Another example is Apple, which outsources manufacturing operations to other companies.

TRADITIONAL VERSUS E-BUSINESS

A *traditional supply chain* is push based, lacks a strategic outlook, and has limited communications with suppliers and customers. It's often vertically organized with the company owning the entire supply chain, including raw materials, manufacturing, warehousing, and distribution. A few large companies dominate the market and numerous barriers are put in place to prevent and discourage competition. These large companies act as a channel master that dictates terms to their suppliers and customer base. They focus on *economies of scale* and have little interaction with rivals.

Traditional supply chain companies aren't customer focused, and have narrow views of customer service. They are *inward-focused* organizations. They limit internal, direct contact with suppliers and customers. The internal corporate staff exercises direct control over decision making and they focus on how operations can be performed less expensively, in less time, and with fewer resources. Supply chain effectiveness is the metric used, rather than customer service performance. A *customer-focused organization* puts the interests of the customer first.

Today, companies have *e-business supply chains* that focus on core competencies. They are virtually or laterally organized and outsource non-core activities. They are also quite lean and agile and join together with partners in a collaborative attempt to grow their businesses by offering low prices and quick delivery. Companies use electronic marketplaces to seek out new customers and market opportunities.

B2B AND B2C E-COMMERCE LAYERS

The B2B and the B2C Internet structure consists of four layers—foundation, application, aggregation, and business. The *foundation layer* includes the hardware, software, and physical resources that are needed to transmit data over the Internet. It also includes the various connectivity applications, middleware, web services, security systems, wiring, fiber optics, routers, and servers that connect in order to operate the foundation layer. The *application layer* includes all web-specific applications and tools for creating interactive websites. This includes commerce tools, web shopping carts, billing applications, search engines, and web development tools. A company has the option of outsourcing this layer to a third party, in which case, it wouldn't be required. The *aggregation layer* includes applications that are designed to pull information and services from various locations and package them for easier access and usage. Portals and intermediaries such as brokers and service providers are considered to be part of this layer. Hosting is very expensive, so companies form larger communities or join consortiums to control costs. The *business layer* includes all exchanges that are involved in buying and selling on the Internet. Companies with a large volume of sales activities need to make a huge capital investment in the foundation layer. Smaller businesses can join exchanges or outsource the business layer to reduce their capital investment.

Exercise 25.1 will test your knowledge and understanding of e-business and commerce. Read each question and write in the correct answer. The answers to the exercise are available from the Web Added Value™ Download Resource Center at www.jrosspub.com.

Exercise 25.1 Understanding electronic business and commerce

Question	Answer
1. What is the electronic business (e-business) type name when two independent organizations join in a long-term relationship to address a specific market opportunity that involves designing, producing, and distributing a joint product?	
2. What is the name of the e-business type that best conducts business transactions electronically?	
3. What is the name of the e-business type that conducts business over the Internet with another company?	
4. What is the name of the e-business type that sells merchandise in a dynamic environment to consumers online?	
5. Which e-business type is considered the sales aspect of e-business?	
6. Which electronic commerce (e-commerce) type looks to purchase products from a pool of suppliers?	
7. Which e-commerce type sells a product to a pool of potential customers using an electronic catalog?	
8. Which e-business type sells a service from a business to an end consumer?	
9. Which e-business type uses an electronic transaction to purchase a product from another business?	
10. Which e-business type uses information and communication technologies to support supplier and customer business buying, selling, and transferring activities over a wireless network?	
11. Why can't a company normally conduct e-business to sell a product to the public over the intranet?	

KEY TERMINOLOGY

Understanding key terms and the concepts they represent is crucial to passing the Certified Supply Chain Professional (CSCP) exam. In this chapter, the important terms are identified in Table 25.1.

Table 25.1   Electronic business and commerce key terminology

Aggregation layer
Application layer
Business layer
Business-to-business commerce (B2B)*
Business-to-consumer sales (B2C)*
Buy-side e-commerce
E-business (electronic business)
E-commerce (electronic commerce)
Economies of scale
Electronic business (e-business)
Electronic business supply chains
Electronic commerce (e-commerce)*
Foundation layer
Inward-focused
Sell-side e-commerce
Traditional supply chain
Virtual organization

*Key term found in the CSCP ECM

CSCP EXAM PRACTICE QUESTIONS ON ELECTRONIC BUSINESS AND COMMERCE

The questions shown in Table 25.2a cover the concepts presented in this chapter on electronic business and commerce. They are examples of what to expect on the actual exam.

Table 25.2a   Electronic business and commerce practice questions

No.	Questions
1	Which of the following isn't a characteristic of a virtual organization? a) Integrated processes b) Identity preservation c) Proprietary information d) Trust between partners and customers
2	An inward-focused company is most likely to look at which metric: a) Efficiency b) Effectiveness c) Customer service level d) Shipping performance
3	The main goal of a business-to-consumer (B2C) business is to: a) Create customer value b) Sell products and services c) Build a trusting relationship d) Eliminate paper transactions
4	Which form of e-business sells directly to the final user through an electronic catalog? a) Supplier b) Nucleus firm c) Business-to-business (B2B) d) Business-to-consumer (B2C)
5	Which business-to-business (B2B) e-business layer consists of applications designed to take information from various locations and package them for easier access and consumption? a) Business layer b) Foundation layer c) Application layer d) Aggregation layer

ANSWERS TO CSCP EXAM PRACTICE QUESTIONS ON ELECTRONIC BUSINESS AND COMMERCE

The answers to the practice questions on electronic business and commerce are shown in Table 25.2b. Any question you answer incorrectly indicates a gap in your body of knowledge and encourages the need for additional study time.

Table 25.2b   Answers to CSCP exam practice questions on electronic business and commerce

No.	Answers
1	Answer: C A virtual organization no longer considers information proprietary. Data is considered open and can be shared among all participating parties.
2	Answer: B Utilizing an inward-focused strategy is how a company's supply chain process can be done less expensively, in less time, and with fewer resources. Supply chain effectiveness is the metric being used.
3	Answer: A Creating customer value helps a business-to-consumer (B2C) business sell more products and services, make more money, and build a long-term trusting relationship. It reduces or eliminates non-value-added activities and makes the online sales experience easier and hassle free. This creates value in the eyes of the customer.
4	Answer: D The key words in this question are *final user*. A business-to-consumer (B2C) conducts business over the Internet directly to the end user. Customers use an online catalog to identify the item they wish to purchase. Business-to-business (B2B) means selling to another business who then sells to an end user.
5	Answer: D This question requires knowledge of the APICS CSCP courseware definition of *aggregation layer*, which consists of applications designed to take information from various locations and package them for easier access and consumption.

26

PROJECT MANAGEMENT

This chapter focuses on project management concepts. It examines project management, the product life cycle, the role of a project manager, the *PMBOK® Guide*, process group activities, and project variance analysis.

PROJECT MANAGEMENT

A *project* is a temporary undertaking to create a unique product (tangible) or perform a service (intangible) over a period of time with a specified budget. It has a defined beginning and end date. The project ends upon achieving all project objectives and the sponsor (customer) either accepting delivery or deciding to terminate the project. An *operation* is an indefinite, repeatable activity that has assigned resources to produce a standard output. It's assigned to a functional manager who oversees activities such as ordering materials, assembling a component, or performing a financial transaction. Resources are assigned to accomplish the task; and the goal is to complete the strategic or tactical objective. Projects and operations interact with each other during project execution.

Project management is an approach to planning, managing, and controlling a project from its beginning to its end. It includes the following components: objectives (*project scope*, cost, time, and quality), management processes (scheduling, budgeting, and *project life cycle* phases), and levels (strategic and tactical). Project management also regulates the project through five processes (stages)—initiating, planning, executing, monitoring/controlling, and closing.

The role of a *project manager* (PM) is to recruit, organize, and manage the project team. This person must provide leadership, influence, communicate with stakeholders, and coordinate the project management process. The PM must also be able to obtain stakeholder consensus, manage the project scope, achieve the project objectives in a timely and cost-effective manner, utilize resources, perform strategic and tactical planning, and incorporate lessons learned from prior projects.

The *Project Management Institute* (PMI®) created the *Project Management Body of Knowledge* (*PMBOK® Guide*). The guide is a global standard providing rules and characteristics for project management processes. It identifies 10 project management Knowledge Areas. They are integration, scope, schedule, cost, quality, resources, communication, risk, procurement, and stakeholder.

Two inputs to the *PMBOK® Guide* processes are *enterprise environmental factors* (EEFs) and *organizational process assets* (OPAs). EEFs are internal or external factors that influence a project and are outside the control of the project team. Examples of them are organizational cultures, government regulations, resource availability, and political or economic conditions. *Organizational readiness* refers to the organization's ability to accept and implement change. OPA outputs include policies, procedures, processes, rules, standards, templates, methodologies, and the organization's historical knowledge (lessons learned). This assists an organization in achieving their goals and objectives and can be divided into two categories. The first category is policies and procedures, which includes processes, plans, and general guidelines. The second category is a corporate knowledge base. This includes a centralized storehouse of tools, techniques, and project-related information—such as risk registers, historical project data, or lessons learned summaries that were created during prior projects. This prior data can support the current project implementation by saving time, effort, and money.

PROCESS GROUP ACTIVITIES

The *PMBOK® Guide* explores five Process Groups. They are project initiating, project planning and design, project execution, monitoring/controlling, and project closure.

Project initiating is the process of defining activities that are required to begin a project and includes writing the *project charter*. A project charter provides an overview of the project along with its direction, accountability, objectives, success criteria, and expected outcome. Other activities in project initiating include assigning a PM, defining the project team and their roles, establishing a budget, and obtaining management approval.

Project planning and design is the process that details how to turn strategy into a tactical plan. It defines the project scope, which includes what needs to be accomplished along with project goals, deliverables, finalized budgets, schedules, and time frames. The plan needs to include current and future information system architecture requirements before initiating the project. Project planning and design also identifies quality standards, staffing, the communications process, risk management, the procurement process, and how to manage stakeholder expectations.

The outcome of this step is a *project management plan*. In this step a *work breakdown structure* (WBS) details the required work necessary to achieve project scope. It takes the activities and tasks, time frames, and resources and breaks them down into smaller, more manageable pieces. It also displays their durations, dependencies, and resources. The WBS shows planned labor and material costs by task, level, and total project.

Project execution is the performance of activities and tasks that are defined in the project management plan. This step requires the longest amount of time and consumes the most resources. The PM has the responsibility of ensuring that the plan adheres to its budget and assigned resources. Quality audits need to be performed to validate that work is being performed to scope. The PM also needs to manage change requests to minimize scope creep and to keep the project on time and within budget.

Project monitoring and controlling is the ongoing collection and aggregation of performance data. This data is used to consistently evaluate the plan status in terms of time, budget, and resources. A variance analysis is performed to identify any deviations from the original plan. The PM and team meet frequently to review plan progress, address any identified budget or schedule deviations, and take appropriate action to resolve issues.

Project closure occurs when all planned activities and tasks have been properly completed and the customer accepts the product or service. The contract is closed out, final payment is made to the contractor, and the team is disbanded. A finalized report is prepared that includes lessons learned, and it is then issued to the project sponsor.

Exercise 26.1 will test your knowledge and understanding of the various project management process groups. Read each question and write in the correct answer. The answers to the exercise are available from the Web Added Value™ Download Resource Center at www.jrosspub.com.

Exercise 26.1   Understanding project management Process Groups

Question	Answer
1. A project manager (PM) is assigned during which Process Group?	
2. A quality audit is performed during which Process Group?	
3. A request to make a work change request is typically submitted during which Process Group?	
4. A user makes a request to change a report layout. During which Process Group activity does this occur?	
5. Collecting performance data on project status is performed during which Process Group?	
6. During which Process Group activity is a final report issued?	
7. The project scope is assigned during which Process Group?	
8. The work breakdown structure (WBS) is developed during which Process Group?	

VARIANCE ANALYSIS

Earned value management (EVM) is used to track scope, schedule, and cost deviations. It uses planned, earned, and actual values to perform project measurement calculations. The measurement first calculates *planned value* (PV), which is the budgeted amount and time frame for the scheduled activity. For example, a project has a $5,000 budget to rebuild four machines, and it's scheduled to take eight weeks. It's now four weeks into the project. PV is calculated by taking the scheduled completion time frame of four weeks, dividing it by the eight week schedule, and then multiplying it by the budgeted amount. It's equal to scheduled completion of four weeks, divided by the total schedule of eight weeks, times the budgeted amount of $5,000. The PV is calculated to be $2,500 ((four weeks ÷ eight weeks) * $5,000 = $2,500).

Another measurement is *earned value* (EV), which compares budgeted work performance to actual work completed to date. For example, it's determined that the repairing of four machines is 55% complete. EV is calculated by taking the budget amount times the actual percent complete. EV is calculated to be

$2,750 (budget of $5,000 * 55% = $2,750). The final measurement is *actual cost* (AC), which is calculated by accumulating all actual costs to date (labor and materials). The actual cost is reported to be $3,100.

The PM uses PV, EV, and AC to determine if a *schedule variance* (SV) or *cost variance* (CV) exist. These calculated variances are used to identify if the project is achieving its planned scheduled date and if it's adhering to its planned budget. Failure to achieve the schedule and budget leads to delayed implementation and cost overruns.

In the previous example, the project was planned for eight weeks, and four weeks have elapsed. SV is calculated by subtracting PV from EV (EV of $2,750 − PV of $2,500 = $250 (ahead of schedule)). CV is calculated by determining the difference between EV and AC ($2,750 − $3,100 = −$350). The project is currently $350 over budget. These identified variances are used to calculate the schedule performance and cost performance index values.

The *schedule performance index* (SPI) is calculated by taking EV and dividing it by PV times 100% (($2,750 ÷ $2,500) * 100% = 110%). A number of less than 100% means that the project is behind schedule and a number in excess of 100% means that the project is ahead of schedule. *The cost performance index* (CPI) is calculated by taking EV divided by AC (($2,750 ÷ $3,100) * 100% = 88.7%). A number of less than 100% means that the project is over budget and a number in excess of 100% means that the project is ahead of budget. This example shows that the project is currently ahead of schedule but over budget. It also means for each spent dollar on the project, it's only returning 88.7 cents, but for every estimated hour of work, it's performing 10% better than plan. However, from a risk management viewpoint, the PM needs to immediately take corrective action to resolve the overspending issue.

Exercise 26.2 will test your knowledge and understanding of how to perform the different variance analysis calculations. Read each question, perform the calculation, and answer the questions regarding the results. The answers to the exercise are available from the Web Added Value™ Download Resource Center at www.jrosspub.com.

Exercise 26.2   Understanding variance analysis calculations

Question	Answer
1. A project has a $10,000 budget to develop and build two custom machines for a customer. The project is scheduled to take four weeks. It's now two weeks into the project. Calculate the planned value (PV).	
2. A project has a $10,000 budget. It's determined that the project is 35% complete. Calculate the earned value (EV).	
3. Calculate the schedule variance (SV) of a project based on the following data: • Percent complete = 40% • Earned value (EV) = $3,500 • Planned value (PV) = $5,000 • Actual cost (AC) to date = $3,000	
4. Calculate the cost variance (CV) of a project based on the following data: • Percent complete = 40% • Earned value (EV) = $3,500 • Planned value (PV) = $5,000 • Actual cost (AC) to date = $3,000	

Continued

5. Calculate the schedule performance index (SPI) of a project based on the following data:
   • Percent complete = 40%
   • Earned value (EV) = $3,500
   • Planned value (PV) = $5,000
   • Actual cost (AC) to date = $3,000	

6. What does the schedule performance index (SPI) number of 65% tell the project manager (PM) about the project?	

7. Calculate the cost performance index (CPI) of a project based on the following data:
   • Percent complete = 40%
   • Earned value (EV) = $3,500
   • Planned value (PV) = $5,000
   • Actual cost (AC) to date = $3,000	

8. What does a positive cost performance index (CPI) tell the project manager (PM)?	

KEY TERMINOLOGY

Understanding key terms and the concepts they represent is crucial to passing the Certified Supply Chain Professional (CSCP) exam. In this chapter, the important terms are identified in Table 26.1.

Table 26.1   Project management key terminology

Actual cost (AC)
Cost performance index (CPI)
Cost variance (CV)
Earned value (EV)
Earned value management (EVM)
Enterprise environmental factors (EEFs)
Operation
Organizational process assets (OPAs)
Organizational readiness
Planned value (PV)
Project Management Book of Knowledge (*PMBOK® Guide*)
Project
Project charter
Project closure
Project execution
Project initiating
Project life cycle

Continued

| Project management* |
| Project Management Institute (PMI®) |
| Project management plan |
| Project manager |
| Project monitoring and controlling |
| Project planning and design |
| Project scope |
| Schedule performance index (SPI) |
| Schedule variance (SV) |
| Work breakdown structure (WBS) |

*Key term found in the CSCP ECM

CSCP EXAM PRACTICE QUESTIONS ON PROJECT MANAGEMENT

The questions shown in Table 26.2a cover the concepts presented in this chapter on project management. They are examples of what to expect on the actual exam.

Table 26.2a   Project management practice questions

No.	Questions
1	The project manager (PM) is using earned value management (EVM) to monitor the project status. Where is EVM best used? a) Controlling b) Monitoring c) Variance analysis d) Throughout the entire project
2	When is a business system project considered to be completed? a) When the client says it's complete b) When the system has been installed c) When the project team is disbanded d) When all project plan activities have been completed
3	An operation has all of the following characteristics except for: a) Ongoing duration b) Standardized deliverables c) The use of permanent manufacturing positions d) Being overseen by a project manager
4	Which of the following isn't a project management best practice? a) Holding meetings to gather percent complete estimates b) Clearly delegating responsibilities c) Keeping the project management plan updated d) Everyone working towards the same plan

Continued

5	What is the best reason why a project life cycle (PLC) is split into phases?
	a) To better control the project
	b) To standardize work assignments
	c) To manage the project budget and time frame
	d) To manage team member activities
6	Which of the following isn't an organizational process asset?
	a) Procedures
	b) Methodologies
	c) Lessons learned
	d) Organizational readiness
7	Which Process Group turns strategy into tactical action?
	a) Planning
	b) Initiating
	c) Executing
	d) Controlling
8	When is the project implementation phase completed?
	a) When the sponsor has accepted all deliverables
	b) When the system has been installed
	c) When the project team is disbanded
	d) When all activities have been completed
9	The _____ is used to determine if the project is ahead or behind schedule.
	a) Schedule baseline
	b) Schedule variance
	c) Total schedule status
	d) Schedule completion status
10	Based on the presented project information, determine the current project status.
	Actual cost (AC) = $435,000
	Earned value (EV) = $416,000
	Planned value (PV) = $459,000
	a) Behind schedule and over budget
	b) Behind schedule and under budget
	c) Ahead of schedule and over budget
	d) Ahead of schedule and under budget
11	A project has a schedule performance index (SPI) of 101% and a cost performance index (CPI) of 83%. What can you determine?
	a) Currently ahead of schedule but over budget
	b) Currently ahead of schedule and under budget
	c) Currently behind schedule but under budget
	d) Currently behind schedule and over budget
12	What tool is used to establish a logical activity framework for a project?
	a) Process routing
	b) Network diagram
	c) Resource breakdown structure
	d) Work breakdown structure (WBS)

ANSWERS TO CSCP EXAM PRACTICE QUESTIONS ON PROJECT MANAGEMENT

The answers to the practice questions on project management are shown in Table 26.2b. Any question you answer incorrectly indicates a gap in your body of knowledge and encourages the need for additional study time.

Table 26.2b   Answers to CSCP exam practice questions on project management

No.	Answers
1	Answer: D Economic value added (EVA) is used to track and measure a project's progress at any given point in time during the life of the project.
2	Answer: A A business system project is considered complete when the customer says it finished, and not before.
3	Answer: D An operation uses a functional manager while a project uses a project manager (PM).
4	Answer: A Gathering percent complete estimates at a project review meeting is a pitfall. This type of information should be collected before the meeting. The meeting attendees should only be discussing substantive issues and risks.
5	Answer: A A project life cycle (PLC) is split into phases for control purposes.
6	Answer: D Organizational readiness is an enterprise environmental factor (EEF). Organizational process assets include policies, procedures, processes, rules, standards, templates, methodologies, and the organization's historic knowledge (lessons learned).
7	Answer: A During the project planning and design activity, strategy is turned into a tactical plan to identify how to complete a project successfully.
8	Answer: A The project implementation phase is completed when the sponsor (owner) agrees to accept the project.
9	Answer: B Schedule variance (SV) is used to determine if the project is ahead or behind schedule.
10	Answer: A The project is behind schedule and over budget. Two calculations are needed to answer this question. The calculation for scheduled value is earned value (EV) minus planned value (PV) ($416,000 − $459,000) = −$43,000 (behind schedule). The calculation for cost variance (CV) is earned value (EV) minus actual cost (AC) ($416,000 − $435,000) = −$19,000 (over budget).

Continued

11	Answer: A
	The schedule performance index (SPI) is calculated by taking the earned value (EV) divided by planned value (PV) and the cost performance index (CPI) is calculated by taking the earned value (EV) divided by actual cost (AC). A calculation that shows an answer that is less than 100% means it's behind schedule or over budget. An answer greater than 100% means it's ahead of schedule or under budget. A project that has a schedule performance index (SPI) of 101% and a cost performance index (CPI) of 83% means that the project is currently ahead of schedule but over budget.
12	Answer: D
	This question requires knowledge of the APICS Dictionary definition of a *work breakdown structure* (WBS). A WBS is a hierarchical description of project activities shown level by level in a greater amount of detail which establishes a logical activity framework. A network diagram is a graphical tool that shows the dependencies between project activities. A resource breakdown structure breaks resources into categories to support the project.

27

CSCP PRACTICE EXAM

This test is designed to help our readers prepare for the Certified Supply Chain Professional (CSCP) exam. We suggest that you take it in one sitting and allow yourself 75 minutes. The questions found in this practice exam haven't been based on any actual certification exam. We have no knowledge of any CSCP certification test questions. Our practice exam has been designed solely to help identify gaps in your body of knowledge based on information found in the APICS CSCP exam content manual course outline and key terms list. If you want to improve your readiness, you need to go back and study your identified gaps because these are your areas of weakness.

We wish you the best of luck on passing the APICS CSCP exam and earning your certification. If our study guide or these questions have helped you pass the exam, please let us know. Thank you.

Howard Forman
David Forman
PIM Associates Inc.
pimassociates@yahoo.com

CSCP PRACTICE EXAM (75 QUESTIONS)

The CSCP Practice Exam questions presented here in Table 27.1a cover various concepts, terms, relationships, and calculations that have been presented in this study guide. The answers to this CSCP practice exam are available from the Web Added Value™ Download Resource Center at www.jrosspub.com.

Table 27.1a   CSCP practice exam (75 questions)

No.	Questions
1	A company has received 100 customer orders during the month of November. Each order had two line items with a November ship date. Ninety-six of the orders had both line items shipped in November, three orders had one item shipped complete in November, and the other unshipped items were shipped in the following month. The last remaining order was cancelled because it couldn't be shipped complete in November. What was the fill rate in November? a) 96% b) 97% c) 99% d) 100%
2	In Hofstede's cultural dimension study, a manager *telling an employee what should be done* may become an issue with supply chain management implication in what area? a) Culture b) Uncertainty c) Individualism d) Power distance
3	Which ISO standard is designed to help an organization manage risk? a) ISO 31000 b) ISO 9001:2008 c) ISO 14001:2004 d) ISO 26000:2010
4	The triple bottom line (TBL) requires a company to have a close connection between all of the following direct goals except for: a) Social b) Economic c) Environmental d) Labor regulations
5	The ability to provide a chain of custody for finished products, raw materials, and components used in the manufacturing process is best called: a) ISO 31000 b) Lot control c) Traceability d) Product differentiation
6	A service company has decided to implement a Six Sigma program. They developed a process flow that identified five customer information points during order entry. How many defect opportunities will exist during order processing? a) 1 b) 3.4 c) 5 d) 17
7	Which of the following isn't true about a responsible landfill? a) Least desirable option b) Turns waste into reusable resources c) Minimizes required disposal space d) Generates high emissions during incinerations
8	A product with high value density and low packaging density will best be shipped: a) Direct ship to customer via air b) Direct ship to customer via rail c) Direct ship to customer via truck d) Direct ship to distributor intermodal

Continued

9	If a computer company offered customers the opportunity to upgrade to a larger monitor for $50 more in order to reduce excess inventory, the process would be called: a) Cross-selling b) Demand shaping c) Demand replanning d) Inventory optimization
10	Calculate the forecast for Product 123 using exponential smoothing based on: Alpha factor = .4 Old forecast = 700 Actual demand = 800 Seasonal index = 1.11 a) 700 b) 740 c) 760 d) 943
11	Which of the following is the primary cause of the bullwhip effect? a) Order batching b) Inflated lead times c) Lack of collaboration d) Demand forecast errors
12	What is the primary output of the capacity requirements planning (CRP) process? a) Work center load report b) Capacity available report c) Work center leveling report d) Revised schedule of planned order releases
13	A company implements a 10% reduction in its order quantity, but annual demand remains the same. How will this impact ordering costs and inventory levels? a) Order costs will go up and inventory up b) Order costs will go down and inventory up c) Order costs will go up and inventory down d) Order costs will go down and inventory down
14	The Supply Chain Operations Reference (SCOR®) Model provides a unique framework that helps to link all companies together in a unified structure except for: a) Metrics b) Communications c) Business processes d) Technology features
15	In what supply chain management (SCM) stage has technology permitted the enterprise to start to reach further and to move faster? a) Extended enterprise b) Multiple dysfunction c) Integrated enterprise d) Semi-functional enterprise
16	What is the name of the term associated with supply chain management (SCM) software applications where users have the ability to flag the occurrences of certain supply chain events to trigger some form of alert within another supply chain application? a) Supply chain visibility (SCV) b) Supply chain management cost c) Supply chain event management (SCEM) d) Supply chain operations reference (SCOR)

Continued

17	Management assigned you as a project manager (PM) to improve the functional operation of the order entry process. What action should you first take? a) Prepare a budget b) Define the project scope c) Define the implementation time frame d) Determine the needs of the functional area
18	Which of the following SCOR metrics measures responsiveness? a) Perfect order fulfillment b) Order fulfillment cycle time c) Upside supply chain flexibility d) Upside supply chain adaptability
19	What is the last step in an ISO 31000 process framework? a) Assess risk levels b) Monitor the process c) Determine risk response d) Place risks in appropriate context
20	What or who may override a global sourcing decision? a) Plant manager b) Local business requirements c) Corporate social responsibility policy d) Material requirements planning (MRP) supplier selection
21	In which customer relationship management (CRM) element is the development of lifetime customers found? a) Collaboration b) Sales operations c) Relationship building d) Customer information dissemination
22	What is the focus of improvement efforts in the Theory of Constraints (TOC)? a) Defects b) Performance c) Minimum throughput d) Maximum system output
23	During its manufacturing process, a company has a by-product leftover. It finds another company willing to use this by-product as a raw material in their manufacturing process. This is an example of: a) Recycling b) Waste disposal c) Waste exchange d) Hazardous material
24	Where does a company report a violation of their intellectual property (IP) in the European Union (EU)? a) Court systems b) Customs department c) Department of Homeland Security d) National Intellectual Property Rights Coordination Center
25	A company that uses customer relationship management (CRM) to capture information about every interaction with customers is best using which of the Four Ps? a) Price b) Product c) Placement d) Promotion

Continued

26	Calculate the mean absolute deviation based on the forecast difference for the last four actual demand periods. They are 3, −10, 9, and 2. a) 1.0 b) 4.0 c) 6.0 d) 8.0
27	A company decides to use a commitment decision point to improve its buyer-supplier relationship in an attempt to minimize disruptions to its demand data plans. Which of the following is most likely not true? a) It specifies the communication methods to use b) It utilizes firm, planned orders in the slushy zone c) It develops a formal process to support the collaborative effort d) It defines expectations in a trading partner agreement (TPA)
28	Work center 100 had five machines running 40 hours per week. The department was expected to produce 200 pieces per the routing standard. However, they actually produced 220 pieces. The department lost five pieces during inspection. Calculate the efficiency of the work center. a) 10.0% b) 91.0% c) 107.5% d) 110.0%
29	What is the best reason to perform cycle counting? a) Counts are distributed evenly b) Annual inventory adjustment elimination c) Physical inventory elimination d) Timely detection and problem correction
30	Which is the most common type of mathematical model used in supply chain management (SCM)? a) Conceptual b) Optimization c) Heuristic algorithm d) Linear programming
31	A web-based service that provides a range of information, tools, and links between sellers and buyers is best called a: a) Portal b) Web browser c) Trade exchange d) Virtual private network (VPN)
32	An application hosted on a remote server and accessed through the Internet would be called: a) Business-to-business (B2B) b) Lines of operations services c) Software as a service (SaaS) d) Universal description, discovery, and integration (UDDI)
33	A company can benefit from a reverse supply chain in all of the following ways except for: a) Making money b) Reducing consumer pressure c) Reducing government regulations d) Being seen as a good corporate citizen
34	A company that earned its ISO 9000 certification has demonstrated: a) Use of Six Sigma b) Implementation of a quality management system c) It's following a quality process d) It has a good quality reputation

Continued

35	All of the following are key principles addressed in the United Nations Global Compact (UNGC) except for: a) Labor rights b) Human rights c) Anticorruption d) Stakeholder rights
36	A shift to a customer-focused corporate culture will most likely require: a) Extensive organizational change b) Involvement of the internal customer c) Involvement of cross-functional teams d) Implementation of customer relationship management (CRM) software
37	A company has decided to increase the number of distribution centers (DCs) from three to four. Its total safety stock (SS) levels will be: a) Increased by a factor of two b) Increased by the square root of three c) Decreased and the percent can be calculated d) Increased and the percent can be calculated
38	What is the most compelling difference between a third-party logistics (3PL) and a fourth-party logistics (4PL) provider? a) A third party focusing on cost reduction b) A third party performing a function c) A third party acting as a general contractor d) A fourth party acting as a general contractor
39	Which Incoterm® makes it difficult for a buyer to verify freight and insurance charges? a) Cost and freight b) Carriage paid to c) Cost, insurance, and freight d) Carriage and insurance paid to
40	The correlation coefficient is shown as zero. What type of linear relationship exists between the variables? a) None b) Positive c) Negative d) Both positive and negative
41	A design team working with a customer reduces the amount of product packaging cardboard by 20%. They are using: a) Design for assembly b) Design for reverse logistics c) Design for the environment d) Design for manufacturing and assembly
42	A volume commitment decision point is established in which time zone? a) Frozen b) Slushy c) Liquid d) No-fly
43	Which of the seven basic tools of quality is most likely the starting point for a continuous improvement program? a) Histogram b) Check sheet c) Pareto chart d) Scatter chart

Continued

44	Which negative indicator in the cash-to-cash cycle time metric can be improved through improved forecasting? a) Inventory b) Safety stock (SS) c) Inventory turns d) Accounts payable
45	A company has decided to reduce the number of bottle caps used in its filling line from six to one. This is an example of which design concept? a) Universality b) Modular design c) Raw material reduction d) Component commonality
46	Equilibrium is best explained when which of the following occurs: a) Supply exceeds the level of demand b) Supply matches the level of demand c) Demand matches the production capability d) Product pricing becomes acceptable to the customers' base
47	Which of the following provides a unique warehouse management identity for each item and not just its product class? a) Product code b) Harmonized code c) Universal product code (UPC) d) Electronic product code (EPC)
48	What is the best opportunity to minimize environmental impact? a) Reusing materials b) Returning materials c) Reducing materials d) Recycling materials
49	Which standard is solely focused on improving working conditions at all retail and manufacturing organizations? a) SA8000 b) ISO 26000 c) ANSI Z.10-2012 d) United Nations Global Compact (UNGC)
50	What is the focus of the Sarbanes-Oxley Act? a) Protect investors b) Segregation of duties c) Corporate governance d) Avoid conflict of interests
51	Which of the following isn't identified as a continuous process improvement (CPI) approach? a) Six Sigma b) Just-in-time (JIT) c) Theory of Constraints (TOC) d) Total quality management (TQM)
52	A natural disaster can impact product variability. What will be the best way to mitigate this effect on product demand? a) Increased safety stock (SS) levels b) Develop an inventory build plan c) Build up inventory in anticipation d) Develop a risk management plan

Continued

53	A shipment begins in China and is placed on a ship that sails to the United States. Upon landing, the shipment is placed on a train bound for New York. Upon arrival in New York, the shipment is then placed on a boat sailing for London. This process best describes which type of bridge? a) Sea bridge b) Land bridge c) Lean bridge d) Mini land bridge
54	Which document may be used to transfer a title? a) Order bill of lading b) Ocean bill of lading c) Statement of liability d) Straight bill of lading
55	What is the major difference between multiple and simple regression? a) Simple regression has only one variable while multiple has more b) Simple regression doesn't have any variables while multiple does c) Both simple and multiple regression have more than one variable d) Simple regression has more than one variable while multiple has only one
56	A company is looking to improve its overall business plan, demand management, and sales and operations planning (S&OP) processes. What type of planning is best suited to accomplish this goal? a) Master planning b) Master scheduling c) Resource planning d) Consensus demand planning
57	Material requirements planning (MRP) system nervousness can best be reduced through the use of: a) Allocations b) Safety stock (SS) c) Planned orders d) Firm planned orders
58	In a long-term option contract, who has the greatest risk if demand uncertainty exists? a) Buyer b) Seller c) Supplier d) Buyer and seller share risk
59	Who is the intended audience for a technology audit? a) Upper management b) Financial department c) Sarbanes-Oxley auditors d) Information technology (IT) department
60	Which step in the product life cycle (PLC) is essential to cultivate brand loyalty and develop lifetime customers? a) Decline b) Growth c) Introduction d) Development
61	What needs to be thought out early before implementing a specific supply chain strategy successfully? a) Database requirements b) Hardware requirements c) Software system requirements d) Information system architecture

Continued

62	All of the following are forms of automatic identification systems (AIS) except for: a) Smart cards b) Optical scans c) Voice recognition d) Electronic data interchange (EDI)
63	What is the best reason for the existence of the North American Free Trade Agreement (NAFTA)? a) It creates jobs b) It eliminates tariffs c) It reduces logistics costs d) It increases tariff revenue
64	Which of the following isn't an action required by a company to support Customs-Trade Partnership Against Terrorism (C-TPAT)? a) Assess the supply chain in accordance with C-TPAT guidelines b) Submit a supply chain security profile questionnaire c) Develop and implement a supply chain program d) Require customers to participate in the program
65	A company plans to implement a program to create a sustainable lean workplace. The implementation effort best begins with: a) Mura b) 5S c) Kaizen d) Management
66	An organization's strategy to address supply chain risk will most likely include which of the following? a) Risk strategy plan b) Risk response plan c) Risk contingency plan d) Business interruption plan
67	Which transportation mode has relatively high variable costs per hundredweight (CWT)? a) Trains b) Water c) Pipeline d) Motor carriers
68	A positive trend will impact a moving average forecast in what manner? a) The forecast won't be impacted b) The forecast will always be above actual value c) The forecast will always be below actual value d) The forecast will be equal to actual value
69	The best objective of the executive sales and operations planning (S&OP) meeting is to: a) Recommend changes to the resource plan b) Define new product introduction plans c) Authorize changes to the production rate d) Prepare an updated financial plan

Continued

70	In what period and for what quantity will the first distribution requirements planning (DRP) planned order receipt be required?

OQ = 25

Lead time = One Period

Demand time fence = two

		Periods			
		1	2	3	4
Gross Requirements		25	25	40	0
Scheduled receipts		10			
Projected Available	30				
Net requirements					
Planned order receipt					
Planned order release					

a) Period one—25 pieces
b) Period two—10 pieces
c) Period two—25 pieces
d) Period three—25 pieces

71	Aggregate inventory management is primarily concerned with: a) Forecast accuracy b) Financial impact of inventory c) Customer service requirements d) Operational impact of inventory
72	A process that creates, produces, and delivers a product to the end user is best called: a) Value chain b) Value stream c) SCOR model d) Supply chain model
73	What is the key reason for failure in a balanced scorecard (BSC) approach? a) Communication b) Information flow c) Inconsistent tactical goals d) Cross-functional team ownership
74	The output of advanced planning system (APS) short-term optimization and simulations are input to the: a) Resource plan (RP) b) Production plan (PP) c) Master production schedule (MPS) d) Enterprise resource planning (ERP) system
75	A company deciding to make a capital investment in an e-business initiative must justify the project in all of the following ways except for: a) Decreased facility costs b) Decreased inventory costs c) Decreased transaction costs d) Decreased transportation costs

28

APICS CSCP TEST
READINESS ASSESSMENT

This chapter focuses on determining if you are ready to take the Certified Supply Chain Professional (CSCP) exam.

CSCP TEST READINESS

Quite frankly, no one ever feels 100% *ready* to take the APICS CSCP exam. We all have doubts and fears regarding our ability to pass. However, if you have:

- Reviewed the APICS CSCP Exam Content Manual (ECM),
- Read the APICS CSCP Learning System,
- Answered the questions at the back of each chapter,
- Learned the key terminology,
- Reviewed at least 300+ APICS CSCP Learning System online practice questions,
- Reviewed this study guide and taken our CSCP practice exams (both within the pages of this book and online at jrosspub.com/testbanks), and
- Identified gaps in your CSCP body of knowledge and studied them,

then you are just about ready to take your exam.

To validate your readiness, three final preparation steps are suggested. First, did you completely read the APICS CSCP Learning System and this book, do all of our exercises, take our end of chapter specific topic practice tests and our 75-question CSCP practice exam, and study your identified gaps? Did you take advantage of our study materials that are available online at jrosspub.com/wav and utilize our online test bank found at jrosspub.com/testbanks? Second, if the answer to all of those questions is yes, then log into the APICS CSCP online system and take the APICS CSCP online 50-question post-test. Third, if you scored 80% or higher on the online test, then take the 50-question APICS practice exam consisting of retired CSCP test questions. If you are able to answer 80% of those questions correctly, then you are ready to take the exam. Don't take the retired practice test unless you have scored at least 80% on the post-test, because this means you have a lower probability of passing the CSCP exam. It's best to delay taking the retired practice exam until you have studied your identified gaps. Please note that the APICS CSCP online practice tests and the retired questions test are only available to those individuals who have purchased the APICS CSCP Learning System ($995 for Plus members as of January 2018 plus shipping and handling), and have authorized access to the online portion of the system. If you don't have this online access, you should consider purchasing the program at apics.org. Additionally, there are hundreds more practice questions available from our online test bank at jrosspub.com/testbanks. Consider spending a few dollars here since these questions are typically harder than those found on the actual exam, and students who do well on these questions have a high likelihood of passing the actual exam on their first try.

What do you do if your score is between 65% and 80% on the post-test or the 50 retired questions test? We suggest the following:

Review each incorrect question and ask yourself, "What did I do wrong?" Table 28.1 is a check sheet to record and organize the reason behind each incorrect question. The specified reasons might be that you didn't know a concept or definition, misread the question, selected the second-best answer, didn't know a formula or calculation process, or had no idea of the answer. Identify each APICS CSCP Learning System module and chapter in which the errors occurred. Put a check in the box that best describes the reason you got a question wrong. A review of this check sheet will identify the gap areas in your CSCP body of knowledge. These are the areas where additional studying is required. Study these gaps, and when you have finished studying, then take the CSCP module or post-test again. Did your score improve to 80%? If your answer to this question is yes, congratulations, you are ready to schedule your exam. If not, then you need to continue studying until you can consistently score 80% or higher on the practice tests.

Table 28.1 Check sheet

Incorrect Question Reason (Gap)	Number of Occurrences
Misread the question	
No idea of the answer	
Didn't know a concept	
Didn't know a definition	
Selected the second-best answer	
Didn't know how to perform the calculation	

If you consistently score less than 65% on the practice questions, don't take the exam. The probability of your passing is low. Go back and continue reviewing the CSCP Learning System and our book. When you have reread the APICS CSCP Learning System and our book, retake the various tests. Based on your score, follow the previous instructions.

29

APICS CSCP EXAM TIPS
AND WALK-THROUGH

This chapter focuses on how to prepare and take the APICS Certified Supply Chain Professional (CSCP) certification exam. It describes a suggested process to increase your probability of passing the exam. It walks through the exam sign-in process, the exam itself, and how to enhance your probability of correctly answering questions.

THE NIGHT BEFORE

It's the night before the APICS CSCP exam and you are feeling nervous and worried. You have spent endless hours reading, studying, and taking practice exams. Don't try to spend all night studying, as you either know the material at this point or you don't. However, a little time reviewing your CSCP dictionary terms and creating a list of a few to be used for the exam can be helpful. A few areas to study are takt analysis, return on investment (ROI), sales and operations planning (S&OP), and the various enterprise resource planning stages. Study this sheet when you arrive early at the test center, but don't bring it into the room with you!

After your study list has been made and reviewed, collect everything you need for the exam. First, make sure you check your CSCP e-mail confirmation and take a moment to validate the date, time, and address of the exam center. Second, check that you have the two required forms of identification that are approved by APICS (one must include a photograph), directions to the exam center and knowledge of public transportation or where to park, reading glasses (if necessary), and a basic calculator that has a square root function. Third, plan appropriate clothing attire, and think layers. The exam center may be too hot or cold for your taste, and you don't want to get distracted. Fourth, APICS permits the use of an English-to-foreign language dictionary (if English is not your primary language), so make sure to pack one. Unfortunately, the *APICS Dictionary* can't be used during the exam. Finally, try to relax, take it easy, go to bed early, and get a good night's sleep. It's strongly recommended that you eat breakfast or lunch before you take the exam since its three-and-a-half hours long. Remember, your brain requires a constant supply of energy, so it's important not to become fatigued from lack of sleep or food.

THE EXAM CENTER AND COMPUTER TEST PROCESS

Plan to arrive at the exam center forty-five minutes early. Remember, traffic delays, not being able to find the exam center, or failure to find a parking spot can create anxiety. Don't procrastinate! Arrive early so you can relax and then take a few minutes to review your study list.

The exam center is often located inside an office complex, so make sure you know the name of the company and the correct floor. Early mornings, evenings, and weekends are usually the busiest times at exam centers, and not all locations have weekend hours. Allow sufficient time in your planning for standing in line. Tell the exam center contact the exam you are taking and be prepared to present your identification. They will enter your information into their system, confirm you are scheduled to take the CSCP exam, validate your identity, and take your picture. A copy of your picture will later appear on your exam result printout. Don't forget to smile.

Except for the aforementioned items, the exam center doesn't allow anything to be brought into the testing room. This includes your cell phone, computers, tablets, purse/wallet, picture identifications, keys, food, watch, drinks, tissues, jacket, an APICS Dictionary, or the CSCP Learning System. These items must be placed in an outside storage locker in the exam center and a key is provided to your assigned locker. Don't bring anything extremely valuable that you might worry about. The lockers can also be quite small, so don't bring anything large, such as a laptop computer, into the testing center.

For complete information regarding the CSCP testing process, download and read the bulletins for the CSCP exam in North America or the CSCP exam outside North America. If you are unsure of anything, or if you have any questions, contact APICS customer service.

Once you complete the sign-in process, you are almost ready to take the exam. After checking in, you will be asked to sit down and wait for your name to be called. When they call your name, depending on the exam center, you will either be given a dry erase board and marker or a clipboard with two pencils and scrap paper. The proctor will then escort you into the room and assign you a seat at a computer station. The computer station has a keyboard underneath the desk, but it's only used by the proctor to log into the system. A mouse, located on the top of the desk, is available for your use. There are two side walls at your desk so you can't see the computer or the person next to you. A noise cancelling headphone or ear plugs may be available for your use.

The CSCP exam can be a fearful and frustrating experience. Don't get upset if you find your mind going blank or total panic sets in. This happens to numerous exam takers. Take a deep breath and exhale slowly. Repeat this breathing exercise a few times until you calm down. Remind yourself that you read the CSCP Learning System, this study guide, took numerous practice exams, studied your gaps, and you're prepared!

Before you look at the first exam question, perform a memory dump by writing down (on the white board/clipboard) the key concepts you studied right before you entered the exam center. Refer to this memory dump during the exam; it can be very helpful.

The proctor doesn't provide any instructions on how to use the computer to take the exam. They will instruct you to click on the computer screen *begin* button (or something similar) and the system will require you to answer a number of verification questions. The first questions will ask you to confirm that your information regarding your name and exam are correct. Next, you are asked several questions regarding why you are taking this exam, ethnicity, gender, and age. It will then ask if you want to take a tutorial or not. If you say yes, it will walk you through the exam-taking process. Even if you have taken a computer-based exam before, it's often a good idea to view the tutorial. The time you spend viewing the tutorial doesn't count toward your exam time.

After you have finished the tutorial, the next screen will ask if you are ready to begin the exam. Once you click begin, the clock starts. Depending on the test center and computer station, you will observe two icons on the top of the screen. The first one shows the question number you are on, and the second one shows the time remaining. You can shut the time icon off by clicking on a button if it becomes a distraction.

On the middle of the screen you will see the question itself; and directly under the question, there will be four radio-type buttons (small round circles) that display the four answer options as "A", "B", "C", and "D". Click on the button that best answers the question. You can choose to answer a question, flag it for later review, or proceed to the next question without taking any action. Flagging allows you to think about your answer, and, its possible you may find a hint on how to correctly answer this question later in the exam.

On the bottom of the screen, you will have four options:

1. MARK—flags the question for later review
2. NEXT—takes you to the next question
3. PREVIOUS—takes you back to the previous question
4. END EXAM—takes you to the completion screen

Upon selecting *end exam*, you will see a *review* screen that shows you a summary page that lists the questions you have answered and those you haven't. It will also show how many questions you have flagged. You will be given an option to review flagged questions, review unanswered questions, or review everything. Remember, you can go to the review screen at any time and select a question you want to go back and answer.

When you are ready to complete the exam, the system will ask you if you are ready to submit your answers. You will be given the option to say *yes* or *no*. If you say *yes*, the system will display a reminder to inform you of flagged or unanswered questions that should be completed before you exit the exam. Remember to answer all questions, even if you need to guess since you aren't penalized for wrong answers. If you hit *no* by accident, you will have an opportunity to cancel this transaction and return to the flagged questions. If you are sure you have finished the exam, hit *no*. The system will display a screen that informs you to contact the proctor to obtain your results. You can now inform the proctor that you are finished.

CHANGES MADE TO THE APICS CSCP EXAM

The APICS CSCP exam underwent a major revamp in 2016 and a minor one in 2017. The number of questions was reduced from 175 to 150 and the names of the modules were changed. Module 1 is now called *Fundamentals of Supply Chain Management*; Module 2 is *Supply Chain Strategy, Planning, and Execution*; and Module 3 is *Supply Chain Improvement and Best Practices*. The first module consists of approximately 35 questions; the second module, 64 questions; and the third module, 51 questions. Some topics will cross modules. In addition, 20 of the 150 APICS CSCP questions are designated as pre-test questions. These pre-test questions are trial questions and don't impact the exam score. If you answer them incorrectly, you aren't penalized, and if you answer them correctly, you receive no credit. Unfortunately, the pre-test questions can't be identified by the exam taker.

It's important to note that if you are using an earlier version of the APICS CSCP Learning System to study for the APICS CSCP exam, you will be at a disadvantage when answering questions. The 2016 and the 2017 courseware added quite a few new concepts, deleted some, and changed others. It's strongly recommended that you use the most current version to prepare for your exam.

The APICS CSCP questions are based on materials outlined in the APICS CSCP Exam Content Manual (ECM). APICS has stated over the years that the CSCP exam and the ECM are in sync. However, APICS has also stated that questions can come from CSCP reference sources. This means that a few questions may be based on material that is not found in the CSCP Learning System. Don't be upset if you find a few questions that you can't answer. This is quite normal. A complete list of reference materials can be found in the ECM section of the APICS CSCP Learning System.

SEGMENT THE EXAM

While you can't outsmart the APICS CSCP exam logic, you can improve your probability of selecting correct answers. Consider using a few or all of our suggested strategies to help you select a correct answer. First, consider using the Pareto analysis concept to segment the exam into three parts. Consider that 50% of the questions will be basic concepts and key terms; 30% will be moderate to hard concepts, calculations, and knowledge of relationships; and 20% will be difficult situational type questions. The level of question difficulty increases as you go from "C" type questions to "A" type questions.

If you want to improve your probability of passing the exam, try the following approach. First, go through the exam and answer the "C" type questions in your first pass. Look for questions that are designed to test your knowledge on basic concepts and dictionary terms. If you have previously studied and learned the concepts and terms found on the APICS Key Terminology List, and the lists of terms found at the end of each chapter in this book, you should be able to quickly and correctly answer a high percentage of these questions. Answering these questions first will improve your confidence and prepare you for the harder ones to come. The goal is to answer approximately 75 questions in the first hour.

The next step is to start answering the moderate to hard "B" questions. These questions are more challenging, but if you know your calculations, and have studied the CSCP Learning System exhibits and relationship charts, you should be able to answer the majority of them correctly. The APICS CSCP Learning System Instructor Visual Book is also a useful study tool, but is only available if you attend an instructor-led course. There are a number of exercises in this book to assist you in learning the various calculations and relationships. Be sure to utilize them as you prepare for the exam. The goal will be to answer at least 45 questions in the second hour.

If you have learned the basic concepts, key terms, calculations, and relationships, you should be able to answer approximately 120 questions in the first two hours of the exam. Assuming that you have answered 85% of these questions correctly, this means that you might have 102 correctly answered questions. You now have 30 difficult questions left to answer, and 90 minutes to complete the exam. This allows you plenty of time to finish. At this point, we suggest you take a short break. Ask the proctor for permission to leave the room, get a drink of water, splash some water on your face, stretch, or just relax for a moment.

This should help clear your mind. However, keep in mind that the exam clock continues to run, so don't take too long.

The final part of the exam will now be spent answering the "A" questions. These are the most difficult situational types of questions. They will require that you spend extra time reading them, thinking about what the question is really asking, and determining the correct answer. Remember, you have plenty of time to answer them, so don't rush. If you can correctly answer 60% of these questions, you will have another 18 correct answers. This will give you 120 correct answers, or approximately 80%. Don't be concerned if you need more or less time than is suggested for each category. If you need additional time, take it, but be sure to keep in mind how much time remains.

EXAM QUESTIONS

The CSCP exam normally has a few questions where you need to perform actual calculations, while others will focus on the process or results. These questions will examine your knowledge of the formulas and the logic and purpose behind the calculations. APICS can test you on variations of the formulas, the calculation processes, and their results as presented in the CSCP Learning System.

The way you read the questions and answers on the CSCP exam will often determine if you pass or not. Read each question slowly, read it again, and then ask yourself what the question is looking for. Look for key words to help guide you toward the correct answer. A key word is a hint to answering the question. Words like *all*, *never*, *always*, *most likely*, *except*, and *best* will help you to eliminate answers or let you know that more than one answer may be partially correct. Look for words such as *communicate, collaborate, strategic,* and *global*, as well as various time frame references, because they can direct you toward the correct answer.

APICS likes to use the technique of negatively structured questions. The following are a few examples of negative wordings: *which of the following isn't true for a company using . . . , would most likely not use this . . .* , or *but not at the exclusion of . . .* Many test takers misread these types of questions—so read them slowly and carefully. When you answer this type of question, look for the pattern of answers that are the opposite of the question being asked. It's always easier to look for the three answers that are true and then select the remaining answer.

For example: Which item is most likely not yellow?

   a. Lime
   b. Lemon
   c. Banana
   d. Apple

Understanding that lemons and bananas are most likely yellow, it's simple to eliminate those answers. An apple can sometimes be yellow, but isn't yellow 100% of the time. Therefore, it's easy to pick lime (a) as the correct answer. Yes, some bananas, apples, and lemons can be green, but a lime is green all of the time. Don't overthink the question, don't think of rare exceptions, and don't consider your personal work experience or knowledge. If you do, the odds of selecting an incorrect answer increases.

ANSWERING EXAM QUESTIONS

Each APICS CSCP exam question is written in a multiple choice format, composed with four possible choices. The question has one correct answer, a second plausible answer may appear to be correct, and two incorrect answers. The question and some answers may contain distracting, unnecessary information that is designed to point you toward an incorrect answer. It's important to identify and ignore this information and select the *best* APICS answer. Start with the "D" answer option and ask yourself if this answer is correct or incorrect. If you think it may be correct, leave it alone for the moment. If you feel it's incorrect, then eliminate that answer. Repeat the process for each remaining answer. This process helps to avoid the problem of selecting the first possible correct answer. Remember, it's always easier to eliminate an incorrect answer than to select a right answer. Don't be surprised if you end up eliminating three answers on some questions.

In a good number of cases, you will be able to eliminate two answers on a question, leaving two answers that might be correct. The following rules will help you to select the correct answer. First, never think *this is the way my company answers this question*. On the exam, only the APICS way matters. Remember, for every question there is a right answer, a wrong answer—and then possibly your company's answer based on the way they do things; an answer according to the APICS Dictionary; an APICS answer according to the APICS Certified in Production and Inventory Management (CPIM) courseware; an APICS answer according to the APICS Certified in Logistics, Transportation, and Distribution (CLTD) courseware; and finally an answer found in the CSCP Learning System. How do you figure out the source of the best answer? Since the CSCP exam questions come from CSCP references, that is the best and only source, regardless of all else.

Another hint is to ask yourself whether either remaining answer applies 100% of the time in large and small companies, in all manufacturing environments, and to all companies regardless of where in the world they are located. If you can't say yes, then that answer must be incorrect and your choice is made. You also need to ask yourself if one answer is always 100% true. If you can't say it's always true, then that answer is incorrect. Finally, ask yourself if an answer is a subset of the other. For example, is "C" part of "A" or is "A" part of "C"? If one answer is part of the other, then the one containing both parts is the correct answer.

Don't be surprised at the end of the exam if there are a few questions that you have no idea how to answer. This is quite common. If you can't eliminate any answers, then select "C" for all remaining questions. Statistically, this may allow you to select at least one correct answer. If you select a variety of answers for each of these remaining questions, you stand a higher probability of selecting all wrong answers. This method is only to be used when you have no idea of the answer, can't eliminate any options, or if you are running out of time. It's better to insert an answer than leave it blank. You aren't penalized for wrong answers, so select an answer for every question, even if you don't know the correct one.

When you have two remaining answers and none of the previously stated rules apply, there is one last suggestion to help you select an answer. This rule applies only if one of the two remaining answers isn't "C". In this case, it's suggested that you pick the longest answer. Statistically, selecting the longest answer gives you a higher probability of selecting the correct one.

When you are completely unsure of the answer to a question, using one or more of these rules can help you correctly answer additional questions. This may be the difference between passing and not passing the exam, so keep these rules in mind. Try applying our various rules to the online CSCP practice questions or with the questions in this book, and see if you begin to answer more questions correctly.

POTENTIAL STUDENT MISTAKES TO AVOID

Review this list and avoid making any of these common mistakes when taking the CSCP exam.

1. Spending too much time on individual questions
2. Not validating the math on calculation questions
3. Quickly reading each question and its answers
4. Not reading the CSCP Learning System at least once
5. Not learning key terminology, concepts, and calculations
6. Selecting an answer without reading the remaining answers
7. Not previously having read the CSCP Exam Content Manual
8. Not validating that the selected answer is the one you meant to pick
9. Not reading the CSCP test questions slowly and identifying *key* words
10. Answering questions based on how your company applies courseware concepts
11. Not using our CSCP online test bank practice questions and the questions found in this book
12. Not considering that some answers can be partially correct and that you need to select the APICS *best* answer

FINISHING THE EXAM

Take the following steps before you exit the exam. First, validate that every question has an answer and that you have answered all flagged questions. The online system will prompt you by informing you that you still have time left to review your work. Click on the box that says *I want to review*, and take the time to conduct a review. Second, go through the exam and validate all calculations. It's amazing how many people make a simple mathematical error. Don't allow yourself to get a question wrong for this type of mistake. Remember, you brought a calculator, so don't do the math in your head.

Do you change an answer or not? As instructors, we recommend never changing an answer unless you find a math mistake or see a later question that leads you to recognize an error. Different instructors have different opinions, but we believe more people change correct answers to wrong answers—and your *gut* answer is right more than it's wrong. Use this theory when answering the online practice questions or the questions in this book. Note if you change correct answers to wrong ones, or wrong answers to correct ones.

One final notation is that the exam center must follow the instructions as defined by the CSCP bulletin. If they deviate from it—if the room is very noisy, too hot, too cold, or if they don't start on time—make sure to register a complaint. The exam center should have an issue form. Request a copy, complete the form, and return it to the proctor. Also, make a point to immediately contact APICS to register your formal complaint and ask them to take corrective action.

30

AFTER THE APICS CSCP EXAM

This chapter focuses on what actions should be taken after the Certified Supply Chain Professional (CSCP) exam is completed. It explores what happens if you don't pass, provides a suggested action plan to help prepare you to retake the exam, and informs you of what to do with your certification when you pass.

AT THE CONCLUSION OF THE APICS CSCP EXAM

Hooray, it's over, the exam is finished. Your results appear on your computer screen and you will know immediately whether or not you earned your certification. A proctor will also print out your results.

NOT PASSING THE APICS CSCP EXAM

The results appeared and you didn't pass. What happened after you studied for so long and so hard? Don't despair, as it's not an easy exam, and one third of the individuals who take the APICS CSCP exam don't pass on their first try.

Complete the following steps to increase your chances of passing the exam the next time around.

- Step 1—Look at your APICS CSCP score sheet. In which module or modules did you score less than 70%? These are your weak areas that you need to focus on.
- Step 2—Immediately go through the APICS CSCP Learning System module by module, page by page, and write down anything that you remember seeing on the exam such as definitions, concepts, acronyms, calculations, metrics, relationships, and processes. Pay special attention to all courseware charts and exhibits for clues on concepts you remember seeing. Write an item down even if you think you understand what it means since you may have misinterpreted it. Don't try to write down the actual test questions because you many not remember them correctly, and it goes against the APICS ethics statement.
- Step 3—Repeat the process from Step 2 for the APICS CSCP Exam Content Manual and the key terminology lists.

- Step 4—In a separate column, write down anything you think you saw on the exam that was not covered in your class, or that you don't remember seeing in the APICS CSCP Learning System. These will definitely be crucial points that require further study.

You now have a list consisting of a few hundred terms, concepts, relationships, and calculations. This is your study guide. Don't assume that you fully understand anything on your list—carefully study each item. Review these items until you are confident that you fully understand the material.

In addition to the steps previously mentioned, there are a couple final points you should consider before retaking the exam.

First, did you have the latest version of the APICS CSCP Learning System? Remember that each year APICS adds new concepts and terms. If you saw questions on concepts that you don't remember learning about, reading an older version of the CSCP Learning System might have been the source of your problem.

Second, did you have access to the 1,000 plus CSCP online system practice questions, plus the retired questions practice test? If not, this put you at a disadvantage. Consider purchasing the latest version of the APICS CSCP Learning System or additional time in our test bank (jrosspub.com/testbanks).

Don't be concerned with identifying the correct answer. Try to figure out which answers are wrong and learn to eliminate them. See if you can reduce the number of answers to two or even one. Then, select what you think is the best answer and also identify your second-best answer. If you find that you are consistently picking the wrong answer, then you need to rethink how you are answering the questions and reread our test-taking rules.

In conjunction with the aforementioned steps, if you took an instructor-led course, inform your instructor. A good instructor is often willing to help his/her students by answering questions before, during, or after the course. A number of APICS chapters or third-party organizations will allow you to retake the course at no charge and/or the instructor may offer extra assistance. All you need to do is ask.

One final thing to remember is that APICS has multiple versions of the CSCP exam. In all probability, if you take the exam again, it won't be the same one. Don't focus solely on just those items on your list. Go back and reread the APICS CSCP Learning System, especially the modules in which you had the lowest scores. Make a point of reading the section in this book that describes what to do if you don't score at least 80% on the practice tests, and follow the advice given to you. When you start to consistently score 80%, you are ready to retake the APICS CSCP exam. Good luck.

PASSING THE APICS CSCP EXAM

You passed! Give a silent shout of joy. You have earned the right. It has been a long, hard journey, but you have successfully reached your goal. Let us be the first to say congratulations.

Go ahead and inform your spouse and family, and make sure you thank them for their patience. Next, inform your boss, coworkers, the human resources department, study partners, friends, and anyone else you wish to tell. If you took an instructor-led course, let your instructor know of your accomplishment. Don't forget to update your business card, e-mail signature, resume, and your LinkedIn, Twitter, and Facebook profiles.

Having earned your CSCP certification, you are now eligible to obtain a CSCP certificate. APICS will notify you in a few weeks via e-mail about how to accomplish this. You can select a downloadable electronic certificate you can print yourself, or an APICS printed certificate can be requested via a link located on the *My APICS* certification page. It's recommended to request the APICS printed certification version because it looks nicer in a frame. Make sure to send a copy of the certificate to your manager and your human resources department. Also, please let us know if our book helped you to achieve your goal. Drop us a note at pimassociates@yahoo.com.

Go out and celebrate your accomplishment. You have reached your goal!

Appendix A

BIBLIOGRAPHY

We believe that reading the APICS CSCP Learning System and our study guide will be sufficient for experienced supply chain and operational professionals to earn their CSCP certification. We also believe that attending an instructor-led course will accelerate the learning process. However, the use of supplemental materials may prove beneficial to help increase your knowledge and understanding of selected concepts. In addition to the references shown in the CSCP Learning System, we also used the following:

APICS, *APICS Dictionary*, Fifteenth Edition. APICS, Chicago, IL, 2016.

APICS, *Certified Supply Chain Professional™ (CSCP) Learning System*, 2018 Edition, Version 4.2. APICS, Chicago, IL, 2018.

Arnold, J. R. Tony, Stephen N. Chapman, and Lloyd M. Clive. *Introduction to Materials Management*, Eighth Custom Edition. Upper Saddle River, NJ, 2017.

AT&T, *Statistical Quality Control Handbook*, Eleventh Edition. Delmar Printing Company, Charlotte, NC, 1985.

Kaplan, Robert S. and David P. Norton. *The Balanced Scorecard: Translating Strategy into Action*. Harvard Business School Press, Boston, MA, 1996.

Martin, Andre J. *Distribution Requirements Planning: Distribution Management's Most Powerful Tool*. Prentice-Hall, Inc., Englewood Cliffs, NJ, 1983.

Orlicky, J. *Material Requirements Planning*. McGraw-Hill, New York City, NY, 1975.

Plossl, G. W. and O. W. Wight. *Production and Inventory Control: Principles and Techniques*. Prentice-Hall, Inc., Englewood Cliffs, NJ, 1967.

Porter, Michael E. *Competitive Strategy: Techniques for Analyzing Industries and Competitors*. The Free Press, New York City, NY, 1980.

Simchi-Levi, David. *Operations Rules: Delivering Customer Value through Flexible Operations*. The MIT Press, Cambridge, MA, 2010.

Simchi-Levi, David, Philip Kaminsky, and Edith Simchi-Levi. *Designing and Managing the Supply Chain: Concepts, Strategies and Case Studies*, Third Edition. McGraw-Hill Education, New York City, NY, 2008.

Vollmann, Thomas E., William L. Berry, D. Clay Whybark, and F. Robert Jacobs. *Manufacturing Planning and Control Systems for Supply Chain Management*, Fifth Edition. McGraw-Hill Education, New York City, NY, 2005.

Walker, William T. *Supply Chain Architecture: A Blueprint for Networking the Flow of Materials, Information and Cash*. CRC Press, New York City, NY, 2005.

Wallace, Thomas F. and Robert A. Stahl. *Sales & Operations Planning: The How-To Handbook*, Third Edition. T. F. Wallace & Company, 2008.

Womack, J. P. and D. T. Jones. *Lean Thinking*, Simon & Schuster, New York City, NY, 1966.

Appendix B

LIST OF TABLES AND EXHIBITS

LIST OF TABLES

LIST OF EXHIBITS

APPENDIX C

LIST OF EXERCISES

LIST OF EXERCISES

Exercise 1.1 Supply chain integration types—vertical, horizontal, or Keiretsu
Exercise 1.2 Understanding value chain, value stream, and value stream mapping
Exercise 2.1 Understanding SCOR processes
Exercise 2.2 Level 1 SCOR metrics
Exercise 3.1 3PL or 4PL functions
Exercise 3.2 Waste hierarchy
Exercise 4.1 Warehouse capabilities
Exercise 4.2 Impact of adding/removing warehouses
Exercise 4.3 Understanding various transportation stakeholders
Exercise 4.4 Understanding various transportation modes
Exercise 4.5 Understanding various mechanized systems
Exercise 5.1 Understanding Incoterms
Exercise 6.1 Understanding various ISO and non-ISO standards and guidelines
Exercise 7.1 Understanding the 4 P attributes
Exercise 8.1 Mean absolute deviation calculation
Exercise 8.2 Understanding forecast measurements
Exercise 9.1 CRM strategy by customer type
Exercise 9.2 CRM tools
Exercise 9.3 Four levels of CRM implementation
Exercise 10.1 Product life-cycle stages
Exercise 10.2 Understanding various design processes
Exercise 11.1 S&OP process steps
Exercise 11.2 S&OP process ownership
Exercise 12.1 Understanding material types
Exercise 13.1 PAB calculation
Exercise 13.2 ATP calculation
Exercise 14.1 MRP calculation

Exercise 15.1 Capacity attributes
Exercise 16.1 Takt time calculation
Exercise 16.2 Understanding quality type costs
Exercise 17.1 Understanding single, sole, and multisourcing suppliers
Exercise 17.2 Auction attributes
Exercise 18.1 Understanding various trading partner types
Exercise 19.1 EOQ change
Exercise 19.2 Understanding various inventory functional types
Exercise 20.1 Impact of process changes on a company's financials
Exercise 21.1 Understanding AD-AS model curve shift
Exercise 22.1 Four basic risk response types
Exercise 23.1 Understanding middleware
Exercise 24.1 Understanding RFID tags
Exercise 25.1 Understanding electronic business and commerce
Exercise 26.1 Understanding project management Process Groups
Exercise 26.2 Understanding variance analysis calculations

INDEX